RACE ATTITUDES
IN CHILDREN

RACE ATTITUDES
IN CHILDREN

BY
BRUNO LASKER
THE INQUIRY

GREENWOOD PRESS, PUBLISHERS
NEW YORK

RACE ATTITUDES IN CHILDREN

A COOPERATIVE STUDY MADE, UNDER THE
DIRECTION OF BRUNO LASKER,
BY MEMBERS OF

THE INQUIRY

A NATIONAL ORGANIZATION FOR THE PROMOTION
OF COOPERATIVE STUDIES OF PROBLEMS IN
HUMAN RELATIONS

CONTENTS

PART III

HOW ARE RACE ATTITUDES TAUGHT?

CONTENTS

PREFACE

The present study is one of a number of projects in group inquiry for the purpose of disclosing the roots of social disharmony. Earlier inquiries—some of them on a national scale—had indicated that on the whole attitudes rather than policies determine the relations between different racial and national groups in American life. These attitudes, it appeared, were only in part the result of personal experience; many of them were absorbed from the prevailing folkways and from environmental circumstances. There seemed to be a tendency to rationalize such unconsciously acquired race attitudes into coherent theories or, where they could not thus be accounted for, to allege in their explanation the possession of diverse "instincts." So many and conflicting were the evidences as to the nature of the racial attitudes prevailing in America that it was decided to inquire more systematically into the ways in which they originate. Hence this study of race attitudes manifest in childhood.

There are other reasons for giving special attention to race attitudes in children: Tests of adult opinion have shown that pronounced feelings of aversion or attraction toward other racial groups often appear quite early in life—so early, indeed, that the individual in retrospect cannot distinguish clearly between reactions with which he was born and those which he has acquired in infancy and youth. Teachers, parents, and others concerned with child education seemed particularly anxious to learn more of the processes by which these early race attitudes arise, develop and might, perhaps, be changed.

This concern, rather than a purely scientific curiosity, determined both the content and the method of the project. For it has been promoted to combine the collection and interpretation of data with an educational process. The promoters—a group of social, educational, and religious workers who have pooled their efforts in a national organization called The Inquiry—hope by such cooperative studies as this to discover how the concern of responsible people for something they regard as a problem in human contact and adjustment might at the same time (1) be guided into channels of self-education, (2) become a dynamic of remedial effort on the problems discovered and (3) contribute a nucleus of reliable testimony and suggestive questioning for others who at some later time might wish to take part in a similar quest.

In short, this aim did not permit of a strictly objective method of inquiry looking for verifiable evidence, such as carefully guarded tests in a psychological laboratory might produce. Objectivity was to be secured in a certain measure, however, by setting side by side experiences of a similar kind as recorded by persons in socially and ethnically different environments and with different cultural backgrounds and interests. In this way, it was hoped, a view of the situation might be built up which, without claiming accuracy for every quoted detail, would have authenticity in its larger outlines.

This method of approach—indicated by the threefold purpose of the inquiry—has its drawbacks and its advantages. Provided we do not claim for it too much—and provided the reader remembers that only the individuals quoted are responsible for the opinions expressed and implied in the testimony—it may in the present state of our ignorance even be considered safer than refined methods of research that aim at a direct and precise ascertainment of attitudes and their causes but are as yet far from sufficiently tested. The present literature of social psychology shows a growing awareness to the dangers of relying too firmly on findings produced with inadequate instruments of inquiry. Lacking an established technique, we need not, therefore, apologize if we begin by collecting the ores of experience from which we may hope to pan at least some few gems of real understanding. Moreover, since this study, like every worth-while social study, is made with a view to the formulation of programs of action and of education, the insight which it may afford into prevailing "attitudes on attitudes"—i.e., concepts as to the nature, causes and modification of attitudes—will be a useful by-product.

The nucleus of informational material for the present volume was obtained by means of a questionnaire addressed to participants throughout the country. During the spring of 1925, about eight hundred copies of it were distributed to a list made up in the main of correspondents known to be interested in race relations, and of teachers, social workers, officers of women's clubs, and ministers in contact with adult groups that might be induced to take part in the study. For, through previous experience, it was anticipated that from the give and take of group discussion, if carried on in small and intimate circles, more material information was likely to result than from individual replies to the questionnaire, and that the collection of data would at once arouse interest and invite analysis and interpretation.

A considerable correspondence developed, with the result that later in the same year it was possible to draft a preliminary outline of findings—a document of 46 typewritten pages—which was used to stimulate further group participation. Some fifty or sixty reports were made in response to the original questionnaire, ranging from marginal notes to substantial records of series of group meetings. In addition, many letters were received containing illustrative incidents on some phases of the inquiry, drawing attention to other sources of information or discussing questions of particular interest to the correspondent. Teachers, parents, social and church workers are represented in about equal parts in the resulting body of information and expressed opinion.

A preliminary survey of this material displayed *lacunæ* that could be filled only by reference to published information. For example, a chapter on the racial variations of physiological growth and their effect upon children's race attitudes resulted in this way. Moreover, it was now possible so to rearrange the material as to bring out more sharply those aspects of the subject that appeared of major importance. Thus, the impressions of many contributing observers as regards the ages at which specific phenomena occur indicated a progressive development of attitudes which, once attention was directed upon it, could be traced more accurately. Again, certain influences that at the outset had seemed minor items in the program of inquiry—such, for example, as the effect of segregation—now loomed as of major significance.

Simultaneous with the direction of these group studies, the author took part in other inquiries with somewhat similar aims, conferences of various social and religious agencies on the subject, and parallel studies on the part of The Inquiry itself of the causation of race attitudes in adults. Through these various contacts, including also many individual consultations on institutional programs and the like, additional material became available that has to some extent been utilized in the present study. Of available outside sources of information, other than those named, none have been rejected if they promised to add to the completeness of the picture. As the sources quoted are indicated throughout the text and mentioned in the index, no separate bibliography has been added.

One of the main findings of the study also explains its main limitations: Race attitudes in children do not stand by themselves as a phenomenon that can be fully understood apart from other types of social attitudes. As the study developed, it became clear that an attempt must be made to examine the total impact of the influences which the adult world permits to play upon the young. The ways in which the childish mind absorbs the folkways of the group in which it is nurtured are only beginning to become known. Perhaps the most serious aspect of this process is the degree to which the insinuating tactics of selfish propaganda have succeeded in affecting social teaching. Compared with the problem of preserving the primary functions of public education, the technical task of engineering influences that make for better interracial understanding in the American community plays a relatively minor part.

Nevertheless, the subject of race attitudes offers a convenient opening for the comprehension of the larger educational problem before America and, indeed, the whole civilized world. It is a subject in which many diverse groups are already interested; it is one that permits of a realistic approach toward our social philosophy. It enters into many aspects of our public life and sets ever new and challenging tests of sincerity to oft-proclaimed convictions. It invites the formulation of a gradually enlarging and deepening program for bringing every-day behavior into harmony with these policies and ideals.

The plan of the book reflects both its history and its purpose. The reader who is accustomed to an arrangement determined by a sociological subject division may be irritated by a somewhat different arrangement here followed unless he recalls the discussional uses from which the book has sprung and which it is intended further to serve. The first part shows what the race attitudes of children are, the second how they have been acquired, the third what intentional teaching has gone into their formation, and the fourth how they may be modified. In other words, the table of contents covers the span of a complete scheme of discourse which—according to what is omitted or what is added— may be stretched over a period of hours or a period of years. In a discussion of an important issue we do not limit ourselves to a single mention of a given subject: we may agree on the facts of the case, but then will come back to them to see whether we can discover the latent factors that create the problem. We may return to the original facts once more to examine them in the light of additional data —from scientific sources, for example; and finally we may look at them again to see whether proposed "solutions" really apply. In the present book this dialectic progression has made it inevitable that certain subject matters are referred to more than once. Superficially, the effect may be one of seeming repetition; but the reader who follows the plan of the book will find that, each time a topic is mentioned, a different aspect of it is the real subject under discussion, and the illustrations emphasize that aspect.

Another matter which must be clearly understood lest the contents and the potential uses of the book be misjudged is the absence of any intention on the part of the author or of his collaborators to present a rounded picture of what is in children's minds as regards other races, or of what has conditioned their receptivity. This is not a balanced survey of facts but an effort to clarify a subject by placing into a light adequate for their examination those facts which many people believe to contain tasks and problems. Thus, the question whether the presentation does full justice to the prevailing tolerance and adjustment between different ethnic groups is not to the point. No evaluation of the total impact of race "prejudice" in a situation full of evidences of mutual understanding and appreciation has been attempted; indeed the use of epithets of praise and blame has been avoided. Our concern is not with facts as facts nor with facts as testimony in a court of social justice, but with facts as evidence of what people, rightly or wrongly, see as a problem about which something should be done in the interest of social peace or social progress.

The author is embarrassed by his inability to mention by name the great company of individuals and organizations that have contributed toward the present volume which, in a very real sense, is the outcome of a cooperative venture. Indeed, it is only because the conventions of the publishing trade demand it and because he happens to have directed these studies and assembled the results that he can claim authorship for this volume. Also, grateful acknowledgment must be made to the authors and publishers of extracts quoted.

I feel happily obliged to acknowledge my special indebtedness

to Mrs. Abby A. Rockefeller, for having first suggested and subsequently helped to promote this project; to Dr. Richard Cabot
of Harvard University and Dr. Goodwin B. Watson of Columbia
University, for reading the manuscript and making valuable sug
gestions upon it; and to my colleagues, E. C. Carter, S. M. Keeny
and Professor A. D. Sheffield, of The Inquiry, for counsel and aid
through every phase of this study.

B. L.

New York, January 1, 1929.

PART I

WHAT RACE ATTITUDES DO CHILDREN HAVE?

Once riding in old Baltimore,
    Heart-filled, head-filled with glee,
I saw a Baltimorean
    Keep looking straight at me.

Now I was eight and very small,
    And he was no whit bigger,
And so I smiled, but he poked out
    His tongue, and called me "Nigger."

I saw the whole of Baltimore
    From May until December;
Of all the things that happened there
    That's all that I remember.

COUNTÉE CULLEN.

From *Color,* published by Harper & Brothers, 1925.

CHAPTER I
TYPICAL FORMS OF EXPRESSION

One of the pleasures of constant companionship with children is that of watching their minds grow. Nothing is more delightful to observe than this breaking through of new ideas and the interplay between new experiences and new knowledge. But occasionally we receive a rude shock when the child quite unexpectedly blurts out some opinion or statement of fact that seems to be totally out of keeping with his previous utterances, with the range of his experiences and, often, with the range of ideas within which we have tried to shelter him. This is especially true of the mental associations with which we are concerned in this book. Suddenly, one day, the child speaks of other children, or of grown-ups in ways that show an awareness to differences which we did not previously know he possessed. Here are a few random examples, contributed by parents:

A man of national reputation for his activities in promoting mutual understanding between different classes and peoples one night overheard his little girl in her evening prayer ask the Lord to bless her father and mother, her brothers and sisters, the teachers and all the children at the school, "except that new colored girl in my class."

A six-year-old colored girl who attended a mixed school told her father, a well-known Negro leader, that she refused to have at her party a classmate because she was Jewish.

The five-year-old daughter of a clergyman, when in an argument with a colored maid, called after her, "Nigger," without anyone in the household knowing how ever she got hold of that nickname.

B. was working in a beauty parlor in a large department store in South Dakota. One evening, after she had finished her work, she was standing by the show-case when a little child passed with her mother. As soon as she saw B., who is colored, the child clung to the mother's skirts and tried to hide. As soon as the colored girl was safely passed, the child became quiet again.

A colored high-school girl spoke admiringly to a little girl of five or six years of age. The child evinced fear at the greeting and turned to her mother: "Oh, Mama, the nigger spoke to me!"

3

A little girl, in refusing an offered piece of cheese, said it would make her "dream of colored people." This instance is contributed by a teacher who specializes in child study as illustrating the absence of any direct race prejudice (which would have caused the use of a derogatory term instead of "colored people"), but the association of fear with dark people in the child's dream life.

Here we see among children around five years of age recognition of racial differences in individuals, with an emotional bias in favor of his own and adverse to some other race. No cases are reported in which children become aware of racial difference without a feeling about the matter. Of course, the feeling exhibited in these few illustrations and the many others which can easily be brought together by an average group of parents or teachers, varies in kind and in intensity. In most cases, if not in all, it has been acquired together with the knowledge, an inseparable part of it. The child hears an older child speak disparagingly of some one as a "Nigger" or as a "Dago," and he learns at the same time that there are people distinct from the rest who are called this name, and that it is shameful to belong to that class or group. Frequently the young child is quite unaware of the nature of the distinction; he does not know that a "Nigger" is a person of dark color, or that a "Dago" is a person of foreign blood. This fact is illustrated in the following examples:

A little colored boy, four years old, calls any child who makes him angry a "nigger." He thinks of the word as something to make one angry because he sees other children get angry at being called "nigger."

Johnny, a Syrian aged five, and his boon companion Angelo, an Italian, had been playing quietly on the sand-pile. The two had apparently given no thought to their different nationalities when one day Angelo, turning around quickly, accidentally knocked over the house that Johnny had labored over. One word brought another, and such phrases as "Wop," "Arab," and "Jew" were being flung back and forth. Finally Angelo asked the "teacher" which was the better, an "Arab" or a "Wop." Upon being assured that both were equal, peace reigned for the time being, and both children went back to their play of building sand houses.

When George, a four-year-old Syrian boy, gets angry, he calls other boys of any nationality a "Wop" or a "Jew," whichever comes into his head. He knows that it makes his temporary enemy mad, and that is his purpose.

Edwards, the colored servant at a southern settlement, was sprinkling the sand-pile. Because he would not allow one of the boys, aged five, to help him, the boy called him a "Jew."

The parents had been at the Christmas "assembly" at school proudly to watch five-year-old Johnny. It was natural that at dinner afterwards the celebration was discussed. One of them remarked on the fact that Henry, a class-mate of John's of Jewish parentage, seemed to have enjoyed the singing of the hymns and a little religious address by one of the teachers quite as much as the Christian children. All at once John flared up: "Don't you call Henry a Jew—he is a friend of mine!"

A colored woman writes: There are mountain sections in Virginia and Tennessee in which few or no colored people live, so that a child is sometimes quite large before he ever sees a colored person or has any conception of what they are like. When he is taken to a near-by town he may get his first glimpse of colored people.

I lived in such a town where there were quite a few colored people. One morning, on coming down the street, I heard a group of boys say, "There's one." A dear little boy of about four years ran out of the gate and, catching my hand, looked up very confidently into my face and said, "Are you a nigger?" His whole face was wreathed in smiles, and he was so obviously searching for an answer to his question that one could not but be gentle with him. He skipped on down the street with me, still holding my hand while I explained the meaning of the word he had just used. His curiosity was satisfied, and he left to go back to his playmates. He was friendly and showed no ill-will whatever.

In a small country town in western New York was one very black big Negro who did odd jobs for everybody and was respected and needed by all. The children, who knew him as the only one of the race, were devoted to him. A little fellow, four years old, had a long illness. He was allowed to go out on the front piazza in the twilight but was told not to go in the street. The temptation was too great, and he trotted out of the gate and up the main street. It was almost dark, and looking suddenly up he saw this great black man approaching. He shrank back in some fright and then laughed at himself heartily and said: "Why, Joe, is that you? I thought it was a nigger." None enjoyed the joke more than Joe who told it everywhere.

More frequent than mere dislike is fear in the emotional association of racial difference.

Contempt almost never appears in the emotional association of racial difference among small children. Obviously, the five-year-old has no experiences directly making him aware of the "inferiority" of others, except in regard to the mental or physical inferiority of other children with whom he is in personal contact. He will hurl stones or shout epithets in situations that *seem* to exhibit contempt, but these actions will either reflect attitudes picked up from others or a momentary emotion soon to be forgotten.

As soon as we get to the next age group—say that of the earlier school years—we discover combinations of race attitudes in which fear may still predominate but which increasingly assume a variety of characteristics among which, in varying proportions, may be found combativeness, cruelty, ridicule, unfairness, patronage. As these traits rarely appear in isolation, it is a little misleading to treat them seriatim and difficult to illustrate them with clear examples of incidents in which one or other of them predominates. Nevertheless, we have to make that attempt so that we may recognize the appearance of an adverse racial attitude in a new form when, perhaps, it no longer manifests itself in the form in which it was first observed.

Moreover, while different forms of race prejudice appear simultaneously, the observations made by individuals and groups suggest that there may be a definite progression of reaction, which might be traced through different normal stages of development. (See Chapter IV.) This progression—to judge from such imperfect record of observations as we have—would seem to represent a tendency rather than a law and, therefore, cannot be proved or denied by reference to individual careers or to the observations made in a given community. At this point we can only state the occurrence of such a cumulative development of attitudes as a hypothesis the reasons for which will become apparent as we study separately the different forms that adverse race reactions take.

In Early Childhood

Our evidence does not warrant an attempt to divide the different manifestations of race feeling and the forms in which race attitudes express themselves into clear-cut categories, each with its appropriate age limits. There are books on child study which are built along such clear-cut age classifications; but often they seem artificial if not in obvious violation of common-sense. The only arrangement which the material seems to justify is a rough separation of the phenomena of early youth from those of adolescence; and even then, as we topically discuss the different types of expression of race feeling, we shall not arbitrarily limit our examples to one or the other of these two groups but present the evidence just as it has come to us—and that, in many cases, is without a sufficiently accurate indication of the age to permit a strict separation by age.   We begin, therefore, with the form which is most frequently the first to manifest itself in the life of the young child:

1. *Fear*

Fear is not only the most frequent emotional counterpart of race-awareness in small children, but also the most vivid and most lasting of the reactions experienced in this connection.| The last of the examples given (page 5) is one of many received which illustrate this point. |This fear usually seems to be associated with two elements in the situation: First, the racial group that inspires it must be sufficiently distinct to give the child an exaggerated impression of physical difference.   For example, in the native white American child we are more apt to find such fear for Negroes, Indians and Orientals than for European immigrants. Second, the fear usually is strongly present in the adult environment of the child.\ Gypsies or Mexicans in certain parts of the country are more likely to inspire fear than other physically distinct groups.   In the great majority of instances, there is undoubtedly present a third element, and that is a deliberate effort on the part of *some* adult in the child's environment to implant the particular association between race and fearful characteristics. The surprise of grown-up people on those occasions when their children suddenly proclaim what seem well developed race attitudes may be due to one or both of two things: Either they have been unaware of the attitudes handed on to the child by some one he associates with (a servant, maybe, or some older child); or they have themselves made the association without being conscious of doing so.   For example, being able to make an absolute distinction between truth and fiction, adults will read fairy tales to children without realizing that the attitudes taught by these stories make their impression quite as effectively—and sometimes more so—than those of true stories or deliberate teaching.

The fear thus created may be within limits; it may only be certain types of contact that the child has been taught to avoid—

just as he is taught not to put certain things in his mouth, though he may be allowed to touch them and play with them. For example, in the following instance the child obviously had not been taught that "colored" and "bad" as terms applied to persons are synonymous; but he had been taught that there was something unclean and infectious about colored persons:

A five-year-old whose parents were not aware of having ever taught or suggested to him any kind of race feeling was playing at the kindergarten with a small colored boy. When this child came a little too close to him for his liking, he remarked (in a tone of disapproval rather than alarm): "Look out, little black child, don't breave your black bref on me!"

The existing confusion on the nature of first exhibitions of fear in children in the presence of certain phenomena is simply due to faulty observation; and the controversy as to whether certain fears are instinctive or acquired might quickly yield to agreement if there were a sufficient body of accurate and complete data. Most of the experiences told by parents and others are fragmentary, and we do not know what all the circumstances were. Hence we get false explanations and, what is worse, false interpretations insinuated in the account itself—as for example, in the following communication from a native American teacher who, in assuming her story to be proof of an instinctive race attitude, quite fails to pay attention to possible differences in sound, smell, touch as well as sight:

A baby of one year of age was taken by its parents to visit in a Mexican colony where its grandmother lives. The Mexicans in the colony, with their intense love of children, gathered in a circle about the baby, wishing to fondle it. The child had never before exhibited a fear of strangers; but it cried and during several days of visiting seemed never to overcome its fear of the Mexicans. During the visit, my mother, who was also a stranger to the baby, took it in her arms when it came to our house, and the child exhibited no fear.

Another baby of American parents was born in one of our Mexican colonies. It is now eight months old. It has as yet exhibited no feeling of difference between white and Mexican visitors. All of them fondle and play with it.

This little example is typical for the lack of telling detail without which such an account is, of course, of small value for our inquiry. Apart from possible differences in looks, smell, strange language, which are obvious, any of the following differences may have produced aversion or fear on the part of the first-mentioned baby. The Mexican women may have frightened it by crowding around it. They may have held it differently from the way it was accustomed to be held. The person who was holding the child in the first instance—the mother presumably—may unconsciously have expressed her own uneasiness in the presence of the Mexican women by a slight muscular reflex, a holding back at first from too close contact. Such a movement on the part of the mother, especially when experienced before in a situation which eventuated in a disagreeable experience for the baby, say being clumsily handled by another child—a situation of which the recorder of this incident would have no knowledge—would be quite sufficient in itself to account for the baby's curious behavior without calling in any of the other possible explanations.

It is not our object in this chapter to explain these manifestations, but rather to acquaint ourselves with their nature. At the same time, it is important to point out, even at this stage, that where colored or other people of a very distinct race form part of the accepted daily environment, children are not afraid of them, normally. For example, a well-known Chicago woman, born and reared in the South, writes:

One can fancy the lasting impression made upon children who have often been frightened by the warning: "If you are not good, the black man will get you." I, on the contrary, had such different experiences in childhood with colored people who were so kindly and so human that I find it difficult to enter into this fearful state of mind that has built these notions among the whites. "Harvey," whose homely black face meant to all of us McDowells an honorable, faithful friend, who went through the Civil War with our father, has colored all our relations with Negro men. This type was again brought to my notice when a young colored boy brought a letter of introduction from my Kentucky cousin who said, "I have known this boy's family for three generations and have never known more honorable men, black or white."

In connection with the study of the Chicago Committee on Race Relations, following the unfortunate riots in 1919, a rather full inquiry was made into racial contacts at the schools, and the almost complete agreement of teachers, covering the observation of many thousands of children, seems to be that fear manifests itself very rarely and, where it does, can practically always be traced to some specific environmental circumstance. Here are the only exceptions quoted:

A teacher in a school with 85 per cent of colored pupils told of a little white girl in another school who cried because she was afraid the color from the Negro children's hands would rub off on hers; in her present school she had known no such instances in the kindergarten. This conduct is paralleled in instances in which Negro children who have never had any contact with white children in the South are afraid of them when they first come North.[1]

The word "fear" has been used in the present chapter to cover the various manifestations of reaction—varying from horror to an almost imperceptible apprehension—that have in common the elements of aversion and suspicion. The examples given only illustrate some of the nuances. Obviously, most parents and teachers will become aware only of the grosser forms of disquietude. Other instances of timidity, even when they have become aware of them, they would hardly consider as worth reporting in the present connection. However, in civilized society, occasions which produce real fright, even in small children, are relatively rare; in their cumulative influences on the development of character the much larger number of experiences of milder perturbation are more important. It is necessary, therefore, that we should not dismiss as a matter of minor significance the frequent exhibitions of timidity in the presence of persons of distinct physical appearance or other strangeness.[2]

All observations made carefully and over a sufficient length of time suggest that it is unprofitable to study race attitudes apart from others aspects of child psychology. If most of the noticeable reactions of small children to race are fear reactions, as seems to be the fact, we shall do well to acquaint ourselves more thoroughly with the nature and causes of fear in childhood.[3]

2. Cruelty

Cruelty is not, of course, a separate type of race attitude. Sometimes the term is used solely with regard to the effect of an

[1] *The Negro in Chicago* (University of Chicago Press, 1922, p. 246). For further evidence of this diversity of reaction, see J. H. Oldham, *Christianity and the Race Problem* (1924, p. 31).

[2] See Bertrand Russell, *Education and the Good Life* (1926, p. 120).

[3] See also Sidonie M. Gruenberg, *Your Child Today and Tomorrow* (1913, pp. 79, 83).

action and sometimes with regard only to motive. Thus confusion is invited unless we are aware of our meaning in the present context. We cannot, with the pragmatic nature of the present study, avoid the use of the term for the simple reason that many of those who have contributed material toward it look upon cruelty as a distinct trait which children are apt to develop at a given age and under given circumstances and which, though it affects the child's relation to things and living beings in general, shows itself with special clarity in interracial contacts. It may be suspected, nevertheless, that even in cases where cruelty appears as a motivation and not merely as a result, it does not usually appear unmixed with other motives. Often it is associated with the pleasure experienced in stirring up activity; and mischief and fun normally play a larger part in it than conscious hostility. There are varieties of attitudes which give the effect of cruelty: Indifference to pain suffered by others may have a very different cause from that which produces malicious joy in causing pain. But the more positive forms of cruelty are decidedly rarer than the forms of indifference. A mild impulse to tease may produce effects which exaggerate the seriousness of the attitude in the eyes of onlookers.[4]

This cruelty, according to most observers, does not as a rule manifest itself only in contacts with persons of another race. When it does, the child merely reflects a highly charged emotional attitude in his environment. More often, a child that uses an accepted inferiority of other persons for purposes of enlarging his ego, is selfish also in other respects.[5]

Freud connects the cruelty which, often, manifests itself quite early in life with a "repetition-compulsion"—an instinctive desire for the repetition of experiences even when these have been of unpleasant character. The small child's experiences are for the most part passive; in his play-life he re-enacts them with this difference that he assumes the most active part in the situation in an instinctive desire to secure mastery over it. If he has had the unpleasant experience of persons or objects of which he was fond leaving him or getting lost to him in ways he does not know, he will now re-enact the experience and make it pleasurable to himself by throwing things away or ordering them to go away.

---

[4] For an illustration see Jane Addams, *Twenty Years at Hull House* (1911, p. 255).

[5] Sidonie M. Gruenberg, *Sons and Daughters* (1916, pp. 114-5).

Often he will go on fetching and throwing away things until he has thoroughly mastered the unpleasant feeling associated with their involuntary loss previously. In the same way, when he has been hurt by contact with an object, he will be afraid of it only so long as he fails to recognize its innocuous nature. As soon as he does so, he will repeat the experience of the contact, but in such a way as to be the active agent who makes others suffer. Thus, even in listening to stories, children will normally identify themselves with those who inflict pain rather than those who receive it, unless their sympathies have previously been aroused in an opposite direction. The popularity of slapstick comedy (which, so often, happens to be charged with a tradition of national or racial animosity) may well have for its origin this infantile desire to identify the self with the active element in situations similar to those in which one has been passive in an earlier experience.[6]

Racial difference, it would seem, need not be felt with aversion to produce an experimental frame of mind: Since other living creatures, in the child's experience, have proved helpless when teased, a human stranger also may be expected to react entertainingly to molestation without endangering the child—most often a boy—who does the molesting. If the tentative annoyance should bring punishment, the attempt will be abandoned.

A colored family moved to a small town where there were no other Negroes. They started their small son to school. Every day the boys ran after him with stones and sticks. Finally he tired of this and took enough courage to fight them back. One day he ran other boys home with a butcher knife. After that he was left alone.

3. Combativeness

One element traceable in many manifestations of alleged "cruelty," then, is the impulse of small children to test out their strength. This impulse induces a boy to engage in combat with the forces of nature—especially if he feels that he has more than an even chance on his side. Curiosity as to his own limits of power makes him adventurous; and he measures his strength or his running power, or his power of hurtful epithet, against that of a stranger seemingly his equal or slightly his inferior. The "new boy" has to fight many a battle before he is accepted, not neces-

[6] See also a case told by Kate Holladay Claghorn in *The Immigrant's Day in Court* (1923, p. 105).

sarily because there is hostility toward him but as a measure of "getting his number." But where there is in the environment an element of aversion to the newcomer's race or nationality or other group affiliation, the attitude of combativeness toward him may be prolonged and, later, become rationalized into a conscious antagonism.

"I remember," writes a high-school teacher, "a scene at a roadside in southern New Jersey, where one set of children—from four to ten years old—was standing on a bridge and stoning another set of children who had been driven underneath the bridge and were not allowed to come up. One of the groups was colored, the other white."

This same teacher has from her own school experience come to the conclusion that often there is a latent group hostility which, though it may not show itself for a long time, will suddenly break out on small provocation. Although in the school the color line is not perceptibly drawn, she says, fist fights in the school yard between white and colored pupils as such are frequent. She adds the following suggestive remark:

I have noticed a kind of fascination in contact with other races which seems instinctive but which may readily admit of being turned to fear or hostility by environmental influences.

More frequently we find the belief that there is an "instinctive" combativeness in small boys of a certain age.[7] G. Stanley Hall and other students of children warn us against "repressing" this supposedly healthy outcropping in the child of some quality he has inherited from his distant ancestors. Some books go to ludicrous lengths in associating every stage in the mental envelopment of the boy (girls, somehow, seem to be subject to a different evolutionary law) with some cultural phase in the long history of his race which, for the purpose of these books, seems always to be a Teutonic one.[8]

Combativeness is as natural as eating.[9] Today we look with horror upon practices that were customary among our grandfathers; and the folkways of one civilized people tolerate prac-

[7] See below, p. 62.
[8] See, for example, J. Adams Puffer, *The Boy and His Gang* (1912, pp. 45, 84).
[9] The theory of the existence of an innate combativeness is well disposed of by Richardson and Loomis, *The Boy Scout Movement Applied by the Church* (1915, p. 67).

tices that lead to the police court in another. There are increasing numbers of those who look upon every form of killing as cruel but lack the imagination to see cruelty also in the tortures inflicted by sports that do not kill. As between children of different racial groups, the sight of adult cruelty in interracial treatment is, no doubt, at all ages a strong influence. Rumanian children who see Jews cuffed about and spat upon will be apt to do the same. Where the parents do not care what they say or do to colored servants, the children are not likely to treat them with more respect.

In short, where "cruelty" is exhibited by children in the midst of a violent clash of adult antagonisms, problems are involved that must remain outside the scope of the present volume. For, in those situations, children are part of a psychopathic phenomenon in which differences of age and experience are all but wiped out, a crisis in which not the educator who works most effectively in an atmosphere of tranquillity but the policeman must bear the first brunt. This is well illustrated by the report of the Chicago Commission on Race Relations which describes the participation of children in the riot of 1919.[10]

4. *Ridicule*

There is no absolute line of demarcation between different shades of hostility. Some of the examples adduced in the previous pages to illustrate cruelty no doubt will by others be looked upon as the outgrowths of a normal form of combativeness. A third person may, in the same instance, see an illustration rather of fear which, as we all know, often finds expression in an exaggerated self-assertion. While, thus, there are no absolute distinctions and all the categories must be looked upon as somewhat indefinite, we can discern different tones or hues in the ways in which different children react to different experiences. The terror of the small child who is spoken to by a large and fierce-looking specimen of a race he has been taught to fear is something sufficiently different from the attitude of the boy who throws stones at the stranger in the neighborhood, to make us realize that the emotions aroused in both cases, while related, are really different in character. Again, the state of feeling of the boy who, as a member of a gang, assists in a pitched street

[10] *The Negro in Chicago* (1922, p. 22).

battle is something distinct from that of the boy who, as an individual, throws a stone at some defenseless member of a despised racial group. And this contempt, again, shades over into a less pronounced and less deep-seated attitude of derision when the boy, safely hidden behind a tree, or close to a safe retreat, "calls names"—in a spirit of mischief rather than of malice. Again, the action may be a test rather than an expression of a firmly grounded attitude.

Ridicule of others, especially those who are strange in appearance or speech, arises from group consciousness and appreciation of the values of group likenesses or traditions. It therefore occurs at a later age, usually, than the first manifestations of fear or of combativeness.[11] Whether it be a difference in the color of the skin or in dress, in language or in gait, the small boy (say, around eight or ten years of age) has all the intolerance of the typical provincial or backwoodsman.

Ridicule is a form of expression which may be the symptom of a variety of feelings and attitudes. It may be mere conservatism, it may be slightly tinged with fear—a process of reassurance in the face of a new experience—or it may be a weapon of self-assertion in a situation in which one's own standing, or that of one's group, is placed in doubt.[12] In children all these different attitudes, which we find so well established among adults, are much less developed, more easily interchanged or combined in a single attitude or motivation.

An experienced church worker, for fifteen years a high-school teacher in the anthracite region of Pennsylvania, writes:

Ridicule develops at the age of seven, but at that age is rather a matter of difference in appearance and customs, dress, etc., than one

---

[11] Obviously, deliberate ridiculing of strangers must be distinguished from a mere thoughtless repetition of derisive nicknames which the child has heard in his environment. The latter takes place at a much earlier age. "The children in these kindergartens," says Professor Mary Chaplin Shute, of Boston Teachers College, (in *Childhood Education* for February, 1926, p. 271) "often come to us with prejudices already started by their parents. The hateful names of race contempt, so familiar to us all—Yid and Wop and Nigger and Dago and a host of others—already fall glibly from childish lips, bringing a tragic ache to many a little heart, quite out of proportion to the intentions of the arrogant young speaker."

[12] Recent studies make more emphatic the connection between a sense of humor and a felt need of re-assurance. William H. Burnham, *The Normal Mind* (1925, p. 400), and others look upon it as both a preventive and a cure of a sense of inferiority. In popular mythology, the devil becomes a funny figure as soon as fear of a physical hell is outlived; but also a funny devil has been used on purpose by religious educators to dissipate a false fear.

of race. The unusual provokes ridicule. This changes to hostility later on, about the seventh grade, when the racial feeling first appears in the form of competition. It then becomes a question of fighting for one's rights. There may be an element of jealousy—but it seems more a question of a sense of superiority and resentment at any other race getting ahead in the class.

As to the particular forms in which ridicule shows itself, two factors are of importance: first, the frequent use of racial nick-names before children are aware what they mean or against what group in particular they are directed; and, second, the poetic quality of children's imagination which gives artistic form to their derision.

A western school principal observes that children are apt to name those of *marked* foreign nationality by some nickname and to invent little uncomplimentary epithets that rhyme with this name. This is confirmed by other observers:

An American-born boy of about ten years of age entered the neigh-borhood-house playground. His eyes fell on a couple of little girls of about twelve years of age who were playing jacks. One was a Syrian and the other Italian. The little Syrian girl was a child of very black hair and dark complexion. The boy said, "Huh, you're Dagoes." Although they became angry, they called back in a rather playful strain:

> If we are Dagoes
> You are a Wop,
> We eata spagett,
> And you eat slop.

A southern settlement worker believes that ridicule, in this connection, is usually associated with a selfish interest. She says, "Often an Italian and a Jewish boy will be playing together; they are buddies. But as soon as they fight they call one another by names ridiculing their parents' nationality." She adds that the weapon of ridicule is used only by children from homes or national groups with a low standard of manners in other re-spects also.

Ridicule is a strong weapon for strengthening one's sense of superiority, particularly when those of another race or nationality are known to be ashamed of their descent:

A boy of German heritage hates to be taken for a German or "Dutch-man," as the boys call him. He looks more Irish than German and, being Catholic, is usually taken for an Irish boy. It is quite a joke among the boys who belong to his gang that he hates his nationality, and they often refer to him as "the Irish Dutchman."

Several correspondents have suggested that the derision expressed by small boys for persons of other races or nationalities constitutes an excellent index to the existing race attitudes of their elders. Fashions in nicknames change as the composition of the population changes, or as new immigrant groups, at first distinct in dress, language or status, gradually become assimilated until they are more or less indistinguishable from the rest of the community.

And what about the children of the minority groups who are objects of derision? How does their response in turn affect the development of the race attitude of their school fellows of the majority group? Usually a child who has suffered a mild ridicule ceases to be ashamed of his ancestry, race or nationality as he grows older; and this either for the reason that the group to which he belongs is gradually assimilated by the neighborhood —so that to be an Italian or a Pole is no longer a matter of particular distinction one way or the other—or, more frequently, because as he grows older the child of the despised or ridiculed minority group finds his associations more closely with others of his own group and develops a race pride of his own. At the same time, a sense of inferiority developed in the pre-adolescent years if nourished, as it so often is, by growing awareness of adverse attitudes on the part of others and by an increasing acuteness of the situations in which these attitudes are experienced, is apt to predispose the child to a sense of inferiority that may color his personality for life.[13]

The following examples illustrate a sense of humiliation that may later either be cast off or develop into a bitter sense of wrong which, biting more deeply into the mind, may eventually, unless sharply counteracted, bring about a false sense of inherent inferiority.

A. M. came to America at the age of ten, an Armenian orphan. An aunt desired to have an American home found for him. The boy begged to be placed with a family that would allow him to keep his own name. Within six months of his adoption he was calling himself James. When asked why, he said the boys were calling him Tony or

[13] The permanency of these effects will be further discussed in Chap. XVIII.

Andy; and he wanted a real American name. At the age of fourteen he again changed his mind. He now desired to take lessons in the Armenian language and took pride in retaining his Armenian associations.

A colored woman writes: When I first entered school in the state of Ohio, at the age of five or six years, I knew nothing about a color line. I was something of a pet because I was the youngest in the school at that time. But when I got to be about eight or nine years old, I began to discover that somehow I was a little different from the other children. One evening when going home from school, a girl who lived next door called me a "nigger." We fought it out with fists and feet—I believe I could go to the very spot now where I sat on her prostrate body and pummelled her "good"!

Georg Brandes (the great Danish writer) tells in his autobiographical sketches this scene of his early childhood: "When he walked out behind the servant girl, his younger brother with him, he sometimes heard a boy call after him, and when he turned around he saw a sneering face with drawn mouth and threatening fists. For long he paid no attention; but when the call became more frequent, he asked the servant what it meant. She said: 'Oh, nothing!' When he asked again, she said, 'He is calling a bad word.'

"One day when he again heard the word, he wanted to know what it meant and asked his mother: 'What does it mean?' 'Jew,' said his mother. 'There are some people called Jews? Are they bad people?' 'Yes,' she said, smiling, 'very ugly people they are sometimes—but not always.' 'I'd like to see a Jew.' 'You can do that,' said the mother and held the little boy up to a large oval mirror that hung over the sofa. He cried out, terrified, and his mother quickly set him down, regretting not to have prepared him. She never mentioned the incident."

At one time or another—adds the commentator—every Jewish child cries out like that. It is the cry of one wounded to death. And with this cry the child becomes different.[14]

[14] Dr. Michael Mueller-Claudius, *Deutsche Rassenangst* (Berlin, 1927, p. 111).

CHAPTER II

TYPICAL FORMS OF EXPRESSION (*Continued*)

In Adolescence

We have already seen that a clear-cut division of our subject by age groups is not possible. Manifestations of race feeling which in one case appear early in life, in another are not observed until much later. Though dealing primarily with the pre-school child and the child of the earlier grades, the previous pages have included evidence also that bears on forms in which race attitudes express themselves in the behavior of older children.

Without a definite theory to start with, there are several ways in which we might account for this diversity of ages in the appearance of a particular phenomenon: 1. It may be merely apparent, the result of superficial observation. Children may often have said or done a thing before a grown-up person takes notice of the trait displayed. Again, the particular persons who have taken part in the present collection of material not always have known the children they speak of from birth, but report on incidents noted, whether they have been the first in the life of the child or not. 2. It is obvious that opportunities for the development of attitudes must vary with circumstances. One child, exposed quite early in life to certain contacts or influences, may react before school age in the same way in which another child will react to similar contacts or influences at the age of fourteen. 3. Children may differ in sensitiveness to impressions, and some may react more quickly to certain kinds of stimuli than others. Again, children vary in quickness of expression; and of two children who have the same feeling toward a certain type of situation, one may immediately give vent to that feeling, while the other requires many repetitions of the experience before he will give a first visible or audible sign of reaction to the situation. 4. Some believe that the child is endowed with latent instincts which require, each of them, a specific stimulus to bring them out into the open. Puberty itself is regarded by some psychologists as a time when racial aversions and fears, always present subconsciously, leap into the consciousness and acquire a more prominent place in the emotional life. Both the age of puberty and the rapidity of its development vary, of course, between children (and not only between children of different ethnic groups but apparently also according to place and circumstances). If, therefore, there are such latent tendencies, their presence might account for these variations in the age at which racial feelings first show themselves.

In spite of these diverse explanations, most observers agree that the type of race attitude which expresses itself at each age normally corresponds to a stage of mental growth. We therefore proceed now to describe one form which sometimes arises quite early in childhood but more frequently is first observed in children over ten years of age:

5. *Condescension*

Derision that expresses itself in nicknames may express merely a sense of the strange, on the general assumption that everything different from the accustomed is to an extent inferior. Somewhat distinct from that inclusive contempt of the young child and the backwoodsman is the contempt for specific groups which, because of their associations, or because of special teaching and the absorption of distinct community attitudes, are singled out from the general run of humanity and looked upon and treated as deficient. This contempt for the more familiar unknown usually takes the milder form of condescension. Moreover, as children become more consciously aware of the attitudes in their environment, their ridicule for strangers is apt to give way to a more discriminating assumption of group superiority. However, it must not be assumed from this statement (or from other categories suggested in this chapter) that this transformation *always* takes place, or that it necessarily takes place at about the same age or the same stage of mental maturity. (See, further, Chapter III.) A very young child may observe an attitude of race superiority in his adult environment; and he will as quickly copy the behavior of his parents or of an older brother toward the colored washerwoman as he will copy their behavior toward the visiting minister. Here are some examples in illustration of this point—which is made by quite a number of correspondents:

William, a little boy of three or four, is asked by his mother to bring in his wagon from the yard. He says, "Yes, Mother," then turns to his little colored playmate: "Ernest, bring the wagon up."

The six-year-old daughter of a man prominently identified with a movement for bringing different racial and national groups together in a southern city was playing in the sand-pile on a playground. One of the play organizers remarked that she had on a very pretty dress. "Oh, yes," she remarked in an off-hand way. "Mary made it!" pointing to the colored nurse. "It's pretty good for her, isn't it?"

More usually, the sense of superiority that expresses itself in a patronizing manner seems to come somewhat later in life.

A Jewish girl came to a settlement party. In talking to the head resident, she observed, "This is a nice place, isn't it?" "Why do you ask that? Do you hear anyone saying anything to the contrary?" "Yes, I do. They say there are so many Dagoes here," was her immediate reply.

From the same source comes another illustration of the sense of superiority often exhibited by Jewish children:

Some ten-year-old girls were practicing for an operetta. At one rehearsal several Gentile American-born children were there, children of a higher social type than the Jewish children in the play and very popular generally. At the next rehearsal these children were not there, the leader did not know why. She asked about their absence, when one of the Jewish children piped up: "Let's not have light-heads in this, let's just have Jewish heads."

It is interesting to note that two groups may be mutually patronizing without realizing it. Thus we read in another part of the same report:

A new girl had come to our playground. One of the workers was filling out an application blank for the office. To convince the worker that she was eligible, the girl said: "I don't mind mixing with the Jews."

Professor Bogardus, among various examples collected by him to illustrate the genesis of interracial goodwill in childhood, gives several which point pretty clearly to a somewhat presumptuous sense on the part of the contributor of the superiority of his own group as the principal element in what is described as an attitude of "friendliness" toward the other group.[1]

6. *Rivalry*

We have deliberately avoided, thus far, trying to keep track of the exact point at which one type of racial attitude turns into another. The transitions are too gradual to be noted with exactness, and all we can definitely record is a tendency for certain forms of reaction to appear at one age rather than at another. We are now coming to a reaction which rarely appears before adolescence. Not before he approaches the eighth grade, several observers aver, does the normal American child pay much attention to his scholastic standing; life is full of adventure and interest, and the thought of personal attainment is rather in the parents' mind than that of the scholar. However, an earlier awareness to personal or group rivalry may in individual cases be the product of artificial stimulation (whether intentional or not) on the part of adults, as in the following case reported from Philadelphia:

A colored girl, about nine years old, was quite a problem of discipline in a Philadelphia school. In fact, she was considered a mischievous child by her teacher. At that time there was no segregation, and all the other girls in her class were white. One day, in scolding her about her conduct, the teacher said, "What's the matter with you? Do you think you are as good as these white girls?" The colored child, giving no thought to the import of the question, spontaneously replied, "Why, certainly I do." Upon which the teacher expressed great surprise.

The girl is now a mature woman and says that on that day there awakened in her a sense of race rivalry, and she set out then to let no girl in any of her classes excel her in her work, and that there began to burn in her the fire of racial resentment.

With the onset of personal ambition, and this in athletics quite as much, of course, as in school work—adverse race attitudes receive yet a new tinge: the animosity felt for a rival is accentuated if the rival belongs to a distinct racial or national group, and more especially if he belongs to one of the hitherto despised groups. Thus we get many reports of incidents like the following:

[1] Emory S. Bogardus, "Race Friendliness and Social Distance," in the *Journal of Applied Sociology*, January-February, 1927, pp. 278, 279.

There had been a serious quarrel in the class, and four boys were sent to the principal's office with the report that they knew about the cause of the quarrel and would explain it. Some of the boys reported that the colored boys had started the trouble. "They always start something in that class, Miss A. Why don't you put them out?" One Italian boy, aged twelve, who had been sitting quietly in the corner listening, got up at this point and said: "I'll tell you the truth, Miss A. Joe here (an Italian boy) started the whole thing out on the playground. Didn't you, Joe?" Joe at once acknowledged that he was the guilty party. He said he had not meant to let the colored boys get all the blame for the trouble, but older boys in the class had said to him, "Just let them take the blame."

There is little partiality shown, writes this teacher, until there is a quarrel. Then the colored children invariably stand up for their own and the white children for theirs. Among the boys and girls over ten I notice more race feeling than among the younger ones. I often hear an Italian boy telling another not to play with the "coons" or not to play with a "dirty Jew."

In a grammar school in New England, it turned out at graduation that a Russian Jew was to be valedictorian and a German girl the next highest. However, an "American" girl thought she ought to be second. Others agreed that it was a shame to have both prizes go to "foreigners." The native girl's father happened to be quite influential in town and by pulling various wires induced the school principal to give an additional examination. It turned out that the original choice was upheld, and the German girl again won second place. The "American" girl continued to feel that she had a just grievance, and that the German girl, being a foreigner, should have been made to stand down in her favor.

A Chinese boy was valedictorian of his school class. Members of the class refused to march up to the platform with him.[2]

Of an Italian boy it is reported that much hostility is shown him at school simply as result of rivalry. His American-born class-mates will not tolerate his getting ahead of them in anything. He has not been admitted to athletics or allowed to run for any class office.

An Italian girl had no friends whatever in high school. It became a case of deliberate, studied avoidance. When she walked up to a group, the group would dissolve. The hostility of the other girls showed itself in little meannesses: for example, they would complain that she had bugs in her head when this was not true and when they would not have dared to say this about an American-born girl.

[2] For a similar instance see *The Negro in Chicago* (University of Chicago Press, 1922, p. 247).

The boy or girl who fails often exaggerates the influence which home or race or class have on the relative standing of scholars. The more intelligent pupil of one of the unprivileged minorities will recognize that individual merit is not the only thing that counts, and that he has a special handicap to overcome. But too often a lazy or not particularly bright member of such a minority will excuse his lack of success before his parents and before himself by attributing to his foreign background or the teachers' prejudice or the jealousy of his schoolmates a failure that is at least in part personal.[3]

Care should be taken not to mistake a demonstration of generosity to a member of the other racial group as necessarily a sign of absence of race feeling. It may be the exact opposite. When a newspaper applauds with bold headlines the award of a prize to a colored boy or girl, it may merely be advertising the race consciousness of the committee or the general sense of white superiority in the community, not the absence of that sense.[4] This also holds good if there is a demonstration among the school children themselves. The following paragraph is typical of many contributed to the present study by persons who thought it illustrated absence of race feeling among children:

A Negro boy was on a track team in a high school and did some fine work. When the letters were given out, he received the biggest applause of the whole team. Color made no difference to the boys on his team or to the whole school, and he was treated in every way as a white boy.

"Color made no difference" is a rationalization, not a psychological fact. The school was glad to have this opportunity of displaying its race tolerance; and as likely as not there were anxious moments that not all would play up to this rôle. An extra measure of applause on such an occasion as this often represents a manifestation of fair-mindedness on the part of an audience that is endeavoring to conquer within itself a less worthy attitude.

7. Class Consciousness

The same transition in the trend of the normal American boy or girl from general to specific recognition of racial and national

[3] Graham Wallas, *Our Social Heritage* (Yale University Press, 1921, p. 96).
[4] See p. 113.

differences, from toleration or mild contempt to a more acute hostility, which accentuates rivalry also accentuates the separation into cliques or gangs that takes place in adolescence. The selection of playmates is no longer a matter entirely of individual congeniality, but social preconceptions enter into the seeking and the avoidance of intimacies. To what extent this tendency is a natural development of a child's reactions to the surrounding circumstances and to what extent a tendency encouraged and brought about by a change in parental attitudes as regards the child's associations at earlier and later ages, we shall examine anon. Here we merely note the tendency as parents, teachers, and others have many occasions to observe it.

They (the children of American-Japanese marriages) get along satisfactorily in the lower grades of school. But when Japanese children reach the seventh and eighth grades, we find that race conflict problems begin to arise. White children sometimes say that their parents do not want them to have anything to do with Japanese children, and so race conflict develops.[5]

We teachers find, writes a Buffalo teacher, that most students by the time they reach high school have an attitude of "one-hundred percentism" which takes the ideas of Nordic supremacy and of our national superiority simply for granted.

The play room of a Cleveland social settlement is open every day of the year, except for two holidays, for boys and girls under ten years of age; and the average attendance is seven hundred a month. Here Italian, Slavic, colored and Syrian boys and girls play happily together. There is never a word or suggestion, writes one of the workers, about color or nationality in play or conversation. But from older children in charge of these smaller ones, one hears such remarks as—"My little brother can't come no more because my mother doesn't want him to play with colored children;" or "A colored girl hurt my sister." During several years of experience in working with little children I cannot recall a single instance where a child under ten refused to play with a colored child or with a child of another nationality or, in fact, let it be known that he noticed any difference whatever. I have often noticed boys and girls play together who could not even understand each other's language.

That class consciousness, where there is a condition of race friction in the community, will show itself at a much earlier age

[5] Emory S. Bogardus, "Survey of Race Relations on the Pacific Coast," *Information Service Bulletin* for May, 1926, p. 11.

seems to be one of the showings of the Chicago race relations report.[6] This report further suggests that the race feeling in children, where it is unusual, can often be traced to southern parents.[7]

A great deal has been written about the "gang age" that would be to the point in relation to the present topic. But, as has already been mentioned (p. 13), some of these books grossly exaggerate the sharpness of the differences in attitude at different ages and make altogether too much of the influences of gang psychology upon the mental development of the individual. It is very doubtful whether there is in existence such a thing as a "social instinct"[8] that drives boys (apparently, girls have no exact equivalent for it) together into noisy, combative, exclusive, race- and class-conscious aggregates. The awareness of the normal boy or girl at a certain age to group differences, the beginnings of a conscious appreciation for the appearance, language, customs and manners of his own group and a corresponding contempt for groups that do not share these heritages is easily enough explained, as we shall see later, on purely environmental grounds.

We must at this point confess to a particular difficulty in the presentation and analysis of our material. Too many of those who have contributed to the making of this volume seem to have entirely overlooked the possibility that a race attitude, as expressed in a reaction toward a specific experience or influence, may exist without being also recognized as an inclusion of the *self* within a given *group* in distinction from certain other groups. In other words, the ages at which different symptoms of awareness to individual differences first appear may not coincide at all with the ages at which these differences are first interpreted by the child in group terms. There is reason to believe—and some of the most trustworthy of our observers expressly give this as their opinion—that the age at which children become aware of their racial group membership is several years later, as a rule, than the age at which they recognize individual differences or react in specific ways to persons of marked difference. One correspondent writes:

[6] *The Negro in Chicago* (University of Chicago Press, 1922, p. 246).
[7] *Ibid.*, p. 246.
[8] For a fuller discussion of instinct see Chap. V.

The age at which children discover group differences between people is several years beyond the first classification, generally between the ages of nine and twelve years. This difference is more apt to come as a direct result of educational training in the schools or other institutions where definite educational activities are initiated, though much of this knowledge may originate in the home.

Not often before school age, says a Southern woman. Through parents who are "Babbitts," also through the remarks of "100 per cent American" lecturers, and the like, says a Northern settlement worker.

After going to school and being told about the "cute little Japs," says another correspondent.

The group of New Jersey parents attribute first consciousness of group differences to the teaching of geography, as at present taught, and not to personal experiences.[9] Several in the group testified to their keen interest in the study of race and to the fact·that the definite training given by certain teachers had fixed in their minds the sense of Aryan superiority.

A western woman observes that the observation comes at any time between the ages of nine and fourteen, according to the nature of school arrangements—as for example the picking of partners and the association of differences in appearance and dress with groups of individual children.

The recognition comes usually at puberty, testifies a middle-western teacher, unless brought about previously by conversations overheard, a frequent occurrence.

An experienced teacher advances the opinion that children find out about group differences when they study geography, at the age of about ten, not before. However, in another part of her report it is made clear that in this remark she has in mind the native white child. Those children who belong to races or nationalities looked down upon may be made aware of group differences much earlier:

Ernest, colored, aged seven, was taken on a picnic with his white friend William and his family. The two boys played together until lunch time. When they were called, Ernest stayed far from the rest of the company by himself and had to be much urged to come and sit by William and eat.

Richard, a little colored boy, at the age of five, resented being called a "nigger" by a white child and already had learned that retaliation

9 The effects of geography teaching are dealt with in Chap. XIII.

was useless though he had not at that time learned the difference in races. At the age of six he knew that there were two groups, colored and white, and thereby hangs a tale: When asked whether he knew any of the children in his class, he answered, "No, they are all Jews." As a matter of fact, they were not; but his family had recently moved from a neighborhood inhabited by Negroes and Jews, and the ideas of White and Jew were the same for him.

The superintendent of a mission in the Northwest puts the age rather higher:

I have noticed for several years that Japanese, Chinese and white children study and play together with no hint of differences based on race lines. But as the Asiatic children, or those of Asiatic parentage, grew older and came to the marriageable age, they almost invariably gravitated to their own race. This is especially true of the children of Japanese parentage, even in Hawaii. For long my opinion has been that race instinct was largely responsible for this changed attitude, but after talking with the young people, I am not so sure. I am almost convinced that race has nothing to do with it, per se, but that the separation is caused by our social standards and usages. Society is a most despotic ruler and has decreed that persons of non-white extraction shall not be admitted to good standing in social circles. As soon as the young people of Asiatic descent realize this, they begin to "take their places"—though reluctantly and with some bitterness.[10]

8. *Returning Fears*

While, generally speaking, society permits the self-governing association of boys during the period of adolescence, it throws new safeguards around its adolescent girls. It is only in very recent times that the flocking together of like-minded boys has been recognized as of social significance, and that organizations have sprung up to supervise, so far as possible, the formation of gangs and the processes that determine leadership and activities. With girls it is different. They have always been kept under control, and even now the freedom granted them to find congenial companions is not, generally speaking, nearly as great as that granted to boys. In later chapters we shall have to examine

[10] For especially vivid and detailed examples of the circumstances in which class consciousness asserts itself among adolescents of the white and colored groups, see the autobiographical writings of prominent Negroes, e.g., Robert R. Moton, *Finding a Way Out* (1920, p. 32) ; W. E. Burghardt Du Bois, *The Souls of Black Folk* (1912, p. 2).

the nature of the pressures which society exerts to produce "desirable" racial attitudes in children; here we can only note that girls, as a matter of plain observation, do develop somewhat differently from boys, beginning probably somewhere around the age of fourteen. Several writers on this subject claim to have discovered an "instinctive" adverse reaction to contacts with persons of other races as part of a dawning sex consciousness. However, this theory leaves unexplained why this instinct should not be common to both sexes, or why it should affect the girls of the dominant group in a given community and apparently not the girls of the despised groups. Of course, it is perfectly easy to explain the fear of girls to associate with persons of a despised group on purely environmental and educational grounds; the more so as this fear seems to manifest itself not only in relation to assumedly inferior racial groups but also in relation to persons of despised classes. In other words, the adolescent girl reflects the attitude of her home and set toward desirable marriage.

The part which her changed sex life plays in the matter is by no means clear. But there is at least a faint justification for the belief that racial difference, so far from constituting a cause of abhorrence, constitutes a special fascination for the young girl. In many institutions for wayward girls white and colored girls have been strictly segregated because experience had shown that their intimacy was apt to lead to homosexuality; and from schools for normal girls one frequently hears of the special popularity and infatuation for girls of distinctly foreign appearance, providing their foreignness does not happen to involve a tradition of inferiority. A high-school teacher writes:

The pupils are seated without regard to race, though there are many colored. The white pupils are preponderantly Jewish. I have noticed white and mulatto girls walking through the halls arm in arm. In a room furnished chiefly with single seats but with one settee accommodating several, I have noticed white girls occupying a crowded settee with colored girls when it was quite convenient to take a single seat.

It is worth noting also that the "fear" of adolescent white girls for men of a different color lessens as the two groups approximate in social status. A Western correspondent observes that young people of all nationalities attend the cheaper dances but that "foreigners" are not admitted to the better class of dance halls. A settlement worker expresses a similar thought as follows:

Children become race conscious about the time their mothers begin to worry for fear their daughters will "go with" some boy of different social status.

Another correspondent says: Up to adolescence, most parents pay little attention to the playmates of their children; their new interest at this time accounts for the children's changed attitude.

Similarly a middle western teacher reports:

It is an unusual child who retains a firm friendship with a child of another race after the period of love-making sets in. The boy may still want to retain his "odd" friends, but there is the girl, and the girl's folk, to consider.

A group of parents in New Jersey states on this point:

The situations do not change very much as children grow older. Changes in attitude are due to maturity of outlook and the effect of the unconscious training in regard to the superiority of the white race. An exceptionally broad-minded mother remarks that while she would be quite willing at the present time to entertain at her home a modern Negro musician and composer, she would hesitate to do so ten years hence because her daughter would then be sixteen instead of six!

These opinions are interesting because they show how explanations and causes of child attitudes may have their common source in adult attitudes. It is possible, for example, that special circumstances, other than those hinted at, may account for a return of fear among girls in later adolescence after having been repressed during the school years. It may be that at this age there is more introspection and more willingness and ability than before to speak about oneself and one's mental life. For instance:

Mrs. D. says that as a child she lived in a part of Ohio where she saw no Negroes. At the age of nine, a Negro came to the home of her father, who entertained him, as he was an ardent advocate of social equality between Negroes and whites. She says she immediately felt for this black man a sense of repulsion which she considers innate. She tried to overcome it because he was a friend of her father's, but she could not. Ever since, when she was unavoidably near a Negro, she has tried to get away because she felt an inner distaste. She never told anybody at home about this feeling because she felt it was wrong, but it was always there.

Before concluding this chapter, it may be well to emphasize the difference which additional opportunities of acquiring information or misinformation must necessarily create in the adolescent's racial attitudes compared with those of the smaller child. It is not possible at this point to estimate the relative weight of emotional and of intellectual processes—if indeed that distinction is permissible in analyzing the learning process—but we are apt to mistake the situation completely if we neglect to make allowance for the influences of a purely informational character and speak of the changes of children's attitudes at different ages as though these might be entirely explained with differences in the child's own development.

Unfortunately few reliable data are available to illustrate what adolescents believe concerning the character and value of different racial groups, and the limitation of those that follow is recognized. Isolating the indications of racial attitudes in the responses of 1,110 high-school students (in different parts of the country) to a "true-false" test primarily concerned with international attitudes (and therefore without reference to the American Negro), George B. Neumann arrives at the following conclusions:

The students who have been studied in this investigation show comparatively little strength in their responses to the items referring to racialism. . . . They are evidently clear in their sense of being born mentally superior to the peoples of Africa. . . . Nearly two-thirds of them have expressed this attitude. . . . While there is a tendency, especially in the case of the peoples of India, to regard the white peoples as superior, the distribution of expressions is not far from being equally divided between pro and con.

On the other hand, there is a rather vigorous denial that weak and backward nations are so because they were born mentally inferior. . . .

Such superiority as the students do feel toward other races evidently does not carry with it a sense of right to interfere with weaker peoples on any basis of innate superiority. Their responses to the items imputing inferiority to the Mexicans and to the Chinese because of their apparent inability in government as contrasted with the boasted superior ability of the whites in that respect were on the whole denials of a right to interfere on such grounds. . . .

There is an evident sensitiveness shown by the students in regard to items where the complexes of nationalism and racialism are involved. . . . The tendency is to deny that the best Chinese are superior to average Americans, . . . a tendency to regard the "Yellow Peril" as a serious menace to the white peoples in our generation, . . . a slight tendency to insist that the Orientals be taught that the white race will never yield its dominance of the world.[11]

Here, then, we have evidence that at the time of maturing the more privileged American boy and girl carry within their attitudes germs of conflict: An idealistic humanitarianism is paralleled by an equally idealistic patriotism; both are apt to be somewhat uncertain and seemingly unaware of their sources. Before considering these sources, we shall do well, in the following chapter, briefly to review the development of racial attitudes through the different ages of childhood, as we have found it.

[11] *A Study of International Attitudes of High School Students.* Teachers College Contributions to Education, No. 239 (1926, pp. 44-45).

CHAPTER III

A PROGRESSIVE DEVELOPMENT OF ATTITUDES

Having presented such evidence as has come to us regarding the forms which race attitudes take in children and the ways they express themselves, we will now return to the question, several times referred to, at what ages do different race attitudes first appear? We have sufficiently guarded ourselves against the assumption that our tentative arrangement of the material in itself provides proof that certain attitudes belong to certain age groups. (See pp. 6 and 19.) In fact, we have stressed the damage done to a realistic interpretation of these phenomena by any such preconceived theory. Nevertheless, after considering the material evidence, we are forced to the conclusion that there is normally some relation between age and the form taken by race attitudes, and the behavior in which these express themselves, however vague the lines of division may be and however many the deviations from the norm. We have seen among the diversity of experiences and observations the somewhat indistinct outlines of a progression within which a majority of the observed examples fall; and it is desirable that at this point we should try further to define that outline. The categories which it contains do not necessarily correspond to age; but as we go over them again, it appears that roughly they do correspond to composite stages of maturity within which physical and mental age, kinds and degrees of personal experiences, and variety of impressions and stimuli received have their part. There is no absolute agreement among observers about the ages at which specific trends first become noticeable; but in spite of a certain likeness of American institutions—especially the public schools—conditions vary sufficiently in different parts of the country to account for such differences in judgment. There are no tests by which accurate data on our subject could be secured, and reliance upon judgments always necessitates a certain lack of precision. Nevertheless, it is now possible to summarize what seem to be fairly general agreements in picturing the advance and regression of the different main types of reaction somewhat as follows:[1]

The racial attitudes of children tend to vary at different ages. The small child is more apt to exhibit signs of fear, the child of early school age teasing and combativeness, either associated with or soon followed by a sense of ridicule—more amused than malicious—for strangers in appearance, language or manners. This is the age of "calling names" and throwing stones, of "aping," sometimes of mild aversion which may or may not grow into a more serious dislike for the unlike; many people mentally do not outgrow this age. Under some circumstances, a tendency toward openly expressed contempt gives way at an early age to an attitude of condescension, more often associated with mild derision than with acute hostility.

With adolescence two new elements enter: First, there is more conscious competition for school and athletic honors or for social recognition; and the granting of such honors or distinctions to those who belong to one of the despised minority groups is especially resented. This resentment against individuals, again, is transferred to their group and thus accentuates and embitters the feeling toward it which previously was one of mild derision or slightly contemptuous patronage. Second, the adolescent has become infected by this time with enough of the attitudes of the adult world to become class- and race-conscious. He no longer thinks of himself in purely individualistic terms but recognizes social relations and obligations. Among girls, the age of adolescence is apt to bring with it a seeming return to racial fears which, however, may coexist with a special attraction toward persons of markedly different appearance or race. For both sexes, the age of adolescence also introduces a deeper understanding of history and social organization and an idealistic turn of mind, with the combined effect of mitigating, if not altogether counteracting, the reactions previously noted.

A number of communications from contributors to this volume indicate that a progression of racial attitudes somewhat corresponding to different age groups is surmised, though not systematically tested. A western school principal says:

[1] Reference here, as throughout the larger part of the discussion where not otherwise stated, is to children of the dominant racial group or groups.

Hostility appears in the lower grades among children; I would say, from eight to twelve years of age. In the younger children I see no planned aversion, only what I think is a natural one. As the child gets older, the tendency of cruelty changes to ridicule, and unfairness becomes more subtle. For example, I very seldom have complaints that come from difficulties among the very young children themselves. Most of the trouble comes from the children of the second group picking on the younger ones or among members of the second group themselves. The attitudes named change in intensity, being most intense in the second group. I think the reason for the lessening of this intensity in the third age group is that, as the foreign child advances in age and in school, he becomes more Americanized, and the American child becomes more liberal in his views.

Typical of the opinions of several is the comment of a southern woman, a social worker: "I think these attitudes do not appear until school age, when the attitudes of elders are reflected."

A settlement worker in New York has observed fear of colored people at the early age of two, other reactions from the age of five years up, while the high-school child begins to take on the attitudes of his elders. In the public schools (of New York City), he says, there is usually little race feeling; often a foreign-born or colored boy is the hero of the group. A North Carolina teacher and mother thinks that "adverse attitudes are never shown until the child is old enough to have caught the attitude of older children or adults. My experience is that young children of their own initiative notice little difference as regards racial characteristics." Most psychologists would agree with the statement that children are "born democrats" and entirely free from instinctive reactions to racial differences.[2]

A Pennsylvania teacher says:

As children grow older, they naturally go in groups, and these groups are mostly made up of those of the same general development and, in a measure, are governed by common interests, such as school class, athletic games, clubs, etc. I do not think race prejudice would have as much influence on those groupings as personality.

When my small daughter was younger she made no demands. She accepted friendships without criticism. In her school there were many Italian children from homes of the unprogressive type, and she invariably chose the darkest and most soiled one of the group. Some-

[2] Arland D. Weeks, *The Control of the Social Mind* (1923, p. 235).

thing in the warm, impulsive nature of little Camilla appealed to her, and I encouraged the friendship. Soap and water clean off dirt.

However, that was a year ago. With her many friends, she has gradually begun to make demands, begun to be critical of her playmates. So far her criticisms are kind enough, but as I see her thinking and analyzing, I realize that I have a new task, that of seeing to it that her standard of measurement is broad and tolerant.[3]

A teacher in a middle western city, by means of a test, ascertained the relative strength of race "prejudice" among the members of a lower and a higher grade in a junior high school, with the following results:

	LOW GRADE CLASS		HIGH GRADE CLASS	
	No.	%	*No.*	%
Tolerant to Negro...............	4	15	8	23
Tolerant with qualifications.......	8	30	12	32
Definitely prejudiced	14	55	17	45

A report by a group of southern settlement workers gives the following age tabulation:

SYMPTOM	AGE
Fear	One year or less
Hostility	Six years up (calling names and playing in own group)
Unfairness	(In games, by choosing members of own nationality for partners) disappears when skill becomes a fact, or in games. Sex also figures in this
Patronage	Seven or eight years up
Ridicule	Ten or eleven years and up, when feeling can be put into words instead of action [4]

The settlement report continues:

As regards intensity and number of incidents:
Boys from ten to twelve show adverse attitude to a much greater extent than before or after because of their love to fight; there is more fighting, but not because of greater race hatred.

[3] Roberta Wayne in *Children,* for March, 1927, p. 22.
[4] Other contributors put the age of ridiculing rather lower. But what is here said about the effect of games of skill is an important point. For active hostility, a somewhat later age, that of eleven or twelve, is given by a middle-western teacher who finds "little intolerance that is deep-seated before puberty, among boys. Much the same is true of girls, although I believe that white girls are less inclined to have colored friends than white boys are."

Boys from twelve to fourteen show less hostility because at that time they are more interested in skill than in class distinction.

Girls, beginning at the age of twelve or fourteen, develop intense hatred as adolescence begins and parents fear intermarriage. Often the parents do not tell the girls the real reason but teach ridicule and hate. With increasing age, this feeling is intensified.

As regards the ways in which the adverse attitudes show themselves at different ages:

Boys and girls from six to ten years of age begin to group themselves according to nationality. This is true more in clubs and classes than on the playground because there is more intimate contact in clubs and classes. Whenever there is an argument, names are flung freely at the enemy, whether they mean anything to the child or not.[5]

A western school principal says: "The older child is less out and out in his warfare upon the foreigner."

One correspondent reports a growth of snobbishness up to the age of sixteen when it is apt to become less marked under the influence of religious teaching.

According to a child study specialist, the adoption of more tolerant attitudes on race is normal during adolescence. He says:

Provided that a child has absorbed sufficient knowledge of other races, both from personal contact and abstract training, he begins to reverse his attitudes during the adolescent period. Naturally, this depends upon how much the child is given to free thinking, particularly if he still continues to live in a prejudiced environment.

According to another reporter, the change in attitude follows from the individualism of the small child through the group interests and activities of the middle grades to a second more individualistic period in adolescence; or, expressed in symptoms, the calling of names at the later age becomes avoidance of individuals and whispered gossip concerning them. The element of rivalry also becomes stronger with the increase of examinations and more serious attitude toward promotions.

Possibly in line with this view is the report of an experienced settlement worker that adverse race attitudes lessen in the early teens and then increase again. A social worker among foreign-born women likewise reports a change from ridicule to a sharper hostility which is most intense in the adolescent period. A group of parents agreed that during adolescence a decided tendency

[5] The point here made concerning the difference of contacts is further dealt with in Chap. IV

to segregation shows itself. A middle-western report mentions a colored girl who left in the middle of the senior year in high-school because she was completely ostracized by everybody. In the same way, colored teachers and students in a Pennsylvania city were agreed that the last year in high-school brought a special crop of difficulties, owing to the increased rivalry and the endeavor of both teachers and fellow-pupils to discourage colored students from completing the course.

However, it should be added that other testimony, already mentioned, tends to indicate that about the same age religious influences often begin to bear fruit, and that friendships—not always without a taint of condescension, perhaps—are formed between white and colored, native- and foreign-born girls. (One hears less, both as regards rivalry and as regards such friendships, about boys.)

On the last point in our tentative statement of categories, the occurrence of a change in race attitudes in later adolescence, there is some difference of opinion because at that stage mutually contradictory trends become operative: We have seen that in later adolescence parents and other adults become more watchful over the associations of their girls, and their deliberate instillation of hostility toward class and race tolerance necessarily also affects the attitudes of adolescent boys. For example:

A boy in Pennsylvania who during his early school years freely associated with children of all races and at the age of seven invited a colored girl to his birthday party, would not, according to his mother, at the age of sixteen "tolerate for a moment having a colored girl invited to the house." Other possible changes in attitude apart, he obviously would have been ostracised by his present friends, boys and girls, had they found a lowering of the accepted race barrier in his home.

But at the same age, while the home is apt to exert its influence in the direction of hostility, church and school are more likely to impress the values of tolerance. We have here in many cases a first realization on the part of the adolescent that there is conflict between the attitudes of home and "set," on the one hand, and those of organized society in the larger sense on the other. Mothers, and what they stand for, come to be looked upon as "old-fashioned" when books or perhaps teachers and club leaders introduce the adolescent into the ideology of "world-mindedness." A southern settlement group reports:

As children grow older, parental teaching is replaced by individual experience and ideals, and in almost every case here there is a more broad-minded outlook than there was in childhood when the parental control was greater.

LIBERALIZING INFLUENCES

Again it is necessary at this point to admit that there are many exceptions to the general trend that has been described. While most observers would agree that on the whole the influence of the school is more liberalizing than that of the home, of course individual homes of a "liberal" tendency wage a continual fight against the "prejudiced" attitudes their children are taught at school. Moreover, in some communities—some of our correspondents seem to think they constitute the majority—the school is so thoroughly under the pressure of the predominant home attitudes that its teaching does not in any significant way depart from the mores and tastes of the majority of the "higher" social circles. For instance, a woman who for many years has taught high school in Pennsylvania expresses herself strongly to the effect that the teachers are the determining influence on the race attitudes of children during the adolescent period, and that the teachers are subject to the pressure brought to bear upon them by the parents.[6]

A New York high-school teacher mentions three factors that account for lessened race animosity in the later years of adolescence: deepened understanding, heightened idealism and greater control of personal feelings:

I should say that group differences are early recognized, say at seven or eight years, but not understood. The ridicule and hostility is a matter of emulation up to the age of fifteen or sixteen, when the child develops an interest in individuals as such. These ages for different attitudes differ, naturally, with native intelligence. For instance, the brilliant may have tolerant attitudes based on understanding, long before fifteen. The dull will not outgrow the imitative stage. It is to be borne in mind that tolerance and altruism arise from an ability to think abstractly; only the intelligent can do this. There is, however, no reason why the less intelligent should not be taught better habit formation and given better examples to imitate.

The attitudes, she continues, do change very markedly in adoles-

---

[6] The influences of home, school, church, etc., are more fully discussed in later chapters.

cence; especially if this period of life is spent in high school. Intensity of feeling is replaced by idealism and altruism, which are so characteristic of the adolescent. We observe very little exhibition of racial attitudes in a high school such as ours. This does not mean that antipathies do not exist, but it does mean that they are discreetly controlled and only subtly recognized. Racial clashes as shown in social activities seem to be less marked among high-school students (and ours is an old-line college preparatory school) than they are in real life outside the school.

As an example of awakening religious concern in its effect upon race attitudes, the following, from a letter of a high-school teacher, may be of interest:

I have been told by those who have been much longer teaching here than I that there is more prejudice against the Jewish race than the colored in our schools. I have never noticed any examples of it although I have a large number of Jewish children in my classes. I am very fond of them as they are usually bright and eager, and those just over from Russia and Poland have had such interesting and often tragic lives.

One thoughtful Russian Jew had stopped to ask some questions which biology arouses, such as the difference between Nature and God. That led up to his remarking that religion causes so much trouble and misunderstanding that, if he had not been born a Jew he would prefer not to have any religion at all. A Catholic girl joined in this discussion, and after a time we decided that, despite the external differences, at heart Jews and Catholics and Protestants are all seeking the same God. Then the boy exclaimed, "That is what we ought to teach in schools so that children would respect each other's religions!" This boy also remarked that prejudice made children very rude to each other, and that this could be excused in grammar school, but in high school a boy ought to know better than to call another a "dirty Jew."

The following confession, from a student at a middle-western university, illustrates the effect of intellectual understandings at the time of adolescence on deep-seated attitudes:

Early in my life, as far back as I have any recollection, I was taught to hate the Negro with all the force my childish impulses could muster. To me, all Negroes were fiends and intent upon killing me if ever they obtained the opportunity. While still very much of a child and even in later years I never saw a Negro but what I would tremble with fear and get out of his sight as quickly as possible.

This attitude of hatred for the Negro I developed purely from environmental influences in my home life. The first words I remember having heard my father tell me were to keep away from Negroes, that they would harm me. Whenever my mother wished to instil discipline in me she would threaten that "a big black man would get me" if I didn't behave.

And it was a matter of social environment that caused my parents to take this attitude. A colony of Negroes lived across the river from our home, and we always had considerable trouble with them.

It is clear, therefore, that I was prejudiced against the black race from the start. I had no contact with the Negro. A barrier had been built up for me, and I was isolated from the black race. I was not given an opportunity of deciding for myself whether my attitude was correct. It was a part of my social heritage, and for years I never doubted that it was correct.

However, as I grew older and began to read here and there about social problems and their relation to the Negro I began to have a change of attitude. It did not come suddenly, and even yet my attitude is somewhat influenced by the early training I received. Of course, I soon learned that the sole idea in a Negro's mind was not to go about killing people. That attitude changed early. But still, even after that change, I had a tremendous dislike for all Negroes.

As I remember it, it was in my second year of high school that first I learned of the narrow ideas that I held of the Negro problem. I followed a series of articles that dealt with the situation at length, told how the only solution of the problem was to educate the Negro and give him a chance of rising from his low social position. This, of course, proved highly interesting to me because it was the first inkling I ever had that anyone looked with the least possible hope upon the Negro. Up to that time he was in my mind a social evil which it would be impossible to get rid of.

It was only through continued reading and study that I saw the folly of my stand and that my attitude was based upon a false valuation of the Negro entirely. I learned that if he were given a chance to educate himself he would not be a scourge to the state.

The late Professor Bird T. Baldwin, of the University of Iowa, some time ago described the new idealistic trends in adolescence, without attempting to trace their source, as corresponding to two distinct periods of psychological development. He distinguishes between early adolescence, from twelve to sixteen, a period of moral awakening, and the second period of adolescence, from sixteen to twenty, one of religious awakening.[7]

[7] "The Boy of High School Age." *Religious Education*, April, 1913, pp. 26, 30.

In conclusion, it may once more be emphasized that what has in this chapter been described as, in the main, a process of change is also a process of accumulation—both of experiences and of the attitudes resulting from them. As each age group develops its characteristic responses to racial difference, it does not alto gether throw off the habits of response previously acquired. These live on and, though normally in recess, may be evoked by an especially strong emotional stimulus. An early fear may break out anew or, conversely, the remembrance of an early friendship across the boundary of race may, in the midst of a situation of acute animosity, suddenly be brought into consciousness by a chance resemblance. Here, then, we have inner conflict as the grooves worn into the receptive mind by different impulses and learnings cross each other and invite the flood of new experience to flow through, and imbue with new life, their ready channels. With each growth of mental age and each enlargement of the field of observation, with each new pressure from home or community, the attitude of the individual becomes more complex and more divided. In a community rich in diversity of folkways and interests, the normal child cannot grow up without leanings toward both pride of folk and appreciation for values other than those cherished by his own group.

CHAPTER IV

CHANGING RESPONSES TO CHANGING SITUATIONS

We have so far reviewed the forms in which race attitudes appear in children and the ages at which they are likely first to manifest themselves without regard to the great differences that exist in the occasions that call forth these expressions of feeling. We shall in later chapters have to consider carefully how race attitudes are formed, exactly what mental traits and environmental circumstances, what associations and what teachings produce adverse reactions to the members of a different group. But this present, descriptive part of our survey would not be complete without at least a hint that the various situations in which these reactions express themselves are as important as objects of study as are the forms of expression.

Here are a few examples which illustrate how children's attitudes toward members of other races and nationalities are colored by the circumstances of their contacts:

A child, just over five years of age, has been attending a Sunday school in which there is a Chinese girl who is "made a good deal of" by the teacher. The result is that little Mary talks very often about the Chinese and asks all sorts of questions about the way the Chinese do things. She seems to have already a decided attitude of friendliness toward the Chinese people.

On the other hand, she was overheard to remark: "I don't like Italians." It was found that the experience which lay behind this was that some Italian street laborers had been passing the house several evenings in succession and had apparently made a very unfavorable impression on her by their personal appearance. She said, "Italians are dirty," and again, "Italians talk so funny. Their talk doesn't sound like ours."

A number of cases illustrating this point are given in the report of the Chicago Commission on Race Relations.[1]

A change of residence through removal or through being sent to school abroad or in a different part of the country is, of course,

[1] *The Negro in Chicago* (University of Chicago Press, 1922, pp. 249, 250, 252, 254, 276, 285, 288).

often a marked change of situation in regard to race—either because it brings with it new types of contact or because it involves a change in the surrounding adult attitudes. For example, without ever coming in personal contact with a Chinese, a child would be likely to be influenced toward that race in very different ways in California and in Boston; his attitudes toward "foreigners" as such would be likely to change considerably between an early childhood in a small hill town of Tennessee and a later childhood in Jersey City. The following examples illustrate this tendency:

A Japanese senior in the university here tells me that as a child she had practically no friends among the Japanese, all her associates in school, church, and social life being white children. Only when she came to the United States as a student did she begin to notice that she was not readily admitted to some of the young people's affairs. Being very pretty and above the average in intelligence, she has always been given credit for her abilities, but she found that she was not acceptable in society because of her race. She then drifted to the Japanese, but as she had some European blood in her veins, she was not made to feel entirely at home there either. This girl is now very much depressed because of her social status.

About four years ago my niece, aged eleven, came to America and was sent directly to a school in the South. When a year or so later she joined us in Brooklyn, she amazed us all by her violent protests against the presence of a colored pupil in the public school to which she was going. The family found it difficult to understand this prejudice on the part of the little girl and insisted that she must continue to attend the school, assuring her that colored people were as good as white. By the end of the school year, my little niece admitted that the colored pupil to whose presence she had objected was quite the nicest girl in the class.

This year my nephew had come to New York after a period in the same school in the South. His attitude toward the colored people was exactly the same that his sister had had a year before. When he saw colored people enter the same car on the subway in which we were, he asked what ailed those black people that they dared to come into our car.

The Chicago report contains several instances of the difficulty which colored children from the South have in adjusting themselves to the different race attitudes in the North.[2]

[2] *The Negro in Chicago* (University of Chicago Press, 1922, p. 248).

Several correspondents point out that the contacts in school are, in most cases, conceived of as quite different in character from those outside school. In most sections of the United States, we look upon the public school as a public service like the streets or parks and do not question the right of any group in the community to take advantage of it. We look differently, however, upon contacts outside the classroom. Even on the school playgrounds the behavior of children often reflects their distinctive social attitudes rather than their sense of common right. A high-school teacher writes:

My own observations indicate that it is quite practicable to eliminate race prejudice as an active force in school matters. Where the problem becomes serious is in matters purely social. Even with complete freedom from racial discriminations in the school, it is but rare that I see colored and white boys mingling in the street, where the boys congregate in the noon period. The colored boys form a distinct group, sometimes on the other side of the street. It is a question with me whether mixed education is likely to touch the social separation of the races.

Still more important, whether desirable or undesirable, is the separation of the sexes. I have no remembrance of ever seeing one of our colored boys speak to a white girl or vice versa. A girl so light as to be practically unnoticed in the classroom among her girl friends will be seen on a social occasion or in the street talking with a black boy rather than with a white one. The dances are open to all, but the colored pupils come in separate groups and dance strictly within these groups.

A colored minister in a city of the Middle West was able, after much saving, to buy a substantial home—not as good a one as a white man could have bought for the same amount of money, not in as good a neighborhood, but still a nice house. He was fair, and as his father was a white man, it was not surprising that his little son was even fairer, with a wealth of blond, curly hair, while the little daughter was unmistakably colored. At school it happened that the little boy played most often with a group of white boys whereas the girl played with other colored girls; it was not generally known among the children that they were brother and sister. This came about naturally, not from deliberate choice. Quite as naturally, during the vacation, instead of following his schoolmates to their more distant neighborhood, the boy played with his sister and her colored friends. When some of the boy's white schoolmates happened to find him thus employed, they realized that he was colored and spread the news among other boys.

Soon they made special excursions into the colored neighborhood and called the minister's son all sorts of names, teasing him as only boys know how to tease.

The minister's son was no pacifist. Soon he had a whole string of victorious hand-to hand encounters to his credit, and, of course, the neighborhood sided with him.

Sometimes the effect of the two environments—school and playground—is exactly the opposite of that so far pictured, and for a good reason. Where classes are subdivided so as to separate the more advanced children of a grade from the less advanced or those needing special help because of language difficulty, a certain stigma attaches to room "B" where the foreign children congregate—the more so since many of the foreign children will be above the average age for children in that grade. Yet, in spite of this division, the children of room "B" may be among the most popular on the playground.

I find, writes a western school principal, that when a foreigner proves to excel in athletics, he is generally accepted as an equal, and especially when his personal appearance is good. For example, Tom Coca is a Mexican boy, a very good boxer and a good baseball player. I find that he is generally accepted as an equal among the boys. When the music supervisor cast him for one of the good parts in an operetta, he was accepted by the girls as an equal.

SCHOOL AND PLAY

Of course, to the child's mind, the distinction between school and recreation is not always quite clear, and clashes between groups are apt to happen when there is uncertainty of this kind, one group assuming that a certain situation calls for a continuation of the relationship formed at school, the other group resenting this as an intrusion. Many bloody battles are fought over this issue on public playgrounds. The clubs and classes of social settlements, likewise, are apt to be confused, so far as their social atmosphere is concerned, with the classes at school; and while one group assumes that the same rules of conduct govern in both cases, another may feel that a more exclusive spirit ought to prevail in these voluntary associations. The following incident, from a middle-western settlement, illustrates the confusion in the mind of a race-conscious colored girl, in circumstances in which the institution had done its utmost not to put any pressure upon the children either in the direction of segregation or in that of forcing them together:

Two sewing clubs were meeting in adjoining rooms, one made up entirely of colored girls, the other entirely of white girls. A new colored girl entered the colored club and noticed that all the members of the other club were white. She immediately came down to the office and asked, "Miss A., why did you put me in a separate class with colored girls?" The director asked, "Did I put you in that class?" "Well, no," she said after thinking it over, "I picked it out myself. I joined that class because my friends are in it."

This little example is interesting because the club director evidently is thoroughly satisfied with the outcome. She says, "Mary was very happy during the rest of the time after she realized that she had made the decision for herself." Of course, the fact remains that the settlement—one of the most liberal institutions of its kind—here had permitted and actively encouraged a form of voluntary race segregation that did not exist at school without, apparently, fully explaining to the children of the less favored group the underlying difference in the situation.[3]

Why voluntary association should have a different effect upon race attitudes from that of compulsory association in the public schools is a matter into which we shall have to go more fully later. Here it is important only to point out that practically all the reports received agree that the reaction of children in these different situations reflects the attitudes of their elders rather than their personal experiences.

Children of various races, says one report, are thrown together in school, playgrounds, theatres, public conveyances and in mixed neighborhoods. If the teacher or manager or person in authority in any of the above places shows a tendency to separate children into racial groups instead of making a division according to ability or alphabetical arrangements, or according to the price of the ticket, a child immediately conceives a sense of difference. If, on the other hand, they learn to know each other through normal association where little of the emotional factor enters in, they are apt to assume a friendlier spirit when they meet on a more social basis in the Sunday school, school yard or club.[4]

[3] The question of social segregation is further discussed in Chap. IX.
[4] The influence of the teacher's attitude, looked upon by many as the cardinal point, is dealt with more fully below (Chap. XI, p. 142).

A settlement worker, enumerating public schools, settlements, mission churches, and playgrounds as the chief places where children of different racial groups meet, draws attention to the fact that these opportunities to mix are open only to those of the "lower classes" of society.

Another report regards the contacts made in Sunday schools as not only rarer but also more abnormal than those made in the public schools, because of the smaller number of children of foreign race or nationality and the more forced emotional appeal.

In social settlements race distinctions are often made because they are taken for granted by the directors, not because they are especially desired by the children. There are many mentions of both long-established and recent mixed clubs in the reports of settlements where these have been allowed to grow up.

From a private school which has made it a principle to admit —when necessary by means of fellowships—a proportion of colored and foreign-born children, comes the following report:

In our school we have always a few colored children. They conform to our usual standard of character and academic work. As a matter of fact, the majority that we have in my department have been very high I.Q. children. From time to time, at very long intervals, I have heard some comment, rather than criticism, upon their presence in the school—usually the comment has been that of pleasure. I believe it is true that over a period of sixteen years during which I have observed this situation, I have never noted a single instance in which the children seemed to show any discrimination or barely any consciousness of difference between themselves and their colored classmates. We have never had two colored children who were intimate with each other, but we have had a number of markedly intimate friendships between a white and a colored child. One of these has continued into the college age. I feel perfectly willing to assert dogmatically that race prejudice is entirely a thing engrafted into children by their parents, teachers or general social environment.

I have various incidents which I could relate in regard to the relations above referred to. This last winter, a boy who had never been to school before entered our sixth grade. He became very intimate with a colored boy; they have been almost inseparable during school hours, going about with their arms around each other. The family became familiar, in the midst of accounts of class activities and names of classmates, with the phrase "and my best friend . . ." Toward the end of January, there was a discussion at the supper table one evening which involved some reference to colored people. The boy remarked quite casually, "My best friend . . . is a colored boy." No one of the household had known of this before. His mother said afterwards, she realized that one smile, one exclamation, one surprised question would have done more harm in instilling a consciousness of there being something unusual in the situation than hours of platitudes about its being very nice for him to have a little colored friend, etc., could have undone. She said that of the rather large household not one "quivered an eyelid" or made the slightest sign of surprise, and the intimacy has continued to be spoken of in exactly the same way.

How even on the public playgrounds adult influence may condition the nature of the contacts between children of different races is told by a colored social worker in a large eastern city:

If there were natural race antagonisms in children, the public playgrounds would be the places where these traits would crop' out. In . . . there is a playground which has a colored man as director. Here colored and white children may be seen engaged in all sorts of recreational activities without any suggestion of racial friction. There is another playground in another part of the city where a white man is in charge. At this playground, colored children are not allowed to use the recreation house and are forced to play by themselves. The two playgrounds are similar in equipment, and the neighborhoods are of about the same racial composition. It is quite evident that the condition mentioned with regard to the latter playground is the result of the arbitrary action of the director who has ordered the white and colored children to keep apart. The director of the playground first mentioned states that the white children are as deferential to him as are the colored children, and that there has never been anything of an unpleasant nature due to racial antagonism on the part of the children who regularly use the playground. Sometimes older boys from other parts of the city cause a little friction, but he does not regard this as racial but rather as due to the usual antipathy which boys living in one part of a town have for those of another section.

A group of parents in New Jersey report on this question:

Children of different groups are brought together chiefly through contact in the classroom and in organized play, chiefly in the school yard. They accept this as a part of the school régime. The effect, however, is in the majority of cases only temporary. When removed from the school government, members of the two racial groups do not mingle. In the Sunday school the nature of the contact is slightly different, in that it is closer and semi-social. One woman reported that her little daughter declined to return to Sunday school when a Negro girl was admitted to the class. The same child was accustomed to

Negroes here and there in the public day-school which she attended; but in Sunday school the group was small, numbering six, and the difference was evidently felt.

That the democracy of the public school is felt as something compulsory is also the observation of a western teacher who writes:

In the primary department I see no premeditated or definite aversion. In their games, they will choose a foreigner as a partner just as readily as another; but when it comes to a choice without the supervision of the teacher, as in marching out of the building, or on the playground, I notice that they are not so democratic. She adds: It is the poorer type of the American child that accepts these foreign children as equal —by poorer I mean poorer in refinement.

A discussion group in Cleveland reports on the adverse effects of denominational schools where attitudes to religious differences often assume also a racial character. One member reported that when attending a Protestant school she and her companions were terribly afraid of Catholics, so that they avoided going anywhere near the Catholic section of the town. Later she attended a Catholic convent school and found her prejudice dissipated by acquaintance. A group of Jewish boys was mentioned as having always thought of Christians as "those who spit on the Jews."

The effect of school policy is mentioned also by a high-school teacher in the Middle West, who says:

Children will mix fairly well on the school grounds if there is no positive effort on the part of the school authorities or of such organizations as the Klan to accentuate their differences.

According to the teacher just quoted, there is a decided difference in the nature of the contacts made in that those at school are looked upon as temporary and more or less compulsory, and no lessons are drawn from them as to the desirability of permanent contacts between persons of different racial groups.

For example, my brother had a Negro chum as a boy. When both reached the age of twelve or thirteen, they naturally drew apart. My brother has no color prejudice to my knowledge, but on the other hand he has no interest in the "color problem." His friend is forgotten. No one, while the friendship lasted, taught him a lesson in unity.

According to a well-known educator (reporting the findings of a class of graduate teachers) there is considerable difference between the contacts made in public and in private schools.

In groups in which there were both public and private school children, the former made no objections to associating and playing with colored children, while the latter refused to do so.

The southern settlement report, previously quoted, gives the following illustration of the children's sense of the difference between the various kinds of contact:

In a club made up principally of ten-year-old Syrian girls, two Italian girls who had played with the Syrian girls all summer applied for membership. The Syrian children declared in no uncertain terms, "We would much rather break up the club than let those two girls in." Their argument was, "We play with them on the playground and we have to go to school with them, but in a club it is different." This, indeed, was not a bad argument, clubs *are* different.

The same group reports a case which proves rather neatly that circumstances alter cases:

A Jewish gang and an Italian gang were always "at war." Finally one of the settlement workers took the two leaders by the nape of the neck and said, "Would your two gangs ever join in anything?" One of the gang leaders promptly replied: "Sure—in fightin' niggers."

As has already been intimated, the situations creating contacts change somewhat as children grow older. A western correspondent states:

The foreign child matures sooner than the American-born. They have generally finished their education when they have finished the eighth grade, if they do not reach the age of sixteen sooner, and then they are through with the Americanization process. I find that, instead of continuing their associations, they go back to their own kind as soon as they leave school. I notice this at dances. You attend one of the cheaper dances, and you will find these foreigners, while at the better class of dances you will not find them, even though the dance is public."

PART II

HOW ARE RACE ATTITUDES ACQUIRED?

CHAPTER V

THE PART PLAYED BY INSTINCT

Having observed some of the forms in which adverse race attitudes on the part of children become visible to their elders, having traced what seemed a progressive development of these attitudes through the different ages of childhood, and having noted the differences in the expression of race attitudes that seem to correspond to differences in situations and the contacts they afford, we must now try to discover in what ways these race attitudes have come about.

The evidence already presented, one would think, might suffice to prove the non-existence of an inherent, "instinctive" race attitude of fear or repulsion as part of human nature. More especially, as we see one type of reaction give way to another with the advancing age of the child, and as we see the child react in two different ways to seemingly like stimuli in two distinct situations, we might dogmatically assert that there can be no such inborn trait, and that all the observed responses are the results of acquired habits. Nevertheless, the impression prevails widely that the child is born with instinctive responses of different kinds, one of which is an extreme dislike of and shrinking from persons of markedly different race.

Among the parents, educators and social workers who have contributed toward the present study are many who take that view—who, in fact, take it for granted and try to range the material evidence of their observation into the framework of an assumed law of instinctive racial aversions. Many of them thus regard the manifestations of fear. Those who call it instinctive rarely argue this as a theory; they simply assume its general acceptance and merely endeavor to contribute interesting illustrations of what they believe to be a generally acknowledged fact. Others, likewise speaking of "instinctive" reactions, if closely questioned would admit that they are loosely using a term to which they attribute no specific scientific meaning, but which they, in common with most people, are in the habit of using rather freely. A third group, aware of the intricacy of the subject, remains content to contribute observations without claiming to possess the knowledge necessary for their explanation. Their statements, in some cases, show real puzzlement; for, having had their attention drawn to phenomena open to every-day observation, some of these contributors discovered that what they saw and what others in their environment told them about the behavior of children in this particular regard did not fit in with what they had always assumed to be true of racial feeling. For example, some southern women admit, as a fact not quite easy to understand, that small black and white children readily play together, while several northern correspondents refer to instinctive aversions which, somehow, do not fit into their belief in a perfect brotherhood of man—except on the assumption that some instincts are part of original sin and can be cast out by the right sort of religious training. Here are some typical passages from reports received:

A northern settlement worker says that quite small children show fear of colored people, and sometimes of Japanese and Chinese.

Other experiences are "Children are little animals and, as such, respond quickly to differences in form, language, color, etc."

From our experience and the experience of teachers and others with whom we have talked, it seems to be the consensus of opinion that children have no natural race antagonisms. We are discounting the artificial attitudes which children accept from the teachings of parents or teachers. Even in adolescence, race attitudes are the result of something outside themselves.

A settlement worker says that these attitudes "often are instantaneous" but immediately adds that even "very young children take their attitude from that of their parents."

A southern settlement group say: The idea of instinctive race attitudes comes about because children get the idea so young from parents or other prejudiced adults that adults who try to trace prejudice cannot remember when they were without it.

A grandmother who has been a teacher and missionary for many years and is now connected with an important mission board, writes: I can just say one thing from experience: I do not think that race prejudice exists at all in children. It is wholly acquired. There are decidedly strong antipathies, but they are not based on racial differences, rather on temperamental differences or those which come from entirely different training and environment. My own children loved the little native Indian children quite as much as they loved any other, in fact rather better, I think, because they assumed a little of the domination which young children are glad to assume. The only real antipathy I remember having seen my small boy register was against a very dirty li.tle Irish boy who sat next him at school. He told me one night as we prayed for the children around the world that he liked the children in China, India, Japan—in fact, liked all children except Mickey. It was not at all because Mickey came from Ireland, I am sure, or because of any racial difference, but entirely because he was an unclean and ill-bred youngster. I have never seen any tendency to race prejudice among children. I will go further and say, I think it is not common among youth but a product of the sort of discussion we get, especially along political lines.

I have seen little children in the South who adored their black nurses. I have entertained in my own home groups of from six to ten Chinese girls and have invited, to meet them, the loveliest young women in our community, and they have been more than charmed with each other.

To the same effect, the New Jersey group of parents: Adverse attitudes of children toward those of other races seem to be instinctive largely because adults have placed this meaning upon them; also because the children themselves do not account for any adverse expressions but, imitating the examples of adults, assume that such an attitude is expected.

A Filipino student contributes two experiences which, he thinks, illustrate that the natural attitude of children to those of distinct racial characteristics is curiosity and not hostility:

1. Two years ago, I was in the Y.M.C.A. College Camp at Lake Geneva, Wisconsin; I was attending to the oil lamps in the tents and along the roads. One day, when I was pushing a little cart full of lanterns, a boy of eight years, the son of a "Y" secretary, was watching and following me. I greeted him in a friendly manner and he responded in the same way. He was rather shy before this exchange of "how-do-you-dos." When I started to push my cart for another route, he came along, helping me to push my cute-looking two-wheeled vehicle. Evidently the cart attracted his attention more than my person did. However, he was responsive to familiar conversation about camp life, and finally he asked questions about myself until he found out how many brothers and sisters I had and how old I was, and every last thing about me. The next day he brought his sister, two years younger; evidently he had told her all he knew about me, because after he had

told me she was his sister, she talked to me without any further ceremony. "How are you, Polly Peanut?" Her brother had told her what my nickname was, but I could not imagine why she called me Peanut besides. I asked her why. She replied that I was as brown as a roasted peanut, and that she liked peanuts.

2. One day I was washing an automobile for a lady instructor at the University of Illinois. While I was getting ready for the hose, two little girls, about four and six years old, asked me what I was doing. I told them in good American accent. The elder one remarked that I did not speak like a "Chink" and did not look "like colored." Then she said that I did not wash my face "good," because I did not look white enough.

A California group produces two seemingly contradictory statements:

Most of the group think repulsion is learned, not inherited. A teacher with missionary experience told of repulsion as a girl of nine at being touched by a mulatto barber in Ohio. Her father was a Union soldier and insisted on no race distinction. She thinks the repulsion was natural. Later she overcame it.

A white baby of a year and a half, states another report, used to pick out colored people in the subway of New York and smile at them as a mark of special favor. This was because of acquaintance with her grandmother's Negro butler.

We have no evidence pointing to adverse attitudes as "natural" or "instinctive," writes a high-school teacher. Our school policy is based on the view that adverse attitudes are deliberately inculcated, and are to be eradicated as soon as possible.

Many of the examples given throughout this book in tracing some of the adverse race attitudes to the influences that caused them, and especially those contributed by groups and individuals, strengthen the impression that these attitudes are acquired. The idea that they are native or instinctive, as we found one of these groups saying, often is due to the fact that those who hold this opinion cannot recollect what happened to them in early childhood.

THEORIES OF INSTINCT

The theory of instinct is just at the present time one of the most controversial topics in the whole field of psychology, and perhaps no particularly useful contribution can be made to the disentanglement of contradictory definitions, observations and explanations in connection with this present study. Nevertheless, we must try to acquire at least a tentative knowledge of the nature and functioning of instinct as a preliminary to a profitable dealing with those particular manifestations of the child mind with which we are primarily concerned in this book. Obviously, if we remain too hazy on this point, many parents and teachers will have good reason to reject in its entirety as "unsound" what follows in subsequent chapters, whether in the form of explanation or of suggestion for the educational treatment of racial attitudes.

Several possibilities are open to us. First, we may, with Thorndike, reduce the application of the term "instinct" by distinguishing it from two other types of original tendencies, "reflexes" and "inborn capacities." He says:

Three terms, reflexes, instincts, and inborn capacities, divide the work of naming these unlearned tendencies. When the tendency concerns a very definite and uniform response to a very simple sensory situation, and when the connection between the situation and the response is very hard to modify and is also very strong so that it is almost inevitable, the connection or response to which it leads is called a reflex. Thus the knee-jerk is a very definite and uniform response to the simple sense-stimulus of sudden hard pressure against a certain spot. It is hard to lessen, to increase, or otherwise control the movement, and, given the situation, the response almost always comes. When the response is more indefinite, the situation more complex, and the connection more modifiable, instinct becomes the customary term. Thus one's misery at being scorned is too indefinite a response to too complex a situation and is too easily modifiable to be called a reflex. When a tendency is to an extremely indefinite response or set of responses to a very complex situation, and when the connection's final degree of strength is commonly due to very large contributions from training, it has seemed more appropriate to replace reflex and instinct by some term like capacity, or tendency, or potentiality. Thus an original tendency to respond to the circumstances of school education by achievement in learning the arts and sciences is called the capacity for scholarship.[1]

John B. Watson rejects both the term "instinct" and its implications current in popular applications of the term:

[1] Edward L. Thorndike, *Educational Psychology*. Briefer Course (Teachers College, Columbia University, 1914, p. 4). We will not follow this educator's further analysis of what he calls the "social instincts" because, pubished more than a decade ago, these applications do not coincide with more recent theories.

Man is an animal born with certain definite types of structure. Having that kind of structure, he is forced to respond to stimuli at birth in certain ways (for example: breathing, heart beat, sneezing, and the like). This repertoire of responses is in general the same for each of us. Yet there exists a certain amount of variation in each—the variation is probably merely proportional to the variation there is in structure (including in structure, of course, chemical constitution). It is the same repertoire now that it was when the *genus homo* first appeared many millions of years ago. Let us call this group of reactions man's *unlearned behavior.*

In this relatively simple list of human responses there is none corresponding to what is called an "instinct" by present-day psychologists and biologists. There are then for us no instincts—we no longer need the term in psychology. Everything we have been in the habit of calling an "instinct" today is a result largely of training—belongs to man's *learned behavior.*

As a corollary from this I wish to draw the conclusion that there is no such thing as an inheritance of *capacity, talent, temperament, mental constitution and characteristics.* These things again depend on training that goes on mainly in the cradle. The behaviorist would *not* say: "He inherits his father's capacity or talent for being a fine swordsman." He would say: "This child certainly has his father's slender build of body, the same type of eyes. His build is wonderfully like his father's. He, too, has the build of a swordsman." And he would go on to say: "—and his father is very fond of him. He put a tiny sword into his hand when he was a year of age, and in all their walks he talks sword play, attack and defense, the code of duelling and the like." A certain type of structure, plus early training—*slanting*—accounts for adult performance.[2]

One need not agree with Professor Watson's sweeping denial of the inheritance of psychological traits along with physical traits distinctive of racial or family strain to admit that he is right when he criticizes the adherents of various theories of instinct for failure to check these up by fairly obvious inductive tests.[3]

Freud still uses the term "instinct" in a meaning which is more fundamental, more primitive, more expressive of the central dynamic principle or energy in organic nature than the meaning attached to the term by the behaviorists. There is, of course, no

[2] John B. Watson, *Behaviorism* (People's Publishing Company, New York, 1924, p. 74). Chaps. V and VI of this work deal very fully with the question, Are There Any Human Instincts?, which, as seen from the above extract, is answered in the negative.
[3] *Harper's Monthly,* July, 1927, p. 230.

getting away from the hypothesis of instinct if we make it, as he does, almost synonymous with the libido.[4]

As Freud has pointed out, the use of biological terms is apt to mislead us into a false analogy between the functioning of mental processes and the functioning of physical processes. For the purpose of our study it is important to keep in mind that we are not concerned with instincts in a state of uncontrolled nature—as we expect to find it in the lower animals—but with instincts operative in the peculiar conditions that surround the exercise of all biological functions within the controlled environment of a highly complex human society.[5]

Expressed in another way, are we not in danger of over-emphasizing the non-intellectual aspects of mind? There is ample excuse for it, for it is only in the last generation or so that the emotional and subconscious activities of the *psyche* have been systematically studied, and that discoveries in this wide range of inquiry have placed other psychological studies somewhat in the shade. Nevertheless, it is well that we recall to our minds the onesidedness, and therefore misleading nature, of preoccupations with "instinct," for example, at the exclusion of study of the controlling factors within which instinct functions and, as Professor Coe suggests, perhaps changes in character.[6]

The present knowledge of the part played by instinct in social attitudes has been well summarized by Professor Ellwood in a recent book. Its wider diffusion should go far to eliminate that false conception of a mysterious, unfathomable, widely specialized instinct that too often obtrudes into the discussion of race attitudes and falsifies our interpretations of these attitudes in their various forms of expression.[7] The importance of the factor of

[4] The history of the psycho-analytical development of inquiry into the nature of instincts or instinct, and its tentatively furthest advanced hypothesis is given in Sigmund Freud's *Beyond the Pleasure Principle* (1925, p. 64 *et seq.*). In this book, the author permits his imagination free range and, without binding himself to his tentative findings as beliefs or convictions, suggests the possibility of the truth of the ancient assumption of a primary duality or polarity of all nature, caused by a disruption of living substance into small particles at the time of its animation, and a subsequent striving for reunion by means of the sexual instincts.

[5] George Albert Coe, *The Psychology of Religion* (University of Chicago Press, 1916, p. 24).

[6] *Ibid.*, p. 141.

[7] Charles E. Ellwood, *The Psychology of Human Society* (1925, p. 277, *et seq.*). Readers who are especially interested in the questions raised in this chapter will find a useful history of thought on the nature of instinct in E. C. Wilm's *The Theories of Instinct* (Yale University Press, 1925). (This author, who is professor of philosophy at Boston University, has in preparation a volume on *Instinct and Intelligence*.)

instinct in the race attitudes of children lies chiefly in the erroneous conception of its nature which prevails among parents and
teachers. Our reports contain many instances in which faulty
educational or administrative policies were adopted because of
such errors.[8]

These errors, while they affect the treatment of fear and other
reactions in early childhood, are especially pronounced in the
treatment of combativeness. (See p. 13.) Since that subject has
received excellent, detailed treatment in a book recently published [9] and is further discussed in another connection below (page
190 *et seq.*) we can conclude this chapter with the bare statement
that the "fighting instinct" does not exist.

[8] Typical is the expression of opinion by a school principal, reported in *The
Negro in Chicago* (Chicago University Press, 1922, p. 248).
[9] William G. Carr, *Education for World-Citizenship* (Stanford University
Press, 1928, Chap. V).

CHAPTER VI

THE PART PLAYED BY PERSONAL EXPERIENCE

Many observers feel that the growth of racial attitudes in children coincides with a progressive series of discoveries which include both a recognition of facts that have always been present and open to view and the forming of conclusions from new personal experiences. It is a little difficult to make a clear distinction between the different types of experience from which a child garners new attitudes toward people, whether favorable or unfavorable. Not only do they coincide to a large extent, so that it is impossible to say whether a new observation, a new assimilation of teaching or a specific incident and the conclusions drawn from it are the major element; but with the conception which educators now have of the process of learning, all the child's reactions to outside influences must really be regarded as experiences of learning, the reading of a book and the enjoyment of a moving picture as much as an altercation on the school yard or foreign travel. Nevertheless, before discussing organized ways in which children are influenced, we shall in this section try to distinguish between different types of experience and learn how they influence the child mind in their different ways.

1. CONTINUOUS CONTACT

We cannot, in this study, assume agreement on the proposition that a long acquaintance with members of another racial group in situations that make for favorable appreciation is immunity enough against the formation of adverse attitudes. In fact, too many cases are illustrations of the exact opposite: People who have every reason to be well disposed toward the members of a given group in a change of circumstances forget all their knowledge and open their minds to prejudices as though they had had no previous experience at all.[1] On the other hand we can

[1] We need only recall the attitudes assumed in many American neighborhoods during the late war against residents of German descent or name. The irresistible power of propaganda and mutual patriotic incitement of normally sensible people made them blind to the well-known virtues of Hans, the butcher, and Friedrich, the barber, and made these inoffensive citizens appear conspirators, spies and traitors to their own adopted country.

all recall examples of the way in which an early happy experience may color a racial attitude for life.

A student writes:

I have an intense and unfailing sympathy for people of the colored race and a feeling of almost personal injustice on hearing them "run down" in conversation by the white race.

The primary basis for this seems to be an early acquaintance with a colored girl of my own age. I was raised in a small town where there was no colored element at all. There was one family of which the father was an educated mulatto, one of the best and most successful lawyers of the district, and the mother was of pure white stock of the best around. They had lived there for years, their parents having been of that region so that they were accepted without much thought. They went to one of the Protestant churches where the woman was very prominent. There were three girls all of whom were very brilliant and surpassed their school-mates so that there was probably a feeling of jealousy more than anything else.

The youngest girl was of my own age, and their house was next to my father's office down in the center of the town, so that very early we became close friends. I was absolutely ignorant that there was any difference between us as my family had very wisely not discussed the matter. So, for about two years before we started to school, we played together a great deal there in the office and were as congenial as any of my other friends. But when it came time for us to start to school, my family thought that I should be told that she was a colored girl and, although they did not want me to abuse her in any way, I should not make her my best friend because there was a difference. They realized the difficulties of the situation but felt that I should know the facts. I will never forget the feeling that I had and how I cried for hours because I felt so sorry for the girl. At first I absolutely refused to believe it, but of course that did not last long. I could not see why, when I liked her so much and we did so many things alike, it made any difference at all.

As school years went on, I never changed my mind about liking her, and it always seemed so unjust that there should be any feeling against her, although I realize now that there was very little in comparison with other cities and conditions. Once, another girl and I were invited to this home for dinner, and we were allowed to go and had a very nice time. There was nothing different from what we were used to at all, and we did not have any sense of doing anything unusual. But when we went home, in a spirit of fun of course, people would say: "Well, do they eat with their fingers at ——'s or do they do so and so?" Those questions always made me very angry, and, as I mentioned above, I always felt that it was almost a personal insult, and I tried to defend them as much as possible.

This friendship was broken off when I was ten. We went to a city where the atmosphere toward the colored was very different and there was absolutely no sense of equality at all. Naturally, I absorbed certain attitudes of discrimination at school, but the feeling of sympathy was there at the bottom and tempered those later attitudes.

An Ohio college student wrote the following class paper on My Attitude Toward the Negro:

Until the age of seven I had never seen a Negro person and therefore I could not have had any favorable or unfavorable attitude for them before I came into contact with them. As the saying goes "First impressions are lasting," and in my case with the Negro this has proven itself true.

About the year 1913 a great number of Negroes who were seeking better working and living conditions migrated from the South. Cleveland seemed to be ideally located, so that many of them chose that city as a settling place. At this time there happened to be a small one-family house vacant in our neighborhood. Since this house had been an exceptionally good place to play hide-and-seek, we all looked with horror to the day when some one would rent it. One day, much to my sorrow, I saw a large moving van unloading an abundance of furniture, and it was obvious that some one was moving into the house. In vain I tried to locate some of the new comers, but none could be found. My brother, who was two years older than myself, was hopefully praying that the new neighbors would include several new boy friends, while I on the other hand looked forward to meeting at least one new girl friend. That evening I heard my parents discussing at great length the new strange neighbors. The conversation, as I remember, ran something as follows: "The grocery man has promised not to sell merchandise to these new people for that would drive away his trade!" The next morning a close neighbor paid us an unusually early visit. The discussion ran in the same channel—the new neighbors. My curiosity was reaching its climax. Who were those new neighbors, and what were they like? Just as I was starting off to school, I saw a little girl making her exit from the much talked-about house. My first glance at her caused me to start back a bit. Perhaps I rubbed my eyes, for it was impossible to believe what I saw. Little cork-screw curls and a tan face,—that new girl must have forgotten the exact date of Halloween! However, as she turned to look at me, I met a great big smile beckoning me to come across the street. If I did have some fear of her, it had all vanished, and my curiosity was leading the way.

I immediately decided that I liked her, but unfortunately the beginning of a friendship was delayed, for Mother had forbidden me to associate with the new neighbors' girl. My inquiries of why and wherefore were futile. Although I could not associate with Eulah, I always met her cheerfully and did not hesitate to walk to school with her, that is, when Mother was not on her guard. The following summer I became ill and was unable to attend school for two weeks. One day, Mother came into the room carrying a small rubber ball which Eulah had sent to me. Although Mother did not look very much pleased, I knew that she liked Eulah's thoughtfulness. Each day after this one I received a little note from my conscientious little friend. The first day that I was permitted to leave the house Mother accompanied me on a little visit to Eulah's home. I learned that during my absence from the group, all of my friends had discovered that Eulah was a "nice" girl and had eagerly accepted her as a real friend. When I entered high school we moved from this neighborhood, but Eulah's friendship has never been forgotten.

As new experience often succeeds in changing one's attitude, I feared that some day I would also learn to dislike the Negro as most of my friends do. However, my experience with a group of Negro children at camp this last summer has left no negative effect. In fact, instead of any dislike appearing, I have become very much interested in the Negro problem as a whole. Since Negroes are constantly migrating from the South to the North, the problem is presenting some real difficulty. Whether future contact or knowledge of them will change my present attitude is very difficult to foretell.[2]

As for experience of racial difference and its effect upon the child of a minority group, there are many revealing references in autobiographical literature—especially in the writings of American Negroes and of Russian Jews.[3]

2. Observation

Quite a number of contributors to the material in hand find that a child of normal curiosity will investigate for himself, in

[2] See also Lillian D. Wald, *The House on Henry Street* (1915, p. 163).
[3] See W. E. B. DuBois, *The Souls of Black Folk* (1912, p. 2). An example of a remarkably accurate observation will be found in a recent book by a German *Gymnasial-Lehrer*, Dr. Michael Mueller-Claudius—*Deutsche Rassenangst* (1927, p. 93 *et seq.*), which describes in detail the emotional life of sensitive Jewish pupils in their contact with Gentile ones. He traces the growth of race consciousness to an accumulation of experiences, each producing a rising sense of being different. These experiences often are the cause rather than the result of group enmity which is the adjunct of isolation.

so far as opportunities permit, the peculiarities that distinguish those who are obviously different from the people he is accustomed to. This open-minded attitude of curiosity is given as the opposite of the various forms of adverse race attitudes that have been described in previous chapters. A western school principal writes:

I find another attitude not mentioned in your questionnaire, working just in the opposite direction as far as results go. I find that curiosity goes a long way in causing children to be friendly to children of other races, and especially to those of a race with which they are not familiar. For example, a little Mexican girl, dirty and ragged, was at first a great curiosity, then treated as a baby by all the class; but after they became familiar with her, the other children dropped her, and I notice that she does not play with them now. A little Japanese girl caused the same curiosity at first and is still accepted as an equal. Both these cases are in the primary department. I find that the child is more ready to accept as an equal a child of a nationality with which it is not familiar. We have more Russians and Mexicans, and these always remain Russians and Mexicans (associating with their own groups), with few exceptions for which there are always noticeable reasons.

There seems to be common agreement that children in the lower ages—say up to that of eight—only exceptionally take note of racial differences, and that they are often quite ignorant of the significance of differences in personal appearance.[4]

The following case seems to place the learning of race through curiosity and observation at an exceptionally early age.

Howard W. Thurman, a Negro student at the Rochester Theological Seminary, commences an article on "College and Color" in the April, 1924, number of the student magazine as follows:

Not long ago I spent a week-end with a friend at whose church I was scheduled to speak. My presence in the home was quite a curiosity to his four-year-old daughter. She had never seen my like before.

I made several friendly overtures, and at length she said, "Have a seat over there," pointing to a large Morris chair. As soon as I was seated, she jumped into my lap, took both of her hands, rubbed them on my face and then examined them to see if any of my color had been removed. Discovering no change in my face and no stain on her

---

[4] See Chap. I, p. 4, et seq. Also E. S. Bogardus, in *Journal of Applied Sociology*, May-June, 1925, p. 378.

hands, she asked with great earnestness and anxiety, "Are you black all over?"

"Yes."

"Are you black under your collar?"

"Yes."

"But I know you don't have black feet?"

"Certainly."

"Did you have to be black? Why aren't you white like Daddy?"

After this grilling cross-examination our friendliness increased, and when I left the home, as far as I could see her from the distance, she was waving a fond good-bye to the human being she had discovered under a black skin.

The article continues to compare this simple reaction—first shyness mingled with fear, then first-hand investigation, inquiry as to whether the deviation from the norm was voluntary, last dismissal of the difference as beside the point and judgment by the qualities the individual had in common with her father—with what the writer calls the "heroic absence of this attitude both on our campuses and in our national life." [5]

The following instances are given as typical of many reported cases in which children of foreign race or nationality are especially popular among their school fellows because of their strangeness until the novelty of their peculiarity in looks, language and manners has worn off and they are judged by the normal standards of child society:

Mary, a little Russian Jewess, was a member of clubs in a large social settlement. She was adopted by a cultivated woman who moved in the most exclusive set of the faculty of a large university. Mary was in school with the children of these faculty people and, after a few weeks, was the leader in all the children's activities. She was the favorite among them and taken into all their small clubs—this when she was twelve years old. She had great charm and personality.

Sylvia, a little Finnish girl, was adopted at the age of seven by a college woman. Sylvia has no charm of manner or mind, and though beloved by her adoptive mother and a great joy to her, is not accepted with any sort of joy by the nieces and nephews of the woman. They say Sylvia is "different," although every effort has been made by the adult members of the family to adopt the little girl.

[5] A similar story is told by a colored professional man, Joseph C. Carroll, "The Race Problem." *Journal of Applied Sociology*, January-February, 1927, p. 269.

Wilhelmina, fourteen years old, is a remarkable full-blooded Indian girl, brought up on a reservation. When she had gone as far as the school there could take her, she was brought, with some trepidation, into a church boarding school in the West where the Indian is not looked upon with favor. Within three months, Wilhelmina was the most loved girl in the school. Her leadership was unquestioned. She was the inspirer of games, the teller of wonderful stories, beloved by all the school.

A western correspondent attaches more importance than others to personal observation. She says:

I believe that the child mind is governed to a very great extent by the appearance of the foreign child. This is especially true of children of the lower age groups. They are usually much more willing to accept as an equal the foreign child that dresses as they dress. Apart from that, absence of mention and therefore of conditioning is more frequent than the other domestic influences named.

Unfortunately, this correspondent rather contradicts herself in the one example bearing on this point which she gives:

An English boy came to our school recently. His appearance was distinctly different, more so, I think, than that of the average other foreigner, but he was accepted at once and, having beautiful manners, has been a very good example to our boys.

Recent studies of children's play activities indicate that there are racial differences in this respect which the observant child, if in contact with children of other ethnic groups, is likely to notice. Whether there be no certain explanation as yet for specific differences—such as the marked poetic creativeness of Negro children —or explanations that have to do with distinctness of cultural background, the child of the dominent or privileged group will be likely to experience a sense of strangeness which, too often, through outside influences, is converted into a sense of superiority. Lehman and Witty explain the Negro child's preference for playing school as a compensatory activity in the face of conspicuous lack of success in academic achievement.[6] In the same way, they explain an excessive indulgence of the Negro child in boxing as a compensatory demonstration of equality where real equality with

[6] Harvey C. Lehman and Paul A. Witty, *The Psychology of Play Activities* (A. S. Barnes & Co., 1927, p. 146).

children of the white group, or the sense of it, is lacking.[7] On the other hand, denial of equal opportunities to participate in athletic contests is held responsible for a notably lesser interest on the part of the Negro child, as compared with the white, in watching such contests.[8]

3. CUMULATIVE EXPERIENCE

Just as in adult life changes of opinion may come about either through the gradual acquisition of knowledge until the pressure upon one's preconceived ideas has become irresistible, or through a sudden conversion, so race attitudes in children may be the result of cumulative experiences or of a single forceful experience, and we shall do well, therefore, to look at these two causative factors separately.

The following examples illustrate the gradual growth of racial attitudes as similar experiences enter into the awareness of children—in most cases, accompanied, of course, by other influences that tend in the same direction:

With regard to the Negro pupils, writes a high-school teacher in a northern city, any discrimination made, it seems to me, is rather on a social than a racial basis. With regard to the Jews, it seems to me that one finds much less prejudice among school children than among adults, and what there is seems to be largely earned.

I have never had any pupil object to sitting beside a colored child. None but cleanly colored children come to high school. I have had them object to sitting beside Jewish children who were dirty and odorous, but only because they were dirty. I have never seen a white and a colored child close friends and rarely Jewish and Gentile children, but it takes a unity of interest along many lines to make chums.

They do not mix very much in their social clubs, that is, their sororities and fraternities, but in such clubs as Bird, Latin, Current Topics, etc., they make no discriminations. When, however, there comes to be a preponderance of Jews in a club, there is a tendency for the others gradually to drift out, not, apparently, from any feeling against the Jews but because it has become less enjoyable to them.

Racial consciousness seems stronger on the part of the Jews than on that of the others; in class elections, when there is a majority of Jews in a class, they usually elect a Jewish president; the opposite condition does not seem to be so apt to exist. Of late there has seemed to be a tendency in the general organization elections to split up along

[7] Harvey C. Lehman and Paul A. Witty, *The Psychology of Play Activities* (A. S. Barnes & Co., 1927, p. 155).
[8] *Ibid.*, p. 160.

racial lines, one party putting up a Jewish ticket and the other a Gentile ticket.   Looking back over the development of this condition and trying to see the facts with scientific accuracy, I feel sure that it arose from racial consciousness on the part of the Jews rather than from any racial attitude on the part of the others. At the election, a few terms ago when this condition first became evident, the Jewish party got out much propaganda in the form of handbills urging the pupils to be above racial or religious bias and to vote for their (the Jewish) ticket. The other party made no reference to racial division, did their boosting along the old lines only and, when they were defeated, took it quietly. Their regret seemed, in fact, to be not so much that their party was defeated as that this racial consciousness had gotten into the school.

On Jewish holidays the attendance is cut down to about half. The remaining pupils are quite apt to exclaim over how pleasant it is and wish that it could always be like that.

Miss —— (a public-school teacher) felt that this was the chief reason for any antipathy shown by the children of her school to the Jews. She illustrated with the following incidents:

1. The sixth grade had dramatized a story in their English work. Wishing to raise money for some purpose, they gave it in the auditorium, charging admission. One little Jewish boy remarked afterwards to the evident disgust of the others that he did not know as he had gotten fifteen cents worth out of it.

2. During the war the children were asked to take home handkerchiefs to hem for the soldiers. Little Abe had recently had some toy taken away from him as a punishment. He told Miss —— that if she would give this back to him he would take home twice the number asked. Other pupils showed disapproval.

3. Mrs. C. said that her daughter had developed much antipathy to the Jewish children due to unpleasant personal experiences. Constance said that the lunch room was clean and usable on Jewish holidays. In reply to the mother's urging that she go about quietly (she has heart trouble), she said that it was impossible as the Jewish children rushed about so that you had to rush. In her official class, the ticket agent was a Jewish boy. Constance bought a ticket, and the agent was unable to make change. After putting off giving her the change for several successive days, he said that he did not owe her anything and became very insolent when the teacher tried to force him to pay the money due.[9]

[9] This contribution illustrates the difficulty of securing objective evidence on our subject. It is quite possible that the reporter herself has an adverse attitude toward Jews which may, or may not, have been caused by her actual cumulative experience as a teacher.

A club of attractive Italian girls, some working, some attending high school, were considering new members for their club. Two names were suggested, and the club leader was conscious at once of a chilling of the atmosphere. Finally, the president of the club spoke up: "Those girls will not be suitable members." "Why?" asked Miss S. "They won't cooperate well." "What makes you think so?" "Because we know all about them."

Feeling that the girls were avoiding a discussion of the real difficulty, Miss S. continued the questioning, and at length the reason came out. "They're Jews, and Jews and Italians don't mix well. Besides, if the girls come in, they'll want to bring more, and pretty soon they'll run us."

When this feeling had come out in the open, adds the reporter, a settlement worker, there was a heated discussion, and they decided to ask the two Jewish girls to join the club since there were no good reasons for barring them.[10]

The following example illustrates the formation of favorable attitudes as a result of personal experience:

During the winter evenings when it was disagreeable out of doors, I would get permission for four or five negro boys and girls to play with me in the library or in the nursery. Here we would play games: jack-straws, blind-man's buff, checks, checkers, pantomime, geography puzzles, conundrum matches, and spelling bees. Frequently I would read the negroes fairy stories, or show them pictures in the magazines and books of art. I remember how we used to linger over a beautiful picture of Lord William Russell bidding adieu to his family before going to execution; and how in a boyish way I would tell the negroes the story of his unhappy fate and his wife's devotion. Another favorite picture was the coronation of Queen Victoria. How we delighted in "Audubon's Birds" and in the beautifully colored plates and animals in the government publications on natural history. The pleasure was by no means one-sided. To our hotchpot of amusement and instruction the negroes contributed marvelous tales of birds and animals, which more than offset my familiar reminiscences of Queen Victoria and Lord Russell.[11]

[10] As has been stated, only the individuals quoted are responsible for the views expressed or implied in the testimony. If their attitude toward Jewish girls was the result of experience, the Italian girls seem to have had a real reason for not wanting them in their club; whether this reason was a "good" one, depends entirely on the value of the contrary reasons advanced for letting them come in.

[11] Professor George T. Winston, "The Relations of the Whites to the Negroes," *Annals of the American Academy of Political and Social Science,* XVIII, July, 1901, p. 106.

4. DRAMATIC EXPERIENCE

Even children—or perhaps we should say, especially children—at times experience a conversion on the strength of a single experience with strong emotional content. It has even been suggested by one contributor, with much experience among children in religious and social work, that racial attitudes may lie dormant as instincts but only begin to express themselves as specific stimuli in the nature of a strongly emotional personal experience, arouse them and call them into consciousness and expression. Without endorsing that theory, we shall do well to look at a few authentic examples where racial attitudes have apparently broken out suddenly in the wake of an impressive personal experience. The contributor who makes the suggestion just noted, herself tells the following incident:

For a year, a group of white children and colored children played together at a Saturday morning play hour. Apparently there was no race feeling. Part of the white children attended a garden club in the same settlement. At the end of the year, the leader of the garden club, who could give but one afternoon a week, chose the colored children for her club for the next year. At once all the white children, even those who had not been members of the garden club, banded against the colored children.

"Eat and Beat the Chocolate Babies," was their rallying cry, and garbage from the street cans served as ammunition. After a time the more intense feeling seemed to die down, but not until the colored children had stopped coming to the play hour. No threats were made against them in the play hour, but the colored children simply chose not to come.

Experiences of shock, according to a middle-western high-school teacher, have an important part in forming adverse attitudes in children which, however, in the overwhelming majority of cases he attributes to adult influences:

I took a beating by a colored girl when a little boy—it was merely a beating to me. But girls have told me that fright at a certain Negro has prejudiced them for life.

It is important that, before proceeding to further evidence on the influence of dramatic incidents upon attitudes, we remind ourselves that there is always a tendency in recollection to exaggerate the importance of individual occurrences that have left a strong emotional influence, and to minimize the slow, almost if not quite unconscious accumulation of impressions of a more general nature. Of all forms of fiction, the autobiography is, perhaps, the most fictional, for here the writer, instead of merely inventing incidents (or permitting his sympathy with certain characters to work out their destinies), actually makes himself believe what he wants to believe about his past and the influences that have molded him. The self-deception that goes into the writing of autobiographical essays is often well illustrated in papers written by sociology students in response to professional requests for this sort of introspective study of attitudes. While it is difficult to spot, an over-simplification of influences may, perhaps, be surmised in such papers as the following:

I have several Jewish boys in my chemistry class, writes an Ohio teacher. Try as hard as I may, I cannot seem to give them the same attention and fair treatment as the other boys. I frequently find myself marking their papers lower, and talking harsh to them when I couldn't do the same with Americans. These boys are intelligent, polite, and friendly—but they are Jews. Why should I hate that word, or that race?

I can see only one reason. In my childhood, I only was acquainted with one Jew, a bachelor junk dealer. When just a boy, an old citizen of the village died, leaving as a heritage to the town an old Revolutionary cannon, unmounted. The cannon was not appreciated by the town, and was left lying in the jailyard for several months. We had finally asked the councilmen for it. We laid large plans for a fort, and big battles. We went after it with a stove truck. It was gone. The marshal had sold it to the Jew for 40 cents to get it out of the road. We could not coax him to sell it back, or give it back. He probably sold it for much more. We lost our cannon. A Jew was responsible for spoiling our plans.

Unpleasant racial sense impressions personally experienced in the early years of life are many. Sometimes fear is aroused; again, disgust. In either case there is a sensory image that is often described as "horrifying." (See Chap. I, p. 7.) The fact that these images were experienced in childhood gives them a more or less permanent character.[12]

[12] E. S. Bogardus, "Social Distance and Its Origins," *Journal of Applied Sociology*, Jan.-Feb., 1925, p. 221. This passage is illustrated by illuminating extracts from student papers.

Whether the children of the less favored groups acquire specific race attitudes more often from a gradually growing awareness or from incidents that suddenly illumine a situation that had not previously come to their consciousness, we have no sufficient evidence to know. But probably, where the racial minority group is both a large one and one markedly treated as inferior, the child will from a very early age be made to feel the difference of his group from the dominant majority.

The two following examples very briefly recall the fact that corrective experiences also may often be in the nature of a conversion. In the first of these cases, the corrective element is a situation in which a misunderstanding involved in the unfavorable attitude is strikingly cleared up. In the second, it is difficult to say to what extent the change in attitude was directly the result of the incident or indirectly the result of the incident in its effect upon adults who influence the child.

A family of Italians moved into —— and bought a restaurant there. There was a boy of about fourteen in the family. He started in school where he was called names and insulting remarks were made about him. Finally he decided to make a place for himself in the school, so he fought the boys who had thrown insults at him and was the victor over them; and so he gained the respect of his classmates.

In Cleveland, Ohio, a Slav family moved into a neighborhood of American-born people. This family was of a high type, but the neighbors were unfriendly to them and practically shunned them. When school started, a boy from this family happened to be in the same room with a boy who lived in the same block. One day, the American boy fell and sprained his ankle on the way home. The Slav boy helped him home. From this on, the two boys gradually became friends, went to each other's homes and had a good time together. The American boy says that he considers the Slav boy one of his best friends, and through the friendship between the two boys the Slav family has been taken into the life of the community.

SUMMARY

To recapitulate what we have learned from the evidence presented on the part played by personal experience in the formation of race attitudes by children, we find, first, that it is practically impossible neatly to dissect the factors that have been operative in any one case. Personal experience never is the only influence to which the child reacts at a given moment. It may, however, stand out against a neutral or hostile background of adult attitudes as an effective stimulant or corrective. Without at this point entering into a discussion of the disputed question whether the child is born with a specific instinct of racial like or dislike, fear, aversion or special attraction toward members of other racial groups, we find that the belief in the existence of such instinct or instincts in itself is a powerful factor in shaping the child's attitudes; when that belief happens to be contrary to personal experience, it is as often the experience that is discounted as the belief.

Without stretching too much the framework of a logical structure of categories, we find that, instinct apart, personal experience as a maker of race attitudes may conveniently be examined with a view to the relative importance of long continued contact with members of other groups, of conscious observation, of cumulative awareness to specific experiences, and of single, forceful incidents. Our evidence is neither voluminous enough nor sufficiently detailed to permit an appraisal of their relative importance. We can at this point merely draw attention to the fact that it is possible to make such classifications as this, and that if we desire to create a practical technique for dealing educationally with race attitudes it is almost indispensable that further and more sustained efforts be made to collect and analyze evidence on this question. As we shall see in later chapters, much well-meant educational labor at the present time is ineffective because it is not based on an accurate knowledge of the weight to be attached to different elements among the influences that make up the child's reaction to his environment. Unless we know, for example, whether individual contacts can and normally do offset the influence of adverse attitudes in the home, it is hardly worth while to engineer such contacts for the child in school or church or settlement. Unless we know something of the respective force of incidents of conversion and of a succession of less impressive experiences, we can hardly formulate a practical, corrective program for the eradication of undesirable attitudes.

We must remember, in passing, that children obtain a large part of their equipment in fixed ideas and prejudiced opinions neither from direct personal experience in the narrow sense, nor from grown-up people, but from other children. This, of course, only removes our inquiry one step further back; for we now have to explain the attitude of the other child; but it is necessary to remember that such chains of influence exist and that one task for the engineer of social opinion, so far as children are concerned, lies in dealings with the association between children.[13]   This task takes on a very practical form when we have to consider the influence, for example, of classmates from a part of the country that is especially prejudiced against one racial group or another.   It does not take much imagination to foresee what would happen within half a generation to the country's attitude toward Japan if the well-to-do people of the Pacific coast were, as a matter of policy, to send their children to eastern schools.   In fact, it is already evident what the increasing prosperity of the South in recent years, with its concomitant of a greatly increased proportion of southern students in the schools and colleges of the Northeast, is doing to the attitude of that part of the country, or rather of its social upper crust, toward the Negro!   From reported examples that bear upon this point, we choose the following as illustrating how, concretely, children react upon each other in this way:

A little white son of Ohio was visiting in a southern city.   One day he was somewhat noisy in his play on the street, near a sanatorium for colored women.   The Negro physician in charge came out and asked him to play less boisterously.   Next day, the lad was again passing the place, this time accompanied by a little white southern boy.   Both were shouting.   Suddenly, the northern boy remembered the request of the physician.   "We must be quiet or we'll disturb the sick ladies in the hospital."   His companion was dumbfounded.   He stopped short, sat down on the curbstone, rested his cheek on his hand and assumed an air of the utmost disgust.   "Say!" he ejaculated, "you make me sick!   Calling niggers ladies!"

As to the relative strength of adult influences and the influences of other children on race attitudes, the opinions of contributors to this study are divided.   One correspondent, a high-school teacher, observes that, while children absorb race antagonisms from their school fellows, the influence of adults in their own home upon them is by far the more effective.   To judge from the volume of evidence submitted, this seems also to be the experience

[13] One of the most interesting chapters in the history of human culture is the handing on of games from one generation of children to another—often through hundreds of years—without adult participation.

of other teachers and workers among children. However, it is not impossible that their observation is faulty, and that trained psychologists, studying the same situations, would assign more weight to the mutual impact of attitudes derived by children from their own experiences.

CHAPTER VII

PHYSIOLOGICAL DIFFERENCES AND THEIR EFFECT

Apart from the situations in which the child recognizes social distances between his own racial group and others are situations in which actual physical or mental difference—whether recognized or not—is the divisive influence. If for biological reasons the little colored boy at a given age tends to develop in a different direction from his white playmate, there will result a growing change in mutual attitude, and this quite independent of possible outside influences. Whether such tendencies exist is no longer open to doubt. Even those students of the subject who are most careful to allow for the effect of environment and folkways on differences in intelligence and capacity recognize that the larger racial categories, at any rate, exhibit inherited differences of temperament which seem to persist in various types of environment and through the stages of growth from childhood to maturity.[1]

In line with this trend of discovery, but based upon an unusually sympathetic observation rather than upon scientific measurement, Dr. Michael Mueller-Claudius has recently elaborated a theory which would account for certain race attitudes in children even though their causative factor would rarely occur isolated from others. His study of German and Jewish boys of the adolescent and pre-adolescent age groups led him to believe that the Jewish child enters at an earlier age into the mental states connected with puberty, and that the resultant divergence in feelings and interests may be large enough to set him apart and estrange him from his classmates.[2] He says:

Puberty and the preceding period of indifference . . . often appear much earlier in the Jewish child than in the Gentile. Although no

[1] S. D. Porteus and Marjorie E. Babcock, *Temperament and Race* (1926); especially Chaps. XVII and XVIII, where also references to other literature will be found.
[2] *Deutsche Rassenangst.* (Berlin, 1927.)   Chap. III, *Tragoedie zwischen Kind und Rasse.*

doubt the climate exercises a retarding influence upon the tempo of this development in the Jewish as well as the non-Jewish child, it remains evident that the period of puberty occurs considerably earlier and progresses more rapidly.

The purely external differences in time cut in queer and tragic patterns across the social-psychological experience of children and from this tragic entanglement assume an importance which from a physical point of view alone would not inhere in them. . . .[3]

Unverified, so far, by a larger range of observation, it is difficult to assign to Dr. Mueller-Claudius' theory its relative importance among the many factors which we have seen to enter into the situation. Whether Jewish children mature sooner than Gentile children is still an open question; at least conditions in this respect are different in the United States from those in Europe—a circumstance which suggests environmental rather than racial causative factors.[4]

While there is an immense literature on the physical and mental growth of children of different nations and races,[5] few comparative data seem to be available on the ages and rates of pubescence in different peoples. There is reason to believe, however, that indirect evidence on this matter is contained in the comparative findings as to growth; for, it is a well-known fact that growth is accelerated at puberty,[6] so that if during the early years of adoles-

[3] Agaih, this author describes in detail the shift in relationships between Jewish and Gentile children as, first, the dullness and later the heightened mental activity of the pubertal stage separates the physiologically more advanced from their schoolmates. The effects on interests, associations and group attitudes are finely observed; but since they refer to a special case peculiar to German conditions we refrain from quoting these observations at length.

[4] Records made by N. V. Zak in Russia, thirty years ago, are still quoted because of lack of more recent authoritative data: e.g., by Bird T. Baldwin in the *Physical Growth of Children from Birth to Maturity*, University of Iowa Studies, First Series, No. 50, June 1, 1921; also by G. Stanley Hall in *Adolescence* (1904), where the passage quoted will be found in Vol. I, p. 8. Franz Boas finds the contention unproven, *Anthropology and Modern Life* (1928, p. 174).

[5] Baldwin, *op. cit.*, lists 911 titles on the former subject alone.

[6] "During adolescence the rate of growth is considerably accelerated, and decreases again rapidly after sexual maturity has been reached. Thus the curve of growth represents a line which possesses a very high maximum at about the fifth month of fetal life. It decreases rapidly, and has a second although much lower maximum shortly before sexual maturity is reached, and not long afterwards reaches the zero point." Franz Boas, Remarks on the Anthropological Study of Children. (Transactions of the 15th International Congress on Hygiene and Demography, Government Printing Office, Washington, 1913, p. 413.)

cence Jewish children tend to exceed Gentile children in height but are overtaken afterwards, it is fairly safe to assume that, other factors (home environment, nutrition, etc.) having remained unchanged, the Jewish children have entered the state of puberty at an earlier age or have passed through it at a more rapid rate, or both.

Opinions are divided as to the extent to which these differences, where they appear, must be accounted for by environmental differences in the larger sense and by heredity. Hall believed that the latter played the larger part.[7] Baldwin notes the enormous variety of stages and rates of pubescence in school children but apparently has not analyzed them by race or nationality, a procedure which might have thrown light on the causes of variability.[8] The disputed question as to whether there is a relation between the age of maturing and the ultimate attainment of height and weight is answered in the negative by more recent comparative studies.[9] Professor Franz Boas, of Columbia University, has perhaps gone furthest of American investigators in bringing into a revealing relationship the factors of growth, pubescence and race. From a series of investigations made for the United States Immigration Commission he concluded that differences in growth and age of pubescence observed among Europeans vary with climate, diet, clothing, and customary treatment of children rather than with race.[10] In America, the main factors of difference, likewise, are environmental.[11] Other investigators do not agree with Boas' statement that the relationship between early arrest of development and racial traits has never been proved, but feel that there is ample evidence for it.[12] Professor Melville J. Herskovits, on the

[7] *Op. cit.*, Vol. I, p. 30.
[8] *Op. cit.*, p. 191.
[9] Ethel M. Abernethy, "Correlations in Physical and Mental Growth," *Journal of Educational Psychology*, 1925, p. 466.
[10] *Changes in Bodily Form of Descendants of Immigrants* (Columbia University Press, 1912, p. 1).
[11] The main findings of many earlier investigations (see especially Franz Boas and Clark Wissler, Statistics of Growth, U. S. Bureau of Education, Chap. II of Report of Commissioner of Education for 1904, Government Printing Office, 1905, p. 46; "The Growth of Children," *Science*, Vol. XXXVI, No. 937, December 13, 1912, p. 817; Remarks on the Anthropology and Study of Children, Transactions of the Fifteenth International Congress on Hygiene and Demography, Government Printing Office, Washington, 1913, pp. 418 and 419) have been summarized by Professor Boas in his new book, *Anthropology and Modern Life* (1928), Chap. VIII.
[12] See, for example, S. D. Porteus and Marjorie E. Babcock, *Temperament and Race* (1926, p. 230).

strength of a body of accurate recent data, shares Boas' disposition to look upon the undoubted differences in ages and rates of growth and ages of pubescence between different racial groups as largely requiring no other explanations than those of differences in environment, economic status and folkways. Two of his recent studies have yielded the following results:

I. Colored boys grow faster in height and weight to the sixteenth year than White boys.

II. The differences in variability between children of these two races, whether expressed in terms of standard deviation or the coefficient of variability, are not sufficient on the strength of these admittedly limited data, at least, to allow of explanation on other grounds than differences in economic background, place of birth and different social conditions.

III. Colored boys show the same acceleration in growth characteristic of White boys during adolescence, which, however, occurs approximately one year earlier even though the Colored boys come from a poorer economic level than the White boys to whom they are compared.[13]

I. When compared to poor public-school children of the same racial type, colored orphanage children are lighter in weight and smaller, year for year, from the fifth to the sixteenth year.

II. This may be attributed to the environmental difference between institutional and home surroundings.

III. Differences between orphanage and public-school colored children are, on the whole, about the same as those between well-to-do Jewish children and Jewish orphans, thus giving support to the hypothesis of distinct racial growth-curves for the various groups in our population.[14]

We are confronted, then, with the probability that there are differences in the rate of physiological development of different groups which usually correspond to differences in the rate of physical growth. But whether these groups are classes or races further inquiry must show. Again, mental ability grows about at the same rate, and reaches its maximum or maturity at about the same time, as physical growth.[15] We have, therefore, quite aside from the question of the relative maximum of attainment,

[13] "Observations on the Growth of Colored Boys." *American Journal of Physical Anthropology,* Vol. VII, 1924, p. 446.
[14] "The Influence of Environment on a Racial Growth Curve." *School and Society,* Vol. XXII, 1925, p. 88.
[15] Arthur I. Gates, *Psychology for Students of Education* (1923, p. 428).

substantial evidence that the rates of mental growth differ for different ethnic groups, as now constituted by unscientific, popular distinctions, at any rate up to the age of maximum physical development. It is unquestionable, moreover, that the differential rate of growth is most accentuated in the early years of adolescence. Anthropological findings here entirely bear out the observations of Dr. Mueller-Claudius and of many other teachers who have noted the tendency of boys and girls, grouped according to age in public- and Sunday-school classes, to break through the earlier social groupings and form new ones in the years of adolescence.[16] Baldwin says on this point:

Physiological age has a direct bearing on physical training and directed play. Not only do children naturally play with boys and girls of their same physiological age, but the types of games in which they participate are dependent upon the age of physiological maturity. . . .

Physiological age is, the writer believes, directly correlated with stages of mental maturation. The physiologically more mature child has different attitudes, different types of emotions, different interests, than the child who is physically younger though of the same chronological age. . . .

The mental age of the individual bears a direct relationship to the physiological age as indicated by height and weight. The results show that at each chronological age the physiologically accelerated boys and girls have a higher mental age than those of the average or below the average physiological age. The girls, when classified on this basis, show a higher mental age for a given chronological age than do the ʾoys. Girls are on the average mentally older than boys.[17]

One of the most careful studies of the relation between chronological and physiological age in the mental development of children is that recently made by S. D. Porteus and Marjorie E. Babcock among school children in Hawaii. While the results of the various tests applied were almost negative in indicating a difference in racial capacity—in so far as allowance could be made for environmental factors—they did show a marked influence of different rates of physiological maturing upon intelligence and competency.[18]

[16] See Frederic M. Thrasher, *The Gang* (University of Chicago Press, 1927, pp. 37, 74, 80, 82). Also Harvey C. Lehman and Paul A. Witty, *The Psychology of Play Activities* (1927, p. 47 et seq.).

[17] *The Physical Growth of Children from Birth to Maturity.* University of Iowa Studies, First Series, No. 50, June 1, 1921.

[18] *Temperament and Race* (1926, p. 227).

PHYSIOLOGICAL EFFECTS ON SOCIAL DISTANCE

The influence of differences of physiological age upon attitudes and voluntary associations between members of different racial groups in adolescence also is shown to be probable by recent findings.[19]   All these data and suggestions, while awaiting further corroboration, throw light on one of the central problems in connection with the race attitudes of children—namely, the undoubted existence of individual and group differences in physical and mental development which, looked at from a purely biological point of view, appear to the layman to prove racial inferiority or superiority.[19a]   The significance of the fact that Negroes are more frequently retarded than white pupils in a given school will not be lost upon the observant child who, encouraged by the prevailing adult attitudes, will be led to believe that here is evidence of innate differences.   However, the extent to which such observations influence attitudes is almost wholly unexplored.   Even recent studies of the differences in the emotional and volitional reactions of children of different racial stocks often fail to look to a difference in physiological age as a clue suggested by the data.[20] That there are as yet no reliable norms for different stages of physiological maturity is the complaint of Dagny Sunne, of Tulane University, who has tried to bring a similar emotional and volitional test of white and Negro adolescents into relationship with it, but was confronted with results so divergent as to prevent the formulation of positive conclusions.[21]   In this, as in several other recent studies, there is wholesome—if for the moment discouraging—insistence upon the importance of such environmental factors as schooling, social restrictions, taboo and situation.   And yet, discredited as these generalizations are, too often popular comparisons of racial groups (especially when strongly pro-this and anti-that) continue to speak of the "emotionality" of this race, the "instability" of that or the "inadaptability" of yet

[19] Ethel M. Abernethy, "Correlations in Physical and Mental Growth." *Journal of Educational Psychology*, 1925, p. 546.
[19a] See also Morris S. Viteles: "The Mental Status of the Negro." *Annals of the American Academy of Political and Social Science*, Vol. CXXXX, No. 229, November, 1928, p. 166 *et seq.*
[20] See, for example, a study of "Racial Differences as Measured by the Downey Will-Temperament Test," by John H. McFadden and J. F. Dashiell. *Journal of Applied Psychology*, Vol. VII, 1923, p. 30.
[21] "Personality Tests: White and Negro Adolescents." *Journal of Applied Psychology*, 1925, Vol. IX, p. 256.

another.[22]   An excessive stress on the factor of racial heredity at the present time completely obscures the seemingly dominant influence of environment, economic status and group traditions —in such matters as clothing, food, child labor and recreations, etc.,—upon differences in growth and scholastic attainment.   For almost twenty years it has neglected the findings of Professor Boas, who, in one of his earlier studies, said:

Statistics which I have had occasion to collect recently seem to show that the development of children of immigrants is the better the longer their parents have been in the United States.   I presume this merely suggests that the economic well-being of the immigrants increases, on the whole, with the length of their stay here, and that the corresponding better nutrition of the children results in better physical development.   Whether, however, the whole change can be explained adequately in this manner is open to doubt.   It is quite possible that the type may undergo certain changes due to environment.[23]

The same thing is also true, of course, of Negroes who have migrated to northern cities from less favorable southern environments.[24]

Professor Herskovits, in a letter to the author (July 5, 1927), says with reference to the explanation of growing social distance between children of different races but of the same chronological age with their different rates of physiological maturing:

The explanation of differential growth rates is made very often, and associated with it, it is also often claimed, are psychological differences in development.   None of these claims as to the latter point have been established, to the best of my knowledge. . . . (Reference to Boas' work on the growth of Jewish children and the effect of environment on them.)   It is this difference that environmental changes may make on growth curves within a given group that makes me doubt so much the theories which have been based on differential racial growth rates.

[22] Statistics of admission to hospitals for the insane are an unreliable source of evidence for two reasons: Institutional provision is not in all parts of the country alike for all classes and ethnic groups.   Insanity often results from maladjustments to which, because of differences in economic and social status, one ethnic group may be more subject than another.

[23] "Race Problems in America."   Science, Vol. XXIX, No. 752, May 28, 1909, p. 843.

[24] See W. A. Daniel in T. J. Woofter, Jr., Negro Problems in Cities (1928, p. 188).   Also Charles H. Thompson, "The Educational Achievements of Negro Children"; Annals of the American Academy of Political and Social Science, Vol. CXXXX, No. 229, November, 1928, p. 193 et seq.

In short, with all their divergencies and complications, it does seem to appear from recent experimental studies that none of the factors named can be neglected. It is a misfortune that the focus of attention upon race rather than the totality of possible hereditary and environmental differences has, in so many comparative studies of scholastic attainment and mental qualities, led to a mere piling up of data which, as they become more accurate, also show up the unreliability of earlier findings.[25] The seeming contradictions of testimony are, to some extent, explained by the variety of situations and environments in which these tests are made. Intelligence testers rarely claim for their findings a validity beyond the particular limits of the test. Obviously it would not be fair to them to take their conclusions as though unconditioned and to compare them as such to show the absence of agreement. A more valid criticism would be that, in spite of a large volume of research, no technique has so far been invented for distilling from conditioned findings generalizations which could be used for fairly comparing the results of different studies.

Whatever one may think of the value of these mental tests, and however large an allowance one may make for differences in their accuracy,[26] faults of method or smallness of numbers, in some cases—it is quite clear that they are confusing partly because they are based upon chronological and not upon physiological age. To group together all Negro children in the public schools of a Northern city in a comparison of their standing with that of white pupils is a procedure that disregards every one of

[25] For a compilation of seemingly contradictory findings from recent intelligence tests comparing Negroes and whites, see *Opportunity* for July, 1927, p. 190. Commenting on this testimony, the editor says: "The personal honesty of none of these students would be questioned. But who, in the midst of such confusion of findings, would dare venture a conclusion on the basis of them, before a group of impartial scientists?"

[26] While it is possible, theoretically, to guard against subjective bias in the application of these tests, it is not usually practicable with the conditions under which children are examined. For example, C. B. Davenport and Laura C. Craytor, in a paper on "Comparative Social Traits of Various Races," *Journal of Applied Psychology*, Vol. VII, 1923, p. 127, after making the most positive statements as regards the rating of children of different national groups in pertinacity, humor, frankness, suspiciousness, sympathy, loyalty, generosity, obstrusiveness, coolness—a medley of unrelated qualities—add a footnote to the effect that "the probable errors and the standard deviations upon which they are based are probably influenced, to some extent, by the fact that different teachers rated the different individuals; and one set of teachers rated a larger proportion of the German students than another set which treated, say, a larger proportion of the Irish. . . . It is true that the different pairs of raters did not rate an equal proportion of persons of the different nationalities. . . . This introduces a further error."

the important factors that have significance: physiological age, environment, early training, diet, habits, and race itself; for, only a small proportion will represent pure Negro stock. But the greatest injustice is done when colored pupils from good homes, perhaps families established in the community for many more generations than a majority of white families, with a background of well-being and middle-class comforts and culture, are grouped for statistical purposes with the children of recent migrant families from the South, subjected for generations to serfdom and the physical and mental conditions of the poorest type of peasantry.[27]   There is no difficulty in securing similar evidence on the effects of environmental influences on the scholastic standing of immigrant children.[28]   Of recent comparative studies, few have been on a sufficient scale to produce reliable results, and nearly in every case the group divisions made for comparison have been somewhat arbitrary.[29]   It is only lately that length of the family's residence in this country is taken into account when contrasting the children of immigrants with those of native parents. One student finds:

The mental differences between the American-reared descendants of foreign races, viewed among themselves, are so small as to be practically insignificant.

The mental difference between the American-reared children of foreign races and children of Anglo-Saxons, whether judged by the fresh-

[27] This is clearly brought out in *The Negro in Detroit*. Report prepared for the Mayor's Interracial Committee (Mimeographed), Detroit Bureau of Governmental Research, 1926, Section VIII, p. 3 *et seq.*, and in the Chicago race report, *op. cit.*, page 261 *et seq.*

[28] See, for example, Henry Pratt Fairchild, *Immigration*. (Revised Edition, 1925, p. 270), also Franz Boas, *Anthropology and Modern Life* (1928, p. 54 *et seq.*).

[29] An example of this type of study is that of the "Intelligence of Full Blooded Indians," made by Thomas R. Garth, of the University of Denver, *Journal of Applied Psychology*, 1925, Vol. IX, p. 382, in which he admits that the difference in social status between white and Indian children is enormous and, finding no way to get around this obvious obstacle to a true comparison, selects his cases from a United States Indian school—seemingly not reflecting that the children here, while somewhat familiar with white American cultural standards, are subject to the exceptional strain of re-education and adaptation to experiences totally at variance with those of their earlier years. In spite of this flaw, he comes to such conclusions as that "the approximate I Q's of full blood Indians of plains and southwestern tribes is 69," but adds : "Because of differences in social status and temperament we cannot conclude that our results are true and final measures of the intelligence of Indian children." And yet, his conclusions are published as though they had some objective value ; and the average reader will quote Garth to the effect that "the mental age of these Indians and whites in the United States, grade for grade, stands in the ratio of 100 to 114, the whites being 14 per cent better than the Indians."

man or by the junior scores [in high school], is equally too small to be significant.[30]

It is only in late years that a serious effort has been made by students of this subject to eliminate from the comparison of intelligence levels of different racial groups even the more obvious factors that tended to falsify the picture. Intelligence quotients for children of different national groups were given out as though they necessarily represented innate differences. Gradually cautioning clauses were added, leaving it to the reader to interpret these figures with due regard to factors as to whose weight he was not informed (for example, social status of parent, length of residence in this country, etc.).[31] At last, we have the beginnings of comparative studies in which at least a beginning is made to evaluate the other than racial factors that enter into the relative standing. For example:

[30] "Intelligence of the First Generation of Immigrant Groups." Gustave A. Feingold, *Journal of Educational Psychology*, February, 1924, Vol. XV, p. 75. The above is one of several interesting conclusions based on the results of a modified Army Alpha test given to 2,353 high-school pupils of English and Scotch, native American, Jewish, German, Danish and Swedish, French, Irish, Polish, Italian and Negro descent. The inclusion of Jewish children in the statements is surprising. More frequently, in similar comparisons, Jewish children of immigrant parents and from non-English-speaking homes show a relatively high score which singles them out from other immigrant groups and calls for special explanation. The influence of recency of residence has been shown by Stephen S. Colvin and Richard D. Allen in "Mental Tests and Linguistic Ability." *Journal of Educational Psychology*, 1923, Vol. XIV, p. 1, summarized by S. D. Porteus, *op. cit.*, p. 354.

[31] A typical example: Miss Katharine Murdoch, of Teachers College, introduces "A Study of Differences Found Between Races in Intellect and in Morality" (*School and Society*, Vol. XXII, November 14 and 21, 1925) with the words: "The report is presented with the belief that the conclusions here reached were true in the year 1923 of the inhabitants of the city of Honolulu. *The reader may judge for himself* whether the differences found are innate differences, and *it is left to him to judge* also to what extent the inhabitants of Honolulu are typical and therefore representative of the races from which they have sprung." (P. 628. *Italics ours.*) Now, how is the reader to judge these determining factors? Obviously, he is in no position to do so. In spite of this, and in spite of other references to differences in social status, urban and rural environment, etc., the investigator presents conclusions that in no way are weighted by considerations of that kind; and the reader who disregards the initial warning will quote her as saying, for instance, that "the Anglo-Saxons clearly excel all the other races in general intelligence except the Orientals" (p. 632); or that "the Portuguese group shows up the worst in these results for moral traits. In no one of the measures, unless indeed we should consider negative self-assertion as a virtue, does the average of this group reach the Anglo-Saxon median" (p. 662). Or he may believe the study to have proved that "race-crossing produces offspring with mental abilities between those of the parent races; but more nearly like those of the inferior race"—when he does not know what particular position in society and what attitudes toward them people in Honolulu incur by racial intermarriage (p. 662).

In recent years there has been a tendency to establish race norms on the basis of mental tests given to representatives of various races who have emigrated to the United States. The results of tests made of groups of children of foreign-born parents have been stated and comparisons made with the distribution of intelligence in groups of children of American-born parents. So far as we have been able to ascertain, except in the case of Negro children[32] no attempt has been made to check up the influence of factors, other than that of race, which might quite as well account for the differences which, it has been assumed, were traceable to race alone. Particularly is this true in regard to the part played by social status. Much has been written about the effect of social status on the median intelligence in any group of American children, little or nothing has been said as to how much this may account for the low or high median score or median intelligence quotient in groups of children of other races.[33]

A statement follows of a study taking full account of the social status of five hundred children tested, 191 of them of native white parents, 87 of Italian and 71 of Negro parents—with this general summary of result:

It is apparent that such differences as we have between the Negro and Italian children and between these and children of native-born white parents are not nearly so striking as the differences between children of the same race but of different social status. Of the two factors social status seems to play the more important part. To such an extent is this true that it would seem to indicate that there is more likeness between children of the same social status but different race than between children of the same race but of different social status.[34]

Porteus quotes an interesting study of Japanese children which tends to indicate that the social status of the parents is a more important factor bearing upon intellectual status than race—but which, of course, might also be quoted as evidence of biological

[32] Dagny Sunne, "A Comparative Study of White and Negro Children." *Journal of Applied Psychology*, 1917, p. 71.
[33] Ada Hart Arlitt and others, *Journal of Applied Psychology*, Vol. V, 1921, p. 179.
[34] *Ibid.*, p. 182. Another clear case of differences in social status is that observed by Gilbert Brown in connection with a mental test of immigrant children. (*Journal of Educational Research*, 1922, Vol. V, p. 324, as summarized by S. D. Porteus, *Temperament and Race*, 1926, p. 353.) While only the low rating of the Italian group is explained with low social status, it is probable that further inquiry would have revealed a more recent residence of the non-Germanic families and prevalence of child labor in some of the non-Germanic groups.

inheritance of mental ability.[35]   Not only status but environment
also may be viewed either as a primary factor or as, in itself, a
result of biological selection.[36]   In short, a very small residuum
of acceptable evidence remains when such critical standards as
those of Professor Porteus are applied to all the "findings" of ten
years of mental testing.   We are almost driven to accept, at least
on its negative side, the theory that intelligence has no meaning
at all except in relation to situation.[37]

   Dr. Goodwin B. Watson, in a letter to the author, summarizes
the essential agreements in the welter of testimony:

   Practically all psychologists who have made a careful study of the
evidence are agreed that differences in the opportunity to learn provided by different environments result in different achievements upon
intelligence tests.   The amount of this difference is more when the
tests contain a good deal of school subject matter; it is relatively slight
in performance and non-language tests.   Some experimenters have tried
to compare children of different races from comparable cultural backgrounds.   There is general agreement that, when proper corrections have
been made, differences are very much smaller than they appeared to
be in the first naïve tests.   At the same time it seems probable that
American Indians and Mexicans show even less than the Negro on the
average of the sort of ability measured by intelligence tests.   The fact
of major importance, however, is that the differences within each of
these racial groups are very much larger than the differences in aver-
ages.   A child of any race may be bright or dull.

   From the point of view of our present study, there is another
kind of injustice, due to ignorance of the facts brought out in the
present chapter, which leads to serious misunderstanding and
suffering.   And that is the failure of our public-school system to
make allowance for different rates of physiological growth in their
influence on mental growth.   As several of the investigators point

   [35] *Temperament and Race*, 1926, p. 354.   Elsewhere (p. 204 *et seq.*), Porteus
warns against false conclusions that may be drawn from comparisons of
groups of the same social status when that status is not representative for both
of them.   Obviously, to sample intelligence levels only in a high-school, or only
in a slum, may mean a comparison of exceptional individuals in one group with
average individuals in the other.   But since, as he shows, immigrants (or
Negro migrants) are apt to represent unusual mental qualities, compared with
the majority of their group who stay at home, practically every comparison
between a native and an immigrant group yields results which cannot, without
further tests, be interpreted as relating to the two nationalities or races as such.
   See also Tonan Fukuda, "Some Data on the Intelligence of Japanese Children." *American Journal of Psychology*, 1923, Vol. XXXIV, p. 599.
   [36] *Op. cit.*, p. 212.
   [37] *Op. cit.*, p. 215.

out, both kinds of growth are retarded in the case of the individual boy or girl who enjoys less than the normal advantages as to food, environment and care. This retardation, it seems, can to some extent be overcome—no one seems to be able to say exactly to what extent—by a more rapid rate of growth after puberty. But unfortunately, the Negro or foreign-born child who has been retarded too often experiences every conceivable form of discouragement before he reaches the later years of maturing.[38] It is said in educated Negro circles, for example, that teachers and school principals are lacking in patience when the pupil does not show a brilliance quite abnormal for the mental growth curve of his group.[39] Moreover, real difficulties apart, the regimenting by age which is the foundation of the grade division often requires that older boys of one of the disadvantaged groups be graded with the younger children of the more privileged groups of the community.

In other words, if the tests and studies which undoubtedly will be made on an increasingly large scale in the future should con-

[38] Complaints that normally endowed and even brilliant colored children are discouraged from completing their high-school attendance are frequently made and are sometimes answered with reference to the difficulties really experienced in finding suitable positions for high-school graduates in northern as well as southern communities. Recording a change for the better since the war, which seemed to offer so many new opportunities to the Negro, George E. Haynes states: "In the years past in New York and other cities, Negro boys and girls dropped out of school in the lower grades because, they repeatedly said, there was no use in going any further when a Negro could only get a menial job anyway, and that they were already prepared for that." (Academy of Political Science Proceedings, February, 1919, Vol. VIII, p. 299.)

Professor Niles Carpenter in his recent study in Buffalo found a number of colored workers who felt that in grammar school and, especially in high-school they had been discouraged by the attitudes of both teachers and fellow-students from continuing their studies. But the inability of vocationally reaping the rewards of study—that is, discouragement by their own group on the grounds of adult experience of vocational discrimination—seems to have been the larger pressure. (Nationality, Color, and Economic Opportunity. The Inquiry, 1927, p. 117.)

[39] For evidence on the discriminatory treatment of white and colored children in the matter of stimulation by praise and reproof, see p. 142. The values of different forms of stimulation are still under investigation by psychologists. But while a few years ago no definite relations had yet been established between scholastic achievement and the uses of praise and blame (see Georgina S. Gates and Louise Q. Rissland, "The Effect of Encouragement and of Discouragement upon Performance," Journal of Educational Psychology, 1923, Vol. XIV, p. 21 et seq.), recent experiments seem to have proved beyond doubt that under normal circumstances praise is considerably more effective than censure as a stimulant to scholastic exertion. (See Thomas H. Briggs, in School and Society for November 5, 1927, Vol. XXVI, p. 596.) These findings do not support the statement of Elizabeth B. Hubert (see p. 144) that praise is more effective with colored than with white children. (A special form of discouragement is referred to on page 135.)

firm the tentative findings as regards non-racial influences on mental growth, which we have briefly reviewed, the case will have been established for a significant departure from established school practices. American democracy—an actuality at least to the extent that persons in every way of life are able to understand each other—is largely the result of a school system that does not recognize a class division of society. But lack of allowance for differences in recency of residence, command of the English language, physiological growth curves and other divergences between children of different national and racial groups introduce an artificial sense of class which corresponds to no social necessity. If children of these diverse groups were graded in accordance with their mental ability in relation to stages of progress rather than of chronological age, there might still be distinctions as between the more favored and the less favored social groups, but the distinctions would tend to be less clear-cut. More especially, there would be no erroneous assumptions as to race characteristics to hold back and discourage the more gifted children of those groups that, in the average, tend to be retarded in comparison with others.

But so far as the mutual attitudes of children of different groups are concerned, not only a faulty system of grading but much more the attitudes that underlie it and that also express themselves in a multitude of other ways tend to create channels of division which correspond to no reality of innate difference. As we have seen, separations occur in the voluntary group formations of children that reflect both the prevalent racial attitudes of their elders and the actual divergencies of mental (sometimes, where interest in athletics is strong, also physical) development. To judge from the contributions made to the present study, too little attention has been paid as yet to the existence of these divergencies in intelligence, ability, and temperament during the years of adolescence and their effect upon personal contacts.

CHAPTER VIII

THE ABSORPTION OF ADULT ATTITUDES

To understand how children absorb the attitudes that surround them in their social environment, whether from adults or from other children, requires a knowledge of the learning process generally. We have, in recent years, had an increasing volume of information concerning the inter-relation between content and method of teaching, between intentional and unintentional or attendant learnings, between apperception and habit formation. But we have not as yet a complete analysis of the relationship with which we are more especially concerned in this chapter, namely that between the desired and the undesired influences exerted by adults upon children in situations that do not involve organized education in any form.

Professor Kilpatrick's theory of "attendant learnings" [1] fits those situations in which there is deliberate provision for some process of learning. The attendant learning may at times be more important than the intended learning, but it is after all always connected with a process recognized both by teacher and by learner as a learning process. Now, when we come to the transmission of attitudes by an older to a younger generation, we enter a field in which often there is no deliberate teaching at all, and the whole volume of learning is attendant. Unknown to the adult, the mental process is being stimulated or canalized by activities which, in intention, may be directed to any of a multitude of imaginable ends. From such evidences as are at hand, it is possible to conjecture that probably most of the "teaching" of race attitudes is totally unconscious and unintentional and therefore a process of influencing rather than of teaching in the narrow sense. Most children copy their elders, whether they understand

[1] *Foundations of Method.* (1925.) The term "attendant learnings," as used by Kilpatrick and others, denotes those secondary learnings which practically always accompany the primary learning toward which an educational process is directed; it consists of the formation of habits, attitudes and associations that may either be an intended or an accidental by-product—an addition which often is more important in the total effect of the educational process than the main, purposed result.

93

what these are doing or not.[2]   The total volume of what enters into the attitudes of children by way of this social inheritance, according to some observers, is much greater than the total of their personal experiences and the effects of their observations.

A child psychologist in an eastern city writes:

Behavior, observation and specific unpleasant individual experiences may be the cause of prejudice springing up in the minds of, perhaps, one-third of a given group, but the mind of the other two-thirds is colored by the attitudes of the adult members of their group who discuss people of other races in their home, taking pains to bring to the fore all the more degrading characteristics of the group instead of stressing similarity of their human failings and virtues.   In many homes, persons of another race are always spoken of by the derisive names applied to their group, such as "nigger," "coon," "wop," "sheenee," instead of the more dignified term applied to them in books of knowledge.

The New Jersey group of parents state that children's race attitudes are chiefly conditioned by their observation of the behavior of children and adults.   The group emphasize the imitative tendency in children and record it as their observation that personal unpleasant experiences with persons of other race groups are relatively few and practically of no influence in shaping the attitudes of children.

The influence of talk overheard by children at home, school and elsewhere in which derisive names are applied is only occasional; that of talk in which cultural efforts are humorously treated may be moderately frequent.   Probably few children are often exposed to discussion of other groups that is marked by emotion.   More obviously considerable is the influence of the lack of mention of the existence of other groups in the community.   The children in American residential neighborhoods are growing up to a large extent with the feeling that, while there are many races, one knows about them only from the pages of textbooks and from the newspapers or industrial contacts in life. In many cases here even the attitude of patronage is not known because the existence of other races does not rise to consciousness in the home or through social contact.

The southern settlement group states that children get wrong attitudes from adults and then, when they see displeasing evidence of the characteristics of other nationalities, get their

---

[2] A significant contribution to our knowledge of childish imitation has been made by Sigmund Freud in *Beyond the Pleasure Principle* (1922, p. 15).

prejudices confirmed. Often, however, the adult teaching goes directly contrary to the children's observations. A young child naturally admires the banana man and the organ grinder until he hears his parents or some one of his own group criticize the other nationalities thus happily represented in his personal experience. The group add that unless the child already has absorbed a definite prejudice, he is not likely to condemn a national group as a result of a bad impression made upon him by one member of such a group.

Furthermore, they point out—and this is a matter easily overlooked—that the friction which exists between adults of different racial or national groups in itself may be the cause of disagreeable incidents in the experience of the child which will help to determine his attitude toward the other group.

Another thing to which they draw attention is the different degrees of emphasis with which parents of different national groups influence their children in regard to their attitude toward other groups. For example, in the Jewish homes of a given community there may be frequent references to the religious prejudices against them of the Gentiles, while in the Gentile homes of the same community Jews are rarely mentioned or commented upon as such.

A high-school teacher writes:

Home influence is stronger than precepts laid down at school in forming attitudes. I have been strongly impressed with the imitativeness of children and the strong tendency to imitate other children more than older people; so the influence of one home probably acts through those children to the children of other homes.

These general statements of opinion give an indication of prevailing ideas as regards the relative weight of home influences and other forms of experience. In the following pages we shall endeavor to examine more in detail exactly what types of attitudes the adult environment, especially the home, impresses upon the child, and how.

Unfortunately, the contributed examples of incidents or situations in which children have learned racial attitudes seemingly from adults do not always show how the attitude was transmitted. But after having in this chapter surveyed their content, it will be easier in subsequent chapters to enter more fully into an examination of the exact nature of the psychological contact that has produced the transfusion. We may, however, even at this stage note how powerful is the emotional element in the transmission of attitudes. Writers on race relations often assume that all prejudice is wrong and that all racial attitudes should be tested by the degree of their rationality. But we know of no case in which a generation actually has transmitted its attitudes to the oncoming new generation through any purely intellectual, rational procedure. Without an emotional quality, the attitude itself would normally be without sufficient life to communicate itself to another person; and the response of the recipient or learner, likewise, must be to some extent emotional, if the "lesson" is not "to go in at one ear and out at the other." [3]

Briefly, then, the current talk about "race prejudice" is not very helpful for our purpose. In a sense, prejudice is inevitable in a society in which the conservation of cultural concepts cannot be counted upon to proceed automatically. Wherever different social groups have different valuations for cultural goods and ills, they will endeavor to defend if not aggressively to promote them; and the resulting conflict will be charged at times with emotion. [4] Even where an educational end is rationally desired, the method may have to be an appeal to the emotion. The most effective educational method will be one that uses all resources and integrates them into a coherent system. You cannot convince a small child by an appeal to his judgment that it is wrong to put a dirty object into his mouth. The Child Study Association notwithstanding, you emphasize the lesson with a slight slap on the hand; and the whole of the education of children in the social concepts of the grown-up world to which he belongs consists of reasoning blended with slaps and kisses. Let us, therefore, in surveying the different kinds of attitudes which, intentionally or not, the social group transmits to its young, also take note, in so far as the illustrations permit of it, of the degree of emotion by which this transmission is attended.

1. Emotional Antagonisms

To begin with, we shall take note of situations in which antagonism to members of other groups has been acquired by way

[3] See William Heard Kilpatrick, *Foundations of Method* (1925, p. 35).
[4] Franz Boas, *Anthropology and Modern Life* (1928, p. 194). J. H. Denison, *Emotion as the Basis of Civilization* (1928, p. 465).

of emotional reactions. (See also Chap. VI, p. 73.) The point of interest in this connection is the way in which an attitude which may or may not be rational is impressed upon the child by an appeal to his feelings. A marked antagonism sometimes is inculcated in children as the result of a single incident, such as a crime:

I have always had an instinctive dislike for a negro, writes a student. I was raised in Kentucky, and while that is really not considered very far South every one down there seems to have a marked feeling of superiority over negroes. It is not so much a feeling of superiority with me as an absolute hate and repugnance when I see one. When I was just a child a negro committed an atrocious crime in the immediate neighborhood. Of course, every one knew about it, and on every hand I was warned against and even guarded from the sight of a negro. I always have a dread of one, no matter how I meet one or under what circumstances.[5]

When a child, writes another student, I was told by both mother and father how the Indians of North Dakota (in pioneer days) would come into the homes and demand things to eat and drink, and that if they would not get what they wanted they would molest property, and in some cases would carry off the children and let them starve. This has always put a fear into me as I dreaded the thought of being kidnapped away from my parents.

She then gives the following incident which, re-inforced by the subsequent talk in the home, sufficed to create a strong race antagonism:

When about six years old, mother had taken me with her to visit one of the neighbors. It was getting dusk when we left the neighbor's house, and as there were no roads, only paths, we had gotten lost. In the distance mother spied a couple of Indians, she became very frightened and ran (dragging me along) to hide behind a big rock. This was the fall of the year, and we became very cold and frightened, but mother would not move for fear that she would get too near an Indian camp, and there we would have been captured. We stayed there (behind the big rock) until daybreak, and then mother could see our house about two miles in the distance, which we walked to as fast as we could as we had to pass near an Indian camp. This experience in the wilderness, being so cold and uncomfortable, hiding from Indians

[5] Because it may have a bearing on the race attitudes of writers quoted, their spelling of race names has been retained in this book.

in the dark, has always put fear into me. Even now (in college) I think of the Indians as ugly men who are thieves.[6]

The following examples show the transmission of strong antagonism in individual cases where it may not be shared by the rest of the community or the set.

Walking across the playground, a settlement worker found a little Italian boy crying bitterly. She asked what was the matter. "Hit by Polish boy," the little man repeated several times. Inquiry among the bystanders showed that the offender was not Polish at all. Turning again to her little friend, she said, "You mean, hit by a big, naughty boy." But he would not have it thus and went on repeating that he had been hit by a Polish boy. This struck the worker as so curious that she made inquiries about the little fellow's family. She learned that it lived in the same house with a Polish family and that the Italian mother, by constantly quarreling with her Polish neighbor, had put into the heads of her children the notion that Polish and bad were synonymous terms.

Two other examples will help to show how home influences of this kind operate:

Mary, five years old, shrinks back and clings to her mother when she sees another child who lives a few blocks away, saying, "She's 'talian." Her mother and father had been discussing in her presence the small section of Italians near by, resenting the fact that they were there. And Mary had been told to avoid the children because they were dirty and "not nice." At the age of seven her prejudice was even stronger.

Tom and Elizabeth lived in a New England town where they had seen few Negroes. At one time their mother hired a woman to do some cleaning. She asked her her name, and the woman replied, "Mrs. Anderson." "But what shall I call you?" the mother said sharply. "What is your first name?"

When the colored woman had left the room, Tom asked his mother why she would not call the new cleaning woman, Mrs. Anderson.

"Because I will not call any nigger Mrs. Anderson or Mrs. anything else. They ought to be kept in their place. New England spoils them." [7]

---

[6] Deliberate, in the same way, is the attempt to create racial fear in an adolescent girl, described by Mary White Ovington in *The Crisis*, April, 1927, p. 61.

[7] The report of the Chicago Commission on Race Relations contains several examples that illustrate the transference of an emotional race antagonism from adults to children: *The Negro in Chicago* (Chicago University Press, 1922, pp. 241, 245).

We must content ourselves in this and the following sections with describing situation of *apparent* response to adult feelings and attitudes, for, unfortunately, a more scientific inquiry into the exact nature of the reaction or the relative strength of different forms of reaction is as yet in its earliest stage.   Tests made of the response of children to facial expressions of emotion [8] indicate that laughter, pain and anger are understood at earlier ages than fear, surprise and scorn.   But this experiment was made with photographs, and no allowance was made, in the conclusion named, for the child's lack of practice in interpreting two-dimensional representations—with the result that, obviously, those emotions register earliest in life that are most sharply caught by the camera, that is to say, those emotions that produce the most marked facial distortions.   But what really counts is the child's reaction to the total gesture, seen three-dimensionally and in motion.

2.   INSTITUTIONALIZED ANTAGONISMS

It would not be difficult here to present a process exactly the opposite in one respect of the one just described, and one far more normal and widespread.   What the child acquires from his adult environment in racial attitudes are much more largely acceptances than specific reactions.   A situation involving mutually antagonistic attitudes between two racial groups may be so much regarded as a matter of course by every one in the child's environment, that no one talks about it, that few are consciously aware of it.   Since he has no opportunity to learn, in such cases, how either his own or the other set of people feel about their relationship (which rests upon a "maladjustment" often only in contrast with an abstract ideal of social harmony, but not in relation to an actual state of balance), the child does not have his attention directed toward the existence of a "situation" and so develops no attitude toward it.   A majority of people thus live to a ripe old age without ever becoming aware of elements in the social arrangements or traditions of their community which, ideally considered, evince injustice or neglect.

Those who travel from one part of the country to another and notice interracial adjustments different from those to which they are accustomed at home, are apt to forget this and immediately

[8] Georgina S. Gates, "An Experimental Study of the Growth of Social Perception." *Journal of Educational Psychology,* Vol. XIV, 1923, p. 453.

to accuse those who to them seem to offend against justice, of selfishness, greed, lack of Christian morality, and what not. When the process happens to be reversed, these same people may be astonished to find themselves subject to the same moral indignation. Thus mutual recriminations result between North and South and between East and West that generate antagonism but not understanding.

For our present purpose, the prevalence of an injustice or mutual animosity in the group relations of a community is of no relevance unless in one way or another it comes to the attention of the child in the form of specific experiences and situations towards which he will react in ways that may be observed. In other words, the particular relationship in which injustice, neglect, or long-standing distrust is an element must be one within the child's field of perception, and it must be one in which adults display a feeling which transmits itself to him, to follow Professor Edward Cary Hayes' classification, either in the form of suggestion, or in that of sympathetic radiation, or by way of imitation of acts which, in their turn, reproduce feelings. But it may also be a situation in which the child reacts to an expression of a sense of injustice on the part of members of the other group without awareness of it on the part of members of his own group. For example, a child may first learn about the way in which a social arrangement discriminates against the members of a racial group other than his own by hearing what classmates of that other group are saying about it or what their parents are doing about it. This, however, is the more exceptional point of contact. More normally, it is the emotional intensity with which adults of his own group either defend or resent an intergroup arrangement or an incident arising out of it that makes a child conscious of the arrangement or the issue and colors his attitude toward it. Here are a few typical situations of the kind that cannot fail to influence the attitudes of children in one of these ways, even if they do not immediately register in their minds:

In a southern community, a Negro girl won first honors in a widely organized spelling match in which white children competed. Several papers decried the results and insisted that the authorities had committed a grave error in holding such a contest.

In this city, writes a social worker from Pennsylvania, we have a school where the punishment for colored children is not undertaken by the teacher but by the janitor. Just yesterday one of the colored children was punished, and the teacher told him that he ought to be sent back South where the K.K.K. could take care of him; in fact, that all Negroes ought to be sent back there so that the K.K.K. could handle them. If he had his choice, he would send all the Negro boys back there so they could be "lynched," as that was the thing they deserved.

The difference in treatment of colored children as compared to white in this school has caused so much disturbance that the colored community and the colored branch of the Y.W.C.A. and the Negro's Protective Association have written to the Board of Education asking for a special meeting to adjust these matters.

I might also add that no colored woman is allowed to teach in the schools of ——. The colored girls feel no incentive in going through school, many of them saying that it is wasteful for them to go through school since they could be nothing but servants after they finish school. The request of the colored community for a colored teacher to teach at least colored children was refused.

One of the local children's agencies a year or two ago made up Christmas packages for its wards. All of the girls within a certain age group were given soft warm wool scarfs. There were grey scarfs with black stripes and there were gay ones of red, blue and green. Apparently unconscious of the incongruity of their choice, the committee sent the dull-colored ones to the foreign girls.[9]

What the children of the dominant group learn from institutionalized forms of neglect, such as have just been described, cannot be stated with certainty. Opinions are divided among the contributors to the present study as to whether children can be conscious of the existence of "foreign" groups in the community with which they have no contact and yet be without an unfavorable attitude toward them. A study group of southern settlement workers remark on this point:

Prejudice is not created by lack of contact in itself. The child must have been taught directly or indirectly what to think of the other group, or have had unfavorable personal contacts with it to acquire a prejudiced attitude toward it.

[9] Anne H. Roller, "Wilkes-Barre: An Anthracite Town" in *The Survey* for February 1, 1926, p. 537. See also an illustration case in Bruce McKinney, *My Neighbor, the American Indian* (Home Missions Council, 1922).

With this statement (which is illustrated by experiences used in other connections in the present volume) several correspondents agree from the vantage ground of their own observations. On the other hand, a child psychologist states:

When no mention of any kind is made of the existence of other groups that live in the community, the child is apt to develop a distinct sense of superiority toward them which makes it impossible for him to sympathize with them, especially if they do not dress, talk, look or act like the people he has learned to look upon as the only people in the world.

Whatever the exact nature of the reactions produced by these situations, it is clear that it does not require incidents highly charged with emotion to give an unfavorable tone or predisposition to the child's attitude toward a group in the community that is kept at a distance socially. The social order itself conveys lessons that are absorbed without conscious learning. This is especially true when that order does not cover all contacts with the mechanical precision of a caste system equally recognized in constitutional and in common law, or when it is broken every once in a while by an eruption of rebellion against it on the part of the disadvantaged group or set aside by the uneasy conscience of members of the dominant group. As likely as not, what first brings the uncodified arrangement to the child's attention is an exception or a temporary mishap to the orderly functioning of the "adjustment."

Since these social agreements or impositions will be considered more fully in their effect upon children (especially in Chaps. IX and X, which deal with the forms of race segregation that are most likely to come to the child's attention), we shall here merely note their existence and their obvious influence in distinction from that of other factors in the total situation.

3. RACE PRIDE AND DEFERENCE

Closely linked up with the content of the previous subsection is the type of situation in which the sense of racial superiority or inferiority colors the attitudes of a group toward members of other groups—or of one specific other group. There is a great deal more of variety and shading of emotional dynamic in these attitudes than is usually supposed. Violent race conflicts between two large groups in a community may obscure the existence of quite a nexus of group attitudes, ranging from milder forms of suspicion to different degrees of sympathy and friendship. The experiments made in typical communities with Professor Bogardus' social distance tests and other questionnaires [10] show an enormous variety of degrees in like and dislike in the attitudes of any single group toward the members of all the other groups that make up the community. We can here only single out for illustration some of these attitudes and the ways in which they transfer themselves in typical situations into the consciousness of the young. Let us, first, look at the general attitude of race pride and see how adults transmit it to the younger generation: [11]

A few mornings ago, in front of a movie theatre, two small boys were engaged in a friendly wrestle,—one boy was white, the other colored. A crowd, mostly white with a scattering of colored men, was enjoying the struggle for supremacy. The sun was hot, each of the boys was being punished, each showed gameness. Busy men stopped to look on, probably the bout would develop into a fight,—the savage instinct still lingers in the grown-ups. We like to see human beings maul each other. The little tots had their partisans on strictly racial lines of cleavage. Race supremacy was the issue in the minds of the crowd. The white boy finally got the colored boy down and held him with the "nelson." The whites applauded; the colored people looked discomfited. The colored boy made a desperate effort to rise. The white boy was coached how to hold his advantage. Each boy began to give way his self-control, anger was plainly seen. The colored boy finally got a hold on the ear of his opponent who winced with pain. Several cried out "Break the nigger's neck!" The colored people present evidently were saying the same thing in their hearts as to the white boy. The colored boy had remained under the bottom all the while, the man under the bottom is not necessarily the more punished. Blood is seen on the face of the white boy. Passion is aroused in the boys, and among the spectators more cries of "Break the nigger's neck" were heard. A kindly faced man stepped forward and told the boys to get up, they had done enough. The races had met; the odds favored

10 For applications of social distance tests, see The Inquiry's publications: *What Makes Up My Mind on International Questions* (Association Press and Woman's Press, 1926), *All Colors* (1926), etc. An analysis of the results of an attitude study of some magnitude is made by Goodwin B. Watson in *Orient and Occident* (American Group, Institute of Pacific Relations, New York, 1927, Mimeographed).

11 The story of the first Negro business venture in promoting the sale of colored dolls is to the point. It is told by W. D. Weatherford in *The Negro from Africa to America* (1924, p. 427).

the whites. The majority of the crowd was satisfied. The whites were happy; the colored people were humiliated. The boys walked away apparently as good friends as ever. Rancor was in the breast of every white man; rancor was in the breast of every colored man.

The boys engaged in the scuffle were as good friends as ever. They are of tender years. We grown-ups alone showed prejudice,—each of us was guilty of race prejudice. Numbers alone made the difference.[12]

I have heard a little Polish boy returning from school ask his mother: "Is it true what the teacher says—that Columbus was no Pole?"

"That is right," said the mother. "He was a Genoese."

"Oh," replied the boy, "I thought that all big men were Poles."[13]

How a foreign-born group may catch the spirit of a typical American environment is illustrated in the following case:

The children of Mexican families in a Southern Californian town caught the spirit of the town when the Mexican colony ostracized a Mexican girl for marrying a Negro. The children call her "nigger" across the street. Their families are mostly Chihuahuans from a province where prejudice against Negroes is rare.[14]

The following example briefly illustrates a situation into which we shall have to enter more fully in a later chapter, namely the disparity between a strong race pride in the home and a somewhat different racial attitude in the community:

A graduate at one of our women's colleges, the daughter of cultivated Germans, told a friend: "My father made me learn German and always was wanting me to read it. I hated to have anything to do with it. It seemed to me something inferior. People in the West call a thing 'Dutch' as a term of scorn. It was not till I was in college that I realized what German literature and philosophy have meant in the world, and that to be a German is not a thing to be ashamed of."[15]

---

[12] From the *Indianapolis Ledger*, quoted in *Opportunity*, October, 1924, p. 313.

[13] *The Living Age*, March 14, 1925, p. 590.

[14] A typical example of the absorption of race pride in the parental home, without any particular effort to rationalize that feeling as the outcome of some specific teaching or event, is given by Professor Bogardus (who, curiously enough, includes it in a collection of cases illustrating favorable interracial attitudes, unmindful, apparently, that the student who wrote it speaks of his own national group) in the *Journal of Applied Sociology* for January-February, 1927, p. 274.

[15] Emily Greene Balch, *Our Slavic Fellow Citizens* (Charities Publication Committee, 1910, p. 414).

A complement to the preceding example is the following, which illustrates the reaction of a child whose home reflects the normal race attitudes of the community toward the exaggerated racial pride of individuals:

When I entered elementary school, part of the first grade's requirement was study of German. I remember how frightened I was of Herr Sheribb, as he was called. He was a short, thick-set, heavy-bearded man with a rather cruel mouth and a pointed mustache. From the first I didn't like him. His voice was harsh and guttural and he would become inordinately angry if some little tot was unusually slow in learning. When his temper got the better of him he would call us all manner of names in German which sounded anything but complimentary, and his frown was terrifying. Then, too, he never tired of extolling the German youth—how apt at learning—what great universities and schools Germany had—what a great country Germany was, and how stupid we were because we found the German language difficult.

When Herr Sheribb left, his position was taken by a Mrs. Reid. I at once felt a dislike for this woman. She, like Herr Sheribb, was squat and fat. Her black hair was always untidy, and she used musk for a perfume. Whenever I detect the odor of musk I think of Mrs. Reid and that horrible aroma of which she was so fond. When German ceased being a requirement—I was then in the third grade—I quit taking the language with a sigh of relief in escaping from Mrs. Reid.

Even though not taking German I still had proceeded to build up a healthy hate for the nation. There was a boy who lived next door whose grandparents had come from Germany and, inasmuch as his grandfather was still living with the family, the grandson had his head so filled with the greatness of Germany and the insignificance of America, that I heard of nothing but the wonders of Germany from this boy. However, he and I never got along very well together, and consequently I angered at everything he said in praise of Germany. These factors, rather than the propaganda of the war, served, I believe, to make me dislike Germany and Germans.

It has been said that no racial group is so humble as not to look down upon some other group as inferior to itself. Even where the local community does not permit of such comparisons, the despised and oppressed race will discover and transmit to its children an attitude of contempt for at least a limited class of people as "poor trash."

Nevertheless, a sense of inferiority is a very real condition, and no matter how disguised it may be by contempt for others or by a studied aggressiveness, it contains those emotional elements that secure its transmission from one generation to another. Most often it takes the form of a frank and unsophisticated acceptance of the dominant group as the superior one. For example, a settlement worker in a middle-western city reports that colored children of all ages prefer white club leaders to colored ones. The question may well be asked, "How did they get that way?" Obviously, they had absorbed from their adult environment the opposite of race pride, namely, a sense of the inferiority of their own group.

Colored children should be systematically taught the truth, and the whole truth—not "protected" against it. The most dangerous kind of protection, in the end, is protection against the truth. They should be taught that there is no virtue in race or color as such; and that the virtue which those qualities seem to have is simply an advantage derivative of the environment. To retaliate by teaching them that black is superior to white simply sets one folly or falsehood against another. Strange to relate, when bright colored children begin to see that the superior position of the individual white man is often due, not to his own virtue, but to an advantage in the environment, those children are disposed to discredit the whole achievement of the white race, and it actually becomes necessary to sober them with the suggestion that after all the Caucasians are perhaps every bit as good as Negroes.[16]

A southern woman recalls an occasion when, as a small child, she referred to a colored woman as a lady and her colored nurse rebuked her, saying: "Only white women are ladies."

Both colored and immigrant children will frequently be found to make allowances for the display of racial prejudice against them on the plea that they themselves have prejudices against other groups. This admission, sometimes obviously stressed, may be merely a disguise for an inferiority sense in the given case. An unusually experienced high-school teacher in New York refers to the mutual tolerance of minority groups among children with very different characteristics as a defensive attitude. She adds:

Among Jewish children there seems to be a tolerance for the Negro that springs, perhaps, from their own difficulties. When the subject of anti-Jewish prejudices comes up, it is almost invariably met with a

16 William Pickens in *Opportunity*, December, 1927, p. 366.

careless pride and a dismissal of the matter as "ignorance." The Jew who deplores race prejudice is quite likely to mention the prejudice of Jews against Christians as the opposite.

4. DERISION

Race pride and contempt for other races are two facets of one attitude, as a rule—but not necessarily so. There are, as we shall see later, in our American life the remnants of a truly aristocratic attitude of *noblesse oblige*. And while such a connection usually exists, it does not follow that the child, in picking up from his elders a sense of pride in his group, will necessarily at the same time learn to look down upon others. The two things, in fact, are often unrelated. A racial group that is conscious of having relatively little to be proud of will nevertheless sometimes have a deep contempt for others; on the other hand, a group which is clearly dominating a community situation may be so secure in its position as to nurse neither grievance nor contempt for any other group. The children of that dominant group may grow up in contacts with those of other groups that invite if not complete appreciation, at any rate a good-humored appreciation of some of the qualities and a predisposition for mutual goodwill.

Situations of this kind are of many degrees of tolerance. Too often when local observers report that mutual respect—each group "keeping its place"—exists in the community, an outsider will discover that important elements in the situation have been overlooked. The element most frequently overlooked and most potent in developing the attitudes of children of the dominant group is that of quiet amusement at the antics of persons who belong to the minority. The "mutual respect" is merely formal; underneath it all kinds of attitudes may be brewing, and the children may learn more from an occasional shrug of the shoulder accompanied by a smile than from the words that are spoken across the dinner table.[17]

[17] The contrast between primary and attendant learning is illustrated in the following incident told in the *New York Evening Post* for February 16, 1927:

The son of the house had made a name for himself in football at his college, and his triumphs were discussed one evening at dinner when the minister was a guest. "You know, Jack," put in the pastor, "athletics are all very good in their way, but your studies are much more important." "That's what Father says, too," replied Jack. "But Father never jumps up and cheers when he hears me quoting Latin the way he does when he sees me score a goal."

Everywhere, children absorb from grown-ups judgments which these have unconsciously formed. That little smile when Sarah, the colored cook, goes out in clothes that are modern and in good middle-class taste; that little frown when the furnace man's son, instead of leaving school the moment the law permits, to work in the factory, talks of high school and even of college; that sharp side remark when the dealer whose price is too high for a piece of furniture that you "absolutely must have" happens to be a Jew . . . all these are action lessons for the small boy or girl, lessons that work and reproduce themselves long after the word lessons in home or church or school have been forgotten.[18]

For this reason, and also because it happens to be a theme to which many of our correspondents have given particular attention, we have here made a special category of those attitudes of contempt and derision which grown-up people transmit to their children in such bewildering variety of ways—some of them, no doubt, unconsciously.[19] The connection between contempt or antagonism and the use of derogatory or derisive names has been explained by Professor Lumley in the following passages:

Laughter is a prophylactic against contamination from without. The ancient Hebrew authorities made much fun of the foreign religions and manners and thus endeavored to keep the people pure. That they did not fully succeed may be shown by many references in the Old Testament. But they greatly retarded the fusion of cultures in this way. And, in the use of this means of protection, they have had an uninterrupted line of descendants.[20]

One of the oldest of practices is that of framing suitable epithets for foreigners. The wide diversities in appearance and manners presenting themselves in the persons of strangers have taxed the ingenuities of persistent name-callers to a quite extraordinary degree. As a result we learn of "pig-eaters," "cow-eaters," "uncircumcised," "barbarian," "jabberer," "bohunk," "wop," "chink," "greaser." Ethnographical works furnish lists sufficient to supplement what may be heard in any city.[21]

The popular assignment of uncomplimentary and hateful names has served always as a protest against social change and thus as a means of social control. We reach this conclusion by the consideration of

[18] Bruno Lasker in *The Womans Press*, May, 1926, p. 332.
[19] Some striking examples are given by Mrs. Sidonie M. Gruenberg, director of the Federation for Child Study, in *The Survey* for September 1, 1926.
[20] Frederick Elmore Lumley, *Means of Social Control* (1925, p. 276).
[21] *Ibid.*, p. 296. See also p. 300.

several facts.   First, a new name, derogatory or otherwise, is always a sign of change.   Old names are sufficient until some unnamed variation appears, then the classifiers set to work; they must locate this new thing and manage it.   Second, there is a striking synchronism between the periods of greatest social variation and those of most prolific name-calling.   When there is an increase in immigration there is a noticeable enrichment of the names applied to foreigners.[22]

The following incident, contributed by a student in the northwest, is a reminder at this stage of a fact which we have already noted in another connection, namely that the handing on of a derisive name does not necessarily hand on to children the feeling that is supposed to go with it.

This happened on a train I was on.   In front of me was a mother with a little girl, about four years old.   The child was much interested in the colored porter who went through occasionally.   He evidently noticed her and smiled and talked to her some.   Finally he told her he had something for her and she happily got into his arms and came back beaming presently, still in his arms, but carrying an orange.   As he put her down she said to her mother, "He is a nice nasty-dirty-nigger, isn't he, Mama?"   The words were all one word to her and were, so far in her life, evidently a quotation of what she had heard him called by the mother.

Two different effects produced by the use of the same derogatory epithet happen to be illustrated by two entirely unrelated communications:

The first one, from a Los Angeles teacher, mentions how a girl in grade II asked for permission to change to another school.   She had overheard her parents call her school a "dago school" because of the large number of Italian and Mexican children that attended it.

The second communication comes from a woman who is now a teacher of foreign-born adults and recalls how, as a child in Colorado, she wanted to be allowed to attend the "dago school," so called by the native people generally, because it seemed to her adventurous at that time to mix with those children, and because her own home did not share the prevailing attitude.

Several correspondents call attention to the fact that derisive place names for the localities where members of a distinct racial

[22] *Ibid.*, p. 300.

group of immigrants generally reside have about the same effect as derisive names for these groups themselves. An unpublished report of the National Urban League mentions that a particularly dirty, squalid neighborhood of a certain northern city is known as "bad lands," and this name attaches to its residents, for the most part southern colored families, recently arrived, that have to seek the homes with the lowest rents. A northern settlement worker mentions "nigger town," "dago shanties," and "the patch" as typical place names which are often used to impress the child with the desirability of keeping away from those who reside in those neighborhoods.[23] In New York, Chicago and elsewhere, neighborhoods have been officially renamed because names that had become unsavory through past associations were throwing a wholly undeserved stigma upon those alien groups that now occupy these areas.

Of the reaction of the disadvantaged groups themselves to derisive nicknames, a recent editorial in *Opportunity*[24] makes the following observations:

There is much sensitiveness to the word "nigger" as a term of contempt, a sensitiveness varying in intensity according to geography and according to degrees of sophistication. It is, perhaps, weakest in the most emancipated Negro circles of the East, and at the same time, paradoxically enough, among the least emancipated Negroes of the South. It is strong generally through the West. An interesting problem of racial psychology is present here. Although the term is in common usage among Negroes in referring to themselves, there is a blind racial ritual on the matter of its use by others with reference to them. . . .

After showing the unwisdom of objecting to terms which represent realities, past or present, no matter how unwelcome the recognition of that reality, the editorial returns to the special objections of Negroes to the use of the word "nigger": With *nigger* there is this difference:

Because it is a corruption intended most commonly as an expression of contempt, it is effective only when it makes Negroes *feel* inferior.

[23] In Pittsburgh, a colony of Italian settlers along an unpaved lane at the bottom of a curving ravine, whose sloping sides offered opportunities for vine-growing, called their street after their home town, Chianti Way. In course of time this was corrupted to Shanty Way—as the street is now known.
[24] September, 1926, p. 270.

The truly emancipated ones who are more certain of their superior absolute status refuse to see or feel a sting in the use of the word. They are doing precisely what the Quakers did.   They are changing the connotation of the word.   "Quaker" and "Shaker" were once words of contempt; "Methodist" was applied in ridicule by Oxford students to the followers of John Wesley; "Gothic" was applied contemptuously at a time when a taste for the classic prevailed; "Whig," "Tory," "Mugwump," were all applied in ridicule.

No one thinks of insulting a New Englander by calling him a "Yankee." . . .

Occasionally a personal experience will provide an antidote to the use of verbal methods by the home in teaching race attitudes to children. Educationally useful accidents like the following do not occur every day, however. It is told by a colored physician in the South:

Two white boys, nine and thirteen years old, were standing on a roadside, seeking a ride. A colored man approached, driving his own car. "Mister, please give us a ride," called out the younger. The car slowed down to take them aboard, when the driver overheard the older boy say, "Didn't papa tell you not to call a nigger Mister?" The face at the wheel hardened, and the car sped away. The two-mile walk to town probably did not reconcile the boys to "papa's" social philosophy.

Of course, the use of derisive names for a group in contempt is only one form of deprecating it in the eyes of children. We have already, in several of the examples quoted, seen how impressions are produced by the association of a group or race term with an unfavorable moral or social judgment. Casual remarks of that kind tend to become stronger as they accumulate in the child's mental vision the details of a picture or, sometimes, as they fasten the habit of associating a given trait with a given racial group. Such remarks in common use are, for instance:

"It was that smoky, we came home black as niggers."

"Rinse those grapes, darling; who knows how many dagoes have touched them."

Religious and racial associations of an unfavorable character often go together. When frequently repeated, they tend to create the impression of permanent and universal traits which the child has difficulty to unlearn completely, even after he has learned through observation or school lessons that the particular associations are temporary or affect only a part of the racial group to which they are applied.   A dislike of Mexicans by Americans in many southwestern communities is undoubtedly caused or aggravated by the current confusion of Mexican nationality and Roman Catholicism.   The same is true of immigrants generally in other parts of the country.

In a certain social institution, Jewish children asked their leader: "Are you going to sing those Jesus songs?"   When they were told "yes," they added: "But it is sin to say the word Jesus."   In the same institution a Polish child refused to speak to Jews.

The association in children's minds of racial groups with undesired moral qualities in its effect upon the attitudes of children who frequently hear it stated has already been illustrated in a number of examples.   The following incident is typical:

In a neighborhood, flowers had been stolen from front yards.   Immediately the blame was placed on the foreign-born children without any previous investigation as to whether some of the native children might not be guilty.   Of course, the children of the neighborhood at once absorbed the notion that foreigners, young or old, are not to be trusted.

This example brings up a difficult point which we must further discuss below.   Supposing there is reason to suspect the foreign-born children whose parents, often, belong to the culturally and morally least advanced groups in the community—is it not quite natural that this association in the minds of both the adults and of the children should take place?   If the children of certain groups usually are the ringleaders in any trouble at school, is it not natural for the teacher to look at them accusingly when a new feat of indiscipline comes to her knowledge?   Would it not be asking for an artificial and not quite practicable observance of interracial neutrality to insist that parents, teachers and other grown-ups should not in the presence of children show their suspicion by word or gesture?   We here merely raise these questions without trying to answer them.

Another rather difficult question occurs in connection with the subject dealt with in this section: Is it wise deliberately to draw attention to the achievements of colored people in order to arouse in children respect for them?   Alas, too often efforts of this kind are in such stark contrast to the actual treatment of the other group that the pedagogic intention is but too plain, and children are not deceived any more by them than are adults. Some teachers make a special point of letting the class know when a colored pupil has done well; but instead of thus imparting to the white pupils the sense of potential equality, she merely imparts the sense of wonder that such a being as a colored child should by a strange knack have accomplished this. In the same way, it is doubtful whether the well-intentioned rules of some of our best newspapers to bring out in their news columns laudable achievements of Negroes really do that race a service. They both reflect and disseminate a prejudiced attitude when they do not take it for granted that colored people will do their share of praiseworthy acts, win their share of prizes, and so on. News paragraphs like the following are common:

NEGRO GIRL WINS $150 PRIZE

Is Adjudged Most Deserving Public School Graduate of Her Sex

A Negro girl, Martha Washington, will receive tomorrow morning from Superintendent of Schools Dr. William J. O'Shea one of the Rebecca Elsberg memorial awards, which are given each school term to the most deserving boy and girl in the graduating classes of the Manhattan public schools. . . .

Supposing next year the newspaper reported: NORDIC GIRL WINS $150 PRIZE—well, you cannot suppose anything like that because it is not being done. The race of the winner is reported precisely to suggest that there is an especially dramatic quality in the fact that a member of it comes out on top. Taken together with items in which the Negro is branded a criminal, the general effect is clear.[25]

[25] The author admits that it is difficult to prescribe a rule for the handling of such items by newspapers. Perhaps the following paragraph from a newspaper code on the uses of the words "Jew" and "Jewish" might be applied also to the designation of other racial groups: "The application of the word 'Jew' or 'Jewish' to any individual is to be avoided unless from the context it is necessary to call attention to his religion; in other words, unless the facts have some relation to his being a Jew or to his Jewishness. This rule should apply equally whether the word is used in connection with some praiseworthy or honorable act or achievement. Thus, if a Jew is convicted of a crime he should not be called a 'Jewish criminal'; and, on the other hand, if a Jew makes a great medical or other scientific discovery, he should not be called a great 'Jewish physician' or an eminent 'Jewish scientist.' In neither case had

the man's Jewishness any connection with his conduct or with the disgrace or honor which that conduct entailed." (*The Interpreter*, January, 1927.) Applying this rule to the mention of Negroes, it would mean that in Boston or New York or Chicago it would be bad taste to state that the winner of a school prize was a Negro, because many colored children win such prizes since they have educational opportunities the same as the white. If on the other hand, in a locality where Negroes have only lately enjoyed educational advantages a member of the race wins such a prize, it may be well worth mentioning this fact as a gratifying evidence of the rise of a hitherto backward group.

CHAPTER IX

INSTITUTIONAL INFLUENCES

1. Social Segregation

We have noted in the previous chapter (p. 94) how lack of contact in itself may more fully impress upon the child the race attitudes of his elders than any positive saying or doing on their part. The learnings of the child directly from circumstances in his environment, unconveyed by the grown-up people with whom he is most closely associated, are so important that we must devote a separate chapter to them. It is easier in later life to discard the specific opinions which school or home has endeavored to impress upon the child than it is to outlive those less defined ideas that have entered into the mental stock through the commonplace arrangements of every-day life. For example, if my parents should happen to feel deeply embittered against a certain immigrant group, I may be able later in life, having discovered the causes of their feeling and also having had quite different experiences myself, to discount and disregard their "prejudice" in what now I conceive to be my own considered attitude. But, having been brought up in a situation in which, under the force of circumstances, members of that group are always in a position that is hostile to the cultural heritages and aspirations of my group, having thus come to associate them with conditions and things I do not care for, I find it exceedingly difficult later in life to adjust my attitude toward that group in a situation where these conditions do not obtain. I shall be likely to continue looking upon these other people as strangers, interlopers, perhaps a danger to everything I value; and even if I do not think this of them, a feeling of aversion, involuntarily entertained, is apt to color my every relation with them.[1]

[1] As Mueller-Claudius has correctly observed (see footnote, p. 66), the symbol of strangeness soon becomes a symbol of evil; and what was seen at first as a static embodiment of these qualities is transformed, under the pressure of adverse circumstances, into the active cause of these qualities in the life of community or nation. It is perhaps this tendency of the human mind that has given rise in every age to the imaginative creation of scapegoats. The unexplainable has to be explained, the undetected criminal has to be found and punished.

But aversion and hostility are not the only attitudes thus absorbed by the child directly from the social arrangement of his environment. Without a word or a gesture, the adult world can and does impress him with the inferiority of this or that other racial group, when it carefully excludes it from those common undertakings or the use of those common services which all other people share, regardless of their age, sex, or social standing. This explains the long historical survivals of social segregations. These taboos cannot be broken from within a society unless circumstances of a revolutionary nature—such as an economic reorientation—compel a change in its social organization. For, the child grown up in a society that segregates a racial group will have had impressed upon him its inferiority or undesirability so strongly that he cannot change his mind toward that arrangement except under the strongest new emotional stimuli.

An eastern social worker among children writes:

Segregation in neighborhoods, conveyances, schools, churches emphasizes social differences and fosters a spirit of narrowness which makes almost impossible adjustment of races that must by the very nature of their environment come in contact with each other because they have no knowledge of each other upon which to base their contacts and are swayed entirely by their own emotional reaction toward the other group.

Another correspondent says:

One of the first things children notice is that colored or foreign children do not attend their church or their school.

Back of this situation, so far as the relation of white children to Negroes is concerned, lies the long history of slave-master relationship during which each generation absorbed quite unconsciously and without effort the attitude of the elder generation and in its turn accepted it as a basic condition of contemporary life.[2]

A few examples will help to illustrate how race segregation carries its own lesson for children of the dominant group without any one necessarily having to comment upon it or to reinforce its direct teaching by a verbal lesson in social amenities.

We will deal, first, with situations that do not involve discrimination in the use of public utilities and services, but situations

[2] E. B. Reuter, *The American Race Problem* (1927, p. 106).

over which those immediately in charge of children have control:

My children always have gone to school with colored children and accept them as simply as they do their white classmates. At noon, those who take their dinners—white and colored, boys and girls—eat together, as a matter of course, all in an informal semicircle in one room under the supervision of one teacher. There is absolutely no race consciousness among the children. There never is any *natural* spontaneous race antipathy between children. They acquire it only after it has been ding-donged into them by prejudiced elders. Then often the lesson is only too thoroughly absorbed and, of course, intensified with all the force of tradition.

But do you think these same children who have just finished lunch side by side could go to any of our ice-cream parlors and get a soda or a sundae together? No, it would be too much for the sensibilities of the adult white people. Really, it is laughable—the utter illogic of it. Or rather it would be if the ultimate result were not so grim and often tragic.[3]

In a Girl Scout camp a girl was expected whom none of the officers present happened to know personally. A bed was assigned to her in a room with another girl of her age. When the newcomer arrived, it was found that she was colored. Of course, her name had not indicated this. She was at once placed in a separate cottage and, at the initiative of the counsellors, her money was refunded, and she was sent home the next day.

The following communication will remind us what this segregation means in permanent influences upon the lives of members of the segregated groups:

A little girl lived with her grandmother in a suburb of a Louisiana city. Under the separate-street-car law of that state, white and colored passengers are separated by means of a movable board, about a foot and a half high, that is fitted by supporting rods into holes in the backs of seats. On the street-car line from this suburb to the city, the two back seats are always provided for colored people, and the little girl had not known of any other possible arrangement when a relative brought her to Brooklyn, N. Y. During the first few days, this colored woman had occasion to take the child on street cars with cross seats similar to those in the Louisiana city. She noticed that the little girl on entering by the rear platform ran and climbed upon the first back seat. At first nothing was thought of this, but when

[3] Quoted from *Haldeman-Julius Weekly* in *The Crisis*, April, 1927, p. 57.

the woman found that the child clung to the back seat even when she herself started farther into the car and that she hung back as if in fear even when she took her by the hand, it became obvious that a great mental impression had been made upon this child, not yet four years old, by the sacredness in which the Jim Crow institution had been held in the South.

We are confronted, writes a settlement worker, with the difficult problem of a largely increasing Negro population in what has heretofore been an exclusively foreign group of nearly thirty nationalities. The question has come up among the staff as to what should be our attitude in regard to sending the children out to our summer camp. So far, none of the Negro children have applied, and we have decided, I am not sure whether wisely, not to urge them to go. It would arouse considerable discussion and opposition among the white families sending their children out, and I question whether this would not foster race antagonism rather than bring about better feeling. For this year, therefore, we have not tried to mix the two at camp. As there are two Negro camps, there is not the great need that otherwise there might be.[4]

Often the policies of a social institution are quite free from an intention of segregating different racial groups; but popular feeling is too strong for them, so that in practice a separation of children along race lines takes place. This is illustrated by the following example:

Colored citizens contributed a considerable amount of money to the erection of the Boys' Club at R. because they understood that white and colored boys would be equally welcome. But after the club had opened, so much feeling developed that a new rule was adopted under which the colored boys have been given exclusive use of the club on Saturday nights, paying $300 a year for the privilege. At other times, colored boys will not go on to the floor of the gymnasium even when they are allowed to do so.[5]

[4] A fuller description of the difficulties in which a social or religious institution finds itself when it tries to avoid the effect of social segregation upon the attendant learnings of its juvenile clientele is given in *And Who Is My Neighbor?* (The Inquiry, p. 174 *et seq.*) That book also contains other illustrative material on the problem here under discussion.

[5] The report on *The Negro in Detroit* (prepared for the Mayor's Interracial Committee of that city) gives several cases in which an intention to provide equally for white and colored children was frustrated by the hostility of rural neighborhoods toward the presence of colored campers. (Mimeographed Report, Detroit Bureau of Governmental Research, 1926.)

It is sometimes said that our churches, more forcibly than any public institutions, impress upon children the lessons to be learned from segregation.[6]

A colored family living near —— Episcopal Church attended services there. One of the children wanted to join the Girls' Friendly Society and was told by the leader: "Why don't you join a colored church? There are several in the neighborhood."

To what extent the desire to segregate native from foreign-born or white from colored children is due to the prevailing view that there are biological differences in moral behavior, it would be difficult to tell. That this motive is of considerable force, there can be no question; and it is easy to see how it arises. Henry J. McGuinn, in his contribution to the Institute of Social and Religious Research study of Negro segregation gives facts which indicate that in the cities surveyed the juvenile delinquency of Negroes is proportionally higher—in some cases three and four times as high—than that of whites. But he shows that the very social arrangements that deprive colored children of the advantages enjoyed by white clearly are the chief cause of this difference.[7]

Quite apart from deliberate segregations, there are, of course, those natural segregations within the community which follow its social divisions, either because of differences in economic status or because groups of the same race, language or nationality tend to live in "colonies." While no one intends these separations to exist, nevertheless they have the effect of associating in the average child's mind the nature of certain neighborhoods with those who occupy them, that is to say dirt and noise with the most recent immigrants (who may also be Negroes from the South) or outlandish institutions with others.[8]

In connection with an industrial study of The Inquiry, a member of the staff was visiting the homes of workers in an industrial city of New Jersey. Going from house to house one Saturday afternoon, she approached the home of a colored family named on her list as distinguished by understanding for the interracial situation. In looking

[6] Fred Eastman, *Unfinished Business of the Presbyterian Church in America* (The Westminster Press, 1921, p. 165).
[7] T. J. Woofter, Jr., *Negro Problems in Cities* (1928, pp. 228, 230).
[8] Compare also what has been said about the influence of deprecatory names for such neighborhoods (p. 109).

for the house number, she attracted the attention of several children playing next door; and when she went up the steps and rang the bell, these little white children called out to her in startled tones, "Missus, colored people live there."

"We have no segregation in schools, theaters, restaurants, or community living," states one of the reports, "but a very real natural segregation is brought about by the high rents in certain sections of the city." This impression of racial segregation is heightened in some cases by the existence of separate social institutions for children of different races and nationalities—necessary perhaps in many cases, but too often continued long after the need of separate provision for the different groups has ceased. In fact, there are sometimes foreign-language institutions which, like foreign-language newspapers, may have no other purpose than that of keeping their clientele loyal to their homeland when, without them, the younger, American-born generation may completely cross the barriers of language, manners, and ideals that separate the different immigrant groups.[9]

The amount of Americanization, in the opinion of other contributors, is much less a factor in segregation than the size of the minority group. Not only do larger groups with similar cultural interests or of similar social status tend to reside in the same neighborhoods, but even when their members have nothing or little in common apart from their skin color or type of countenance (Oriental, Indian, South European), if they appear in numbers, they are apt to be classified and treated by the rest of the community as though they were composing a group of uniform character.

A colored student aptly remarks:

In a community where there are few colored people, prejudice is not apt to be shown so much as in one where there are a large number. A Negro is treated as an individual. My family has always lived in a small town where we were the only colored family. As a result we became well known in that part of South Dakota and well liked. The children knew we were colored, but we never thought of it—there was no occasion for it. However, when we moved to Minneapolis, the fact that we were colored was brought home to us very strongly by white and colored—especially colored—people.

[9] See, for example, John H. Mariano, *The Italian Immigrant and Our Courts* (Christopher Publishing House, Boston, 1925, p. 21).

The effect of numbers shows itself not only in the different degrees to which cities with large or small Negro population will tolerate contacts between children of the two races, but also in the corresponding attitudes of different neighborhoods of the same city.[10] One correspondent maintains that segregation, so far as the foreign-born are concerned, has no influence on attitudes because it is temporary, and only those stay in segregated neighborhoods who are not yet Americanized. Yet, too often that temporary situation creates its own lasting influences; and accepted social segregations are reinforced by direct teaching on the part of parents and others.[11]

The New Jersey parents' group says on this point:

The influence of segregation on the attitudes of children to those of other races is very strong in that the child has the tendency to believe that "whatever is, is right." Finding segregation an established fact in his little world, he assumes it to be the right thing. Sometimes he asks questions: "Why?" but the white adult can always cleverly turn the question aside so that the first impression is that his little white group always knows what is best for the little black or yellow or brown group.

George A. Coe has devoted the greater part of a book to the problem here so simply stated and what it involves for the theory and method of project teaching.[12] He states it thus:

The young encounter moral law, first of all, in the customs, or settled modes of action, of some group—a family, a play-group, children's parties, a school, a church, a city, a business community, and so on. The way in which anything is regularly or statedly done without protest in any group with which a child is associated is assumed to be the way this thing ought to be done.[13]

General Segregations

We have, in the preceding pages of this chapter, dwelt too largely, perhaps, upon those segregations which directly affect the relations between children. We have done this because, un-

[10] *The Negro in Detroit,* Section VII, p. 10. Manuscript Report prepared for the Mayor's Interracial Committee, Detroit Bureau of Government Research, 1926.

[11] Nathaniel S. Shaler, *The Neighbor* (1904, p. 177).

[12] *Law and Freedom in the School* (University of Chicago Press, 1924), especially the middle chapters.

[13] *Op. cit.,* p. 75.

doubtedly, those institutional influences to which children are personally subjected leave the strongest imprint upon the development of their racial attitudes. But at the same time it must be recognized that the whole environment of the child is the material from which he gathers his impressions, from which he gathers an increasingly coherent sense of the attitude of his group to other groups in the community. Not only his playmates, his school fellows, his club at the settlement or religious association, but more and more also his observation of the way grown-up people live and behave gives him a knowledge of race differences as apart from personal ones. He notices that people of dark skin are "jim-crowed" or that they occupy a different part of the town. He becomes aware of the fact that immigrants do not belong to his church, that the clerks in his father's office all talk good English and wear good clothes, while the men in the mill speak broken English and wear dirty clothes. He notices that at the summer hotel there are no Jews, that the well-dressed people who call on his mother do not include Mexicans (if he lives in the South-West) or Portuguese (if he lives in the North-East). He finds that the grown-up people in his set avoid calling certain kinds of people "Mister" or avoid sitting next to them on the street car.

In other words, by a thousand subtle influences he learns to associate race and nationality with social status and, failing contrary experiences, to look upon that association as permanent, inevitable and part of the divine plan that rules the relationships of men.[14]

Curiously self-contradictory is the reply sent by a Pennsylvania teacher who first states, in general terms: "There is no influence on the attitudes of children by segregation, exclusion, or association of race with status" and, later, quotes these remarks of children: "Mrs. B. is moving; every house in the block next to her is filled with Jews." "From —— Street to —— Street is entirely a Finnish neighborhood." "I do hope that G. won't have to go to —— School. It is filled with Finns."

Exclusion from employment, of course, is noticed by children less than exclusion from residential neighborhoods, schools, and churches. But it has its influences:

[14] The nature and consequences of these associations will be more fully discussed in Chap. XVII.

When the children about here play train, writes a correspondent, the small colored boy is always by common consent porter.

Exclusion, according to the New Jersey parents' group, is recognized by the child largely during the adolescent and post-adolescent periods. One of the women present said: "We had three colored girls in our class. . . . Two of them were in the honor group. We all admired them for their achievements, and we liked them *because they knew enough not to intrude.* After further argument, this speaker admitted frankly that she would like the people of other races if they all knew enough "not to intrude."

Eula, writes a Californian teacher, a Negro child of eleven, was in my room at school. It was a foreign school of eleven nationalities in which Mexicans and Russians predominated. Eula's family lived in a better house than did the average family in the neighborhood. Eula was usually better dressed than the other children. While not especially "light colored," Eula was unusually pretty and attractive. Apparently, the children of other nationalities, Russian, German, Italian and Mexican chiefly, felt not the slightest difference between her and themselves. Small childish flirtations between her and the boys in the class were the rule. I wished very much to watch the transition of this child to a higher school where, I was sure, she would be made to feel the color line; but I left the district before this came about.

This chapter, since it is based on reports from many communities, indicates the variety of existing customs and viewpoints on the matter of social segregation in their effect on child attitudes. But since no one community has been studied over a considerable period and no general survey is available for a previous period, it does not show the change that is taking place. This change, we have reason to believe, is in both directions, due perhaps to the greater contact between South and North. It is because of this change that animosities develop; and the school strikes and other public manifestations of the conflict that comes with attempted change (see next chapter) usually are paralleled by, or follow, lesser conflicts in homes and neighborhoods.

Our picture is incomplete also for two further reasons: Students of public opinion are less likely to observe changes in group accommodation that are unaccompanied by friction; thus, practically all our correspondents have failed to note instances in which either between racial groups or within a racial group voluntary segregation for distinct social purposes takes place. Our method of gathering evidence does not ensure that the less articulate group opinion—which is usually the satisfied opinion—is adequately represented. On these points, therefore, further study is needed.

CHAPTER X

INSTITUTIONAL INFLUENCES (*Continued*)

2. SEGREGATION IN PUBLIC SCHOOLS

When the force of law coincides with the pressure of public opinion in keeping the children of different races apart, the lesson learned from the fact of separation is, naturally, even stronger. This is not the place to discuss in detail the arrangement of duality upon which the public school system of the greater part of the United States is built up—though obviously our consideration of the subject under discussion in this volume remains quite inadequate so long as we only deal with the minor manifestations. For the great majority of American children the fact that children of another color do not go to the same school as they do is a lesson which is ineradicable if it extends through the whole period of school attendance.

The inconsistency between profession and practice in the state's attitude toward the children of a minority racial group can hardly escape children when the situation is, for example, like that in California as regards the Japanese and Chinese.[1] If the schools provided for the two racial groups are unequal in quality—that means, in school buildings and opportunities for advancement, the only aspects that are likely to be observed by children—the lesson is even stronger.[2]

[1] Eliot G. Mears, *Resident Orientals on the American Pacific Coast* (University of Chicago Press, 1928, p. 353).

[2] For further evidence on the differences of educational provisions for white and colored children in certain southern states, see a series of articles in *The Crisis,* beginning with the number for September, 1926. The subject is also dealt with in W. D. Weatherford, *The Negro from Africa to America* (1924, Chap. XIV) and in the *Negro Year Book* (Tuskegee Institute). For important statistical data see also the June-July, 1927, number of *The Bulletin,* official organ of the National Association of Teachers in Colored Schools (Tuskegee Institute, Ala.). The data contained in the elaborate report edited by Thomas Jesse Jones for the United States Bureau of Education (Bulletin, 1916, No. 39, two volumes) have been overtaken by a great improvement in both white and colored schools, evidence concerning which will be found in the annual reports of the General Education Board, the Slater Fund and the Jeanes Fund. There is no basis of comparison for Indian schools, in so far as they are maintained from public funds; however, study of them, from the point of view of educational qualities, will be found in G. E. E. Lindquist, *The Red Man in the United States* (1923).

A careful study of these differences has recently been made under the auspices of the Institute of Social and Religious Research by a group of workers headed by Professor T. J. Woofter, Jr., of the University of North Carolina. Their summary findings are as follows:

School funds are not adequate to meet the needs either in the North or in the South. The South, however, is not only poorer than the North, but also less disposed to distribute such funds as are available according to the school population. The Negro schools are a secondary consideration. In comparison with schools for white children they have fewer seats in proportion to the school population, more pupils per teacher, more double sessions, fewer teachers, poorer salaries, fewer and smaller playgrounds, and less adequate provision for the health and comfort of pupils and teachers. They also have few, if any, of the "extras," such as libraries, lunch-rooms, auditoriums and gymnasiums; and the courses of study in the high schools and normal schools are more restricted. In practice, the policy toward the Negro schools is based on a feeling that less care and attention must suffice.

The cities that show the greatest contrasts between the white schools and the colored schools in such items as those mentioned above are not in all cases the cities that show the greatest contrasts between them in current expenditures. The differences are owing mainly to long periods of neglect of the colored schools. The recent comparatively substantial efforts to improve both the white and the colored schools still leave the colored schools far behind the others, which also need to be further improved to bring them up to the best educational and physical standards.[3]

Even where there is no outward difference in buildings and equipment, the product of two schools may be so different in quality as to raise the question whether there may not be unfairness in the assignment of teachers or in other educational provisions. Children may notice that few of the children from the poorer neighborhood graduate into high-school or that they cannot compete in games or win prizes when equal opportunities are given to all. The answer is, of course, that the better neighborhood will normally attract the better teachers, and that standards of attain-

[3] W. A. Daniel in T. J. Woofter, Jr., *Negro Problems in Cities* (1928, p. 201). That equal educational opportunity is not present either in the North or in the South is further shown in the articles contributed by N. C. Newbold and E. George Payne to the special number on the American Negro of the *Annals of the American Academy of Political and Social Science*, Vol. CXXXX, No. 229, November, 1928, pp. 209, 224.

ment to a large extent reflect the cultural status of the adult group. Even poorer equipment may be due less to intentional discrimination than to a difference in the vigor with which parents demand the best for their children.[4] It is important at this point to realize the effect which the large disparity in public expenditure upon the schooling of white and Negro children produces, not only on the difference in the quality of the education they receive but also on the degree with which the school attendance laws are enforced. If enforcement is slack in the case of one racial group in the community the impression, of course, is created—whether intentionally or not—that the children of this group are not worth educating, or that education will not benefit them, anyhow.[5]

We cannot, of course, produce here anything like full evidence either as to the extent of segregation in schools or as to the extent and nature of discrimination in the allotment of public funds to education, but must content ourselves with a few typical illustrations of the kinds of fact that are likely to come to the attention of children and the atmosphere in which they are likely to hear these facts discussed by their elders.[6]

Let two illustrations from the South suffice to recall situations in that part of the country which are all too familiar:

Recently a not inconsiderable town in a southern state built its first elementary school for Negroes. It is a three-room frame building; already inadequate at the start, for it is to house 125 pupils with two teachers. The town had provided no more than the bare building. The Negroes were expected to purchase desks, blackboards and other necessary equipment, as well as pay the teachers' salaries.

Yet this event marked a real step of progress. The whole county only has four schools which colored children can attend, two of them old, miserable, one-room schoolhouses, one an abandoned Negro church, said to be in "perfectly horrible" condition, and one a Rosenwald school of modern construction and equipment. These schools are from ten to eighteen miles apart. The county provides funds with which to keep them open for three months in the year and will pay for another month if the Negroes of the county, who are very poor, will raise the necessary money for opening the schools a fifth month.

[4] This point is illustrated in the Detroit report previously quoted. Detroit Bureau of Government Research, 1926, manuscript report, Section VIII, p. 5.
[5] W. A. Daniel in T. J. Woofter, Jr., *Negro Problems in Cities* (1928, p. 217).
[6] Historical and practical origins and justifications of school segregation policies will be further discussed in Chap. XIX.

There is in this county a small training school for colored teachers under the auspices of a mission board; this is in danger of being closed for lack of local cooperation.

A large southern city recently let the contract for a $250,000 high school for its colored population. According to the authorities, the courses of study at this high school will be liberal, preparing for college entrance. But so great is the prejudice against giving Negroes a general humanistic education that, in order to get approval of the bond issue, it was necessary, writes the reporter, to label the institution an *Industrial* High School for Negroes.

This prejudice is shown also in a complete lack of public provision for the training of teachers. The city in question has about two thousand Negro children of high-school age. Of course, all of these will not avail themselves of the new school facilities. But the total number of colored children of school age is 12,000, requiring at least 300 teachers, if complete school attendance were enforced. Yet the city in the past has done nothing to train these teachers or in other ways to secure teachers of quality.

In this city, there is a small junior college for Negroes under the auspices of one of the denominational missionary societies; this college proposes to enlarge its program to train the teachers needed for the new high school. But the sponsors of the institution are not willing to bear the whole cost without local support. They laid the matter before the school board, before an influential organization of colored residents and before the alumni, threatening to move the institution to another city unless there was more evidence of willingness to cooperate.

The superintendent of schools, though sympathetic, and realizing the necessity of training more teachers, expressed fear that the white citizens, after having voted the high-school bonds, might resent being asked for still further expenditure on Negro education. But he thought that the city might at any rate pay the salary of a teacher of education at the school. The Negro organization pledged itself to vigorous participation in a campaign for funds by the alumni, who themselves undertook to find at least $2,500 a year with the understanding that this amount would be raised from year to year as the extension plan would come more fully into operation.

The influence of racial segregation upon the race attitudes of children—the aspect of the matter which is of primary concern to us in this book—is, as may be expected, particularly great in communities with changing ethnic composition of the population. Where segregation, residential as well as educational, is an accepted practice—whether consented to by the unprivileged or not —we are not likely to have that friction, that emotional stress which is typical of situations where school policy in this matter is in flux. While, in one sense, a long-continued discrimination against the children of a racial group may be more serious in its larger social consequences, the situations of conflict in which white and colored or native and immigrant are marshalling their forces in defence of privilege are more apt to produce incidents that make a deep impression upon young minds. And the fact that different teachers, different school officials and different neighborhoods pursue somewhat distinctive paths in meeting the situation only adds to the confusion and tenseness.[7]

A student writes: I have always been more or less associated with Negroes in school. When I was too little to remember much or to have formed any active dislike, a Negro laundress was working at our house. Lunch was announced and Mother, as a matter of course, prepared a place at our table for her. When my older brother returned from school, he refused to eat at the same table with a Negress. Mother was very angry and embarrassed, but it was a question of excluding her own son or a stranger and a member of another race; so that next week the Negress ate in the kitchen. She offered no protest and seemed to take it for granted. She expected the latter and not the more familiar intercourse with her employers which she had at first been offered.

A mother in Cleveland says that her young son gave up a job because his foreman was an Italian and he "would not be bossed by a Wop." In his case the home training had been in quite a contrary direction, but he had caught the popular prejudice at school.

Bitterness and mutual recrimination must have marked the impression of the following events upon all children affected by them:

Victoria, the capital of the province of British Columbia, has an old and very wealthy Chinatown. A few years ago an attempt was made to segregate the Chinese children in separate schools, because though most of them were Canadian-born, a few who were Chinese-born re-tarded the others. The Oriental children in one of the public schools were asked to stand up. Then the Japanese children were told to sit down. One Chinese boy, sensing the insult, marched out of the room,

[7] W. A. Daniel in T. J. Woofter, Jr., *Negro Problems in Cities* (1928, pp. 182, 183).

and the rest followed him. The Chinese community, led by the Chinese Native Sons Association, which has a few very brilliant and very active members, asked the school authorities to explain the incident. The Chinese school children then went on strike for a year. At the end of the year the older boys were put in special classes, but the Canadian Chinese children went back to the public schools on their own terms, which were "no discrimination in regard to creed, class or color." [8]

Conflicts Between School and Home

Special problems arise when the attitudes toward segregation are not the same in school and home. Sometimes the one, sometimes the other is the more liberal in this respect; but in each such case children are likely to be exposed to an attitude of friction that expresses itself in exaggerated words and deeds of hostility and thus lays deep foundations for those various adverse race attitudes that have been described in earlier chapters. Frequently these conflicts between home and school policy embroil the whole neighborhood or community. For example:

The parents of 160 children carried out their threat yesterday to boycott Public School 5, Webster Avenue and 188th Street, the Bronx. Only sixteen of the 176 pupils transferred on Friday from Public School 33, an imposing new structure at Jerome Avenue and Fordham Road, reported at the fifty-year-old Webster Avenue building.

Although the reason given by the parents for their aversion to Public School 5 was that the equipment of the red-brick structure was antiquated and unsafe, Miss Elizabeth Rottger, the principal, said eighteen of the mothers had told her they did not care to have their children associated with the other pupils there. She pointed out that her school drew many of its pupils from that part of the Bronx, east of the Grand Concourse, where there are many Italians, and that, west of the Concourse, there are a large number of more prosperous Jewish people. . . .[9]

Six hundred white students of a high school in Chicago went on strike on September 22, 1928, because of the transfer to it of twenty-five colored pupils from another high school. In this case, hostilities seem to have been carried on with equal activity on the part of both racial groups outside, and a squad of policemen had to interfere. The whole neighborhood was aroused.

[8] Winifred Raushenbush, "The Great Wall of Chinatown," *The Survey*, May 1, 1926, p. 157.
[9] The *New York Herald Tribune* for February 3, 1925.

Recent unfortunate events in Gary, Ind., likewise seem to point to the presence of community attitudes of which the school system, a brilliantly progressive one in this case, had not taken sufficient cognizance:

At first 800, then 1,400 pupils of the Emerson High School went on strike in Gary, Ind., when twenty-four colored students had been admitted. They were upheld in this attitude by the parents and business men of the community, and this in spite of the fact that white and colored students had for long been admitted to another city high school. The Negro population of Gary is about 15,000. Various explanations have been given of this occurrence. Some hold activities of the Klan responsible. Others hold that it may be "an offshoot of the resentment of white labor against being brought into competition with colored labor from the South." [10] Against this contention stands the fact that in the Froebel High School the children of the very groups are mingling that are most likely to be in severe economic competition. It is more probable, therefore, that class antagonism—Emerson High School has held the state football championship, and the pupils of the Emerson High School are mostly German, Scandinavian and English in origin—is responsible. The protest comes from the older American group rather than from an immigrant one.[11]

In the sequence, the school board has proved that the often espoused ideal of separation with equal accommodation is pure romance—even in a city which has just spent millions on other public buildings. The striking pupils agreed to return on the understanding that the Negro pupils were to be removed as soon as possible to a new temporary school building for colored pupils, under construction at a cost of $15,000!

Here is a case in which the school authorities stood firm:

Parents of the striking students of the John Swett School in Oakland were threatened with arrest yesterday by Fred M. Hunter, superintendent of schools. The charge would be the violation of the State compulsory-education law.

All but thirty-seven of the white students of the school have been removed by their parents as a protest against the continued refusal of the school authorities to deny the eighteen Chinese pupils entrance to the regular classes.

A committee of the mothers of the striking students, armed with affidavits that the superintendent had promised the removal of the Chinese, have canvassed the district in an attempt to have the parents

[10] *New York World*, September 29, 1927.
[11] See the detailed account in *The Congregationalist* for October 27, 1927.

of the remaining thirty-seven white children withdraw them from the school.[12]

In passing, mention must be made of a phase of our subject that is too often forgotten altogether. We talk of separations between racial and national groups, or between natives and immigrants, as though it were perfectly simple to separate the sheep from the goats, as though in any given instance a glance may suffice to establish the group membership of an individual. This is not, of course, the case. Often children are, by deliberate fraud, introduced into circles where contact with their race is taboo. More often still, such introductions are made in all innocence because it does not happen to occur to the members of the minority group that they are under the ban.

The headmaster of a famous private school one day discovered that a little girl whom he had had in his school for some months was colored. No one, apparently, had noticed it either from her appearance or from that of either parent who regularly came to fetch her from school. The headmaster was perplexed because he knew that a majority of the parents of his pupils were opposed to having their children associate with colored children. He was particularly angry with a white clergyman who had introduced this child to him without mentioning her race. The clergyman took the position that it was not his business to make such a statement, so long as he knew the child came from a good, Christian home; neither he nor the child's parents had been aware that the school—in which there were many Jewish and immigrant children—did discriminate against Negroes.

Amateur Anthropologists

Occasionally there are real disputes as to whether a certain child is Gentile or Jewish, native or immigrant, white or colored. Too often, in a case of doubt, the sense that the native or white or Gentile children must be protected at all costs wins over a sense of justice, and because of their looks or for other reasons children are thrown into a group to which, either mentally or physically, they do not fully belong. As Professor Franz Boas has pointed out, there is no way of determining with certainty the racial group membership of any individual.[13]

On a somewhat larger scale are the difficulties which recently

[12] *Daily Californian*, September 30, 1926.
[13] *Anthropology and Modern Life* (1928, pp. 36, 38, 44, 49, 178).

confronted the school authorities of Richmond, Va., when they endeavored to enforce more strictly the law which demands school segregation of white and Negro children.

Richmond is to establish a special school for her racial outcasts— fifty or more small children who have been barred from the white schools because of non-Caucasian blood. These children, most of them apparently of pure white blood, missed school last year because their parents refused to send them to Negro schools. Their parents insist that they are not Negroid but have Indian blood. The State educational authorities, backed by the opinion of the State Registrar of Vital Statistics, Dr. W. A. Plecker, assert that such a plea is a confession of Negroid extraction because Virginia Indian blood for more than three generations has been more than half Negro. Families with Western Indian blood are not barred from the white schools.

The situation followed the adoption of the Virginia racial integrity law in 1924, and it became acute last year. Families with a noticeable strain of Negro blood first were barred from the white schools. In many cases it was necessary to eject children who had almost completed their education in the white public schools—sons and daughters of parents who always had considered themselves "white." Parents of such children had no choice but to send them to Negro schools. Only a few of them did so. The others kept their boys and girls at home, trying vainly to explain why. Embarrassment involved a score of families and gave Richmond a bitter lesson in miscegenation.

The parents besieged the school authorities in their misery and won their complete sympathy. But the city School Board could do nothing for them. And when a desperate mother charged favoritism and informed upon her brothers and sisters and cousins, the authorities were forced to eject their children also from the white schools. Some of the children shown by records to have Negro blood were so white that no one would have thought them other than pure Caucasian.

Several of the families affected had been proud of their Indian blood until the racial integrity agitation disclosed beyond reasonable doubt that practically no Virginia Indian blood subsequent to 1800 remained free from a pronounced Negroid strain.

Indian reservations for more than a hundred years furnished refuge for runaway slaves and hospitality to freed Negroes. The black and the red races in most of Virginia became inextricably mixed. And inevitably the white mixed with the red and black to produce children with clear features, aquiline noses and straight Indian hair. Many of these children became handsome men and beautiful women. They left the reservation and came to the city years ago. Their children were more white than they. And the children of the third and fourth generation took their places with the whites, and in many cases have become valuable citizens with considerable property.

Some of these families will send their children to private schools in the North, determined that they shall keep their status as Caucasians. The Richmond School Board, with the help of the State Board of Education, is to establish a special school for the others in September. There are enough of them to establish a little borderline colony composed of people neither white, red nor black.[14]

A similar case was decided by the United States Supreme Court in a case appealed on behalf of a Chinese school girl against a decision of the Supreme Court of Mississippi:

Martha Lum, a nine-year-old Chinese girl, was excluded from school by the board of trustees of the Rosedale Consolidated High School, solely on the ground that she was not a member of the white race. The Constitution of the State of Mississippi provides for separate schools for "children of the white and colored races," and the state courts held that Martha Lum could not insist on being classed with the whites.

Chief Justice Taft, in delivering the opinion of the United States Supreme Court, on November 21, 1927, said: "The question here is whether a Chinese citizen of the United States is denied equal protection of the laws when he is classed among the colored races and furnished facilities for education equal to that offered to all, whether white, brown, yellow or black. . . . The decision is within the discretion of the state in regulating its public schools and does not conflict with the Fourteenth Amendment."

It will be news to the colored people of Mississippi, a correspondent opines, that they are furnished equal educational facilities. In Bolivar County, where Martha's suit was brought, the per capita expenditure on public schools for white children in 1925 was $43.33; and that for colored children $2.26. Moreover, there is not in the whole state a consolidated rural school for Negroes which Martha could attend instead of the Rosedale school.[15]

We need not adumbrate the picture. The reader will have no difficulty in visualizing the effect which Martha Lum's new status, sealed by the highest court, will have upon her relations with the Caucasian children in her neighborhood or upon the

[14] The *New York World*, August 2, 1927. A similar case, that of the so-called Cherokee Indians of Robeson County, North Carolina, is told by G. E. E. Lindquist in the *Southern Workman* for November, 1928.
[15] A full account of the Negro school situation in Mississippi, the result of a special investigation, is given in *The Crisis* for December, 1926.

racial attitudes of either. In commenting upon this case, *The Survey* said editorially:

The mortification experienced by Martha and her fellow-sufferers at being classified with the colored races is very largely due to this striking dissimilarity in educational opportunity and its obvious result in social status. If facilities for education were really equal, it might in a generation or two become a matter of indifference to parents of Mongolian blood whether their children associate with whites or with Negroes. But unless the American people change the Fourteenth and Fifteenth Amendments by the substitution of concrete for abstract rights, such equality will not even be approached in any of the states that segregate children by races.[16]

We have so far discussed segregation in this chapter as though it meant necessarily complete separation of the pupils of different racial groups. But there are also in existence many systems of partial segregation through the school system, of segregations that are incomplete or that reserve certain courses, activities or parts of school premises for the pupils of the dominant group. It is an open question whether the net effect of these partial forms of exclusion from educational privileges is not as great or, perhaps, even greater than complete separation of the two groups. Certainly the sense of being discriminated against is likely to be greater on the part of the unprivileged group when the situations that bring the difference in treatment to awareness are frequent. The principal varieties of partial segregation are described by Mr. Woofter and his colleagues, whose findings not only give direct evidence of the discouraging effect upon Negro pupils but also indicate the probability of a forceful impression of Negro inferiority made by these arrangements upon white pupils.[17]

We are here, of course, merely stating problems. In later chapters we shall have to consider whether or how, in spite of the real difficulties disclosed, it is possible at some point to protect children from influences that inevitably produce prejudiced race attitudes.

[16] December 15, 1927, p. 368.
[17] W. A. Daniel in T. J. Woofter, Jr., *Negro Problems in Cities* (1928, pp. 186, 187).

PART III

HOW ARE RACE ATTITUDES TAUGHT?

CHAPTER XI

WHAT CHILDREN LEARN AT SCHOOL

In the preceding section (Chaps. VI to IX) we have surveyed what might be called the informal or unorganized part of the education which children receive in race attitudes. It is true, their home, their school, their church or some other organization wishes children to have certain attitudes, and in so far as the children absorb these, a desired educational influence is functioning. But in those situations that have occupied our attention, the teaching of race attitudes was not made part of a system of education; exactly how the child was to acquire the mindsets desired by his elders was more or less left to hazard. We now come to the deliberate devices employed in systematic education to give children specific knowledge of and specific feelings toward other races than their own. And since we have in the preceding chapter considered the learning absorbed by the child from a certain factor in school *organization,* segregation, we will now look a little more closely at the content of what the school offers the children in *method and material.*

Before doing so, however, it may be worth while to examine a typical sample of childish opinion of other races and peoples with a view to disentangling, if we can, those that have been acquired at school from those acquired in the home or on the streets or elsewhere. We may get a hint as to the sources of childish attitudes by carefully noting how children themselves describe their feelings toward other peoples. The following quotations are from the replies of boys to a questionnaire which asked them to write down the names of any peoples that they did not like and to state why they did not like them. Of course, its educational value quite apart, the form of such a questionnaire is very much open to question if the desire is to get an honest opinion. Much more elaborate tests, which avoid the obvious crudity of this one, also have been far from satisfactory as real gauges of opinion.[1] The test under review was taken by a teacher in the choir school

[1] Such a test to ascertain the nature of the problem was tried out by the Committee on Christian Education of the Federal Council of Churches in 1926.

of a church known throughout the country as a center of liberal Christianity in a cosmopolitan city; the answers, therefore, might be expected to be more tolerant than those which a similar questionnaire would produce under average conditions in a public school. This is what the boys say (in their own spelling):

Italians, Chinese, Mexicans, Japs and Portuguese and Germans (Spaniards and Russians being crossed out again after reflection). The Italians are a very unclean and sneaking race. The Chinese and Japs are a stealing and distrustful people. The Mexicans are a stingy and conspiracy people. The Portuguese are a very blood-thirsty and dishonest people. Germans are hateful because of their love for war and bloodshed.

Chinese and Jews. I do not like the Chinese because they are so sly and I am afraid they will plunge a knife into me when my back is turned. I do not like the Jews because they are so tight and because if you are in a subway rush they push you away and are generally disagreeable.

Jews. Because they live in dirty places. Chinese. Because they have such a bad reputation. Niggers. Because they are crooks and too free with razors. Italians. Because they are such a nasty and dirty people.

Neagro. I do not like the Neagro because he fits with rasers and are verry sly. Chinese I dont know but I dont like they thats all. Mexican are verry sly they sneek upon you. Japanese I dont like them. Jews I dont like them. Indians kill the white people and that is why I dont like them.

Italians Irish Mexicans Wobs Chinese Germans. Because some times they swipe and get kind of fresh.

Chinese because of their bringom into our country opium. Irish (South) because of religion.

Chinese Because I do not like to be knifed.

Mexican Because they are lazy, like some of us.

Negroes—Unreasonable dislike probably. (This, to judge from the language and handwriting, from an older boy.)

black race—think thay own the country
red race—thay kill
Chinese—   "   "
Japiness thay steal
Irish—thay swair and lie
Germans—croks

Chinese—to crafty
Cannibal—Eat up people
Serians—not clean people
Germans—War makers
Turkeys—torturers

I don't like Chinese because they stab you with knives
I don't like Italian's because they robb.

Chinese, Italians, Jewish, Russians. Because the Russians and Chinese do a lot of underhand work and the Italians try to make themselves disagreeable. The Jews are always trying to charge more for goods and small things like that.

People: Chinese, Mexican. Race Mongolian, White. I do not like the Chinese because of the looks of the slant eyes gives me a chill.

Jewish A race that believes Jesus was not on earth
Italian to dirty
Black race. Do not know.
Chinese You can never tell what they are going to do next.

Chinese—I do not like the Chinese because they have a certain air about them, a sneaking, slimy air. Mexican—A Mexican you think of as a person who will creep up and stab you in your back. Germans— A German seems to have a nasty disposition. Jews—a Jew is too tight and he goes around always talking about money.

Japanese, Jews, Chinese, Bolshevik. I do not like the Japs because there is something about them that gives one a feeling of distrust. I do not like the Jews because of many of their habits. I do not like the Chinese because they are so backward and refuse to be helped— and have such an aversion to help from foreigners. I greatly dislike the Bolshevists because of their actions in Europe.

Can we know how these adverse attitudes have originated in the minds of the boys? The teacher states: "The answers suggest that the boys had been reading stories of the Chinese which were bloodthirsty. There is no other known source for such ideas." But what were these books, and where did they get them? Can "penny dreadfuls" be held responsible for the views that are displayed in such remarks as on the Jews as "a race that believes Jesus was not on earth," on the Bolshevists "because of their actions in Europe," on South Irish "because of religion," on Mexicans "because they are lazy," on the Chinese "aversion to help from foreigners"?

Teachers' Attitudes

We shall probably have to examine the books used at school
and Sunday school to find the sources of some of these mental
pictures. But we shall also have to examine the teachers. Some
hold that the way in which teachers are recruited in the United
States ensures a maximum of reflection of unintelligent middle-
class attitudes. Against this, of course, it must be said that a
large majority of teachers have had opportunities of a higher if
not a college education. Still, the idea that teachers implant their
personal prejudices in the minds of children is occasionally borne
out by incidents such as the following:

A school superintendent was visiting a city school in Kansas where
two Negro boys were monitors. He unwisely asked a white child if
they did not object to the presence of Negro children and, on being
answered "no," went on to say: "It would never have been allowed
where I come from."

In a high-school in New York state were a number of Italian pupils.
Miss H, teacher of English, frequently showed her prejudices against
"foreigners," especially Italians. In one of her classes she had an unusually intelligent Italian boy. He usually came to class having done
his home lesson, but when he happened to fail in some minor part of
his lesson, the teacher would get extremely angry and send him from
the class. In the same class there were certain American-born students
who came to school day after day without having prepared their lessons; all that happened to them was that they were told, "be sure this
does not happen again." The Italian pupils at this school after a time
became so discouraged in this teacher's classes that whenever they could
they spent the period of her classes working on some other lesson.

A secretary of the Congregational Education Society reports on
conversations between two little girls, eight and ten years of age,
who had recently been transferred from a private experimental
school to a public school of good reputation. Here is part of it:

"This is one thing he (the principal) ought to know! A colored boy
named Richard only went and sharpened his pencil without permission
and he has to stand in class all day long for a week. One day he sat
down to do his work and now he has to stand two weeks."
"He has to stand all day long, day after day?"
"Yes, he has been standing all week; he never sits down.

"One day, in the beginning of the term, he was not paying attention and the teacher shouted at him this way—'You dirty, black, stupid simpleton, I am tired of you. I have had you too long and if you don't mind I will shake the life out of you, and I can do it too.' There are lots of children who do worse things than this, but she does not talk to them in that way. This boy really was not doing anything, but the teacher does not like colored boys, and I don't think the other children in the class like them either. They write nasty notes to the colored children."

"You say she does not like colored boys?"

"No, and she does not like colored girls either. There is a colored girl who is quite big and she is awfully nice to us. She swings us on the swings and tells us stories outside, but in the class she makes faces at the big boys. She makes faces all the time and sasses the teacher so that the teacher does not dare say much to her." [2]

Of course, these instances are exceptional, or they would not have been reported; and the fact that children speak of such happenings at home shows that they produce in them an effect unfavorable to the reputation of the teacher rather than to that of a racial group. Nevertheless, other children in these classes may have been profoundly influenced by the teacher's behavior.[3] According to the Chicago report on race relations, the attitude of the school principal is more important in influencing that of the pupils than is that of individual teachers on the staff.[4]

In many cases a differential treatment of white and Negro children seems to be based upon the prevalent conception that they are different; that is to say, the teacher makes no effort to find out what the capacity of individual colored children is but takes it as a generally acknowledged fact that all Negro children are more stupid or more emotional or less industrious than all white children in the class. The result is either neglect or the application of consciously different methods to the colored pupils —with the result, as recent psychological studies have shown, that Negro children receive less encouragement. One such study revealed:

In schools where Negro children are taught in the same classes with white children the Negro child rarely receives what slight amount of praise is given for good school work. This is not due so much to the

[2] Albert John Murphy in *Religious Education* for February, 1927, p. 177.
[3] Evidence suggestive of this influence has been given in Chap. VI, p. 105.
[4] *The Negro in Chicago* (University of Chicago Press, 1922, p. 245).

fact that his work is inferior to that of the average white child, but may be traced to the presence of racial prejudice.[5]

It has been pointed out that in some cases it is not the home circumstances and early upbringing that tends to imbue teachers with race prejudices but the very system under which they receive their training for their great social function. If the normal school or college they attend permits only association with other students who come from more or less the same class of home, an attitude of aloofness to others may easily develop which at worst is class-conscious and hostile, at best condescending. Existing social attitudes may be sharpened by rigorous exclusion policies; and the students may find it difficult later to adjust themselves to circumstances—such as the public school system of another state —which do not permit of the expression of racial preferences and taboos.[6]

Instances such as those quoted on page 142 probably are exceptional from the point of view of the relative prevalence of adverse race attitudes in teachers compared with the community that employs them. Instances seem to be more numerous in which teachers—with much pains, and sometimes at personal sacrifice— work against prevailing attitudes that they consider prejudicial for a more understanding and appreciative race attitude among their pupils. The following case is in point:

The High School of Y. in California is one of the biggest schools of the city; it has many hundreds of pupils who represent a cross section of the city's social strata, including many foreign-born boys and girls.

One of these is Yuki. She is the second child of a prosperous Japanese family which has six children, all born in America, who speak English without a foreign accent, attend church regularly, own several stores in the shopping district. The eldest son is a graduate of the University of California. Yuki is possessed of a beautiful soprano voice, is always well dressed, gentle and friendly. She made a wonderful record in scholarship during her high-school life, and at the end her credits far outnumbered those of any other student.

[5] Elizabeth B. Hubert, "The Value of Praise and Reproof as Incentives for Children." *Archives of Psychology*, No. 71, July, 1924, p. 60. It is interesting to note that this investigator herself, in spite of a meticulous objectivity in her own piece of research, assumes without evidence as a generally acknowledged fact that Negroes as a race are vain and more susceptible to praise than white people.

[6] In illustration, note the exclusion of colored teachers from a neighboring state from the extension course for teachers offered at Johns Hopkins University, as told in *The Crisis*, January, 1926, p. 145.

The principal of the school announced to the graduation class that this Japanese girl would be their valedictorian. Immediately a storm of protest broke loose. Newspapers took it up; citizens called upon the principal and threatened him; classmates announced that they would not allow a Japanese girl to appear on the platform as leader of the class.

The workers of the local International Institute of the Y.W.C.A. knew Yuki well and admired her. They called upon the principal to get first-hand information from him about the matter. They were pleased to find that he took a strong, clearly-thought-out attitude. He said: "Yuki has made a record of which all Americans with true American ideals should be proud. She shall take her place at the head of the class on the night of graduation, or there will be no valedictorian. These young people must learn to be good sports and fair-minded Americans."

The young Japanese girl did lead her class on the night of graduation and received many congratulatory notes from both Japanese and native Americans. The incident was referred to in many Japanese papers and without doubt found its way across the ocean to their homeland.

The following example further illustrates the pressure often brought to bear on the Pacific Coast upon teachers in regard to race relations:

In Seattle there was quite a stir because a Japanese public-school child in the fourth grade had taken the part of George Washington in a school play. The reporters would like to have made the teacher responsible for this choice, but actually it was the little boy's classmates who decided that he should play the rôle.[7]

How the exertion of influence by a teacher may produce unexpected results, is told by a Wyoming teacher:

We have a Negro girl in the seventh grade. When she first entered, we thought that a little talk upon the subject of her treatment would make matters a little more pleasant for her. The children responded nobly—too nobly, in fact, for one group nominated her as president of the class. Another boy, who comes from a better family than the majority of the class, retaliated by nominating as an opponent to her a moron boy.

[7] William C. Smith, "Born American, But—." *The Survey* for May, 1926, p. 168.

Before considering more in detail the use of the various branches of teaching in the handing on of race attitudes, it may be well to recall briefly what part the American public school as a whole has had in the upbuilding of a democratic, "American" public opinion.

To begin with, the American public school like that of every other country serves, of course, in some of its functions, the purpose of preserving the established folkways. It is the common instrument of thousands of "like-minded" homes to mold their children to the established pattern of their thinking. Since advance is always made by individuals, the school necessarily represents the community in a conservative mood.[8] Kimball Young[9] and J. M. Williams[10] maintain that our American public-school education represents "the mores and folkways which date from an outworn past." It prepares children for the obligations and exigencies of a social life they will never meet. The outstanding problem of the American school system almost from the outset has been how to preserve these traditions in a constant flux of population—involving not only the introduction of hitherto unrepresented folkways and mores through immigration, but also the diffusion of the original settlers and their offspring over a continent with widely differing geographical, climatic and therefore occupational conditions. The situation has been unusual. Hence the importance which the teaching of civics has assumed in our public schools.[11]

1. CIVICS

We come, then, from these general considerations of the part which the school plays in shaping the racial attitudes of children to the influences of specific subjects of instruction and the ways they are handled. But while, for the sake of convenience, we may examine separately what the child learns in the different class periods about his relations to members of other groups, these

[8] See F. Stuart Chapin, *Education and the Mores* (Columbia University Studies in History, etc., 1911, pp. 15, 65, 104). This monograph is an interesting review of the whole history of education and "initiation" as a means of society to perpetuate its mores.

[9] "Primitive Social Norms in Present-Day Education." *Social Forces*, June, 1927, p. 573.

[10] James M. Williams, *Principles of Social Psychology* (1922, p. 367).

[11] The part played by the school in the adjustment between the descendants of early settlers and new immigrants and their children will be further considered in Chap. XXI (p. 294).

separate learnings carry over from one period to the other, from one subject to the next; and it is never possible quite to dissociate what the child learns in a particular class period from what he learns through his associations with his school-fellows and with his teachers throughout the school life. This inter-relation of the "tone" of the school and specific instruction in citizenship has often been pointed out by educators.[12]

When we consider the specific purposes of civics as a school subject, we discover that, in addition to certain practical objectives, it has the definite aim of acquainting children with the political and social organization of the society in which they live, and to dispose them favorably toward it. There are a few modern teachers, at any rate, who would like to utilize the teaching of civics as well as that of other subjects of instruction for the purpose of encouraging in the child a receptive attitude toward any established social fact, and who desire to train him in a critical evaluation of social theories, so that he may the better in adult life apply an informed intelligence to the political and social problems that will face him. But such teachers often seem to overlook the fact that their purpose is incompatible with the one for which civics and history and other social sciences have been included in the school curriculum—not only of the public schools of America but of practically all systems of public instruction the world over. The school is primarily the agent of the state in its character as the organized embodiment of society. It cannot but represent a definite ideal of patriotism and social arrangements and endeavour to safeguard the continuity and robustness of that ideal by impregnating with it the youth of the land. To expect a neutral attitude of the public school toward different theories of social organization would be like expecting a neutral attitude toward different religious faiths in denominational Sunday schools. But there are different degrees of dogmatism. Occasionally it happens that a public authority or a church becomes uncertain in its adherence to traditional ideals and is more willing than is normally the case to permit the presentation of other ideals. More often a church or a school system banks on the accumulated experience and desires to condition children in the direction of what the great leaders in the past have found worth while; but in so doing they do not really wish to immunize

[12] See, for example, Henry Frederick Cope, *Education for Democracy* (1920).

children against new ideas or to make them less receptive to the lessons of their own experience.[13]

Our American public schools have in the course of time been modified in their civic and patriotic objective from the period when they represented the religious, political and social ideals of a simple, homogeneous society. How much they have changed under the impact of powerful influences from every part of the world as well as the influences of changed internal relationships between the individual and the state, we shall realize if for a moment we consider the kind of civic and patriotic attitudes which millions of immigrants have brought with them to this country from the public schools of their homelands. Here we have had represented in our citizenships, and thereby in the government of our school systems, attitudes as deliberately shaped by the imperialism of Austria, by the republicanism of France, by the internationalism of Holland and the great mercantile city-states, the militarism of Prussia, the seething revolutionism of Ireland, the liberalism of England, the progressivism of the Scandinavian kingdoms—and this not merely in the first generation of immigrants but, in diminishing degrees, by generation after generation of citizens of the various foreign derivations. In each of those countries, the public school system had served to create and conserve loyalty to the government.[14]

Under these circumstances, in a country that has had to digest a great mixture of civic and political attitudes created by the school systems of other countries, it is natural that, in the main, the civics class became an instrument for the integration of those attitudes into a single, American pattern. On the political side, the constitutional democracy of the country had to be emphasized in a way in which no other country need emphasize, in the education of its children, its traditional political ideals, because they are surrounded on all sides by its expressions and manifestations. On the social side, the civics class had to work for harmonization of the cultural ingredients that went into the country's "melting pot." There are many divergent judgments as to the success of the public school in doing this. While some critics lament the "failure of the melting pot to melt," others complain that its simmering has too rapidly reduced a rich variety of heritages into a

13 For further discussion of this topic, in another connection, see p. 266 et seq.
14 See William Moore, The Clash (London, 1919, p. 103).

uniform substance of Americanism. More particularly has there been protest against too rapid an assimilation of the youth of the land from the practical standpoint of the integrity of family life. In using the civics class (and the school as a whole) to produce harmony between the children of different groups through the creation in them of common loyalties and understandings, the school too often has lessened the bond that ties the youth to the older generation, and new problems have sprung from the incongruity of homes in which the older members were strangers to the language, customs and ideals of the land, often traditional enemies of their neighbors even, while the younger members spoke the language, knew the systems, held the ideals of the land and felt at home with the children of the community irrespective of their parents' nationality or race.

And yet, there are critics who feel that our country has not gone far enough in placing the public schools deliberately at the service of a process of Americanization. They point to the existence among us of large numbers of day schools under religious auspices, in which a foreign language is used, as evidence of our failure to do what other countries have done: make the nationalization of attitudes the first motive of the school program. Moreover, they point out, citizenship teaching has not yet reached the lower grades, and even in the upper grades is not given the prominence which, as a subject of study, it has attained in certain other countries. In Germany and France, the religious and moral teaching of the school has assumed a definitely patriotic color; every country that has a national church so intertwines religious and civic ideals in the education of its children as to make them indistinguishable; and so, reinforced with a deep-going conditioning of the emotions, the early attitudes toward the established order sometimes become well-nigh unshakable.[15] It has often been pointed out that the Americanization of children of foreign-born parents through the schools, as at present conducted, has its dangers to fundamental social relationships.[16]

To the question, what, more precisely, is being taught in the

[15] For a detailed comparison of our use of the public schools in the Americanization process with the nationalization methods of European school systems, the reader is referred to Frank V. Thompson, *Schooling of the Immigrant* (1920, p. 591 *et seq.*).

[16] See, for example, Thomas Burgess, Charles Kendall Gilbert, and Charles Thorley Bridgeman: *Foreigners or Friends.* (Missions and Church Extension of the Episcopal Church, 1921, pp. 65, 199.)

civics class on the subject of race and race relation, the answer is
—for most communities—nothing at all. What the child receives
in direct instruction about other racial groups is given much
more frequently in the history and geography lessons; and even
there a purposeful teaching of the subject is rare. It is curious,
but a fact, that in a country in which the adjustment of different
national and racial groups forms one of the major tasks of civic
statesmanship, a direct discussion of that topic is usually avoided
in the teaching of civics. Indeed, where it is brought into that
study, it is usually owing to the initiative of a teacher who has
strong convictions on the subject—whether adverse to inter-racial
contact or friendly toward it. Since the war, however, references
to race problems in civics textbooks have become more numerous,
and with them protests from organizations representative of races
and nationalities that feel offended by references to them—or the
lack of such references.[17]

"What up-to-date, inter-racial information is being taught our white
children?" was asked a prominent school principal who was explaining
in public the excellent aims of Quaker schools. "Oh, wherever the
locality will bear it, fine teachers are doing such work through the
South." "But in the North?" With a blank face he answered: "Well,
practically nothing."

A city high school was approached on the same errand. "We are
doing good work along our civic line," proudly answered the fine head
of the History Department. "Come and visit our Eighth Grade class
when it reaches the chapter on Negro sociology. Take our two textbooks
home and examine them." It is with an uncomfortable sense of abus-
ing a kind hospitality that it is necessary, for the sake of the immortal
souls passing through that and similar schools, to record the hollow-
ness of that civic teaching. The Negro chapter of one of the books was
packed with old-time prejudice with just a smear of modern social spirit
at the end to bring it up to date. Long before the student reached this,
however, he had imbibed ideas about the vicious tendencies of the
Negro masses, the danger of reversion to barbarism, etc. And the action of that class? They knew the ill-trained maid in the home kitchen,
the ash and garbage man in the back alley, and their judgment was
based on such experience. Colored people were lazy, over-paid, under-
efficient, impudent and dirty. "We ought, of course, to be kind, but
it is a great pity that we have to shoulder such a burden!" And after-

[17] Bessie L. Pierce, *Public Opinion and the Teaching of History* (1926, p.
199).

ward the gentle little teacher explained: "Well, dear madam, one *cannot* antagonize one's class." [18]

Of course, as the teacher just quoted has stated it, "one cannot antagonize one's class"—at least not a public school teacher, if by class we understand the norm of the parental group. Yet, it is a mistake to assume that the teacher's impulse, in all cases, is to teach democracy and that the attitude of parents is universally more class- or race-bound. Occasionally it is the teacher who, in attempting to instill race pride in his pupils, encounters an unlooked-for resistance on the part of parents who are more liberal.

This was rather amusingly illustrated, one of our correspondents reports, in her community when a white teacher, to be absolutely fair, and to inspire the colored children in the class with the same ambition as the white children, used the expedient of requiring that they read the life of Booker T. Washington while, presumably, the white children were reading some other American biography. The mother of an eight-year-old colored boy remonstrated with the teacher on account of this assignment. She said there was no need to make her boy more race-conscious than colored children need be. The example he was expected to learn from the life of the leader of his own race, she thought, he could just as well learn from the study of the life of a great Greek or Jew.

While racial attitudes do not, in the majority of public schools, form a part of conscious civics teaching, a new and insidious propaganda in favor of racial purity is gaining ground. This propaganda does not openly espouse the cause just named but with text and picture endeavors to imbue the pupil with the sense of the superiority of native-born white Americans over any and all other racial groups.[19]

Even courses in ethics and civics which are intended to create friendliness sometimes do the opposite. A Chinese boy returned to his friend's home in Hartford one day with bright red spots burning through his olive cheeks. In the civics course a brief paragraph was given to other nations to show their good qualities. The glowing

[18] Anne Biddle Stirling, Chairman, Philadelphia Interracial Committee. *Opportunity*, March, 1923, p. 7.
[19] A striking example of this kind of literature is a "visual education" textbook entitled, *We and Our Work* by Dean Joseph French Johnson, of New York University, published in 1923 by the American Viewpoint Society, Inc.

tribute to China was, "The Chinese eat rats." The answer of the state commissioner of education to a letter calling his attention to this was that the author of that textbook was out of town! [20]

When all is said and done, the outstanding criticism which may be made of the teaching of civics in relation to race attitudes is not, however, that it diffuses this or that information which is incorrect or that it encourages this or that attitude which is prejudiced. The chief failure, in so far as there is failure, lies in the divorce of civics teaching from the home and social experiences of the child. Books too often are substituted for the concrete resources of neighborhood and community; and the content of the books too often deals with the remote and impersonal instead of starting from the immediate civic responsibilities of the child and his family and group.

It is a singular fact that the content of school subjects presumed to train for effective membership in society is so frequently determined without reference to the immediate social experiences of the student. Teachers seldom take into account the fact that their pupils are also functioning as members of society and will continue to do so. Hence it is a common occurrence that pupils, finding class-room instruction at variance with the lessons of their experience, lose confidence in school instruction. As a rule, the pupils either do not raise any questions about the contradictions, or soon cease to do so. The teachers, unaware of the conflict, continue their work with results diminishing almost to the point of complete futility.[21]

While this chapter may seem somewhat over-critical in its display of the effects of civics teaching on race attitudes, it must be remembered that here we are concerned with surveying and analysing what people concerned in the matter—not least among them many teachers of civics—recognize as an educational problem that confronts the nation. In a later chapter (XXII) we shall endeavor to recognize the tendencies that are under way to remedy the situation, and the new educational viewpoints which even now are reshaping the whole theory of the relation between social objectives and educational policies and methods.

[20] A. J. Myers in "Literature for Children and Its Influence," in *Religious Education,* April, 1926, p. 219.
[21] History and Other Social Studies in the Schools. Report of a Committee Submitted to the Council of the American Historical Association. Pamphlet. December, 1926, p. 24.

CHAPTER XII

WHAT CHILDREN LEARN AT SCHOOL (*Continued*)

2. HISTORY

For children and for old people, the past is more real than for the hustling adults of middle years who, for the most part, live so exclusively in the present that for them "history is bunk." A child who barely visualizes as distinct personalities the distant aunts and uncles who are constantly in the mouths of those around him may at the same time have a vivid realization of the character and life of some hero in remote antiquity. In his play he will with equal abandon impersonate the corner grocer, the circus rider seen a year ago, a pioneer fighting Indians, a knight at the court of King Arthur or a Roman general—it all depends on the relative depth of impressions produced on him by personal experiences, by stories told him, conversations overheard, pictures seen, and through other channels of perception.

Too often, in thinking of "life experiences" of children, we arbitrarily limit that concept to physical contacts when, as a matter of fact, all learnings are experiences, no matter what their nature. And, the further we go back in years, the less important are the differences between one type of experience and another in their power of producing images and evoking thought. It is for this reason, incidentally, that in later life we are apt to confuse what we have actually seen as small children with what we have been told.

From the point of view of our present study these considerations are significant because there prevails a regrettable disregard, even among teachers, for the weight of the printed word in the education of children. Parents will indulgently smile as the child absorbs attitudes about peoples and situations from the comic page, teachers will use historical textbooks, knowing them to be prejudiced or false on a given point, thinking that later reading will correct whatever false impression may be obtained now. But later reading does not always have this corrective

153

power. It may, of course, substitute a new for an old notion, but the emotional response to an early, gripping situation does not get eradicated except with difficulty. When such a response becomes habitual—as for example, when all literature which the child reads about a given "arch-enemy" of his country, or about a given racial group within his country, is similar in its general tendency, it requires more than corrective information to get quite rid of it and to substitute a different attitude later in life for the one formed now.

A sociologist suggests that, to a certain extent, a teaching of history in the elementary schools that conditions children to acceptance of the folkways and mores of the society into which they are born is as inevitable as it is old. Nevertheless, even at this stage a trend toward more independent thinking might be started for further development through higher education.[1]

Where the conditioning of a child toward love of country, and whatever under the given circumstances may be conceived of as complementary hatreds of other countries, is a definite objective of history teaching, it does become an effective barrier toward contrary influences in later life. Again, where the history that is taught through the years of childhood and adolescence consistently pictures a specific race or nationality as inferior in general, or lacking in courage, or dangerous and bloodthirsty, that impression of that people often will stay for life, later corrective experiences notwithstanding. A well-known geographer says on this point:

I feel outraged when I turn back my memory and think how the imaginative and idealistic years of my impressionable childhood were poisoned by the stuff called history—extensive rehearsals of the way the heroic revolutionary forefathers killed so many, very many, wicked and perfidious British or properly butchered so many barbarous, treacherous and cruel Indians who richly deserved killing. (What are your children getting now?) [2]

On occasion a deliberate one-sidedness in the use of history teaching for racial propaganda may be justified theoretically by the prevalence of propaganda in the opposite direction for which it is offered as an antidote. Such an effort, for example, is the

---

[1] F. Stuart Chapin, *Education and the Mores* (Columbia University Studies in History, etc., 1911, p. 90).
[2] J. Russell Smith, "Racial Superiority," *Friends' Intelligencer*, October 24, 1925, p. 845.

National Negro History Week, observed by Negro schools, churches and social agencies throughout the United States at the instigation of the Association for the Study of Negro Life and History. However, such an enterprise, if sincere, cannot claim impartiality. In this particular case the purpose is frankly stated as follows:

The Negro must either convince the world that he has a record as glorious as that of any other race or remain content with a fixed status of inferiority. The greatest scholars of today are saying that there is no such thing as race in science, and that there is nothing in anthropology or psychology to support such myths as the inferiority and superiority of races. These truths, however, will have little bearing on the uplift of the Negro if they are left in the state of academic discussion. The Negro must learn his past and publish it to this prejudiced world.

Obviously, the teaching here advocated is as prejudiced as that which it desires to replace. The only possible good that may come from it is that it may make some people sceptical in regard to all historical dogma; but it does nothing to create an attitude of real curiosity as regards the subject of the Negro, and incidentally it cannot but sharpen racial conflict by conditioning the children of two racial groups in opposite directions.

At times the propaganda use of history teaching over-reaches itself and fixes in children attitudes that later in life become hostile to new purposes and policies of state and society. This is illustrated by a participant in the present inquiry as follows:

In my childhood we studied a history that gave a great deal of its attention to the Revolutionary War. We played war a great deal, but neither of us older children would be the British—forcing the younger brother to take that part. This set against the British lasted until the outbreak of the Great World War, when we were still youngsters at home. In spite of all the Allies' propaganda that was set going about that time, my brother was quite pro-German until shortly before America entered the war. This was not due to any feeling about war guilt but because he could not "go" anything British. We knew few, if any, English at that time.

The subject of influences on public opinion through the teaching of history has received considerable attention of late because of a number of outstanding controversies between teachers and authors of textbooks on the one hand and educational authorities or self-styled patriotic societies on the other.[3]

Because of the international attention which it has received, the war carried on by Mayor Thompson, of Chicago, against current history textbooks has achieved unusual significance. It discloses that the nature of a country's history must inevitably color the thinking of its citizens generations later—no matter what the current interests of state and society. Thus, as it happens, the relation of the United States toward Great Britain has undergone a progressive change from revolt and a series of wars to close international cooperation. While many critics have deplored the tendency of history textbooks unnecessarily to keep alive unpleasant memories by giving much space to the account of these old hostilities, the new critics would have them dwell less sympathetically upon the British antecedents of the American nation, culture and ideals. They represent—however inadequately or even foolishly—a trend toward the assertion of the other racial, national and cultural traits that have entered into the American scene, especially in these last fifty years, traits to which few of the school histories have done adequate justice.

There is nobility back of the screaming farce of Superintendent Mc-Andrew's trial in Chicago. It is found in the noble desire of the non-Anglo-Saxon peoples to make their way up into a fair co-partnership in the ideals and aspirations of their country. . . . The impulse at heart is clean and true. We do not believe that it is in essence anti-English; it is anti-American-English, anti-dominance by the Anglo-Saxon tradition.[4]

[3] In this connection it is worth remembering that, because of the large size of editions, school textbooks are revised very frequently. Although, in the case of standard texts, the revisions mostly consist of additions of statistics from government reports and other reliable sources, the tendency is for the publisher to hand on to the author criticisms collected by the agents in the field or received in letters from teachers and school superintendents. A recent report on the process states, "Publishers are very sensitive to these scattering criticisms." Competing texts are pulled to pieces in interviews with those who have the placement of large orders in their power; and the texts most closely fashioned to meet the prevailing attitudes and prejudices in a given state or part of the country are likely to have an advantage over others. The sentences or paragraphs that flatter local sentiment are emphasized in sales talks and in digests given to agents. The publishers, as a rule, are more concerned with the craftsmanship of bookmaking than with the objectivity of the contents, says the correspondent who has made this special study; and they are very much averse to the publication of statements that are likely to be regarded as controversial.

[4] From an editorial in the *New York Evening World,* October 22, 1927.

The most comprehensive survey of the propagandist element in the teaching of history, for the United States, is Professor Bessie L. Pierce's *Public Opinion and the Teaching of History,* which contains ample evidence of the different trends of sectional feeling and nationalistic bias that enter into the choice, content and diffusion of history texts and the war raging around them.[5] Other sources are listed and interestingly discussed, with valuable suggestions of his own, by William G. Carr, in *Education for World Citizenship.*[6]

Even those who have no particular fault to find with the patriotic tenor of books on American history often feel that these should be supplemented by books which tell of the cultural contributions made by immigrant groups and the historical developments back of these contributions. The subject is often brought up at teachers' conferences.[7] The textbook question was prominent at the National Education Association Conference of 1928 because of recent Congressional revelations as to the extent of propagandist interference with high-school teaching. Lately the American Historical Association itself has come out with a project which clearly shows that its aim is not to teach a critical appraisal of historical happening but to create appreciation for current ideals of citizenship. At its conference in December, 1926, a plan was made public for a campaign to educate American children for effective citizenship. Professor A. C. Krey, of the University of Minnesota, is in charge of this plan, and a large committee is assisting him in a five-year study of the subject.

As regards actual effects of this type of teaching on the attitudes of children, both teachers and social students possess plenty of evidence. The primary misconceptions that are engendered are amusingly illustrated by this incident:

A little colored boy who lived in a northern city where he had not been made conscious of racial differences had begun the study of American history. One day he said to his father, "Tell me something about our ancestors." The father began to tell about life in Africa, but the boy soon interrupted, "That's not what I want. Tell me about *our Pilgrim ancestors!*"

[5] (1926. See especially pp. 136 *et seq.,* 156, 206, 238, 239, 248, 249, 274, 281, 329, 333.)
[6] Stanford University Press, 1928, Chap. IX.
[7] See, for example, Proceedings of National Education Association, 1915, p. 245.

How history teaching may undermine respect for the home and create socially disadvantageous attitudes has some years ago been described by Grace Abbott, at that time director of the Immigrants' Protective League of Chicago.[8] The same complaint, with special reference to Negro children, is made by a southern writer in a report on public-school textbooks to the Kentucky Interracial Conference:

In no textbooks that your committee has examined is the American Negro shown, in a creditable sense, to the pupil, white and colored, as a people, a race group, with a past and authenticated history of their own in Africa. Again, no textbook that we have examined tells the pupil that practically every people in the world have been enslaved by some other people, at some period in their history; no textbook that we have examined explains to the pupil, white and colored, that slavery is a condition imposed, endured, not necessarily merited.

Your committee, in a word, has found no school textbook which, first, presents and considers the negro as a race group, with the rights and attributes of such a group, and next, as a slave group, contributory to the economic development of America.[9]

The same plaint is made also in regard to the history teaching of oriental children. Professor William C. Smith, of the University of Southern California, writes:

A study of the Japanese children in the schools of California has brought out the fact that in American history they tend to rank very high. But about the history of the Orient they know little and care less; they seem to be more interested in Africa and South America than in China and Japan.[10]

[8] *The Immigrant and the Community* (1917, p. 226).
[9] *The Crisis* for February, 1925, p. 181.
[10] *Journal of Applied Sociology*, November-December, 1925, p. 161.

CHAPTER XIII

WHAT CHILDREN LEARN AT SCHOOL (*Continued*)

3. GEOGRAPHY

Negroes and Orientals also suffer in the estimation of American citizens from an association of ideas which is inculcated through the public-school teaching of geography. To some elements in this situation reference has already been made under the heads of civics and history—for our evidence does not always come in clear-cut subject categories. Tropical climate—absence of clothes—primitive community life—lazy habits—mental inferiority: these are some of the ingredients of a composite picture which too many school children take home with them from the geography lessons on Africa. As a rule those who write the geography textbooks are far behind the findings of recent research as regards the complexity of African community organization, the rigidity of African morals and customs and the variety of race character that is to be found in different areas of that huge continent. So when the term African is used in relation to an American citizen of dusky skin, it often denotes to the public-school child all the qualities of aboriginal life at its most primitive, even when the colored citizen may be almost wholly white with just a little mixture of blood from that intelligent Negroid people, the Zulus.[1]

But the falsification of description by over-simplification or a stressing of what is quaint and strange to western ideas in the school teaching of geography also affects many other groups: the Orientals whose physical characteristics, mentality and histories are all apt to be woven into highly fantastic works of semi-fiction, and also American groups of European descent.

In most of these cases, the propaganda effect of the illustrations, we must presume, is accidental and not intentional. The publishers have learned that well-illustrated textbooks sell better than those that are poorly illustrated or not at all. With the educational significance of this phenomenon they have been less con-

[1] Evidence bearing on this influence has been given in Chap. II, p. 27.

cerned. Yet the subject is a serious one because the picture fastens into the mind of the child more definite impressions than the text, impressions that last long after the text has been forgotten.[2]

And who does not remember the pictures and stories of "native customs" which during school years colored his conception of life in the less accessible countries of Europe? A sociology professor contributes the following auto-biographical note of a student, showing how later experiences may fail to correct the earlier teaching:

When I was a small child I remember studying in my geography about Turkey. The pictures of the costumes of the people fascinated me, and I thought what an interesting country that must be and wished, as we all do, that I might visit the country of elaborate head-dresses and loose costumes.

As I grew up and studied history in high school and later in college my attitude toward the Turks changed, for I learned of the many wicked crimes they committed, of the barbarous warfare they carried on, and that even in their own country they were never at peace.

Several years ago an American friend of mine was teaching in an American Academy in Cyprus and for his Christmas vacation took a trip through Turkey. He described for me the life of the people. Although, as is usually the case, the people were simple folks, their rulers and masters do commit awful deeds, and the living conditions of the Turk are not favorable.

Last year in my travels I met a young Turkish man who wanted to become close friends. He was such a gentleman when I first knew him and treated the ladies with such high respect, I almost changed my mind about the Turk. He told me many things about his country, and I was fascinated by the life of his people. I encouraged him in his work as a student, but on his finding that we could not continue our friendship he, as it were, turned against me and said that he would prefer that I never speak to him again.

Although this gave me a different and broader view of the Turk, yet my attitude remains that he is a foreigner, and while I am willing to share America with him, yet I still feel he is a warlike person, always ready to fight and not to be fair and offer justice to his adversaries.

A colored woman writes:

When I was about to finish the grades, we were studying the races of men in the geography class, and I remember distinctly the picture of

[2] See Frederick Elmore Lumley, *Means of Social Control* (1925, p. 196).

the African savage that was used as our representative. I was quite innocent of the fact that I had the same racial lineage as he. Underneath the picture it said "Ethiopian—he belongs to the most backward race on the face of the globe"—and my white schoolmates turned around to me and said, "Now, that's your folk." Nothing else was said concerning Negroes in any textbook we used, except that they were slaves. This made a profound impression on my mind and resulted, many years after, in my touring the country for four years in a Ford coupé, carrying with me a two-foot shelf of Negro literature in the hope of doing something to offset the silence of the textbooks with regard to the achievements of the colored people.

A public-school teacher refers to the shock which teachers themselves sometimes receive when on occasion they observe the unintentional by-products of learning among their pupils. She says:

Perhaps children do react instinctively against anything which is strange to them. When in an assembly some travel pictures were shown, it was announced that the next picture would be of scenes in Czecho-Slovakia. Immediately there arose an amused and, I thought, a bit scornful laughter. However, this stopped when the picture was actually on the screen, and I heard the exclamation, in a tone of surprise, "Why, they look just like us!"

In this case the reaction was to a strange sound rather than a strange sight, it seems—the difficult name suddenly introduced, not unusual scenes shown on the screen.

Professor Edward L. Thorndike has pointed to paternalism as one of the evil effects in later life of the erroneous attitudes toward other peoples that are so frequently fostered in the geography lesson.[3] F. Stuart Chapin finds that an exaggerated emphasis on one phase of the subject matter of geography—the political—is in itself a cause of distorted attitudes.[4] That a very large part of the erroneous teaching in geography (and other) lessons is simply due to a desire for over-simplification is the opinion of the explorer Vilhjalmur Stefansson, who has recently made a study of what children are taught in our public schools and has reported his findings amusingly but not without showing the serious effect of this misinformation on attitudes toward other races and peoples.[5]

[3] *Principles of Teaching* (1917, p. 190).
[4] *Education and the Mores* (Columbia University Studies in History, etc., 1911, p. 90).
[5] *The Standardization of Error* (1927).

4. LANGUAGE

Several of the quotations in this and the previous chapter contain significant references to the havoc played with the attitudes toward other peoples and races by books which contain imaginary or intentionally misleading descriptions of them. The total impact of a child's reading far exceeds the content of school books, of course. But in this chapter we are concerned only with that reading which directly forms a part of the school teaching, including the supplementary reading of the classes in English composition and other language subjects.

It does not require the description of whole peoples in a piece of literature widely read by children to create a prejudice against them. Often a single character of fiction suffices to fix for many generations popular attitudes toward a racial group. The outstanding example, probably, is Shakespeare's Shylock. For three centuries this classic of the schoolroom, The Merchant of Venice, has taught the boys and girls, not of the English-speaking countries alone, that the Jews are a crafty, designing, usurious cruel people. Shylock became the symbol of a race. And yet, recent research has revealed that the story of The Merchant of Venice antedated the Shakespearean version by three centuries; and that in the story as first recorded by a Cistercian monk the merchant was a Gentile. Shakespeare merely adapted the story to the theater—incidentally creating a dramatic work of masterly construction and beauty—and gave it timeliness by making the principal characters correspond somewhat to those of a recent criminal case in the London courts, in which the principal figure had been a Jew.[6]

The Merchant of Venice has borne the brunt of the battle around prejudicial literature and has almost become the touchstone of educational policy in some communities. The following editorial from a Jewish weekly illustrates both the facts and a typical Jewish attitude toward them:

Information reaches us that the city of Los Angeles, California, has banned the teaching of The Merchant of Venice in its public high schools. This is the second time that Shylock has made an inglorious exit in this western metropolis of sunlight and movies. Fourteen years

[6] The story of this discovery by Harris J. Griston and the long literary search of which it is the outcome, is told in the *New York World* for January 14, 1927.

ago, it seems, the teaching of this play encountered opposition, and a decision was reached by the Board of Education to place a ban on it. But the interdiction proved to be indecisive because the play came back. In commenting on the action of the Los Angeles Board of Education, R. D. MacLean, a veteran Shakespearean actor, points out that The Merchant of Venice is a standard drama and has been accepted as such for hundreds of years all around the world; that, furthermore, the greatest Jewish actors, among them Jacob Adler, Von Possart, Schildkraut, Moscovitch and Warfield, have interpreted the part and were glad to do so. All of this is readily granted, and Mr. MacLean can hardly be blamed for taking up the cudgels on behalf of Shylock as a stage spectacle. The teaching of the play in the high schools, however, is another matter. It must be remembered that Shakespeare puts strong language into the mouths of Antonio and Bassanio. The playwright lived in a period when the stage Jew was an accepted comic character. Only Shakespeare's genius, his intense sympathy with human suffering, his profound understanding of human motive, saved him from going on with the burlesque. He made a human being out of a potential buffoon. When this play is presented on the public stage and witnessed by adults, the part of Shylock (which is naturally stressed) becomes a poignant human characterization and achieves the Aristotelian aim of purging our emotions through pity. During the adolescent period, however, when social and anti-social emotions run high, it is dangerous to place The Merchant of Venice as a teaching vehicle in the hands of any except the most expert and the most broad-minded teachers. An instructor of the Klan variety need but change his emphasis to do deadly harm. The Merchant of Venice should be dropped from high-school lists of required reading in literature. In the colleges and as a classic for the general public it has its legitimate place.[7]

That in individual cases the literature read in childhood really does leave a lasting impression injurious to the formation of attitudes on the basis of personal experience is illustrated in the following communication:

The word "Jew" always awakens in my mind a momentary feeling of unpleasantness. I have never had any experience with a Jew which would arouse this feeling, and I was unable to account for it until I remembered a fairy tale which somebody read to me when I was small. In this story the villain is a Jew, lying, thieving and altogether a despicable character. The study must have made a deep impression on me, and as I had never seen a Jew, my childish mind pictured them all like this one. Later the impression was strengthened by reading "The

[7] *The American Hebrew* for April 22, 1927, p. 889.

Merchant of Venice." I regarded Shylock likewise as typical of all Jews.

Now that I have learned to know Jews, my childish antipathy for them has entirely vanished. I feel toward them just as toward anybody else; in fact, one of my very good friends is a Jewish girl. But still, although I no longer feel any prejudice against the Jewish people, the name "Jew" always arouses for just a moment the unpleasant sensation which is a remnant of my old idea.

For many people, the Spaniards are still to-day the Spaniards of the Inquisition and the oppressors of the Netherlands. It was possible, and almost necessary, during the height of the war propaganda to refer to Germans as Huns, because for English and American public and high-school graduates, the literary associations of the latter people were all unfavorable and those of the former almost wholly favorable. There is no question that a new and popular edition of Multatuli's *Max Havelaar*—a work of fiction that is sure to appeal to teachers of style—will react against the popularity of the Dutch in America; or that Kipling diffuses among us a British-Colonial attitude toward East Indians.[8]

Even in the lower grades, a number of correspondents point out, the books read or recommended for home reading often have influences on race attitudes that are difficult to eradicate later on. Thus a northern correspondent tells this incident:

Catherine, aged five, attended kindergarten and was taught the story of Little Black Sambo who was pictured as a rather stupid and silly boy, doing a series of silly things. There was no lesson of interesting facts to be learned from the story. A white child called Catherine a "nigger," and she reported it to her teacher, who answered, "Well, aren't you a Negro? Aren't you a little Black Sambo?" at which remark the children laughed. Catherine was very much hurt because the children laughed. Her mother took it up with the school principal and pointed out to her that the story was planting in the children's minds the first seed of the idea that colored people were inferior. Little Black Sambo, she pointed out, is rather a silly, uninteresting person; but later when the children can read newspapers for themselves they will notice that one colored man has done one crime and another one another crime; their minds will go back to childhood stories in kindergarten and he will remember little Black Sambo. The ideas will be correlated, and with each additional unpleasant fact that is brought to his notice

[8] See Arland D. Weeks, *Psychology for Child Training* (1925, p. 268).

his opinion will be strengthened that Negroes are worthless. On the other hand, she continued, had the story been told of the life of Booker T. Washington or of Paul Dunbar or Frederick Douglass, and if the newspapers printed in headlines the inventions, musical, literary and scientific accomplishments of Negroes, good opinions of Negroes would be built up. The story of Little Black Sambo also had planted the seed in Catherine's mind that she belonged to an inferior race.

How the effects of early reading wrestled for supremacy in the mind of a child against all the weight of propaganda by school and society is interestingly told by the following correspondent, a student in a middle-western college:

When a very little girl I had enjoyed the German fairy tales. Germany was to me a place of dear old grandmothers, dancing red shoes, and the like.

At the beginning of the world war I heard my father say that it was impossible for the other countries to win against Germany. I can still hear the murmurs of contempt for nations attempting to struggle with so fine a country.

And then, suddenly, people began talking about a ship having been sunk by Germans. Horror was expressed everywhere. America was needed to aid France and England. Germany had become the opponent of liberty.

In the eighth grade the teacher asked one day whether might made right, and went on to show us that Germany was in the wrong. Then movies, speeches, drives contributed to my idea of this symbolical monster clothed in the person of the Kaiser. A shell-shocked soldier came to the school to speak one day. He became excited and described supposed atrocities committed by the Germans. Somehow that soldier made me doubt his story. The fairy-tale Germany struggled for supremacy.

After the war, in high school, Germany did not bother me much— though I seemed to agree that she should be made to pay her share of the war and that of the other countries too.

Then in college I suffered a sudden contempt for war. All influences pointed to the fact that it takes more than one guilty party to make a war. Study of German philosophy brought back my respect for Germany. But it is the old Germany of which I speak. The Germany of the fairy tales will persist.

A new element of danger has been carried into English teaching by the rapid extension of "public speaking" or "oral English" as a recognized high-school subject. The arts of oratory and de-

bating stimulate the pupil to a clarification of viewpoints and attitudes, and thus help him to form consistent social and political
theories.   But too often they bring with them a wilful exaggeration of arguments that the pupil can count upon as being popular.
In this way, understanding is falsified, prejudices become more
firmly fixed, and feelings of racial antipathy are rationalized into
philosophies.   There has been too little insistence that teachers of
English should themselves have enough critical understanding
of historical and social movements to counteract this natural
tendency by insisting upon the presentation of arguments that
would favor minority opinion or, better still, by insisting upon
accurate knowledge and clear thinking.

Even at its best, debate encourages habits of mind directly
contrary to those which would make for greater interracial understanding and appreciation.   A sociologist says:

Debate has in it precisely that evil quality of which we have happily rid ourselves in the field of science, but from which we still suffer,
often quite tragically, in the larger field of human relations.   It is the
We Win—You Lose attitude.   It is the We Have the Truth—You Are
All Wrong attitude.   It is the attitude of To Us Be the Glory—To You
the Humiliation.   Fundamentally it is an attitude of mutual exclusiveness. . . .

If we are to cultivate that requisite open-mindedness, that "will to
see farther" which is the first essential of the truly international mind,
it is obvious that there must be substituted for the technique of the
debate a technique of social exploration and discussion.[9]

Oral English

A particularly evil effect of a certain type of English teaching
by recital of famous oratory is the substitution of high-sounding
phrases for genuine sentiments.   In a country where the public
school tries to give children of all sorts of national and cultural
backgrounds common ideals it is unavoidable that the sayings
of its great men should become symbols of these common values.
Knowledge of the symbols often is a necessary first step for
getting at the ideas that lie concealed behind them until some
personal experience or more ample reading reveals them.   But
the danger is that the symbols will be handed about as though

[9] Harry A. Overstreet in *Progressive Education* for May, 1925, p. 68.

they were ideas, and that the words of the nation's great statesmen
—their appeals for tolerance and democracy among them—will
take the place of a real appreciation for these ideals.[10]

All this is bad enough but has been made worse still—from the
point of view of realistic attitudes—by the recent deliberate incur-
sion of propaganda into high-school teaching of public speaking.
A prominent professor of this subject at one of the middle-western
state universities, who is familiar with this phase, writes as
follows:

My impression is that certain oratorical contests promoted among
colleges and schools are masking under various pretenses; they pretend
to be one thing and, in my judgment, are something else. There are,
for example, the oratorical contests centering around the Constitution
of the United States. I have so much respect for the Constitution of
the United States that I resent the way in which these contests are conducted. I have read over fifty of their speeches and have listened to
one of their contests. Then I have noted the way in which the speeches
are judged. My observation in this matter is supported by my colleagues in the profession who have read and listened to these speeches.
I am convinced that the people who are sponsoring these contests do
not agree with me as to what constitutes honorable and sincere discussion of issues concerning the Constitution. I am convinced that they
do not want and will penalize at all times any attempt to picture the
Constitution as a growing body of governmental principles. I am
rather strong in the conviction that their purpose and intention is to
spread the doctrine among the young and susceptible that the Constitution is something fixed and irrevocable, and therefore sacred just as it
is. I think it is commonly understood by those who deal in these contests that no speech or speaker will be tolerated in a recommendation
of changes to the Constitution. The result is a collection of speeches
written insincerely and calculated to spread the doctrine that whatever
exists now in America is sacred and should in no wise be subjected to
change.

A recent survey by the American Historical Association shows
how serious is such interference with the primary work of the
schools:

Lay organizations not normally concerned with education, and some
of them distinctly propagandist in their purposes, have devoted increasing attention to the social studies in the school. A casual exploratory
survey shows nearly seven hundred such organizations with more or

[10] W. H. R. Rivers, *Psychology and Politics* (1923, p. 51).

less well-defined interest in social education. Some of these have long concerned themselves with the schools. Most of them, however, developed their direct interest in school instruction during the war, when the importance of the schools was revealed to them. Many of these have continued their interest, and still other organizations have become interested since that time.[11]

Although less authoritative as evidence, frequent rumors indicate that racial and national animosities—and, on the other hand, sentimental exaggerations of ethnic affinities—likewise are fostered here and there by competitive essay writing and oratorical contest. This means of creating public opinion was, of course, used to the full during the war; but it is also being used in peace times in regard to such peoples as the Mexicans and the Japanese.

A closely related evil is the uncritical use of newspaper material for "current history" essay writing which often, with the stress upon effective qualities of style, becomes the very antithesis of care for accuracy of statement.

Apart from conscious propaganda, the newspaper and other material used in the teaching of current events and of English composition is apt to produce unintended "attendant learnings." The difficulty of pronouncing foreign names may produce a sense of aversion. Often the foreigner is represented as picturesque and "queer" rather than as an attractive personality. But above all, the translation from foreign sources often is so faulty as to produce the feeling that foreigners cannot plainly express themselves—that they are "dumb." The schoolboy, reading an account of an international conference or an address by the President of Mexico, does not realize that the text before him is a translation; if the English markedly deviates from what he has been taught to regard as "good" English, if it seems jumbled and ungrammatical, he will put the foreign speaker down as a person lacking in education or in taste. The poor translation will reinforce the impression gained from recreational reading (see below, page 204) that foreigners are inferior to Americans.

But quite apart from these particular dangers, the use of the newspaper in the schools requires care because of the propagandist nature of much that is printed as news. This is not necessarily

[11] History and Other Social Studies in the Schools, Report of a Committee, submitted to the Council of the American Historical Association, December, 1926, Pamphlet, p. 11.

because of influence exerted by advertisers and others, or of party bias, but to some extent is inevitably linked up with the editor's news sources and with the process of news gathering. For example, an account given by a reporter of an event in which natives and foreign-born clash, because of the greater ease with which the natives can explain their side, will almost inevitably be favorable to the natives.[12]

Home Reading

Before closing this section, it is necessary to point out the great importance which the reading of children in school and out of school has in giving a common experience to those coming from homes with very different backgrounds. It is almost a commonplace to refer to the influences of great American biographies— especially that of Lincoln—on the integration into the American community of the children of immigrants. But other books likewise, even books of foreign authorship, if they are read by all children of a given age and grade, have the effect of giving them strong common interests, no matter how diverse the cultural background of their homes.[13]

While attention to the racial content of books read by children is important, those educators and librarians who are making selections of children's books for the purpose of strengthening attitudes of tolerance and international-mindedness do not seem as yet to have paid sufficient attention to the wider implications of their task. If curiosity rather than aversion and appreciation for differences in culture rather than contempt are among the desirable goals, obviously books which have no direct bearing upon racial attitude at all will also help or hinder. Thus, innumerable children's stories stress the virtue of courage, but very few emphasize that of humility. Children's stories are almost entirely individualistic in their ethics, and it is more typically the villains who show a cooperative spirit than the heroes. Thus, the virtues which are most in need of being intellectually grasped and sympathetically felt in an age of complex community structure are least

[12] See Frederick Elmore Lumley, *Means of Social Control* (1925, p. 195).
[13] For graphic illustrations of this influence, see Dorothy Giles, *Adventures in Brotherhood* (Council of Women for Home Missions and Missionary Education Movement, 1924), pp. 106, 112-114. Gratia A. Countryman, "Buying Books for Aliens" (In *Americanization*, Handbook Series, 1917), p. 237.

represented among the attendant learnings of children's literature.[14]

[14] *The Pallid Giant,* by Pierrepont B. Noyes, former Rhineland Commissioner (1926), while not primarily intended for children, is a splendid adventure and mystery story which adolescents will enjoy that teaches without any moralizing the peril of national and racial fears. A reading list compiled by William G. Carr (*op. cit.,* p. 190 *et seq.*), primarily as an aid in teaching international good will, contains many items which will be recognized as being equally effective means for the teaching of interracial tolerance.

CHAPTER XIV

THE INFLUENCE OF SUNDAY SCHOOL

On no phase of our subject is it more difficult to make a general statement of objective truth than on the influence of religious teaching upon the racial attitudes of children. For that teaching not only covers the whole range of attitudes from impassioned animosity to complete personal social fellowship, but it is riddled with inconsistencies. The correspondent who writes, "In Sunday schools tolerance is taught but not often practiced," probably exaggerates a condition that is sometimes present. But then her statement only means that, as a human institution, the Sunday school and the church of which it is a part fall short of their ideal. And what is this other than a truism? However, the notions as to what must be expected from a nominally religious agency in this matter of social education are so confused that it seems necessary to consider briefly the principle of the thing before we turn to the details of our study.

Originally the Christian Church had its work cut out—as some of Paul's letters show—to bring to a common understanding men and women of many different antecedents, including slaves and high government officials, artisans and rich women, who were held together by an overwhelming religious experience but not by similarity of outlook on worldly affairs. Later, extending through the long period of struggle between Church and Empire, the main task of the former was that of deepening its influence in a society which, though nominally Christian, still was dominated by ancient superstitions and selfish group interests. Still later, when practically the whole community had become so organized in and around the Church that even the separate needs of its interest groups (through their guilds) recognized in it the common Mother, the religious ardor expended itself upon church expansion throughout the known world—the conversion of the heathen. It was to this missionary enthusiasm and enterprise that the western world owes its great increase of geographical knowledge at the end of the Middle Ages. And to our day, it is the foreign mission work upon which rests a large part of the educational effort which the Church fosters in its effort to create peace and good-will among men.

But the nineteenth century, with its enormous extension of travel and communication, not only brought the foreign mission closer home and thereby gave greater effectiveness to its work, but it also created a new mission field at home through the large increase in human migration. And the western community is no longer culturally a unit, conscious of its essential fellowship in the midst of many varieties of group associations. In America, the process was accelerated by the comparative ease with which races and nationalities and classes could intermingle. It became easy, in an economic sense at least, for a family to pass from one social status to another; and every once in a while a new group takes form that stands half-way between those formerly recognized as separate "classes." A further complication arose from the emancipation of Negro slaves—a cutting down of legal group separations to which social opinion did not and does not respond with a corresponding abrogation of social caste distinctions.

Within this setting, then, we now have problems in group relationships that did not bother the Church in former times—yet problems as real as any of those which it faced in the days of the Roman Empire or in the days of the Reformation.

While the local community is no longer homogeneous, racially or culturally, a new nucleus has arisen around which centers the social idealism of the people: the nation. The town hall, the court house and the public school are the local embodiments of the new ideal of brotherhood; and the churches—no longer the Church, for its division into numerous denominations was itself an inevitable effect of the new nationalism—are somehow left behind to adjust their teaching as best they can to the concept of nationality. And in this adjustment, the teachings of Christianity on human relations seem, for the great majority of people, to have become of less practical significance than the creeds of their political and economic affiliations.

In this situation it is not surprising that the churches are limiting themselves, generally speaking, to an exceedingly small corner of the field open to them for the cultivation of human brotherhood; that for example they promote energetically foreign mission work but—with some notable exceptions—abstain from cultivating an immense tract of unchristian international relations.

And one reason for this is that the mission flatters the home community, which is always in the position of giver. Thus the national pride taught by the state is mirrored in the teaching of the churches; the social tendency of the school house is transferred to the Sunday school and there receives religious sanction. The Church, as an invisible fellowship, knows only one humanity. The church, as a local institution, is essentially of its time and recognizes the racial and national distinctions in the life and thought of the community as facts which it cannot escape.

The history of the Protestant churches in America in their relation to the Negro problem demonstrates the close connection between church policy and the contemporary social thinking of the community. There is practically no attitude either toward the education or toward the baptism of Negroes which churches have not held and defended at one time or other during the last century as in keeping with their faith.[1]

The most obvious start for a concrete discussion of the race attitudes taught by Sunday school is the question: What racial attitudes influence the membership of the Sunday school itself? Often, in defence of a selective process of enrolling members, the argument is given that the public schools are maintained by the taxpayers and that, therefore, all children have the right to be admitted and taught; but a church is supported from private contributions and therefore is responsible only to its members. But this line of reasoning merely brings back the same question in a different form, namely: Why is the body of taxpayers, including Jews and heathen and atheists of all sorts, more liberal in its rulings as regards school privileges than the church which, presumably, was founded to embody the most far-reaching principles of human brotherhood that have ever been formulated? The only answer, in most cases, is that, after all, the church, as a membership organization, has the general character of a private club, even though its aims are of a religious and ethical character. And a club requires the atmosphere of social congeniality. Having its being in a temporal setting of class or race exclusiveness, the church then proceeds to include the justification for that exclusiveness—either tacitly or expressly—in its teaching of the ethics of human relationships, thus giving a social arrangement of temporal convenience the authority of religious sanction.

Here, then, we have in brief the explanation for such peculiar

[1] E. B. Reuter, *The American Race Problem* (1927, pp. 260, 323).

spectacles as a Sunday school working enthusiastically for the
uplift of Africans in Africa when it would be extremely loath to
permit discussion of the Africans in the back-streets of its own
community; or that of a Sunday school singing hymns of fellowship but ostracizing a stray child of southern Europe that may
have slipped in unawares.   What many—perhaps a majority of—
American Sunday schools teach children is a sense of aloofness,
if not a feeling that their own group is much superior to others.
How this feeling may inadvertently be created through an act of
ill-considered kindness is illustrated by the following communication:

A certain children's club in a northern city represented a number of
different nationalities.   Each girl seemed proud of the fact that her
ancestors had belonged to a distinct nationality that had made distinct
contributions to human welfare.   But a difference developed between
the girls of A. street and those of B. street, the one representing a
slightly more prosperous national group than the other, because one of
the workers connected with the institution had been seen to "hand out
things" to children in B. street.

The way in which the Sunday school is recruited—its exclusiveness in matters of class, race or nationality, or of all three—provides an "attendant learning" that often leaves a far deeper impress than anything that may be printed in the hymn-book or
lesson sheet.[2]
The following experience with a Bible class is reported by a
leader invited from the outside to conduct a discussion:

One of the members commented on the fact that, in a discussion such
as they were having, thinking was always pitched on a high level, but
later on when they confronted actual situations, their behavior did not
show much of the effect of their high thinking.   I was interested to
observe that this particular group, in spite of the way they laughed at
the Nordic myth and proclaimed in various ways the principles of racial
equality, nevertheless revealed a clear Nordic complex for the very
simple reason that, when they were discussing what attitudes they

[2] That children subjected to this double standard may be perfectly conscious
of its essential hypocrisy is illustrated by the well-known verse in a college
song:
> I send my money to Bourra, gar, gar, gar, gar
> Away off there in Africa so far, far, far, far;
> I save up all my pennies and my tin, tin, tin, tin,
> The heathen kid to save from sin, sin, sin, sin.

The Most Popular College Songs (1905, p. 85).

should take, nobody in the whole class ventured to suggest the need of trying to learn what other races had to teach us. The whole discussion was around the question as to the spirit in which we should teach other races what they ought to know.

However, the same report also contains other remarks which indicate that there were also stirrings of self-criticism:

When the respective merits and demerits of patronizing and tolerating other races were considered, one boy suggested as a definition of patronage the following: "To patronize a person or race is to manifest an interest in him or it which you do not really feel. . . ."

One member said at the close of the discussion: "All this is bunk. What we need to do is to bring some people of other races into our group and actually work and think with them. Until we do that, it doesn't matter much what we say."

Impatience with what looks to them like "bunk" in the teaching of interracial friendship is reported by many Y.M.C.A. officers who work among younger boys. The following account from a leader of an adolescent boys' club at South Bend, Indiana, is typical:

At the first meeting to discuss brotherhood, the discussion centered around whether the members of the club themselves were brotherly towards those of other races or nationalities. The group was challenged by one of its members with these words: "We're a great bunch to talk about world brotherhood, let's talk about brotherhood in this town, in this club. Why, a fellow from Hungary or Greece wouldn't have a look in here!"

Boys: "Yes, he would; they don't want to come in."

Another: "Let's find out."

Another: "We ought to stick to our standards of admittance, ought we not?"

Another: "Sure we ought, but can't a foreign boy or a boy of foreign parents come up to our standards?"

Another: "How about colored boys—going to let them in too?"

An hour's discussion, and the group came to the following conclusions:

1. Membership should be open to all boys regardless of color, creed or nationality who come up to our standards, i.e., intelligence and decency.

2. Continue the discussion at the next meeting.

At the next meeting, the group had applications from one Hungarian and one Negro boy. Both had been interviewed and charted. Both ranked very high, in some respects higher than the boys in the club. There was the usual discussion of the candidates and they were voted in. The group was feeling pretty good about it, possibly a little smug, until the discussion was opened and a member of the club started the discussion with this observation:

"It's all very well for us to talk about brotherhood, vote these fellows in, pass resolutions, etc., but it doesn't mean anything, because there isn't a fellow here but feels sure that he is better than any Negro, Jew or Hunky that ever lived."

Another boy: "That may be true, but we can change our minds, can't we?"

[At this point the discussion entered into the question whether human nature can be changed.] [3]

In this connection it should be kept in mind also that the educational tasks of interesting children in foreign peoples and of preparing them for unprejudiced, tolerant and mutually helpful race contacts at home require different methods. The one involves an interesting and sympathetic presentation of information, the creation of positive attitudes where there were no attitudes at all before; the other is largely of a negative character. Before the teacher can deal with the question, "How can we give the child desirable attitudes?" (desirable, that is, from the point of view of the church), he has first to face the question, "How can we free the child from the prejudices handed on to him by his environment? How can we prevent him from acquiring or retaining undesirable attitudes?" And with these questions we are at once involved in a necessity to define values. What attitudes are desirable, what attitudes undesirable? By what standards do we divide the desirable from the undesirable or the more desirable from the less desirable ones?

It will be admitted that church people rarely face the dilemma that arises from the contrast between the standards of value that inhere in their religious faith and those that inhere in their cultural traditions and tacit creeds. Usually, a native, white American community seeks to defend certain cultured heritages; but these heritages are not the same in Vermont and in Virginia, in northern and in southern California, or in any other two contrasted regions; and they are not necessarily Christian. They are not necessarily democratic either. For example, on Christian

[3] *Christian Citizenship* (an organ of the National Council of the Y.M.C.A.) March, 1927, p. 2.

and democratic grounds, the members of a church may desire that their children should associate with the children of other groups, if only in order that they may, by personal appreciative understanding, be prepared for contacts with them in adult life. But on the grounds of the integrity of their folkways, out of loyalty to the cultural heritage of their group, the same parents may hesitate to have their children associate with other children whose influences might "corrupt" their manners, language, habits, and even morals.

In this dilemma, most churches rely on magic. They permit the arrangements and, sometimes, the teachings of the church to be permeated with the prevailing temporal public opinion in the community but expect that somehow the educational result will be modified in the direction of a more inclusive sense of human fellowship through a singing of hymns, a reading of Bible texts, and a rehearsing of lessons. Occasionally, the miracle happens; but on closer examination it will be found that the particular teacher who called forth among his pupils that larger vision, that greater passion for righteousness, or that more inclusive human love, was himself already outside the walls of the defensive group psychology that held the community within their thrall.

Having said so much as to what seems to be the predominant situation in American Sunday schooling, we must also mention the occasional exceptions, especially where they represent an intentional pioneering in new group relations in the face of a contrary social opinion. Thus, a western Sunday school teacher writes that she has two Japanese boys in her department:

All the children love them and treat them just as well as any one in the class. I have tried by the use of stories and pictures and songs to show God's love for all children—and care for all—and the brotherhood of all children. But not seeing my children in their day-school contacts with colored children, I cannot be sure whether the lessons in Sunday school really form their attitude toward other races.[4]

While examples of this kind are too numerous to require illustration, nevertheless—our correspondents in different parts of the country seem to agree—the opposite condition, adaptation of the church in its membership and teaching to the race attitudes

[4] Examples of a more systematic planning of ways in which the contacts and teachings of Sunday schools may be integrated in a race-educational program will be given and examined in Chap. XXIII.

that prevail in the community, is more frequent. Exactly what the attendant learnings are which children take home with them from the Sunday school and its lessons cannot easily be ascertained. But a number of participants in this study have contributed illustrations of child attitudes in the making of which, they think, the positive or negative teaching of the Church has had a part. For example, the pastor of a large Protestant church in one of the most cosmopolitan neighborhoods of New York told this incident against himself (showing his awareness to a situation in his own church which, in an institution of that kind, probably no individual could have altogether prevented):

We have had great difficulty, because of our old-fashioned, inadequate premises, to fit in the different services for which there was a demand. Between 3 and 8 P.M. each Sunday there were held services in the Lettish, Esthonian, Italian, Russian, Chinese and Polish languages as well as, of course, English. The different congregations were always jealous of each other and tried to secure for their separate purposes the maximum use of the premises, so that the difficulties were greatly increased.

One Sunday afternoon, while several services were going on in different rooms, I was annoyed to hear some noisy goings-on in the gymnasium the use of which on Sundays was against the rules. I found in possession a little group of Lettish children, dismissed a little while ago from their Sunday school. They were enjoying a game without restraining their voices or other noise-producing organs. I said to them, "Don't you know that Mr. X is conducting a service just above the gym? You ought to be ashamed." "Oh," they said, "that don't matter, them's only Esthonians."

A teacher in a middle-western high school, in connection with a test of racial attitudes in two of his classes, endeavored to get light on the racial ideas of children absorbed through their religious training. He writes:

That religion is compatible with either side of the color problem, as it has been with either side of every great social problem, was aptly portrayed.

A girl writes: "When Noah sent Ham he banished him and turned him black because he sinned, and the Negroes are descendants of Ham. So I don't think we are on equal standards." Another young lady feels that "if whites would treat the blacks right they would get along better.

There will be black people in heaven, and the whites won't never get there if they don't want to go to the same school." [5]

A church woman speaks of the "many stories" brought by her youthful clients "of pagan rites practiced by other racial groups in the community and of unclean food eaten by other peoples." She wonders what part home or church may have played in bringing a little girl of her acquaintance to the point of leaving a group of which she was a member:

She stopped me one night on the way out and told me she could no longer come to club. "Why?" I asked. "I don't know, but I can't go wid no Yids at all. I think it's because they spit on Christ and worship dirty animals."

A story told by Lillian D. Wald in her autobiographical book also may serve here as similar "circumstantial evidence":

An Irish boy observed to one of our residents that on Easter Day he intended to kill his little Jewish classmate. Having had long experience of the vigorous language and kind heart of the young Celt, she paid little attention to the threat, but was more startled when the soft-eyed Francesco chimed in that he was also going to destroy him "because he killed my Gawd." "But," said the teacher, "Christ was a Jew." "Yes, I know," answered the young defender of the faith. "He was then, but He's an American now." [6]

Exactly how such an anti-Jewish bias may be strengthened by a Sunday school teacher through mere haste to get away from a disagreeable, and perhaps to him difficult, subject, is illustrated by one correspondent as follows:

A Sunday school in a wealthy suburb of New York furnished the setting for an interesting question from one of the kindergarten children. The teacher was talking about Jesus' love for little children. One five-year-old volunteered the remark, "He doesn't love Jews, does he?" The teacher seized upon this statement with great rapidity and answered: "Jesus loves everybody"—and hurriedly passed on to what she considered more important.

That the teaching of racial antipathies, where it takes place, is unintentional—or at least a product of loose thinking or con-

[5] David H. Pierce in *The Crisis* for June, 1923.
[6] *The House on Henry Street* (1915, p. 302).

fusion on the part of the Sunday school teacher—and not deliberate, seems to be the general verdict. What they find in most instances is expressed by two witnesses:

The influence of the churches, says a middle-western high-school teacher, is generally to give the white Protestant child a feeling of superiority, of being the elect. Others are newcomers, outsiders, to be either welcomed or rejected, but not to be met as equals.

The president of a southern college for Negroes writes: As far as I have observed, no attempt is made in the public schools or in Sunday schools to teach the children what should be the attitude toward the opposite race. I have never heard the question discussed in any Sunday school I have attended in this state. It seems to be taken for granted that each race is to work out its own destiny separately from the other —white people looking upon the Negroes as trustworthy servants.

Occasionally, conferences with ministers and Sunday school teachers reveal that even those who are working together in the same church have the most diverse notions of what their common creed implies in duties of interracial tolerance. In more than one case, members of The Inquiry, in conducting discussions on race relations in a church, discovered that the attitudes of the officers of the institution ranged all the way from those of the Klan to those of, shall we say, the I.W.W. (for there is no Christian sect which as such goes quite as far as that industrial body in the denial of racial separations).[7]

A Californian minister, reporting on a discussion of the questionnaire used in the present inquiry by a group including teachers, parents and others, puts in the forefront his observation that "the group had not all realized that Christianity has any thoroughgoing connection with the race question. It was by no means agreed that race prejudice is opposed to the Christian ideal."

Like other persons, religious teachers are loth to admit when they have been in error. As a member of The Inquiry staff, the author has sometimes used the occasion of meetings held in churches to correct false impressions concerning the racial characteristics of other peoples: it is often difficult to convince people that Turks do not alternate in moods of lust—which they are supposed to gratify in large harems—and of cruelty—which

[7] Typical cases of this sort are described in detail by Bruno Lasker in the *Religious Education Journal* for October, 1926.

they are supposed to gratify in tormenting Christians. The ministers themselves have been so thoroughly propagandized on this matter that they cannot see the truth—even when, for the sake of comparison, the habits and deeds of other peoples of the Near East are drawn in for illustration. They never accuse Americans of Nordic ancestry of innate cruelty even when made cognizant of the deeds committed by them against Indians. In that case they know that not cruelty but fear was the predominant motive. Graham Wallas says on this point:

> On the practical point, whether the stronger race should base its plans of extension on the extermination of the weaker race, or on an attempt, within the limits of racial possibility, to improve it, Christians have, during the nineteenth century, been infinitely more ruthless than Mohammedans, though their ruthlessness has often been disguised by more or less conscious hypocrisy.[8]

Not only ignorance and confusion, but occasionally distinct prejudice on the part of the teacher himself, are among the elements that create the Sunday school pupil's attendant learnings. One cannot prove this by actual instances because other adults are rarely in the room when such influence is exerted; but a few illustrations may again be given as possible circumstantial evidence:

> I have been amazed to hear ministers preaching to their congregations, and teachers instructing their Sunday schools, that Jesus was rejected by His people—"Christ came to His own and His own received him not." This declaration is less than just to the memory of those Jews who *did* receive Him, who were the first to preach the gospel to the Gentiles.
> If Jesus was misunderstood, hated and rejected by Jews, He was also loved and accepted by Jews, who by "their love, faithfulness and courage, gave Jesus Christ to the nations, and who with their life and death paid for what Christians now call their own."
> It is the Church of the Middle Ages, with its bigotry, and fanaticism, its hatred and persecution of the Jews, that has erected a wall of partition between Jesus and His people.
> I have never heard of a Greek being accused of killing Socrates although he was tried by five hundred judges, every one of them a Greek, and more than half of them condemned to death the great phi-

[8] *Human Nature in Politics* (1921, p. 301).

losopher. Yet if you ask a Christian schoolboy who killed Socrates he will not say the Greeks. Ask him who assassinated Julius Cæsar; he will not say the Romans, but Brutus, Cassius, and the others. Ask him who assassinated Abraham Lincoln; he will not say the Americans. But if you ask him who crucified Christ, he will not say the Roman soldiers, but the Jews. I asked a schoolboy in New York whether he meant the Jews of Harlem or of Brownsville. He answered that he did not know which of them killed Christ. . . .

I have heard ministers preach that when Jesus was nailed to the cross the Jews reviled and mocked Him, but they never state that those who were grief-stricken and lamented the tragic death of their teacher and friend were also Jews.[9]

The New Jersey parents' group agreed:

As far as educational influences are concerned, up to the present time no effort has been made in school or Sunday school to overcome adverse race attitudes. One might almost say that in school adverse attitudes are engendered; in Sunday school no Christian emphasis is laid on the brotherhood of man racially. Missionary instruction is given, but its purpose is to emphasize the supremacy of the white race. Always the chief idea stimulated is that of "sweet" patronage.

The influence of the Bible on race attitudes has never been analyzed. It presents questions of staggering difficulty to the psychologist and the educator. For whatever the earnest religious frame of mind in which the Bible is read may add to its influence, in kind this will be similar to that of other types of historical and poetic literature. Just as the reader identifies himself with the evangelists of the New Testament in their charge against the Jews as the people who killed the Savior, he will in many more passages identify himself with the "chosen people" in its hours of oppression, of triumph, of intimate communion with the All-Father. This tendency of the reader to identify himself with the hero of the story and his kin is so strong that

[9] Max Hunterberg, in *Christian Work,* December 5, 1925, pp. 576, 578.
This writer and others who voice the same complaint fail to mention the mitigating circumstance that the Bible record itself is full of condemnation of the Jews in this matter. In all three synoptics, the rejection of Christ by his own people is explicitly connected with Isaiah's strong language. Where the religious teacher referred to above is at fault is his lack of distinction between national self-accusation and outside attack. No sensible person will quote the preachments of Savonarola or of Luther as evidence of the base character of the Italian or the German people; on the contrary, the looming up of great prophets who chastise their own countrymen will usually be emphasized in the historical teaching so as to make for appreciation of that people's healthy core.

again and again sects have arisen, many of them surviving to
this day, that identify themselves with a "lost tribe" of Israel;
and this identification, in the case of the Mormons, for example,
or of various Anglo-Israel societies which still flourish, is producing a sense of kinship and warm affection for the Jewish
people in our time.   The force of this sympathy tends to be
particularly strong, of course, in the more remote regions of
America where the Bible still holds its old place as almost the
only source of family reading.   But even here, in spite of Funda-
mentalist revivals, the door is now so open to modern contacts
and influences as to counteract that impulse.   Exactly to what
extent the reality of concrete experiences cancels this indirect
influence on racial attitudes would be worth a careful investigation.   As we shall see in later chapters (XIII and XVI), the impact of literature upon national and racial sympathies often is
strong enough to offset the learning from personal observation.
But too little is known as yet as regards the conditions under
which that impact is most effective.

One correspondent invites attention to another effect of school
and Sunday school.   She says, "They incline to bring out distinctions rather than likenesses." [10]

Religious Literature

What are the central educational departments of the various
denominations doing to promote the teaching of Christian attitudes toward people of foreign nationality and different race?
Or rather, what part does the literature disseminated by these
departments play in influencing children on matters of race?
The question is difficult, because only a painstaking general survey would reveal the extent to which and the ways in which the
services and literature offered by these departments are actually
used in Sunday school work.   Moreover, it is difficult to separate
the influences that flow from a helpful textbook from those that
have other sources.   Again, it is only indirectly that sometimes we
can trace a specific influence.   We know, for example, that in
comparison with those who have had no Christian upbringing,

---

[10] For further illustrations of probable reflections of church teaching on
children's attitudes toward race and nationality see the following Inquiry
publications: *And Who Is My Neighbor?*, p. 173 *et seq.*; *All Colors*, p. 70
et seq.; *Why the Church?*, p. 22, and the two pamphlets: *The Fairfield
Experiment* (1927) and *How Catholics See Protestants* (1928).

the graduates of Sunday schools tend to have a more kindly attitude toward strangers and are more disposed to seek the ways of peace in cases of conflict. After all, the judgment of pastors and Sunday school leaders counts for something, and their testimony as to the value of certain textbooks, certain types of project teaching, and the like, is evidence of a purposeful and successful use of this literature.

On the other hand, an examination of many Sunday school books, pamphlets and leaflets which have the special purpose of teaching race tolerance indicates that both locally and nationally the pedagogical problems involved have not as yet been thought through.

As an outcome of this recognition by leading personalities in religious educational work reference must here be made to the conferences and investigations of the Commission on Christian Education of the Federal Council of Churches, in which a program of education for better race relationships is taking first place. This commission has endeavored to ascertain, by means of a written test, how young people between twelve and twenty years of age respond to typical situations in racial group contacts. And its frank discussions have done much to clear the way for a new type of program on the basis of up-to-date educational psychology.[11]

Two interesting papers based on an examination of Sunday-school literature from the point of view of its teaching on interracial and international relations, were read at the Toronto convention of the Religious Education Association in 1926. In answer to the question put to her, Has the Missionary Movement Promoted World-Mindedness at Home?, Mrs. Sophia Lyon Fahs reported, in part:

Until within the last few years, it was the exceptional piece of missionary literature that told us adequately facts about the social and cultural life of the non-Christian peoples apart from their religious superstitions, although startling details were recounted showing the great differences between these far-away folk and us. Compare the autobiography of John G. Paton, a missionary classic of twenty years ago, with *Moana*, the moving picture of life in the South Sea Islands. The missionary gives us nothing but a series of pictures of tragic situations in which he is the central figure and all of which have to do with

[11] Some of the concrete suggestions made by members of this commission vill be given in Chap. XIX.

religion. The moving picture leaves us fascinated by the skills of the islanders and at least respectful of their social institutions. . . .

Up until a dozen years ago, missionary literature consisted principally of addresses and stories picturing the tragic in the life of foreigners. Peculiar customs were described as a stimulus to interest, but the major emphasis was on dire need. "The poor, dark, idolatrous heathen" were held up as the objects of our pity. We were given the dreadful details of foot-binding, the sadness of child marriage, the dreary bleakness of the zenana, the hair-raising distresses of witch-doctoring, and the vanity of idol worship. The heart wrench of a grievous theology, the death-rate of the heathen millions and the ticking of the watch were brought together for dramatic effect. . . .

In these later years, missionary writers are more hesitant in picturing the tragic and the evil in the lives of the people to whom missionaries have gone. Descriptions of unsanitary conditions, of the degradation of women, and of the cruel effects of ignorance are glossed over or repudiated altogether. We are given, instead, the fetching fairy stories and legends of all nations.[12] The poetry, the art, the happiness, the love and the charm of foreign life are so exhibited that children are apt to feel the reverse of the attitude Robert Louis Stevenson suggested in his poem:

> "Little Indian; Sioux, Crow,
> Little frosty Eskimo,
> Little Turk or Japanee,
> Don't you wish that you were me?"

Very few missionary books, however, are ready to picture the ethnic religions in this rosy light. . . .

For example, most of our church schools gloss over the facts in Hebrew· history showing Abraham's worship of trees and stones, and Jacob's household gods. Most biblical teachers have condoned Hebrew human sacrifice, magic, animal worship, and sacrifices to the dead. In fact, we have tried to make ourselves believe and we have told our children that these Old Testament worthies worshiped "the heavenly Father," while at the same time we have been condemning in pitying terms the very same forms of idolatry practiced among tribes of the present day. May not the worship in the temple of heaven in the classic period of China's history have been as worthy as that in the ancient temple at Jerusalem? Yet the two are never associated in the minds of our children. The Pharaoh Ikhnaton who preceded Joseph

---

[12] Other impartial surveys of recent missionary literature yield a less optimistic verdict. Even in the educationally most enlightened denominational organizations unfortunately the stories, pictures, poems, songs and plays produced for children still too largely are of the kind condemned in this quotation.

and Moses was more of a monotheist than either of the two biblical characters, yet to most of our young people the ancient Egyptian religion means idolatry, and the religion of Moses one pure and undefiled.[13]

From a somewhat different angle is another survey of religious literature for children. Trying to discover the influence of books used in Sunday schools on the creation of world-mindedness, we find, not so much teaching contrary to that objective, as innumerable opportunities missed. Professor A. J. William Myers, of the Hartford School of Religious Education, had a small class of graduate students go over the graded Sunday school lessons, "picking out those which seemed to offer or suggest opportunity for teaching world friendship and also any lessons in other courses of the same nature." With the aid of two graduate students he subsequently studied the selected books and others more carefully and was able thus to report, in part, on Literature for Children and Its Influence:

The first conclusion came as a surprise to most of the class. Nowhere in the graded Sunday school lesson courses is world friendship, in the sense of friendship between nations, races, and religions, consciously taught. Not only so, but lessons where world fellowship seems the inevitable teaching or implication are usually handled without reference to racial, national or religious fellowship.[14]

After a detailed analysis of the contents of some of this literature, he adds these further tentative conclusions:

The fundamental principles on which world friendship is based have been taught through the years, but the consciousness that friendship between races, nations and creeds should be consciously taught is new.

Material obviously suited to the teaching of world friendship was used for the most part to develop a benevolent attitude rather than personal or group friendship on a basis of something like equality of spirit.

The greatest limitation in Sunday school and missionary literature in this respect is that it implies a superiority and a consequent handing out of benefits to the "poor" or the "heathen" of other lands.

[13] *Religious Education* for April, 1926, p. 175 *et seq.*
[14] *Ibid.*, p. 217.

Since no comprehensive survey of the educational literature is available as yet, the present study can only point out that even the admittedly best texts often are unsatisfactory when considered from the point of view of their actual effects, their attendant learnings.[15]

Graver failings also appear from time to time. Occasionally there is loud protest of a minority group that feels offended by a piece of literature put out by a religious organization for educational purposes. This, to judge from several communications received at the Inquiry office, seems to have been the case in Negro circles close to the movement for race cooperation in regard to a Sunday school leaflet issued by the Pilgrim Press of Boston for the Congregational church. It is one of a series of "primary stories" and part of a course. It has a full-page picture of Jesus surrounded by children of the five continents. Four of the children, representing Europe, America, Asia and Australia, are within the embrace of the Master. The fifth, a little African, is lying, entirely nude, in the grass at the Savior's feet. In this case, the stigma of a representation—which may have been evolved after much painful thought of a "tactful" way of avoiding an impression of favoring "social mingling of the races"—is obvious at first glance. But how much of subtle inculcation of prejudice there is hidden away in the letterpress of such Sunday school lessons escapes all but the most vigilant eyes.

The question may be raised at the conclusion of this chapter whether institutions which, as we have seen, necessarily represent the temporal feeling and thinking of their time as well as the seemingly eternal doctrines of their Church are able to lead children in their sentiments and attitudes much beyond those

[15] It has been pointed out, for example, that practically every one of the lessons given in one of the pedagogically most advanced books, John Leslie Lobingier's *Projects in World-Friendship* (University of Chicago Press, 1925), has the net effect of strengthening rather than reducing a sense of racial superiority on the part of the native American class for which the book is primarily intended. Each project makes the child "do something for" the children of other peoples; and even in those cases where contributions of the other peoples or races are referred to, these are obviously of such minor quality as to be unable to stand any comparison with the boon conferred by American mission work. This is true of most books with the same purpose. A number of texts sent to the Inquiry office by participants in the present study as samples of "worthwhile and effective forms of Sunday School lessons and activities" share the general fault and are constructed in a spirit of kindly condescension and not of brotherhood.

prevailing in their home environment. The question has also been asked seriously and will be further discussed in Chaps. XIX and XXIII whether they should if they could.[16]

[16] See also George A. Coe, *A Social Theory of Religious Education* (1917, p. 60).

CHAPTER XV

RECREATIONAL INFLUENCES

1. GAMES AND ATHLETICS

From the Sunday school to the playing field is not a long way nowadays. In fact, the weekday activities of church societies for young people often are so largely recreational that the distinction is practically lost. The songs and yells of a typical Epworth League are no more remote from the current mode in popular music and wit than those of the baseball field. Indeed, outstanding religious leaders, having observed the effect of athletics and play upon the social mores, have frankly adopted them as tools of the Lord and are as enthusiastic today in sponsoring "team play" as their predecessors were in efforts to bring about individual conversions.

Bertrand Russell, like other observers, feels that the effect of games on the formation of social attitudes—especially the claim that they teach cooperation—has been much exaggerated. The kind of group competition which games teach has become more dangerous in the modern world than it was; and "it is more important than in former times to cultivate the idea of cooperative enterprises in which 'the enemy' is physical nature, rather than competitive enterprises in which there are human victors and vanquished."[1] William G. Carr truly observes that games, anyhow, merely provide the opportunity for education in cooperation; the lesson is not absorbed automatically.[2] Moreover, mass production in industry has its counterpart in organized recreation. No longer does the potter fuss at his wheel to produce the perfect individual bowl. There are too many children to lead individually to the Kingdom either of personal salvation or of socialized attitude toward their fellow-men; and so the spell of the crowd is held over them, and they are baptized *en masse* in the waters of a group- and class- and race-conscious code of "fair play." Conformity to the social code has become

[1] *Education and the Good Life* (1926, p. 132).
[2] *Op. cit.,* p. 108.

the pedagogic goal of the football coach; and the mentor has abdicated in favor of the cheer leader.

Conveniently, to fit in with the changed pedagogic outlook of the times, a school of recreational philosophers arose early in the twentieth century to provide a much-needed rationalization for the part allotted in the new pedagogy to organized play. They practically argued away individual differences in children and built up a marvelous parallelism between individual growth and the growth of the human race, according to which each child at a certain stage of his development was bound to show all the traits of a race in the corresponding ring of its slow attainment to maturity. These analogies, at first tentatively advanced by Gulick and others, are becoming more and more refined and—more and more absurd. The individual is completely lost sight of in the visions which some of these writers call up of the ancestral stage of tribal life that enmeshes his emotional life. We no longer need the anthropologist to piece together for us slowly, bit by bit, as evidence gradually accumulates, the life habits of the caveman or the early huntsman; all we need do is to observe the boys of the neighborhood dig themselves into their improvised den of packing cases or follow that gang of little fellows exercising their skill as marksmen with sling and pebbles.

As we have already seen in an earlier chapter (page 61), there was a time, not so long since, when the biological analogy between individual and social growth was greatly exaggerated, when sociologists thought they could explain a phenomenon in the social life by indicating to what stage of individual organic growth the particular phase of social development corresponds in which the phenomenon occurs, and when child study thought to provide a basis for a psychologically correct pedagogy by discovering the analogy in cultural development for each age. We now know that, valuable as these comparisons were, they tried to prove too much, and those who trust them instead of studying the behavior of children afresh in each new combination of social circumstances and racial heritage will go far wrong in their efforts to apply appropriate educational techniques.[3] While there are direct in-

---

[3] The "recapitulation" theory and other theories of parallels in developmental history are critically discussed at length in Kurt Koffka's *The Growth of the Mind* (1925, p. 42 *et seq.*). His studies have led him to adopt an attitude of skepticism toward all these theories and of demand for more evidence before any interdependence between phases of child development and of race development can be regarded as more than interesting hypotheses. He says:

fluences of different phases of physical growth upon functions and interest, the similarity between the resultant phases of social attitudes in children and the phase of a developing culture cycle is not so much because of likeness of the organic process but because the social group in which the child grows up subjects him successively to degrees of social experience and responsibility that somewhat correspond to the degrees of socialization from a primitive to a highly developed community life. The similarity, in other words, is there, but the cause of it is more experiential than physiological.

With these preliminaries—necessary because of the widespread influence which a certain type of literature in the field of recreational psychology has had in fostering an erroneous conception—we can now turn to the evidence more particularly opposite to our study. First of all, on the process of a gradually widening experience of children which needs special provision to ensure that it will not omit opportunities for the development of social consciousness, we have many recorded observations.[4] The dangers of a too limited experience of group association in play have been described tellingly—though in terms now outmoded—by the late Luther Halsey Gulick.[5] The way in which gang loyalty develops has been the subject of several recent studies.[6] The purely accidental nature of a racial or national differentiation in the development of gangs was brought out in an Ohio study.[7]

What, exactly, the relationship of leadership and led involves in these voluntary associations is a subject concerning which there is much haziness. That a selective process is at work, however, will be generally agreed.[8] We are here entering a field of psychological research that has received new impetus from recent social changes. Partly as a result of the youth movement in Central Europe, and partly as an outgrowth of a revived interest in

"One should constantly endeavor to support, to control, and to supplement the results of one branch of developmental investigation with results obtained in another branch; as, for instance, by comparing child-psychology with folk-psychology; but one should never allow oneself to be led into the dogmatic construction of uniformities and dependencies." (p. 48.)

[4] For example, Richardson and Loomis, *The Boy Scout Movement Applied by the Church* (1915, p. 44).

[5] *A Philosophy of Play* (1920, p. 194).

[6] Robert A. Woods and Albert J. Kennedy, *The Settlement Horizon* (Russell Sage Foundation, 1922, p. 74). See also studies of Thrasher, Lehman, Witty, *et al.* (references, p. 83).

[7] M. Lavinia Warner, "Influence of Mental Level in the Formation of Boys' Gangs." *Journal of Applied Psychology,* Vol. VII, 1923, pp. 232, 236.

[8] See Luther Halsey Gulick, *op. cit.,* p. 208.

the manifestations of *eros* in the larger Platonic sense, there is at present a disposition toward an entire re-examination of the leader-group relationship. These studies will not fail, eventually, to affect profoundly the practice of organized recreation. What we know already is that a group of boys or girls that has been formed spontaneously and given the opportunity of acquiring vivid social experience of the kind that leaves permanent impression on mind and character, is not a purely casual or arbitrary compound. The introduction of a foreign element or the artificial reduction of the group to secure greater uniformity of age or temperament or race or creed may completely spoil this social product of the children's own initiative. The self-chosen group or gang is so effective an influence precisely because it corresponds to a want—whether this be conscious or merely a vague longing for social companionship within the natural opportunities of the situation. Its pull and pressure is stronger than that of the adult-made group because of that spontaneity and perhaps also because there is at work a selective process that cannot be reproduced by adults until they know more about its nature.

In some cases, children of mixed parentage, socially and racially —not excluding the more distant racial groups—will compose such completely self-sufficient gangs as have been so delightfully portrayed in some of the earlier films of the Our Gang series of movie comedies. In others a felt need for exclusiveness, along one direction or another, seems an essential connective element of the group. Again, and this seems to be the most frequent form of development, a group which starts in such exclusive forms as are naturally indicated by neighborhood and family ties, through actual experience is induced to widen its formal or informal membership. And occasionally some event of dramatic character suddenly breaks down the invisible barriers that a group of children have thrown up around themselves. Here is an example of a situation in which group distinctions were maintained, in spite of the socializing objectives and efforts of adult organizers, but where at a much higher age level the logic of events melted away the racial exclusiveness:

The athletic club at a certain settlement is composed of young men between the ages of eighteen and twenty-five. There is a membership of about one hundred and fifty. The members are chiefly of German and Irish extraction with a fairly large proportion of American-born Jews of Russian and Polish parentage.

A few years ago when young Italians began to apply for admission to the club there was a strong prejudice against accepting them. Indeed, a boy with an Italian name had no chance. The headworker of the settlement used to argue with the members in behalf of the Italians, citing cases of young Italians he knew who were thoroughly decent fellows, and urged that all applicants be considered on their merits. This had no effect. The club members replied that it was all very well for the chief to talk but that they knew these boys in a way he did not; they worked alongside of them, and they knew that any Italian for the slightest grievance would stick a knife in your back. There was no question about this in their minds.

The headworker concluded that it would be foolish to try to force things by insisting that Italian boys should be taken into the club. However, as Italians began to be prominent in sports generally, and as the club members came into competition with Italian members of other clubs, the prejudice began to break down. They were ready to take in an Italian if he looked like a promising athlete, one who might make some sort of record for the club.

Several correspondents report similar happenings. Excellence in athletics, where the separation of groups is not too deeply set through the influence of old antagonisms or that of widely conflicting standards, is a frequent key to the door of mutual appreciation.

On one of the football teams of a high school in New York state a Negro was allowed to play. He was a fine player, and was treated with a great deal of respect by all members of the team, as well as by the whole school. He in return treated the other pupils with respect. Early in the season, at an out-of-town game, he was badly hurt. He was taken to a hospital; and had to stay there two days. Some of the boys stayed with him until he was able to return. The spirit shown by the whole team was very fine. Later at that school a dance was given to pay his accident bills. This dance, from a financial standpoint, was one of the most successful of the whole year.[9]

Situations for such appreciation, of course, can be and often are successfully engineered.[10]

On the other hand, it must again be pointed out that contacts

[9] For similar evidence see *And Who Is My Neighbor?*, p. 114.
[10] For two excellent illustrations see Peter Roberts, *The Problem of Americanization* (1920, p. 174), and Edward A. Steiner, *From Alien to Citizen* (1914, p. 11); also *And Who Is My Neighbor?*, p. 116, *et seq.*

such as these do not in themselves necessarily prove effective in the creation of tolerant attitudes. A much larger body of fully reported data than is at present available is needed to enable a complete analysis of the type of contact, and the type of adult interference with natural group formation, that will produce such result. Moreover, it must be remembered that the engineering of social contacts through games and athletics is not only a scientific technique but also an art in which even leaders who are sensitive to the imponderables in group psychology are apt to fail through lack of skill. This may be illustrated by the following instance:

It is only within the last twenty years that Jewish boys in New York have taken an active interest in athletics. The settlements that worked among the Jews realized that the boys were devoting themselves to literary and intellectual pursuits and decided, about that time, to stimulate an interest in sports.

I remember, writes the headworker of one of these settlements, one of the first basketball games that our Settlement Athletic Club played with a group from one of the downtown settlements. Their opponents were all Jews, and our Irish and German boys regarded them with contempt mixed with amusement. This was before the game. To their astonishment and chagrin the Jewish team beat them. I thought it was a wholesome lesson but did not anticipate the consequences. The Jewish boys politely said good-by, but not long afterwards they came running back to the gymnasium breathless and demanding protection. It seems that our Athletic Club boys had gone down to the street and waited for the victorious team to appear and then had proceeded to give them the kind of a licking which the rules of the game would not permit on the gymnasium floor.

The difficulties of a national organization which is endeavoring to serve colored as well as white children may be illustrated from the experience of the Boy Scouts:

The chief difficulty encountered by the Scout organization in its effort to enlist large numbers of Negro boys in the South arises from the charter requirement that the consent of troops already existing in the neighborhood must be obtained before new troops can be formed. Groups of Negro boys who wished to organize in Atlanta, Charleston, and Richmond found it impossible to do so because the local organizations were unwilling to allow Negroes to use the title and uniform.

A scoutmaster in Memphis said that white boys would not stand the presence of Negro boys in scout uniforms, and that violence would result from an attempt to organize them.[11]

That the provision of opportunities for children of different racial groups to join in games does not in itself suffice to bring about a friendly intercourse where the customs of the community do not sanction it, may be illustrated by the following extract from an unpublished report of a survey made by the National Urban League in Westchester county, New York:

An attempt was made to establish definitely what use was made of the playgrounds by colored children. Questionnaires were sent to the person in charge of each of the fifteen communities. Only half a dozen responded. But from these, from actual observation, and from reports of the colored people themselves, a few facts were gained:

First, all of the playgrounds are open to all children of all races. One director said: "I know of the existence of no statistics which would enable me to answer your questions, but I will say that all citizens in our community of whatever race, religion, or language, are welcome at all times to our only public park. I am enclosing for your information an account of the last Games Day in F—— Park, depicting a picture of a little colored boy in our midst. . . ." Another said: "They are all welcome in all activities and all teams have colored members." This attitude is typical and is so reported by the colored themselves. The directors who replied said that there had been no friction between white and colored groups.

In spite of this and in spite of the fact that the playgrounds are generally accessible to Negro neighborhoods, they are not well used by the colored children. One community in which Negroes form one-half of the population reports "total weekly attendance 400; Negro 1," although the playground is near a colored section. The town of A. reports the playground attendance of colored children as "practically nil." One reason for this is the lack of any special effort to interest the colored group. Except in this place and a smaller town, nothing has been done to urge colored children to attend or to get their parents to send them. Some of the colored communities are at a distance from the playgrounds, and parents hesitate to send their children. Moreover, many of these playgrounds are poorly equipped and are thus unattractive to any of the groups of children.

An incident illustrating conflicting attitudes on the part of recreation workers to the free association of children from differ-

[11] Henry J. McGuinn in T. J. Woofter, Jr., *Negro Problems in Cities* (1928, p. 249).

ent racial groups is reported by an interracial group in a New England city:

When some colored children came to a public playground in this city, the matron told the white children that no nice children would play with them. The playground director saved the day by remarking to the children when they told him of this that the matron was ignorant and did not know the customs of "nice" people.

How the administration of a park or playground may actually undermine the liberal education on race relations given by a broad-minded school is illustrated in the following incident, which is told by a Californian teacher:

In a small rural school, two Japanese children were in attendance. The teacher of this school was careful to make the children of American parentage feel that the Japanese were a rare addition—especially at times when geography lessons were given. These two children became the pets of the entire school. Their small, doll-like countenances seemed a source of pleasure to their playmates, and they were fondled and petted very much.

On the closing day all the children were taken to a near-by town for a picnic in the park. When they had all donned their bathing suits, preparatory to going into the plunge, the manager told them that "no Japs were allowed." The children were much shocked. Some of them hovered about the little Japanese children all day, trying their best to make them forget the insult.

Where there is compulsory segregation in the use of parks and playgrounds, the implied inferiority of colored children in the minds of white children may be re-enforced by the actual inferiority of the provision made for the colored. To judge from Mr. McGuinn's findings, this discrepancy, both in the physical equipment and in the management of municipal facilities for playing, is very prevalent.[12]

Not only the nature of the effort that would produce contacts between children of different races in such a way as to secure greater mutual appreciation is in question. But recently, after the first enthusiasm over the playground movement had begun to give way to calmer and more searching investigations, some educators have come to question the extent to which the attitudes

[12] Henry J. McGuinn in T. J. Woofter, Jr., *Negro Problems in Cities* (1928, pp. 231-233).

brought about in this way really are carried into adult life as permanent social assets.[13]

This chapter would be incomplete if mention were not made of the fact that the playground may also in some situations be the occasion of the child's first experience of race separation and the arena of his first active part in racial conflict. Surveys made in a number of cities have shown that the public playground often introduces into the life of the child who has mixed with children of another race in school the first consciousness of a social distance between the two groups. Just because its contacts are voluntary, adult opinion forces a recognition of prevailing social discriminations.[14]

2. THE MOVING PICTURE

Observers of child life in our large cities often stand aghast at the mixture of influences that surround the child of school age out of school hours. We often hear the expression, "It is a mystery how any child can come out whole in body and soul from such an environment." But the explanation probably is that only in rare cases does a single experience produce lasting impressions. Looking back, we are apt to exaggerate the influence upon us of specific things seen and heard; their weight in most cases was that of the proverbial last straw, that of a particularly vivid impression on top of many others in the same direction. Thus, probably we must explain such retrospective analyses of race attitudes as the following, written by a student in a middle-western college:

When I hear the word bolshevik there comes to my mind a character I saw in a movie when I was a little girl. The villain was a huge bulk of a person with a thick stubby beard and a mop of unruly hair. He was dressed in a loose smock that was held in at the waist with a wide belt in which was thrust a dagger, and his trousers were stuffed into high boots. He seemed to have dangerous weapons about his person, and his favorite method of revenge was bomb throwing or hand-to-hand combat, with knives. These terrible bombs were always set off

[13] David Snedden, *Sociological Determination of Objectives in Education* (1921, p. 272).
[14] This may be illustrated with an example from Chicago, where the official policy was non-recognition of racial difference until a change was practically forced upon it. See *The Negro in Chicago* (Chicago University Press, 1922, pp. 277-278).

at a certain time, and the suspense was horrifying until help would come at the psychological moment and all would be saved.

Later I learned that bolsheviks were persons very much like our-selves (even last year it was said that some of our professors were sus-pected of bolshevism and went so far as to vote for La Follette) but the thing that made them different from us was that they had radical views about government.   But always at the word bolshevik there flashes on my mind the picture of the bearded, bomb-throwing, dagger-carrying and altogether formidable person of the screen.

The relative vividness of the impression created by the moving picture and by the printed word is strikingly brought out in the following communication from a teacher who overheard two of her high-school pupils discuss the merits of Joseph Hergesheimer's novel, *Java Head:*

One of the girls had read the book, the other had seen the film based on the story.   The first referred to the Manchu woman as having given her new light in her conception of the Chinese.   "But," said her friend, "you should have seen her in the movies!   She was just like all the rest of them.   It's all right to read about them; but I don't like to see them."

Social psychology has made considerable strides since environ-mentalists first endeavored to discover the permanent influences of unwholesome impressions in childhood upon adult attitudes. We now know that the child's mind is more flexible than had been thought.   The mystery of his preservation of fairly healthy and realistic reactions to life in the artificial world of the city only exists when we view the kaleidoscopic picture of successive, single impressions and regard these as the character-forming factors.   But beneath these occasional influences there is a fairly steady current of more or less uniform environmental pulls and pressures, and it is these that create the lasting attitudes of mind, that fix the interests and prejudices, the motives and the habits of behavior.

Sponsors of moving picture censorship sometimes talk as though the influence of a single vicious film could blast the morals of youth.   In fact, as we now know from the more recent studies of educational psychologists, it is rather the frequent repetition of impressions of a similar nature that gradually carves out the channels of response.   That the influence of the moving picture makes for unrealistic, prejudiced attitudes on race and nationality is unquestionably true. This is not, however, because some particular pictures—say, "The Birth of a Nation"—create romanticism and prejudice, but because the great majority of the moving pictures seen by children represent, in regard to social relations, the more romantic and prejudiced currents of public opinion. The participants in the present study are practically unanimous in regard to this:

Movies show foreigners and Negroes as comic characters or to their disadvantage, writes a settlement worker.

The New Jersey group of parents, repeatedly quoted in this book, report: The group considered that in regard to strength and permanency of influence the strongest factor today is to be found in the motion picture where much race discrimination is subtly taught.

A middle-western teacher writes: Movies will use villains who are Mexicans or Italians, or just look foreign. But I feel there is less of this now than there was formerly.

That the moving picture is improving in this respect is the view also of the southern settlement group:

There are good and there are injurious moving pictures. Most movies encourage tolerance because the hero is the hero, no matter what nationality he is. The classics now being produced in moving pictures are doing valuable work. On the other hand, South Sea pictures and other cheap ones do show prejudice, and the pity is that so many of our neighbors see these instead of the better ones.

The distinction here made between classics and "cheap" pictures is not quite clear. There are many South Seas pictures among what are popularly regarded as moving picture classics. It would seem probable, offhand, that, generally speaking, the popular prejudices will be most strongly reproduced in pictures fabricated for the entertainment of the masses. On the other hand, the clients of the dime picture palace are often more tolerant in their social attitudes than those of expensive houses frequented by the middle classes. Here, for example, is a report on a random visit paid to a high-class picture theater in a suburb of New York. There is no reason to believe that this evening's entertainment was in any way out of the usual:

1. In the Pathé News there was a picture of a boys' football match on a lot somewhere in New York, made funny by makeshift imitations

of regular football players' accoutrements. One boy gets away with the ball and makes the goal, all the other boys piling on him as they fall in a heap. Only then is it seen that the boy who made the goal is colored while the others are white—this is supposed to add a special element of humor.

2. In the comedy, a young bridegroom tries to rescue his bride from a harem to which she has been abducted. In a mad race he carries her away until all pursuers are outdistanced. Lifting the veil from her face, he discovers that he has rescued the wrong woman. That she is a Negress, though pretty, is supposed to add special horror to his predicament.

3. The feature picture is "The Midshipman," filmed in and around the naval academy at Annapolis. Only one Negro appears in this picture, introduced without any relation to the story or any probable reason for his presence in a scene where the appearance near a cemetery of a midshipman clothed only in his pajamas and a bedsheet is supposed to arouse superstitious fear. The Negro, in a rôle quite out of keeping with the realism of the picture, has his hair rise, rolls his eyes and flops back stiffly—all in the approved comedy manner.[15]

Here is testimony as to the effect of moving pictures on children:

A correspondent gives a concrete example of international prejudice induced by a film. It occurred in Raleigh, N. C., last month. The film is called "Foreign Devils," and the story is based on the Boxer uprising in China in 1900. It was shown on Saturday night. Next day a teacher in a Sunday School was explaining to a class that children of all countries are children of a common Father. One child responded: "I saw a movie last night, and the Chinese are terrible people!" [16]

Another observer writes:

Foreigners and traveled persons see the need for more information in the making of scenes of foreign countries and foreign peoples. The idea of ridiculing other nationalities and showing only their faults is very irritating. It not only creates a bitter feeling abroad but also becomes partly responsible for the erroneous idea that the average American has of the rest of the world.

[15] The introduction of a Negro to depict fear has become as much a stereotype with producers as that of cigarettes to denote wickedness, of a moustache to denote villainy, of a wide-brimmed hat to denote courage. Soon there will be no need for action; there will be a ready-made symbol for every state of mind, e.g., white-haired Negro: servility or burlesque; young Negro: fear; Negro woman: monstrosity; Negro child: oddity.

[16] *Christian World Education News Service*, December, 1927, p. 6.

Yesterday I saw a motion picture supposed to show scenes in Brazil. It is a brand-new picture, of a reputable make and directed by Charles Brabin. Once more Brazil was shown on the screen as a Spanish-like colony, semi-civilized and disgraced by poverty and fevers. . . .

Let the hero in all pictures be an American, but at least stop showing the rest of the world as a filthy, horrid hell on earth.[17]

An agitation to restrain the showing of motion picture films that tend to create or inflame racial prejudices has lately been carried to the legislature of the State of New York by the American-Irish Vigilance Committee who complain that the existing state law and the city ordinances are insufficient to prevent the showing of pictures which, they deem, hold the Irishman up to ridicule. This activity arose from protests which, made with ink, ammonia, rocks, and other missiles, had led to disorders, arrests and court convictions.

It is not difficult to find proof of the remarkable extent to which moving pictures—and the best of classics no less than the worst of blood-and-thunder films—already have affected popular thinking on race attitudes. Try, for example, the experiment of telling a mixed group, whether of children or of adults, an actual scenario, only with this difference, that the hero is described as a little dark man with a black moustache and the villain as a blond giant. Almost invariably the attempt will result in shrieks of laughter. A hero of that description seems grotesquely impossible.

The foreignness of all non-white races is accentuated by the weird music with which the moving picture orchestra or organist will accompany a scene of folk-life in any part of the world other than Europe and North America. The same drum-accentuated tune does duty for the Hottentot Kraal and the Mexican *pueblo,* for the Chinese market place and the Arab camp. Quaintness is the impression chiefly aimed for, and with it mild compensation for those emotional passions that are ruled out of the humdrum existence of westerners.

After all, what are these entertainments for, the moving picture and the popular play? They must provide vicarious exercise for those elemental emotions that find no outlet in the routine of modern life. Cruelty and sexual passion, the control of power, indulgence in barbaric luxury and splendor—these elements of the

[17] Francisco Silva, Jr., in *New York Times,* July 13, 1927.

successful popular play or film will remain as long as social life and the conditions which it provides for the average individual remain as colorless as they are today.   To ask of the moving picture to become sane and realistic and informing is to ask it to commit suicide as a commercial institution and as a recreational factor for the majority of people.[18]   It is precisely because it can present the unreal so convincingly, because it rolls off in mad frolic and pictures the average man's ideal country in the way he would picture it himself if he had the imagination, that the moving picture has such tremendous appeal.[19]

The question arises whether children should not be kept away from moving picture theaters altogether.[20]   Several of the correspondents who participate in the present study seem to imply that the commercial moving picture has brought into the relations between national and racial groups a new element of discord that can simply be eradicated by prohibiting the attendance of children and adolescents.

But then, are we prepared to apply similarly heroic measures to other forms of recreation that are now open to children? Moreover, can the influence of the moving picture on the growing generation be cut off by merely preventing the attendance of minors?   Does not the influence, to some degree, remain?   Mrs. Sidonie M. Gruenberg, director of the Federation for Child Study, points out that the lurid posters may be worse than the films they advertise, just as the objectionable comic supplement that is forbidden at home is likely to be passed around on the playground.   The time has passed in which the individual home could control influences such as these; and concerted action, through legislative and municipal control, is the only way out.[21]

Cooperative action for the protection of youth is proposed also by many literary people who, in principle, are opposed to moving-picture censorship for adults.   They realize that the point of view that must govern the "liberty" of children can only be an educational, protective one.   But exactly how to combine a system

[18] And yet, a genius can produce very nearly a popular success along these lines, as witness the moving pictures "Grass" and "Chang"—the latter containing not only an unusually appreciative description of native life in the jungles of Siam but actually portraying a supposedly primitive state of culture as in some ways more advanced than ours, educationally most valuable, however, because it stresses the fundamental relationship of all cultural values.

[19] See Frederick Elmore Lumley, *Means of Social Control* (1925, p. 196).

[20] There is considerable support for such a legislative measure in Germany.

[21] *Sons and Daughters* (1916, p. 320).

of selection of moving pictures suitable for children with complete freedom of choice for adults, or even on what principle exactly to separate harmful from innocuous productions, they are not agreed.[22]   Professor Walter B. Pitkin, of Columbia University, who is an authority on the moving picture, writes:

It is time that a new kind of motion picture review be inaugurated. Pictures have been judged mainly from the point of view of adult audiences.   But it must be remembered that average American audiences are composed about equally of adults and children. . . .

We realize that many a picture can please a ten-year-old boy and at the same time bore an eighteen-year-old. We also know that many a picture has a suggestiveness about it that is poisonous to the eighteen-year-old but wholly without effect upon the younger child, whose experience is as yet too limited to appreciate the questionable situation and lines. . . .

To make a thorough job of it, the critic of motion pictures for children really ought to present two orders of comment: he ought to appraise the films from the point of view of the impression they make on children under twelve years of age and then again from the point of view of children over twelve. . . . The effects which pictures produce upon the younger of these groups . . . deserve the more serious consideration and the more careful protection, for they are much more impressionable than their older brothers and sisters. Pictures mold their habits of thinking and acting more profoundly. Unfortunately, their welfare has been least of all considered in the production of pictures.[23]

[22] The explorer V. Stefansson, in *The Standardization of Error* (1927, p. 66 *et seq.*), shows how misleading even "educational" films, widely used in schools, can be—illustrating this thesis with the description of Eskimo life in the film, "Nanook of the North."
[23] *Children,* for March, 1927, p. 38.

CHAPTER XVI

RECREATIONAL INFLUENCES (*Continued*)

3. READING

The difficulty of the home in protecting the powerful influences on the child which the outside world effects by means of print is obvious when we consider for a moment the vast array of outdoor advertising. We can protect our children individually against the consumption of dangerous wares, but we can protect them only by social measures against the advertising of these wares.

So far as the present inquiry is concerned, none of the participants seems to have discovered sinister influences on race attitudes through the poster. Nevertheless, subtle influences emanate from it now and then which, innocuous in themselves, tend to confirm impressions obtained in other ways. Again, reference in this connection, as in that of the moving pictures, must be made to the romantic fiction that is spun around the peoples of foreign lands. One whose only education in human geography was taken from colored prints—including advertisements of every kind, booklets of transportation companies and the recruiting posters of our government—must remain ignorant of the vast advances made in adaptation to western standards in living and working conditions the world over. To him the peoples of the greater part of the world would be naked savages, to him the Orient would be a vast pageant of ancient ceremonial, and the well-dressed blond European or American the only representative of wealth and effective control.[1]

If he reads newspapers and magazines, especially those of the more popular kind, impressions of this sort will be driven home by a thousand hints and implications.

As we have already discussed—in the section on English teach-

[1] When travelling, try this experiment: Compare the proportion of decidedly blond and brunette persons in the car with the proportion among the portraits of the car cards. (Or the colored advertisements and illustrations of a magazine may be used.)

ing (Chap. XIII, p. 162)—the influence of books on the race attitudes of children, we need not here go over the effect of reading for recreation; for, although there are differences in degree between the effectiveness with which the school-book and the voluntarily chosen story-book impregnate the juvenile mind with adult prejudices, in kind the two forms of attitude absorption are much alike. There are, however, other readings and other contacts with the printed page. There is, for instance, the trash especially printed in enormous editions on cheap paper to meet the special needs of impecunious ten-year-olds. The faults of the worst of romantic fiction are here outdone. In the "penny dreadful" and in the detective story, racial controversies as such, of course, rarely appear—except in the background of a situation of intense struggle between individuals. But all the popular prejudices, in so far as they are widespread and not merely those of a small section of the country, are utilized to the full to make these stories, mostly the mechanical output of a sordid form of industry, as palatable as possible. For example, picking up a recent issue of a detective story magazine, we read:

"A lone drink did not suffice the midget. He used a water tumbler, and speedily stowed away a pint of the liquid fire. In the case of a white man, such indulgence might have caused sensational results. The midget, though, was Chinese, which meant that his nerves were not highly organized—that he was virtually immune to stimulants."

In the same story, the chief criminal is a Chinaman who wades in blood, kills his partner in crime to save himself and has no other ethical code except that he honors his ancestors. There is also a petty thief who steals from the Chinese super-criminal; he is a Negro. These three characters—each of them a shady criminal—are the only non-Caucasians in a story that plays in an American mining camp.

Probably both author and publisher would be surprised if told that they are implanting race prejudices in the minds of their readers.

One of the worst features of popular literature for children, from the point of view of racial attitudes, is the pigeon English or ridiculous diction that is put into the mouth of foreigners. Even where the the conversation is carried on in a foreign country and in a foreign tongue, the talk of the American traveller— supposed to be translated, often, from a language with which he cannot be perfectly familiar—is rendered in faultless English, while the native, presumably speaking his own tongue, is translated in what conventionally is regarded as a Frenchman's or a Kaffir's way of making himself understood in English. By this device the sense of superiority over the foreigner is, of course, insinuated in a way that does not easily come to the child's consciousness.[2]

A large mass of slowly poisoning literature is much worse in its total impact upon, say, race attitudes (to stay within our immediate subject field) than an occasional extremely vicious piece of writing of a more obviously dangerous and inciting character. The German government has recognized this in including every kind of "trashy" literature in its recent legislation for the protection of youth from nefarious printed matter. Intensive studies by specialists had shown that the clearly obscene book or one directly inciting to crime was merely the outgrowth of a much larger semi-obscene and semi-criminal literature. The deterioration of taste through the large consumption of trashy literature in youth, they found, was a greater social evil than the surreptitious circulation of something so filthy that every decent citizen would agree to its suppression. In an earlier chapter (p. 140 *et seq.*) we have seen from the answers of a typical group of boys in a cosmopolitan community how completely the prejudices absorbed from literature of this kind turn children, in the pre-adolescent years, from appreciation for the actual facts of racial and national characteristics, even though they may have easy access to them.

Children read the "tabloid" papers to an extent quite unknown in the days when even the most popular newspapers presented their news in long columns of text. The items are short, the headlines large and many; and the pictures attract. Millions of children in this way were introduced into the mazes of the Rhinelander trial and other scandals in which race psychology played a part. But even if there were no references to racial and national differences at all in this type of journalism (and because of its production for mass consumption there are relatively few), their general effect is to foster prejudice, cruelty, and fanaticism in human relations—the very ingredients from which group antagonisms are built up. Again, it is the general effect on children of this miscellaneous reading rather than a specific influence on racial attitudes that is productive of the greatest harm.

[2] See also the remarks on translation in general, p. 169.

There are those who contend that all these influences are present in the child's environment anyhow; that these sheets of sordid reading merely give back to the public what it already fabricates itself in nasty gossip.   Many hold that the great advance made in recent decades to overcome illiteracy has in itself been a factor making for prejudice.   The illiterate person trusts his own experience and observation to a larger degree, they say, than the newspaper reader who permits his mind to be swamped by prejudiced propaganda and becomes a willing register of unassimilated sensations.[3]

While most of the racial propaganda that finds its way into the recreational reading of children is either unintentional or diffused without any special regard to age, sex or stage of mental development, one occasionally hears of a more deliberate choice of books for children to condition their racial attitudes.[4]

While this chapter was being written, a curious illustration of the extraordinary variety of by-paths to race prejudice through miscellaneous reading came to the author's attention.   To improve his handwriting, a schoolboy on vacation was asked to copy every day a page or two from whatever book he happened to be reading.   This is one of the "exercises" he sent in:

We can fix no bounds to Nature's conforming power.   She has produced certain vertebrates, such as the mud-turtle and the hellbender, so eminently adaptive to circumstances that they are equally at home whether immersed in air, water, or mud.   And there is the Chinaman, who, being of a breed that has been crowded and coerced for thousands of years, seems to have done away with nerves.   "He will stand all day in one position without seeming in the least distressed; he thrives amidst the most unsanitary surroundings; overcrowding and bad air are nothing to him; he does not demand quiet when he would sleep, nor even when he is sick; he can starve to death with supreme complacency."   A missionary says: "It would be easy to raise in China an army of a million men—nay, ten millions—tested by competitive examination as to their capacity to go to sleep across three wheelbarrows, with head downwards like a spider, mouth wide open, and a fly inside." . . . From the first chapter of *Camping and Woodcraft*, commonly called *Kephart's Manual*.[5]

[3] See Everett Dean Martin, *The Behavior of Crowds* (1920, p. 272).
[4] See the example referred to on page 98, footnote 6.
[5] Horace Kephart, *Camping and Woodcraft* (1921, Vol. I, p. 18).

4. THE FINE ARTS

In addition to prejudicial "literature" there is prejudicial "art."

An immigrant recalls that his only knowledge of the American Negro, prior to his migration to this country at a mature age, consisted of the impressions which he obtained from those once popular colored lithographs of scenes of Negro life which are seen throughout Europe and, more especially, in the sea ports. Very crude, these pictures nevertheless are not without artistic value; and, in fact, since the craze for collecting American antiques began, some of these prints have become rare and expensive. There are, however, on the market reproductions of these prints which are very popular; probably hundreds of thousands of children in Europe, potential immigrants, derive their only knowledge of the American Negro from this source.

Goya in Spain, and Hogarth in England, two centuries before the moving picture, invented the comic strip—or its analogue in those days, the series of small paintings that tell a story. In the long line of succession between these masters and Bud Fisher were innumerable comic stories with quite definitely prejudiced lessons in ethnography. One recalls, for example, the enormous vogue, a generation ago, of the illustrated sheets with the children's song about "Twelve Little Nigger Boys." The comic strip today is regarded by many as a decided influence on both the social attitudes and the behavior of children.

A southern settlement group reports: The comic newspaper supplement is one of the most injurious influences. The Italian banana man whose cart is always turned over by boys, the German Katzenjammer Kids, the red-nosed German, and the Englishman with the monocle have created definite prejudices.

I have noticed, writes a church worker, that small children are strongly influenced, in an undesirable direction, by the funny sheets.

One correspondent quotes a Negro theological student at a Christian Endeavor conference as complaining that "everything evil is painted black; and the Negro is thought of as evil because he is black." He told of a picture he had seen in which the devil was not only depicted as black, but also with kinky hair and thick lips.[6]

---

[6] This complaint only refers, of course, to the "art" of the last two centuries. A comparison of Flemish, Italian and German paintings of the fourteenth and fifteenth centuries representing the Adoration of the Kings—for long the most popular of all subjects—shows an effort, both realistic and

It would be unfair, of course, to deny that in this matter corrective influences are at work today which go far to counteract the tendencies thus deplored. To come back to the moving picture for a moment, it is true that we have educational films and news films which, by simply telling the truth about foreign peoples, provide a corrective for the fiction told by the feature film and the comedy. Not all these realistic films do so, of course, for in the selection of material the foreign representatives of the great moving picture corporations will be inclined to have an eye for the romantic, for that which, though fact, yet is likely to please their American audiences with their preconceptions of the conditions. So, in oriental scenes, for example, those rituals will be given prominence that most correspond to the ideas of the West as regards Asiatic splendor and quaintness. That a street car winds in and out the milling crowds of a Chinese street scene is an unavoidable "anachronism" in the eyes of the photographer, rather than an important element of the picture.

Similarly, in story book and newspaper and magazine the normal child finds many correctives for the erroneous impressions produced by the comic strips. The photogravure section, however, also results from a process of selection and, therefore, is subject to the same tendencies as the news film. It is absolute fact so far as it goes, but often it does not go nearly far enough in giving the objective truth—for example, of the conditions found by a travelling expedition or of life in a tropical country.

The political cartoon is normally of little interest to children. But occasionally these ephemeral works of art are so graphic and simple and brought to the child's attention so forcibly that he cannot help but notice them. This latter condition is in operation more especially if a newspaper cartoon is reprinted by a magazine that has other elements of interest to the child or which he is obliged to read in connection with a school lesson. (Of course, this only applies to children of the higher grades.) The cartoon often is an effective means of driving home a prejudiced point of view. The caricature of the German and the Turk which it fastened into people's minds helped to win the

reverential, to portray Caspar as nearly a Negro, with all the characteristic features, as the artist, who in many cases had never seen a person of that race, was able to contrive. One cannot help feeling in looking over a series of such paintings (at the Metropolitan Museum in New York, for example) that they are primarily and not accidentally expressions of a deeply religious concern for human brotherhood. The devil, in some of the art of the Middle Ages, has the Mongolian features of the Hun.

war. Try to remember the kind of Japanese or Mexican you
have come in contact with through your newspaper! Imagine the
effect of these repeated visualizations upon those who may have
few occasions to rectify the impressions of racial or national
character created by them! [7]

Lately, the governments of the world have taken a hand in
utilising the opportunities provided by the dissemination of millions of postage stamps for purposes of visual education. The collection of postage stamps is sometimes recommended as an occu-
pation for children that widens their international understanding
and sympathies. It has been pointed out, for example, that the
beautiful stamps of Persia or of Liberia will leave the impression
that these countries have standards of beauty and of technical
excellence no less than the countries of the West about which
one hears so much more. But, alas, it seems that the governments of nations have recognized the propaganda possibilities of
this medium, and the stamp collector is more and more to be
impregnated with the attitudes which the bureaucracy desires
to create.

While our American government, so far, contents itself with
a variety of patriotic appeals—taking historic events for the occasion of special issues—the British assures the world, by means
of a super-stamp, that British Goods are Best; and the German
attempts to correct the world's judgment of German character
by portraying poets and philosophers on their most popular
stamps. (Curiously enough, a recent series also includes a member of the Hohenzollern dynasty, Frederick the Great—evidently

[7] How the newspaper cartoon may be utilized by an interested party to
prepare unawares and bit by bit a public opinion as yet hostile to the political
policy it favors is illustrated with particular effectiveness in the case of American relations with Mexico. Not long ago, in connection with the Nicaraguan
trouble, a daily newspaper published a cartoon in which Uncle Sam was
represented in the general shape of the map of the United States (a profile
facing east) in such a way that Mexico became the tail of his coat. Nicaragua
and Mexico, represented by relatively tiny figures, got up like bandits, were
pulling at these coat-tails. This picture was reprinted in the *Literary Digest*
and later, in whole-page advertisements of the most influential daily papers of
the country. The "attendant learning"—whatever the immediate object of the
cartoon—was: "Of course, really, when you look at the map, Mexico and
everything down to the Panama Canal really is part of our country—some
time or other we must occupy these territories that ought to belong to the
United States."
If the reader will watch, he is very likely to find the same idea incorporated
in other, similarly deceptive but plausible cartoons in the course of the
next few years until large sections of the American people will have become
accustomed to the idea that these territories "by rights" ought to be under
the Stars and Stripes.

less a gesture of royalist sentiment than a re-assurance of self-respect by a much maligned people.) The latest Turkish series includes a stamp picturing an important bridge entirely constructed by Turkish engineers. A new series of Belgian Congo stamps shows scenes of native life.

Another educational use of children's interest in postage stamps is described by Dr. H. A. James, formerly headmaster of Rossall, Cheltenham and Rugby:

An experiment has been made during the last four years in distributing some of the commoner foreign and colonial stamps (nearly 40,000) among certain elementary schools. The stamps have been utilized under the direction of the teachers by the children who fasten them in appropriate positions in their books of notes relating to the respective places, historical events, customs or products, etc., as shown in the design.

The experiment has been found helpful to teachers and of interest as well as pleasure to the pupils. To the latter the stamps give a sense of reality, especially when good and clear postmarks are retained uncut. . . . Under the experiment no encouragement is given to the children to become stamp collectors in the usually accepted sense of the word.[8]

Another powerful form of public propaganda through educational uses of art is the decoration of public buildings. We rarely think of this as an influence on race relations; but that it has such effect cannot be doubted. Apart from the decoration of school buildings—which rarely goes beyond the use of conventional material used in visual instruction—there are the monuments, and the sculptures and friezes on public buildings. Visits to the public buildings that house organs of the national and state governments usually produce in children a sense of awe because of the unaccustomed size, materials, and acoustics. The beautiful groups symbolical of the contributions of the continents to the welfare of the world that flank the Custom House in New York, the friezes of the University of the State of New York, the statues and paintings in many of the public libraries and post offices of the country, the decorations of the Library of Congress, the statuary of the Capitol at Washington and of the state capitols, all have their lessons. How many such statues, groups, friezes or other public works of art do you remember that sympathetically portray the contributions of the Negro to the commonwealth? And

[8] *The Spectator* for November 26, 1927, p. 926.

how many do you remember that so portray the Indian? The contrast is startling. The Negro is almost completely absent from our public art; and the Indian is everywhere.

Because of the historical significance of much mural painting it is natural that the American Indian should hold a conspicuous place in the mural art of this country. The Indian's position as original inhabitant, and his first and subsequent contacts with the white race have been portrayed. . . .

Another phase of the subject is being emphasized at present, and that is the essential picturesqueness of Indian physique and the beauty and poetry of much of his primitive life. The newer painting is being done by men who have looked beneath the surface details and have sounded the individual quality of Indian character and feeling, and it often reflects the modern aspect of the red man's adjustment to the changed conditions that white civilization has forced upon him. In this latter phase the Indian is receiving more of the treatment that is due him as an interesting art model. He is advancing from the cigar-store sign to a distinctive place in American decoration. . . .

All of these Indian murals and others that might be described reflect the appealing qualities of the red man, qualities that are being more generally appreciated now that most of the old glory has departed. Mural decorations attract popular attention, and they may fittingly reflect the dominant atmosphere of a community and so present a distinctly local appeal. . . .

Modern painters of Indians are showing that the red man was not only a picturesque figure, but that he had an art and a philosophy remarkably well advanced for his material development.[9]

There are many available series of colored prints, of a size suitable both for home and class-room decoration, that portray sympathetically different types of workers; and, of course, series of prints illustrating foreign landscapes (including also railroad posters) often are effectively used to interest the child in foreign countries. But there are not so many pictures of artistic merit that can be used to make children pleasantly and constantly aware of the interdependence of different peoples and races.[10]

Other official forms of visual propaganda are limited to specific groups and purposes. Apart from the recruiting posters—with

[9] Rose Henderson, "The American Indian in Mural Decoration," in *The Southern Workman* for March, 1927, p. 113.
[10] One such set of posters, illustrating ten nationalities in characteristic costumes and activities, is published by the National Child Welfare Association (70 Fifth Avenue, New York).

their often by no means accurate representations—we have had, in war time, a regular avalanche of posters addressed to investors, to housewives, and to other sections of the people. From the point of view of race relations, these posters, in so far as they touched upon that subject, were decidedly liberal. For, all sections of the mixed population of the country—other than, perhaps, alien enemies—had to be won for a wholehearted support of the war. Not a few national and local posters prominently figured men of foreign or even Negroid features in uniform. The immigrant was wooed by means of flag displays in which high honor was done to countries and nationalities previously little known. To make the picture complete, American Indians in full rig were hired to harangue the crowds.

At the same time, strenuous efforts were directed toward the Americanization of immigrants, and many of the handbooks published by national and state authorities, owing to their handsome make-up and illustrations, are household treasures to this day. In this literature, of course, the inclusiveness of American racial and national sympathies was stressed, and even those sections of the Constitution which are most openly disregarded in some parts of the country were brought out for the occasion in bold type.

Since the war, propaganda of this kind has suffered a considerable slump, and the weeds over the war gardens also cover a wartime growth of splendid social sentiment. The flags of other nations are less frequently displayed today, few are the colored prints that show swarthy men in uniform. Few booklets with sayings of Lincoln and poems concerning the unimportance of the American's family tree and social status are distributed to school children to take home to their foreign-born fathers.

And that brings us to another part of our subject, the child's part in the dramatization of the traditional American race tolerance through play and pageant.

5. Plays, Pageants, and Living Shows

Santa Claus, with his long white beard and gayly puffed cheeks is a descendant of the pre-historic medicine man who dons mask and ceremonial robe to impress the traditional mores of the group upon the younger generation. Always has "dressing up" been a favorite method of fun-making. Always has it been, also, a prime ingredient in social education. The Greek vintner put on the scarecrow mask that had done good service in ensuring a plentiful crop of grapes and led the dance around the wine-press. His clowning became the rite of the Dionysian festival and the origin of drama. He had many and strange offspring.

If you want to add to the gayety of a situation by dressing up, you will seek to represent a gay character. Now, there are two obvious ways of achieving that result: Either you will make up as a character already known as funny or you will take a particularly staid and dignified character and caricature him. The foreigner always is funny to the stay-at-home; if we are not afraid of him, we are amused by the quaintness of his appearance, manners or language; if we *are* afraid, grotesque imitation will help to overcome fear. The circus clown, made up with flour, is an abstraction of humanity that will not frighten even small children. The small boy, who does not mind frightening others, paints his face black.

Most people are afraid of darkness and love light. In the mythology of the nations, the gods are light, the evil spirits dark. In the middle ages, there were mystery plays around the feast of Epiphany, and the Three Kings, representative of the three principal racial divisions of mankind, were much in evidence. (We know of the gorgeousness of these spectacles from many paintings.) What is not generally known is that in some of these plays the comedy element was not wanting. While Melchior and Jasper maintained their dignified parts, Caspar, the African, became the buffoon. He was the original "coon," so to speak, though that word is a modern American addition to the language of comicality.[11]

American also is the present-day meaning of "minstrel"—originally simply a servant, *menestrel,* employed by the medieval baron as a musician and entertainer and, later, a wandering singer of ballads. The American minstrel show was no more, to begin with, than a carefully picked group of Negro slaves whose plantation songs had given pleasure to their master and, therefore, were employed to entertain his guests. It is probable that originally their

[11] A reminder of these old Christmas plays will be found in the Punch and Judy show, the *Kasperle Theater;* but here a transformation has taken place in that the original buffoon, Caspar, is now the hero of the piece and, as such, must needs be white to secure the sympathy of the crowd; and a new black figure is introduced (in addition to the devil who, of course, also is black) to be pummelled and thrown about.

contribution to the festivities was of a simple musical character; but even in those days many considered it a ludicrous sight to see the Negroes produce song, "just like white men." The guests laughed, and the entertainers, anxious to give pleasure, more and more enlarged the ridiculous and bizarre behavior connected with their singing that seemed to be so much appreciated. Hence the minstrel show—and hence, further down the lineage, the extravagances of the present-day jazz band. Minstrel shows in our day are composed nearly always of white men. The typical occasion is a lodge meeting at which the members must do something to entertain their guests. Since not all of them are individually gifted, a group of them together will sing comic songs. Musically considered, their entertainment amounts to little. So they blacken their faces, perform some antics and thus "get away with it."

Now, from the point of view of our study, this custom of blackening the face to denote tomfoolery—exasperatingly in evidence these days as an almost universal substitute for wit and clever caricature at carnivals where the more genuine humor of other ages demanded a more diversified harlequinade—has the unfortunate effect of perpetuating the association between colored skin and supposedly empty head. Even settlements and churches have been known to get up minstrel shows, quite oblivious of the "attendant learnings" of these entertainments which are so contrary to their conscious teaching on race relations. The minstrel leader often will endeavor to speak with a Negro accent so as to drive home still further the clownish character of the race; and of the jokes that pass between him and other members of the cast, many tend to be in the same direction.[12]

The stage Jew and the stage Irishman, of course, also have their influences on the racial attitudes of children, and so have other extravagant persiflages of that sort. Tests as to the origins of pronounced prejudices in young people frequently point to

[12] Incidentally, it may be remarked that jokes told at the cost of a specific racial or national group, while they may have some relation to its real character, usually are of so general and widely applicable a nature that they would fit almost any other group in the same general cultural relationship to the group of the humorist. The stories told about Irishmen in England resemble those told before the war about Poles in Germany and about Hungarians in Austria—not to go back into the literary records of antiquity. Stories told about Negroes in America are much like the stories told by Europeans about Chinese coolies or by the ruling classes about peasants anywhere. Jokes about Jews are more nearly unique because the relationship of Jews to Gentiles is common to many countries and somewhat different from that between other majority and minority groups.

impressions received early in life from vaudeville and burlesque characters. Probably recollections of that sort are rationalized into an importance which they do not really possess in comparison with other early influence; but these stage representations undoubtedly play their part in reinforcing a misunderstanding of racial or national character already present in the community. Sometimes they are part of deliberate misrepresentations; but with the enormous economic progress made by all racial types in the United States, the commercial theater no longer dares deliberately offend even one of the minority groups. This was recently pointed out tellingly in an editorial article, entitled, "The Comic Alien Passes," in the organ of the Foreign Language Information Service:

The recent levelling of a once-famous playhouse on the Bowery in New York calls to mind a rapidly vanishing phase of popular American entertainment. What has become, one wonders, of the orange-haired Irishman who walked the boards of that demolished institution, to the huge delight of some of our fellow-countrymen, a generation ago? And of the round-paunched "Dutchman," his contemporary? And of the successor of both, the Jewish peddler with his seedy derby pressed snugly down over nape and ears, and his eloquent hands in perpetual motion? They do not seem to have moved, like the opera of the same period, to other quarters farther uptown. They have been swept off the scene, leaving hardly a trace, along with the gas lamp, the horse car and the cigar-store Indian; swept clean not only off the obstreperous burlesque stage but out of the joke book, the comic strip and the fiction magazine as well. . . . The ancient jests have become too stale to laugh at. That the erstwhile alien who served the clown for model now sits in the audience probably takes some of the zest out of the performance. Doubtless, also, his name and the tone of his voice have a soberer ring. The time was when merely to pronounce Rafferty, Dinkelspiel and Cohen was enough to make some older inhabitants smile. Now that Hon. Michael Rafferty presides at the county court house, Mr. Hans Dinkelspiel edits and publishes the local newspaper, and Mr. David Cohen is a leading business man in town, they are somewhat feeble stuff for vaudeville. Most devastating of all to the comic sense, the younger Allens, Lowells and Eliots have grown up together with the junior Raffertys, Dinkelspiels and Cohens, have gone to the same public schools and played on the same teams. Their funny bone was dulled from birth. They cannot even become hilarious over some newer arrivals in the neighbourhood, such as the Palotellis and the Stanowskys.[13]

[13] *The Interpreter,* February, 1926.

The worst caricatures of racial character, as we have seen, are not always found on the public stage but often in private entertainments—sometimes under the auspices of organizations that do not have the faintest notion of the propagandist nature or effect of these entertainments.

This is not the place to review particular plays from this point of view, but it is interesting to note that different parts of the country will judge differently as to the influences of specific plays, according to the nature of their own situations and tendencies. For example, a southern group of participants in the present study, who condemn Eugene O'Neill's "All God's Chillun Got Wings" (for a sympathetic representation of interracial social contact which has brought similar condemnation from other parts of the country also) share the strong feeling of their section against *all* racial intermarriage and, for this reason, also condemn "Abie's Irish Rose." On the other hand, the more current verdict of that almost miraculously successful play seems to be that it makes for greater harmony between groups—in fact that the long run of this play and its large crop of imitative productions is directly due to the fact that it has caught on to a new mood of tolerance not previously made use of on the American stage in so popular a form.

The whole subject of the influences on group attitudes exercised by dramatic presentations deserves careful study. The impressiveness of the play is, for obvious reasons, even greater than that of the moving picture. Here real people are seen to express themselves, often with inciting passion, in situations that are recognized as falling somewhere within the orb of the individual spectator's present or potential life experiences. Why it is—but it seems to be an unquestioned fact—that Shylock leaves a deeper impression as a racial type than Othello, we do not know. We do know why it is that in the modern comedy colored actors occasionally may appear in the character of a servant but never in that of one of the leading figures—and we also know how this perpetuates in the average mind the association between color and social status. We also know that a certain type of play has contributed to the current misunderstanding, if not fear, of the Oriental. On the other hand, why are Negroes commonly banned from worthy participation in the caste of serious plays when they are welcomed as, probably, unique entertainers in musical shows? Do we not here have merely an embodiment, in modern form, of the doctrine that it is contrary to the social mores to take seriously a member of one of the lower castes, but that it is perfectly proper to employ him to amuse?

Though not directly connected with the stage, one form of entertainment must be especially mentioned as a cause of much racial prejudice: the presentation of more or less primitive tribes in the performance of their native dances and ceremonies. There are dignified shows of that sort—one recalls, for example, an open-air performance of an Indian troup to the words of Longfellow's Hiawatha that made the round of the country some years ago. But too often these performances are both degrading and misleading. First of all, the ceremonies of the African, Indian, Singhalese or Arab group are in themselves exaggerated in the direction of primitiveness. War dances are performed that may have a faint resemblance to the genuine thing but which are tuned up to what an American or West-European audience expects of wildness (again a matter of compensation, largely, for the lack of excitement in their own lives). Moreover, these shows are often associated with a circus. (Barnum and Bailey at one time took a magnificent Bedouin camp all over the world alongside their ordinary show.) The chief of a tribe, comparable to the respected head of one's own local government, appears as a circus performer to do his stunt. The medicine-man, comparable to the head of one's church, appears as a sort of conjurer. The religion of the tribe is dragged into the dirt—in so far as it is visibly represented —as for example, nearly always in the case of Arab or Indian or Mohammedan performers. Its private and domestic life is opened to the public view in the form of a caricature of the real thing. A particularly insidious association occurs when these shows are held—as is so often the case especially in the cities of Europe— in a zoological garden where the railed-in camp of the "children of nature" suggests to the youthful mind a close analogy between their character and that of the wild animals in their adjoining yards. Indeed, often the animals of their native landscape—wild and domestic—form part of the ethnological exhibit, and so the sense of relationship is reenforced.

Even more frequent than exhibitions of this sort are, of course, the lesser exhibitions of wild men at country fairs. Grown-up people may know that neither the racial nor the personal character of these viciously snarling strangers corresponds to the barker's description of it. But children do not know; and the man-eating Bushman will for long remain in his imagination the typical Australian native when he is merely a harmless colored man from Tennessee, who longs for the barbecue of his native town. Another educationally bad exhibit is the ball-throwing game in which a Negro puts his head in and out of a series of holes in a wooden background and the player attempts to hit it with a hard baseball—three throws for a nickel. This degrading type of game fosters the erroneous impression that, somehow, the colored man is of different physical make from the white and does not feel pain in the same way.

We have so far confined ourselves to those type of plays, performances and public games which children are likely to witness. What about their own play-acting? Left to themselves, children will reproduce in their play what they have heard and read and seen. In other words, when undesirable racial attitudes show themselves in their imitative games, this is only secondary evidence of undesirable impressions absorbed somewhere or other. So much has been written on this subject that we need not go into it here in any detail. It is worth pondering, however, how many occasions are missed, occasions when the play activities of children might be utilized to produce mutual appreciation between members of different national and racial groups. Occasionally, a natural disregard of racial differences in the games and plays thought out by children is frowned upon and actively discouraged by their elders to whom these divisions represent important social factors. Such an incident is reported by a colored social worker, as follows:

In the Junior High School of C. there are as many colored pupils as there are white. A short while ago, the teachers arranged a play in which several of the children were to take part. Some of the important parts were assigned by the teachers to colored children. After rehearsals had progressed for some time, the principal ordered that the parts be recast; only one colored girl was kept in the play, and she was assigned to the part of maid to one of the white girls who was cast for a special part. When the parents of the colored children discovered what had happened, they protested to the principal who said that the parents of the white children had objected to having their children in the play on equal terms with colored children. There had never been any sign of the white children themselves objecting to having colored children in the play.

Since this incident, there have been several unpleasant situations.

One might be mentioned as an outgrowth of the incident described: The school has a baseball team of which it is very proud. The principal catcher was a colored boy, and two or three other colored boys were on the team. When the team played a neighboring school, not one of the colored boys was in the line-up.

6. Toys and Games

It has been observed that white children often are exceptionally fond of dark dolls, whether in the form of caricatures—golliwogs —or of real dolls with pretty features. Just now an entirely pretty type of black doll with fuzzy hair, dressed in ordinary baby and small-tot clothes, enjoys a considerable vogue under various trade-names such as "Chocolate Drop." Of course, colored children have always played with white dolls. But too often parents are uneasy at the display of real affection for the dolls that represent the opposite race and endeavor to foster a race pride by insisting that they be assigned secondary parts in the child's games. Several years ago, when Garveyism was at its height, a Negro firm placed a large order in Germany for colored dolls of a superior type. They at once became very popular, and many concerns, both in Germany and in America, now supply them to a steadily growing market (growing largely, no doubt, owing to the increasing prosperity of American Negroes as well as their increasing race consciousness).[14] During the war dolls dressed in the traditional peasant costumes of many peoples became popular in the general atmosphere of sympathetic interest for small and oppressed nationalities. In this way, a more diversified ethnographic interest was introduced not only in the wealthier private homes but also in the play-rooms of Sunday schools, social settlements and kindergartens and, in a few cases, in the permanent collections of local museums. At the present time, a special effort is under way, under the auspices of the Committee on World Friendship of the Federal Council of Churches, to secure an exchange of dolls between children of different nations—more especially the United States and Japan—dressed in the costume of their countries.[15] Inexpensive Japanese and Chinese porcelain

[14] See p. 103, footnote 11.
[15] An effort such as this seems to be self-defeating when it assumes the character of a diplomatic ceremonial. That this has been the case with this doll exchange is obvious from the report (New York Times, November 26, 1927) that high officials in the Japanese government have collected for official presentation in America elaborately dressed dolls valued at two hundred

dolls had always been available and no doubt have contributed toward the creation of sympathy with the Orient. But it is only where dolls of obviously foreign racial physiognomy are given to children in the sort of clothes which children themselves wear and to which they are accustomed that they are likely to enter into their real affections. Probably it is a mere accident of industrial development that in the past Germany supplied the West with its flaxen-haired, blue-eyed dolls; it would be interesting to know, if this could be ascertained, what influence this simple fact has had upon the growth of our American pro-Nordic prejudice!

Any large toy shop will produce evidence of the expression of race prejudice in other toys and games. The trade is not, of course, responsible for the sentiments that make up an educational by-product of its wares, whether it be a game of skill in which dark-featured figures are the targets or an ornamentation in which Mongolian features are made ridiculous. Its backing often is respectable enough. The following, for example, is one of "Some Favorite Garden Games" recommended by the Children's Encyclopedia:

AUNT SALLY

Aunt Sally is a black doll. She wears a white cap on her head and a white cape on her shoulders, and carries a pipe loosely in her mouth. Her body is only a stick with a pointed end, and when this is pushed into the ground she is ready for the fun to begin. The players stand at a distance of some yards and, each in turn, throw at the pipe with a number of short, stout sticks. Those who knock it out of her mouth the greatest number of times win the game, but those who cannot aim straight must not be surprised if Aunt Sally seems to smile at them.

Miss Mary Chaplin Shute, of Teachers College, Boston, has this to say on the commercial aspect of the matter:

Our toy merchants will cease to present us with "mammies" and "coon dancers" when we adults cease to act as if the race they claim to represent is capable of nothing but serving or amusing the white race. No one objects to a child's love for her Mammy doll, but all thinking people ought to object to a child's unconscious assumption that to wait on "white chillen" is all a Negro woman is fit for.[16]

dollars each to "represent" each of Japan's forty-seven prefectures, six large cities and two colonies, and that the director of the Bureau of General Education of Japan accompanied the shipment of these dolls for their exhibition at the City Hall in San Francisco.

[16] *Childhood Education* for February, 1926, p. 273.

7. Ceremonials

Public parades and ceremonials offer opportunities for displaying the interdependence of peoples and races of which we rarely take sufficient advantage. Liberal use of the French flag was made, for example, in association with the American, in decorative schemes to celebrate the successful exploit of Colonel Lindbergh; but except in one of the colonel's own speeches, there was not sufficient recognition for the variety of contributions from different countries that had made his transatlantic flight possible. Again, while the army and navy often get the lion's share in patriotic parades, these serve but rarely to make us aware of the multitude of racial and national influences that have made America what it is. On this point Miss Shute says:

We still need to give concrete emphasis to the bravery of our soldiers and to the significance of our country's institutions through pictures, songs and stories, and the creation of monuments; but it surely can be done without stress on war as in itself noble, and without the type of blatant glorification of our country which inevitably throws contempt on every other. Pictures of the brave soldiers and fine public buildings of other countries, and a stirring parade in which many of our "playfellows'" flags were carried alongside Old Glory might do more than we realize to help our little folks to take some of the first steps toward the much-desired goal of "international thinking." [17]

In other words, the emphasis here as in other things is not on desirable omissions, on less of stimulants to patriotism, but rather on the addition of elements which would purify the love of country and the pride of race by giving it the proper setting of appreciation for greatness, virtue, skills, wherever these may appear in our world.

It is generally assumed that plays and ceremonials in which children take part as representative of different races and peoples make for greater international and interracial appreciation and friendship. Many people hold this view quite uncritically and without a grasp of the difference which the kind of representation of each group must necessarily make educationally.[18] For example, there may be an artificial separation and group classifica-

---

[17] *Childhood Education* for February, 1926, p. 275.

[18] This shortsightedness is very similar to that signified earlier in the chapter on Sunday Schools (p. 183 *et seq.*) as regards the intended and the real effect of some of the texts and pictures in use.

tion when, as a matter of fact, the children of the different groups in their ordinary activities think of themselves as a single class or school. One correspondent says:

These things foster orthodox customs and uphold racial feeling. On the other hand, organized recreation and especially association at camp help to break down prejudice.

Another, a high-school teacher, is merely doubtful as regards results. He says:

Ceremonies, plays and the like give liberals a pleasant thrill. But it takes more than an occasional get-together. I am very sceptical of the permanent influence of joint-religious meetings, of Jew-Gentile church interchanges, union services, joint banquets, etc. They do no harm, they influence a few—but it takes more than that. You may say, "everything helps," but that is not the issue. I would answer: Give us a national policy for reducing racial and religious friction. If we rely upon private resources, we are insincere in our faith. I feel no solution is possible so long as we have colored schools, Catholic schools, and public schools tinged largely with Protestantism. I want parochial and racial schools abolished. I want children together.

Others, though they do not express themselves as forcibly, on the whole share this point of view. They feel that ceremonies and pageants to emphasize oneness are empty gestures—and felt by the children to be such—when they stand out against systematic segregation in every-day life. On the other hand, the extent to which people can become oblivious to segregations sanctioned by tradition and public opinion is extraordinary:

An international pageant was observed on a playground to which colored children were never admitted; but some of these got near enough to watch it over the railing. No one in that neighborhood seemed to recognize anything incongruous in the situation.

Similar efforts at dramatic education with a higher age group, at college, often meet with resentment on the part of the students. On one recent occasion a group of Chinese students refused to go on the stage in old Mandarin costumes because, they said, what they needed was more recognition of their real, present-day interests by their fellow-students, not more recognition of their difference of background. A South African student at a large university voiced the feelings of many when he objected to being continually "toted around" with Canadians and other Colonials as a member of "the British Group"; he had enrolled in the institution as a student, he said, not as an exhibit.

But there is an even greater danger in many dramatic enterprises of the kind under review. Too often they engender not international friendship but unmitigated snobbery. "America," in the person of the oldest or prettiest or most popular pupil, drapes the Star-spangled Banner around the lesser nations of the world, as though to protect the poor dears. Or children dressed up as American missionaries enter the jungle and cure all the ills of a Hindu community—which is represented as without the slightest vestige of a civilization of its own. The Negro boy who always thought of himself as an American, suddenly is forced to appear half-naked as an "African." A Chinese group, children of respectable parents, are made conscious of the failings of their nation in the matter of opium indulgence or superstition.

Always, without exception almost, native American children— especially those of "Nordic" ancestry, are given an intensive feeling of the superiority of their own group over the other groups. They are reminded, possibly, of the duties they owe other peoples, but never of their own humble racial history—so recent, alas, when measured by truly historical standards. We have yet to come across the pageant in which a British-colonial group is made up in part of convicts and indentured servants, or a scene representing the true native background of other early continental settlers.

Very different, both in feeling and in influence, are those efforts that are now increasingly being made to have children of foreign parentage produce dramatic masterworks of their own nation. Here the selection of a handful of pupils because of their Italian parentage, let us say, is not arbitrary or derogatory to their dignity as future American citizens but, properly handled, gives them and their national group a deserved glory and recognition in the eyes of their fellow pupils as contributors of distinctive cultural values. Such plays may make children aware for example, that the Italian immigrants carry in their blood something of the glory that was Rome. On another occasion they realize, as they did not realize before, that the great figures of the Old Testament are not extinct in line but that little Moe and little Isidore, so far from belonging to a second grade of American families, really are aristocrats by as much right as the little boy who traces his descent to the *Mayflower*. These relationships are made dramatic and become effective influences on group attitudes —but only, this cannot be too often stated, when the educational project is worked out with full consideration of all its secondary learnings.

This involves, for example, a selection of heroes in international pageantry from the point of view, not of their outstanding racial significance and character, but from that of their most inclusive human significance and character. Not the Russian peasant but Tolstoy, not the Indian coolie but Mahatma Gandhi, not the drink-sodden denizen of the Glasgow slums but Sir Walter Scott are figures which the American child must visualize instantaneously when Russians, Indians, Scots are named if his reaction is to be appreciative in the highest sense. Of course, there are many degrees between the highest and lowest personifications of peoples. And no hard and fast rule can take the place of tactful selection of material in relation to the specific psychological situation.[19]

Another danger, too often not even thought of, is the use of a pageant to stress a totally superficial community of interest as between different national groups in American life.[20]

Instead of stressing an unreal and materialist individualism through which each American, after shedding all his Old-World associations, becomes purged as it were of his separateness and becomes a full-fledged "one-hundred-per-center," a pageant can point to the actual cultural wealth which this country enjoys owing to the diversity of its constituent populations—a very different thing from merely insisting on either likenesses or unlikenesses.[21]

8. MUSIC

Though incidental reference has already been made to the subject, it is necessary to add to our catalogue of recreational influences on race relations a special word about music. Foreign sounds, it would appear, arouse more fear than foreign sights. The visible physical strangeness, after all, is only partial; and only

[19] See some pertinent remarks by George Becht, at that time of the Pennsylvania State Board of Education, in *Americanization Handbook* (1917, p. 232).

[20] This has been tellingly illustrated by Walter Lippmann in *Public Opinion* (1922, p. 86).

[21] Edwin Greenlaw, *The New Significance of the Community Pageant* (War Information Series, No. 16, University of North Carolina, 1918, p. 16).

the youngest children are without similar earlier experiences that help to range the new phenomenon into the general cosmos of their known world. Not so with sound. The weird music of the Chinese flute or the African tom-tom stands by itself as a new experience; and only a sight of its source makes it understandable. Hence, the incidental "native" music tends to heighten the sense of difference from the tribal group on exhibition; and the deliberate wildness of the rhythms that accompany the introduction of the wild man from the antipodes or the showing of the film of aboriginal life strengthens the impressions of savagery which, of course, the performance is intended to convey.

On the other hand, foreign music—and most often vocal music —when properly transcribed into the familiar language of European-American musical art, tends to make for sympathetic appreciation. A Turkish march as conceived by Mozart, Chinese motives as transformed by Vincent d'Indy, American-Indian tunes as worked up by Edward A. MacDowell provide an esthetic pleasure which rebounds to the credit of the race that is supposed to have contributed it. Exactly the same effect is produced, of course, by fake national music, as in so many Arab love songs, oriental dances, and the like—so long as the deception lasts. It is not so much awareness to the artistry of these compositions, however, that creates the attitude of sympathetic interest as awareness to its common humanity. The music must, therefore, not be too remote from the recognized musical forms; and the sentiments it expresses must not be too remote from those commonly experienced. Dance rhythms must invite to dance. Themes must not be too much repeated except with pleasantly stimulating variation; different parts of the composition must be recognizably set apart. For example, in the original form Japanese string music, one of the world's finest products of musical imagination and artistry, according to some of the most advanced of western musicians, falls as a strange and hideous medley of noises upon less educated western ears and so contributes nothing at all to sympathetic understanding.

Apart from the influence of music on the widening of appreciation, we also have to consider the words associated with it. Reference has already been made to certain dramatic developments from the group singing of slaves on American plantations. But apart from the minstrel group, the plantation "darkey" ballad and the city Negro's "coon song" also have had an independent development through the printed music sheet and the victrola record. It is only in recent years—and this, very largely, because of its enthusiastic reception in Europe where the American form of race prejudice did not exist—that the greatest musical contribution of the Negro, the spiritual, has found appreciation among us. But the kind of music that did not involve any need to take the Negro seriously always has been popular in America. What interests us in the present connection is the fact that, though it originated with the American Negro, the light, amusing music of dance and song became one of the factors that keep down the opinion that white America has of the Negro race. Presumably the words written or sung by the earlier Negro singers themselves tended to be derogatory of the mental and moral character of their own race—as, of course, humorous ditties usually are; but the vast production of "coon" songs by white musicians was far worse, for they recognized no lower limits at all to permissible forms of derogation. Reputable college songbooks will contain such songs as "Kemo Kimo," "Some Folks Say a Nigger Won't Steal," and worse. Let the reader to whom considerations of this sort are strange imagine for a moment a popular song book used widely in British homes in which the American is held up to scorn and ridicule!

To what extent derisive songs of this sort are balanced by appreciative songs that bring close the common humanity of the Negro—as in "Swanee River" or in "Old Black Joe"—it would be difficult to say. There has always been appreciation for the Negro lullaby because it recalled to white children the pleasant memories of their "mammies," and because motherhood does not evoke thoughts of animosity. Thus, even modern songs of this nature, such as Ethelbert Nevins' "Mighty Lak a Rose," are popular.

But there is a new race consciousness among American Negroes that makes them frown upon the wide appreciation of songs that paint the Negro, while sympathetically, yet within too narrow limits of social status. They consider the rendering of dialect overdone. An increasing number of them object to songs that portray human beauty or virtue as necessarily white—as for example in the well-known gospel song, "Wash Me and I Shall Be Whiter Than Snow."

A New England contributor to this study, widely known as a pioneer in the movement for wholesome recreation, writes with reference to objections of the kind mentioned in this section that "songs hurt as much as they help the cause of race harmony." On the other hand, the movement to make better known the folk songs of other nations, started during the war, has made great strides and unquestionably has made for international appreciation.

Special collections of songs of different nations for children almost always dwell on themes that give pleasure, are edited in such a way as to make the tunes easy to grasp, and therefore do contribute toward better international and interracial understanding. Educational effort in this direction has been exceptionally intelligent and successful.

CHAPTER XVII

SOME UNDERLYING PROBLEMS

After having surveyed the parts played by home, school, church, and other environments upon the race attitudes of children, we shall summarize in the remainder of this section some of the influences which different factors have in common, so that we may more fully understand the nature and the limits of the educational task before us.

It may be contended that the picture so far presented has been too dark, and that the child's environment contains far more influences that make for intelligent interest in strangers, for appreciation of differences, and for a sense of justice as between strong and weak individuals and groups than have been described. But this book is not primarily intended to give a "fair" picture of the situation for general informative purposes. Its aim is to clarify the problem in such a way as to set out in high relief those aspects of the situation that seem to call for purposeful social and educational engineering. The arrangement of the book, therefore, somewhat departs from that of most textbooks in that each step of the discussion creates the incentive for the next, and in that the procedure as a whole represents a dialectic progression from the recognition of an evil to suggestions, even common agreements, as to effective or promising remedies.

To recall our progress thus far: In the first section we reviewed the attitudes which children have been observed to display at different ages toward members of ethnic groups other than their own. We did not at that point attempt to explain these attitudes or to estimate their relative prevalence. In fact, we set out to present, in the main, those race attitudes in children that give concern to public-spirited parents, teachers, social workers, and others. In the second section, we endeavored to get behind the seemingly obvious explanations—which often are incorrectly stated—to the major sources of the attitudes found. Thus we obtained a picture of the part played by personal experience, in the narrower sense of the word, and that played by other influences. In the third part, the present section, we have reviewed some of the ways in which race attitudes are actually taught, whether intentionally or unintentionally, through the influences that are brought to bear on the social education of the child. Here we surveyed the fields of concern rather than the situation as a whole; and for this reason our picture may in places seem an unduly pessimistic one.

Before we can proceed to the next part of our study in which we shall endeavor more systematically to consider the solutions to many of the problems raised—solutions which, for the most part, are already exemplified in actual life—it is necessary in two further chapters to summarize and discuss those underlying factors that make up a common task for parents and teachers.

We may begin by asking all the various interested parties the same question:

What Are Children Made to Feel?

What are children made to feel they will lose, or gain, by free association with children of other racial or national groups? The answers to this question will give us the background of parental and educational intentions against which to set a summary account of what actually happens in their minds. Unfortunately only a minority of the correspondents have addressed themselves to this question.

The New Jersey parents' group, looking upon their own actions in the light of these questions, found occasion for self-criticism:

In the majority of instances, the children are not made to feel that they are given *anything* by free association with children of other races. It is America's shame that her training, even in the public schools, and especially in the private schools, tends more and more to exclusion. Most children of the exclusive group are made to feel that they will lose social prestige by free association.

The southern settlement group comes to similar adverse conclusions:

Children are made to feel that they will lose their standing with their own family and friends. They are also afraid that they will lose pride in their own people. Where they are made to feel that they will gain by such association, it is chiefly for personal gain, often with a selfish motive.

One report puts special blame on mothers who, in teaching their children, insist overmuch on the loss of cultural advantages, manners, and morals through association with children of other groups. Another says:

Children are taught that they will lose their coveted social position in their own group if they are seen too often in free association with members of the other group. They should be made to feel, instead, that they would gain in their knowledge of people, that their own culture might be enhanced by the valuable contributions of their foreign-born neighbors, and that their loss of petty, narrow social relations would result in the larger social vision of human brotherhood.

A college student writes: My father, being a country doctor, often took me with him on his rounds when I was a child. I was especially interested in his colored patients and felt very kindly and sympathetic towards them. Once, at a large celebration at a local park, I wished to take in my arms a cute little colored baby who was there with its mother. My best girl friend, a neighbor's daughter, exclaimed in horror when I voiced my intention, "If you take that child, I'll not be seen with you." So I had to stifle my natural impulse.

This may be an exceptional case, though, in view of previous criticism, it is worth remembering that other correspondents also lay emphasis on attitudes taken by children, not only from grown-ups but from older children or those of their own age.[1]

The educational difficulties which often arise from the child's free associations outside the home cover, of course, a much wider field than that of attitudes on race and nationality. In fact, it is not too much to say that these are merely incidental to that fundamental problem of modern education: the conflict of standards as between the different social influences brought to bear upon the child—the opinion-making efforts of home and church and school and street, and the divisions even within each of these categories. One of the principal causes of unhappy home life is the conflict of desires as to the child's social attitudes, either between the parents or between relatives of two generations. Serious divergence of social standards as between the larger categories of social contacts is now the normal rather than the exceptional condition in an average American community. Social democracy is forever in conflict with exclusiveness along one line or another; and ideals of loyalty to family and church

[1] See George A. Coe, *A Social Theory of Religious Education* (1917, p. 106).

and comrades and country cannot be combined when each of these social groupings has a different objective in demanding loyalty.

What children "are made to feel" concerning the group contacts themselves is a matter of frequent conflict. The school or playground often goes much further than the home in making the child embrace an inclusive ideal of democracy in his personal relations, and the church may give authoritative sanction to friendships entirely at variance with the anxious efforts of the home for maintenance of distinctive group standards.[2]   Again, sometimes school and church are not nearly as liberal in these respects as parents—especially foreign-born parents—who are taking seriously the ideals of American democracy as described in official handbooks for immigrants.   A New York settlement worker writes:

Sometimes children are made to feel that their capacity for charity will be increased by patronizing such and such foreign or Negro group —provided they do not get close enough to "catch some terrible disease" or acquire livestock with which Negro and foreign groups are supposed to be infested.   It is impossible for a child not to associate dark skins with dirt.   Add to this the "onion breath" of the Italians and Jews, and the child gets a physical repulsion which bears out his suspicions.

FALSE ASSOCIATIONS

The last paragraph may serve as an introduction to the major subject of the present chapter, namely the astonishing ways in which complicated associations between concepts seem to take place in the child's mind.   The mental processes by which experiences or isolated bits of information are associated to form generalizations are surprising to the adult—partly, perhaps, because usually he has lost that flexibility and tension of mind that makes them possible, and partly because it is difficult for him to follow in imagination a piecing together of widely separated bits of experience without the large mass of other intervening experiences which in his own case would serve as links between them.   The research of educational psychologists has brought to light much concerning the nature of association that not only

---

[2] For discussion and examples of the associations which different forms of social segregation induce children to make between race and social status, see Chaps. IX and X.

teachers but all who are in contact with children should know.[3]

The reason why children and simple people seem to be making more rapid associations of individual experiences with previous knowledge or impressions is that their mental life is free from those interferences which in the more complicated adult both lengthen the time of reaction and introduce during that time interval deviating associations. The child's associations are healthy, normal, to be expected; and it is we who are surprised by them that are tortuous in our mental associations.[4]

That the associations often are unfortunate is not the fault of the child's mentality, but of the contacts he is permitted to make —including the overhearing of adult talk and the witnessing of unconscious displays of adult attitudes. Even among educated parents the curious notion often prevails that children are blind and deaf except to those sights and sounds that are intended for them. The same mother who brags about the quickness with which her child picks up information will, in an unguarded moment, act or gossip in the child's presence as though he had no apperceptive ability at all. She will, maybe, spend much time in telling stories with a moral lesson—such as kindness to all living beings—and soon after herself in the presence of the child commit an utterly thoughtless, cruel act. And so, not only in the school or on the street but in the home itself, the child meets with those contradictory influences that give so much trouble to those responsible for his social education.

Partly, then, through deliberate efforts to foster certain attitudes, but much more largely through the child's own logic, and contrary to any definite intention on the part of his educators, certain associations between race and social values are created that tend to become stronger as experience accumulates additional seeming evidence around each association, faulty though it may be.

1. Association of Inferiority with Physical Characteristics

The earliest form of such association, which sometimes, as we have seen, occurs even in infancy, is that of agreeable or disagreeable qualities—first seen from a selfish personal point of view,

[3] See the illustrations quoted on p. 104.
[4] See William H. Burnham, *The Normal Mind* (1925, pp. 491, 494, 497, 681).

but later seen as social values—with distinctiveness of physical appearance. A number of examples of this mental process have been given incidentally to the discussion of other phases of our subject. The nature of the association is described in the following contributions of corresponding groups:

A New York discussion group, in connection with the present inquiry, focussed its attention on the question, "Are differences in appearance instinctively felt?" [5] The group disagreed on this matter. A majority felt that differences in color, language, and other racial or national attributes raised an unconscious barrier to full appreciation; but two or three strongly opposed this view. They brought out that the feeling of native white children that children of other races are not equal to them is at least partly due to the fact that they usually are acquainted with those members of the other races that belong to the less cultured groups.

The New Jersey parents' group, which has been repeatedly quoted, writes on this point: The group was quite certain that children absorb from their environment associations of material and moral inferiority with physical characteristics. In the minds of children, and even of adults, skin of another color is somehow associated with the idea of uncleanliness. One teacher said that four students in her class had expressed themselves as quite willing to associate with Japanese, Negroes or Jews "if they were not dirty."

A school teacher in a Cape Cod town complains that she has a great deal of trouble with her pupils because of the presence in the school of Portuguese children. These Portuguese, she says, "are from the Cape Verde Islands off the coast of Africa, and the Negro blood is pretty well distributed among them. The white children think the others are Negroes. I have had such a time making them understand they are not 'darkies' but Portuguese!"

Southerners present at a New York discussion said it was inevitable that the child should associate inherent inferiority with a race very different in appearance when the members of that race always occupy an inferior position. They spoke of the fact that the southern children

[5] Incidentally it may be pointed out in this place—though other quotations from the findings of discussion groups in this volume might serve equally well —that the value of this type of evidence is distinctly lessened by the failure of the participants to distinguish between arguments that can fruitfully be pursued on the basis of their personal experience and those which require recourse to testimony from specialist sources. In the present case, for example, a question of psychological fact is considered that involves disputed theories as to "instinctive" feelings and "unconscious" barriers concerning which there would have to be agreement before the group could speak the same language.

love their mammies but in other respects maintain attitudes which northerners would condemn as "prejudiced." The connection between race and status expresses itself, they said, in the fact that there is practically no dislike of Negroes in the South when and where they occupy lowly positions, but that it becomes marked when and where members of that race rise to social prominence.

How children are impressed with the talk about "dark" people and are apt to associate what is said about them in fairy tales or in other connections with the Negro race, is illustrated by a colored woman who writes:

My family and our neighbors, who are fair in complexion, have living near us a white family with several small children. Evidently these children have been advised that, even though our skin is as fair as theirs, we are entirely different from them and that we shall harm them in some way. One of these children, seeing one of the neighbors on the front steps of her home, looked up at her and said, "You won't hurt us, will you?"

A colored member of a discussion group in Cleveland rather humorously spoke, when this question was reached, about the advantage to members of her race to be seen carrying Spanish books. The suggestion of a possible connection with Spain (or with Latin America) seemed at once to inspire a more neighborly attitude on the part of the whites.

In another discussion, an Indian student at a theological seminary was mentioned who was given a position as supply teacher in a high school. Among the pupils of his class many foreign nationalities were represented. In spite of this fact, the man from India aroused a great deal of curiosity, probably because his skin was very dark and his hair black and smooth. When he first tried to teach his class, he could make no progress because he felt the hostility to his race. But after the novelty had worn off, the pupils discovered that they had a very fine and interesting teacher.

The peculiar twist by which, in the very effort of trying to impart to children desirable habits and moral attitudes, parents and teachers again and again do the exact opposite has been illustrated by many examples in previous chapters. Here, because it shows how a false association in the grown-up world is often handed on from generation to generation, note may be taken of a particularly striking instance:

Children, a "Magazine for Parents," has made its appearance in 1926, with the avowed object of helping parents in the many trying tasks of bringing up children. With an imposing array of editors, consultants and advisory editors, this magazine, among other things, occasionally deals with the subject of children's attitudes. Yet, in a story published by that magazine in April, 1927, the inference is plainly intended that a colored skin is a particularly dirty one. The illustration to this story (p. 27), in which a little blond girl, dressed in white, is seen kissing a ragged colored child, is captioned: "Mary Ellen perpetrates her ultimate hygienic atrocity." The question is, why could she not have perpetrated it on a dirty, *white* urchin? And the answer is that popular opinion requires the portrayal of the "ultimate" in personal uncleanliness with Negro features, and this with no justification whatsoever.

Several correspondents point out how much more effective than anything "said" in creating associations between color and inferiority on the child's mind is the actual fact of discrimination which he observes in his immediate environment:

I know white mothers who are perfectly willing to have colored nurse-maids to help them care for their children during the latters' most tender and impressionable years, but are scandalized at the idea of colored teachers in the public schools. According to them it is quite all right for a child of four or five to be put under the influence of a mediocre and frequently rather undesirable type of colored girl, but quite horrifying for an older child to be carefully taught by a thoroughly prepared, well-educated, finer type of Negro. I fail to see either the good sense or logic of such an attitude. Even more untenable is the position of those who prefer colored maids in a household, but resent the idea of colored stenographers or of colored trained nurses.[6]

The following quotation shows in an interesting way how an association once formed is brought to bear by the child on new information presented to him, sometimes to the utter puzzlement of adults who do not know the stages of association through which some startling concept or judgment has come about:

Some time ago in North Carolina I was called upon to give some educational tests in our County Training School which represents the best of our rural and small-town schools in this state. These were merely to examine the progress which the children in the upper grades were making in silent reading and fundamentals of Arithmetic, but they brought sharply to my attention evidence of attitudes of thinking which I claim are prevalent and dangerous.

Monroe's Silent Reading Test has a paragraph worded about as fol-

[6] Quoted from *Haldeman-Julius Weekly* in *The Crisis*, April 1927, p. 57.

lows: "Aladdin was the son of a poor tailor. He lived in Peking, the capital city of China. He was always idle and lazy and liked to play better than to work. What kind of boy do you think he was? Indian —Negro—Chinese—French or Dutch?" The child was to show how well he had read and retained the meaning of the paragraph by underscoring the proper word.

At the first school tested, many of the children underscored the word "Negro," and in scoring the test such a response would have merely been rejected as wrong and showing that the child to that extent lacked ability in reading. But! Many of the rest of the responses testing ability to understand even more complex paragraphs were correct!

I was puzzled. At the second school visited I was still more puzzled by a similar reaction on the part of many of the students, some of whom I knew personally to be bright and above the average. At the close of the test I called on one fine, bright boy about twelve years old and asked him why he thought Aladdin was a Negro. Without hesitation he looked into my face and frankly said, "Because he was lazy." There you have it!

At all the other schools I gave slips of paper to all the children and asked them to tell me why they answered question Number — as they had. I still have some of those slips of paper which gave me such naïve and frank replies discovering to me the existence of a fact that I may have suspected but conclusive evidence of which I never had had before.

The following are typical of the replies which they wrote for me: "Because Negroes like to play better than to work." "Because most Negroes are lazy." "Because Negroes do not like to work." "Because most Negroes are poor," etc.

Here were bright children, many of them in some of the best schools, who so frankly accepted certain popular beliefs unfavorable to the group that they simply could not make the very obviously proper response to a simple paragraph that included the word "Negro." [7]

2. *Association of Inferiority with National Origin*

There is no agreement as to whether this type of association is as widespread as association of inferiority with physical characteristics. Obviously, it is at a more advanced age that children become aware of differences between their own nationality and others in those things which one may either take pride in or be ashamed of. We have seen how varied are the influences that give children an opinion about some other group. Usually a number of such influences are exerting pressure in the same direc-

[7] William Albert Robinson in *The Crisis* for April, 1924, p. 275.

tion: Differences in physical appearance, even if only slight, are accentuated by foreign speech; and a natural sense of strangeness is reenforced by what one learns about the other's religious affiliation, his political views, or the history of his country. The difficulty of distinguishing between these factors in the child's association between foreign race or nationality and social inferiority is brought out by a teacher who writes:

A solitary, stupid Negro will lead children to say that all Negroes are pretty dumb. Children look upon Jews as smart, but resent seeing too many honors "copped" by them. Those who cannot speak English are considered ignorant. If the foreigner is also dirty, so much the worse for the child's impression.

A specialist in child psychology says:

If a child is once told that because a man is black he is inferior, he will constantly associate with any person of this color inability to do certain things that can be done by members of his own group. In the same way, children learn to associate inferiority with the country from which these same groups have come. The fact that these people may have been slaves at some time in their history gives them the idea that all people hailing from that country are of the same origin and therefore unable to rule themselves.

The southern settlement group reports, rather cryptically:

Armenians are sympathized with because of war publicity. Polish people are always referred to as inferior because of their checkered history as victors and vanquished. Americans are looked up to because of their history and political organization.

The New Jersey parents say:

Association of inferiority with the countries of certain racial groups is very general among American children. The parents felt that this was due to the fact that children in the majority of cases see only the lowest classes of foreign races. It was the opinion of the group that such associations came chiefly through personal experience on the part of children.

I was born in a small Ohio town, writes a student. During my early childhood I had never seen a foreigner. I had seldom heard them mentioned, but when I did they were referred to as "dagos," "hunks" or "wops." Stories have been told me concerning a group of Italians who had been given permission to go into a clover field and had eaten all the clover blossoms. Also, I had been told that they lived almost wholly upon bread and molasses.

Some few years later, I lived in a town close to a railroad. During one summer a crew of small, dark-skinned Italians camped just south of town. Each day they would carry loaves of bread and molasses from the store to their camp. I was almost convinced that all foreigners were a lowly class of people who lived on almost nothing. I felt that these men, who could live so cheaply, were taking work away from my friends.

During my early college days I became acquainted with some foreign students who were trying to get an education. They were working hard and seemed to have the same difficulties I had. Later when I was in Christian work I came in contact with many foreigners. Many of them were hard-working people, and many were trying to be real Americans. Many of them were living on as high a plane as the working class of Americans in the same town.

I met, worked with and associated with hundreds of foreigners. But if the word "foreigner" is now mentioned there flashes into my mind the picture of those small Italian workmen who lived on bread and molasses

A contributor who for some years was a kindergartner in a public school in the vicinity of New York contributes the following detailed account in illustration of the association between inferiority and country of origin that may be implanted in children early in life:

We had in our kindergarten children from twenty-nine language races, with a slight preponderance of Italians and Germans, in two groups totalling over one hundred. At that time I had the younger group of children, i.e., those from four to six years of age. Two boys came together there who had never known each other until a few days before coming to school since one of the families had just moved into the neighborhood. One of these, the older, was Italian, and the other, *if I recall correctly*, was Bohemian.[8] The Italian child was swift in his action, keenly intelligent, quick to learn, and exceedingly hot-tempered. He was handicapped by speaking no English and being thrown with a large group of children most of whom had never been in kindergarten before and amongst whom many native tongues were spoken. The younger boy was phlegmatic, slow to pick up ideas even from sign lan-

[8] In a later interview the correspondent admitted that the parentage of the child may have been Jugo-Slav, which would better explain the antagonism described.

guage, physically slow to act, given to observing rather than doing what the other children were doing.

The older boy, in spite of speaking only Italian, announced in reply to the Italian question "What is your name?"—"Jeemie." We called him Jim. The younger child for many days refused to answer to his name, which I have now forgotten, and held himself isolated from the group.

Suddenly one day when the fifty children were gathered in a circle seated in small chairs, and when for a second my back was toward the child whom I could clearly see in the large mirror over the piano which I faced, Jim made a sudden dash across the diameter of the circle and before I could reach him was vigorously tearing the hair out of the other youngster's head. When I sought to find out what the trouble was, and got another child to interpret my English questions in Italian, Jim's sullen reply was, "He called me dago." This was the beginning of a long feud between these two youngsters which lasted throughout that six months' term, through the following summer and came back into the kindergarten next fall. It seemed to be quite a mutual affair. On one occasion I recall that Jim came "armed to the teeth," and in the course of the usual "quiet time" when all the children had their hands down on the table feigning sleep and actually relaxing under the influence of soft music, Jim rushed around the whole hollow square of tables in order to attack the other boy with a quite formidable knife which he had purloined from his mother's kitchen. His gesture and the force of his blow were sufficient to have done real damage had not my assistant been within hands' reach of the child he attacked. In fact, we had to keep constant watch of these two children all the time they were in kindergarten lest James harm the other one. Always the attack came from him and not always could either of the teachers find out what was the spark which started these attacks. Gradually the virulence of the attacks wore down under the social pressure of disapproval from teachers and from other children, this seeming to have much more effect than any amount of punishment for the boy.

In the course of the first six months I made numerous visits to both families to try to ascertain the background of the children's antagonism and found that there was a family antagonism which extended to vocal reprisals from one back balcony to another, to door yard fights between the mothers, to threats between the fathers, and even the neighborhood siding with one or the other of the families in their arguments. Intelligent mothers in the neighborhood told me freely that it was the common opinion that the actual incidents that caused the scraps were never enough to amount to anything, that the two families hated each other because one was Italian and the other Bohemian, and that it was an absolutely unreasoning race prejudice. When after I had had no contact with the children throughout the summer, they came back into the kindergarten, I soon noticed that there was an aggravation of antagonism, that apparently much of the effect of social pressure during the previous fall had worn off, that as the children were growing older their antagonism was growing bolder. Naturally I was curious to see whether this same antagonism extended to other races insofar as these two boys were concerned. It did not seem to be so with either. What I did notice, however, was that the Bohemian boy gradually learned to recognize other Italian children in the kindergarten as Italians and, though his antagonism to them was mostly sullenness and not accompanied by flashes of anger as when for instance Jim got in his way in playing a game, he still seemed to have no use for any Italian children. And his most frequently spoken American word for many months was "dago." I never could find out where he got the term. Jim, on the other hand, because of sheer personality, soon won over the kindergarten children as a group out of their original fear because of his temper and his use of fists and other weapons, to a grudging admiration and later to a very great appreciation of his leadership.

Before the end of the second term I had found a real field for Jim's activities through his quality of leadership and finally made him so feel his responsibility for the group that it was possible for me to leave the fifty children working busily under Jim's direction or supervision, go to the school office—a distance of about two blocks because of our large building—transact some small item of routine and return to find the group atmosphere entirely undisturbed, every child busily happy and even the little Bohemian child quietly lost in the group. I felt quite triumphant when by the end of the second term I had aroused in Jim a sense of personal responsibility for developing certain powers in the Bohemian child. I even found it possible to get Jim to take the Bohemian child off to a corner of the room, work with him possibly on some handwork problem, leave him and come back to him, and in general take the big-brother attitude toward the child. By this time most of the Bohemian boy's sullenness had worn off and he seemed to have absorbed the group attitude toward Jim, at least to the point of tolerance, though I never could detect any evidence of admiration or particular loyalty on his part as I did on the part of many other children.

I have never been able to adequately explain this incident. It typifies more or less the thing I was constantly observing as a kindergartner among foreign children. I never saw so strong a case as this one, though I must have handled between 2,000 and 3,000 children in the course of my teaching. Always in the early days of the mingling together of a new group of these foreign-speaking children, most of whom were second or third generation foreigners even though their tongue was foreign, I found all sorts of evidences of antagonism which at least seemed to me to be racial. These I found flourished as the term proceeded, sometimes growing more acute because of unpleasant personal qualities in some child originally disliked because he was a "dago," a "dutchie," etc., sometimes wearing away because the child possessed a fascinating personality or was able to do more or do something better than the other children. Always I was able to trace in the more acute cases of antagonism the influence of the family use of terms of opprobrium, or in the family scraps of parents or older children. I found that my whole bag of tricks and my whole knowledge of social psychology stood helpless often in specific cases until I had gotten the mother into the mothers' club, and had made the unhappy child proud of her by praising her fine cake, admiring some beautiful piece of handwork or in some other way getting the group of other children's mothers to recognize the unhappy child's mother.

The following incident illustrates the reflection of such associations between nationality and moral qualities upon members of the group subject to such mistaken identities:

Naideh, the only Turkish girl employed as a member of the staff by a certain American organization in Turkey, was beloved by all the girls and adults with whom she was associated. One day a large sum of money was stolen from the office while four of the native members of the staff, including Naideh, were in the office. Several days went on, and as the money did not return, the matter had passed. Naideh, whom we would have trusted in any situation, came to the director and gave her the amount of money which was stolen. She had not taken it—that we all knew—but she said: "If you do not take this money I shall leave. I was in the office when it was taken; it was due to my carelessness, and besides all the others think I took it—for I am a Turk." [9]

3. Association of Inferiority with Foreign Habits

Half-way between associations of values with physical appearance and with what is known or surmised as regards national origin are those associations that have to do with language and manners, clothes, diet, forms of recreation, and other aspects of culture. Here the personal experience of the child counts for much because it is in significant details of difference that the

[9] Prof. Bogardus has collected retrospective reconstructions of associations of this type on the part of students, three of which happen to relate to Turks. *Journal of Applied Sociology,* January-February, 1926, p. 220.

strangeness of members of another group is recognized as such. Peculiarities, whether they stimulate fear or ridicule, are combined in the child's imagination into new fictional culture patterns; he reconstructs for himself a picture of a group or a people from the little that has come to his attention. Often, however, the secondary knowledge that comes from reading and teaching and from the absorption of adult attitudes is woven together with the results of personal observation into a pattern which, thus made the more complete, also is the more firmly fastened and the more difficult to correct by later and better knowledge.

IIere is a typical example, which shows this combination of personal observation and hearsay in a single imaginary picture of a group:

Deborah had, with great interest, been watching the gardener set out trees. When she came in, she blew her nose, to her mother's consternation, without using her handkerchief. "Why, Deborah," asked the mother, "what made you do a thing like that?" "I saw Tony do it," replied the child. "But, Deborah, only dirty Italians do nasty things like that."

Some time later, Deborah heard her mother discuss with friends the influx of Italians in the neighborhood. "Oh, I know about Italians," interrupted Deborah, "they are people who blow their noses without handkerchiefs."

Attitudes to those speaking a foreign language, according to a number of answers that deal with the matter, seem to be quite similar to the attitudes aroused by strange habits, clothes, etc., eliciting fear in very young children, chiefly ridicule in those somewhat older and, perhaps, a more virulent dislike later.

A member of the Cleveland discussion group formed a minority of one in insisting that children are not nearly as much prejudiced by differences of skin color as they are by differences of language. She had proved this to her own satisfaction, she said, on a recent trip to Europe. While in Germany, her four-year-old son was full of fears because he could not understand the language, and he still feels resentful against having to hear languages he does not know. Other members of the group, while admitting a childish dislike of foreign languages, attributed this to a dislike of differences in ways of thinking. American children, they say, create inferiority complexes in other children by ridiculing their language; children like to be like others and do not even want to think differently. Indeed, they do not like to be singled out for any reason. One member remembered how deeply mortified she was when the school superintendent picked her out in class for recognition because he knew her father.

Differences in dialect are effective because they mark a person off not only as an outsider but, often, as one belonging to a distinct, inferior social class. This is perhaps more marked in foreign countries with their larger class and geographical stability (*vide* George Bernard Shaw's *Pygmalion*) but is very obvious also in a typical old New England community—where the "old" families speak a pure English while immigrants speak modern American—and, of course, in the South.

A little boy, reports a Pennsylvania woman, says: "Grannie, you talk just like the colored people. They say, 'for keeps,' white people always say 'to keep.'" That in this young mind there had taken place a threefold association between class, race and idiom was made clear on other occasions when this boy and his small sister refused to eat with the maids or reproved their mother for washing dishes.

As for association of inferiority with strange customs, a colored man of good standing who holds several degrees from prominent universities states that he dislikes the Chinese to this day because when he was a boy he was told that the Chinese ate rats. (See also the comment of boys given, p. 139 *et seq.*)

A group of pupil-teachers, coming to this point in their discussion, agreed on the finding that there is no such thing as race prejudice. The whole difference, they conclude their report, amounts to economic and educational difference. We always tend to look down on those who work for us. These are usually of a different race, hence we look down on these races.

Less categorical is the report of the southern settlement workers: Visitors to our settlement think all dark people are Italian and all light ones American. Many look upon foreigners as immoral or subnormal because they have large families. Large men, to them, are German because of their impressions from the comic supplements. Children, for the same reason, think of Jews as shrewd or trying to get something for nothing.

Whenever children here want to imitate a Jew, they use their hands when they talk. Children in our neighborhood enjoy foreign food. Often when a child comes in with a piece of foreign food, "like we eat in the old country," the other children yell, "halvers of that, Joe," or

"You know me, Mike." They only make fun when they associate ideas with the comic supplement where Italians eat endless spaghetti, etc. If a boy doesn't remove his hat at once, "He must be a Jew."

Groups in New York and New Jersey dwell on the importance of difference in clothing. The former reports:

Children are likely to absorb the idea that anything not American is necessarily of a lower type of development. For example, children do not as a rule notice the features, but they do notice the clothing and the way the hair is kept and the general appearance. Anything different from the Anglo-Saxon is apt to seem amusing.

An unpublished report of the National Urban League points out that the differences in manners and customs which children observe often are merely temporary while a group, new in the community, adjusts itself to the prevailing tone and standards. It says, concerning the Negroes of Milwaukee:

The crimes for which they were arrested are not serious ones but those which would naturally result from the conditions under which they live and, in the case of Southerners, simply misunderstanding of the code of manners of the North. Yelling and boisterous play in the streets, loud and noisy behavior, unnoticed in the South, are an offense in a Northern city. It is here not so much a question of criminal nature as of manners.

Yet, these distinctions between temporary and permanent characteristics of the various national or racial groups children cannot make. And even the adults who endeavor to create in the child's mind associations between nationality or race and moral or cultural standards often fail to consider the injustice of their own judgments in this respect. The following illustration will fittingly remind us of a common method by which the adult environment impresses upon the child the permanent association between foreign habits, which may be temporary or only those of a part of a group, and national or racial inferiority, which is considered permanent and true of the whole group.

A girls' club at the summer camp was singing as they watched the sunset from the end of a wharf. Some youths came up and jeered at them. The woman in charge of the club, much annoyed at the interference, said, "Those fellows are a nuisance. They may be Dagoes."

There happened to be in this group Italian girls to whom such a remark could not but be offensive. An older woman who had spent much effort in getting girls of different nationalities to rid themselves of prejudices and accept each other as equals was even more shocked. She explained that the young men did not look in the least like Italians or, indeed, anything but the native American "hicks" they probably were. A private conversation with the girls' leader, who had invested them with a foreign nationality, revealed that she had had very little contact with the foreign-born, had absorbed the attitude of contempt for all foreigners current in the particular native American Protestant church circle to which she belonged, and was not even aware of the fact that the term "Dago" had a national, as apart from a class, significance.

A social worker who has spent years in getting members of different nationalities in a typical industrial community of the East to appreciate each other and get on together, reports this conversation with one of the most cultured of native American leaders in the town:

My family have worked hard to attain our culture. It would be endangered, lowered, if we associated with the foreigners and other uncultured people with whom you are seeking to bring us together. As it is, our children learn slang and low ideals too readily; they would be culturally corrupted if we let them come into contact with the people whom you represent.

Lest our examples give too one-sided a picture of unfavorable reactions to other groups that result from associations between race or nationality and varying levels of cultural achievement or moral character, we must remind the reader that the formation of these pictures is by no means limited to so-called native white groups or even the older established immigrant groups in the typical American community. There are plenty of evidences to show, first, that foreign groups often, by the same process of association, arrive at a similar judgment of the native whites, and, second, that by the same process, class distinctions also arise within the same nationality or race.

As regards the first, a typical example was contained in a recent editorial in the *New York Times* (for February 1, 1926):

Deep in a Surrey birchwood, almost pathless, where one finds by luck rather than by direction the camps and caravans, the first English Gipsy school has just been opened. Must Gipsies, too, go to school?

In childhood, if we used to fear, how thoroughly we envied them. The abundant young, presumably "stolen," were exempt from compulsory washing and roamed the greenwood, careless of truant officers. How good the soup smells, stirred in the pot dangling from the tripod by an eldrich hag, her tatters rich in sky and sunset. Alas! Gipsies are "progressive." . . .

It is some consolation that the pride of old descent and separate tradition is still strong in the Romany breast. A mother in her dingy bracken hut, with its central fire, speaks her aversion of common schools: "I have brought up my children with care. What I dislike about schools is that well-brought-up children will have to associate with brats who come from piggish surroundings." [10]

While we cannot in this chapter pursue the devious ways in which both parents and children arrive at their cultural valuations, their effect upon the relationship between foreign-born children and native or fully Americanized adults is worth noting. The manners and not the intellectual powers of the teacher and settlement worker seem to be the stronger Americanizing influence on children.[11]

[10] For an interesting illustration of early association between class distinction and manners within a national group, see Jane Addams, *Twenty Years at Hull House* (1911, p. 103).

[11] T. S. McMahon, *Social and Economic Standards of Living* (1925, p. 150).

CHAPTER XVIII

THE EDUCATIONAL TASK

Some readers may have opened this book with the question: Why should we be concerned so much with childish attitudes? Will not later experience correct them in so far as they require correction? Or they may have put their doubt in these terms: Why set up this separate discussion of influences that misdirect childish attitudes toward other races when, as a matter of fact, the same influences are operative, in different degrees, throughout adult society? Is there any reason why this business, more than any other, should be attended to early in life? Moreover, *can* it be attended to early in life when home and school and church and the other agencies that influence the attitudes of children are by no means always agreed as to the direction in which they wish to influence them?

We feel that the preceding pages will to some extent have answered such questions as these. They have at least indicated, if they have not proved, that there are urgent reasons for dealing with race prejudice and every mental attitude connected with it as early in life as possible. The very fact that many teachers, parents, ministers, and social workers have asked for such a study as this and have taken part in it, and the multitude of books and articles bearing upon it which we have been able to quote on one phase of the subject or another show that there exists at least of a good *prima facie* case for such a contention. But now we can go further and say that the bulk of the information available justifies the general feeling that here we have a problem somewhat distinct from that of general race prejudice, though a part of it. We have discovered, first, that children react somewhat differently to contacts with persons of other races and nationalities than adults—and differently at the various stages of growth—and, second, that educationally the problem of modifying undesirable racial attitudes (as we must call them for short though now we know them for something much more diverse and complicated) is a different one at different ages.

248

Psychological research amply confirms these deductions from our material. First, on the negative side, the special danger that education may be perverted into an attempt to fasten on the plastic mentality of children all the prevailing adult prejudices of their time and place unless counter-influences are set to work, a danger which many believe to be a disastrous reality in present-day America, is thus expressed by John Dewey:

The plasticity of the young presents a temptation to those having greater experience and hence greater power which they rarely resist. It seems putty to be molded according to current designs. That plasticity also means power to change prevailing custom is ignored. Docility is looked upon not as ability to learn whatever the world has to teach, but as subjection to those instructions of others which reflect *their* current habits. . . .

When we think of the docility of the young we first think of the stocks of information adults wish to impose and the ways of acting they want to reproduce. Then we think of the insolent coercions, the insinuating briberies, the pedagogic solemnities by which the freshness of youth can be faded and its vivid curiosities dulled. Education becomes the art of taking advantage of the helplessness of the young; the forming of habits becomes a guarantee for the maintenance of hedges of custom.[1]

Professor Kilpatrick points out that not only the content but also the method of education in vogue at any place or time reflects the cultural ideals of the adult world, so that seemingly there is no escape for the child at all.[2]

PERMANENCE OF ASSOCIATIONS

As to the question, how much of the learning in the years of childhood carries over into adult life, no accurate data are available; and psychologists who express themselves on the matter seem to be disagreed. This whole matter of permanence of associations in memory has, however, received an enlightening new interpretation by the *Gestalt* school of psychologists, who explain the retention of associations by the transformation of their ingredients into a single common pattern or configuration.[3]

[1] *Human Nature and Conduct* (1922, p. 64).
[2] William Heard Kilpatrick, *Foundations of Method* (1925, p. 109).
[3] Robert Morris Ogden, *Psychology and Education* (1926, p. 184).

PRIMACY OF EARLY ASSOCIATIONS

Likewise, it is still an open question whether first impressions are more lasting than later ones. Professor Thorndike's more recent experiments indicate no advantage in this respect for first words or numbers in series due to their position. Experiments to test the doctrine of primacy—"other things being equal, the association first formed will prevail"—lend no support to it, he says.

In general, the first connection shows no greater potency over the connections immediately following it. In general also the first connection shows no greater potency over those following it than the nth experience shows over those preceding it. On the contrary, in four of the six experiments there is much greater resemblance to what comes after than what comes before.[4]

Ogden, on the other hand, takes the accepted view that first connections with a situation are more important for future reactions than later connections. He says:

The importance of primacy for pedagogy can hardly be overstated, because if the first impression of a new subject of study is incorrectly apprehended, or bungled in the behavior that belongs with it, the confused or distorted impression left upon the memory may be a serious hindrance to subsequent steps in learning. . . .
The striking pattern of what, at the time, seems to be an original idea may have a tenacity in memory out of all proportion to its significance.[5]

It is possible that the apparent conflict of these testimonies may be explained with differences between types of experience. Professor Thorndike's experiments had to do with measurements of strips of paper and areas of surfaces, with representation of sounds by letters and the combination of letters to make words. Here the emotional excitement incident to first contact is at a minimum. On the other hand, meeting for the first time a living creature different from anything one has ever seen, or a human being of previously unknown physical proportions, produces a shock which, in common parlance, makes a "deep impression."

[4] E. L. Thorndike, "The Influence of Primacy," *Journal of Experimental Psychology,* October, 1927, pp. 18-29.
[5] Robert Morris Ogden, *Psychology and Education* (1926, p. 199).

This difference in types of experience would explain why, Thorndike's findings notwithstanding, first associations of race or nationality with an unpleasant experience, picture, or descriptive epithet often outlasts innumerable corrective experiences and teachings. But it is also true that this applies not to all but merely to some of these early learnings—not to those casual inferences which the southern group has in mind when it denies their serious significance but to the acute incidents of felt injustice or antagonism which, as some members of minority groups declare, have supplied them with the fuel of inner revolt or the stimulus to emulation for many years.[6] For, if it is because of their vividness that early experiences have so great an impact upon the mind, then it is, again, the most vivid among them that will form lasting patterns of associated ideas.

Impressions that are received with marked pleasure or displeasure are more lasting than those received in a state of affectional neutrality. This is especially the case when impressions are colored with emotion, although if the instinctive nature is too deeply stirred the articulateness of the figure will be impaired. Of impressions made under strong emotion one can often remember a frustrated desire, or the exultation of a satisfied want, without being able to recall the articulate details of the experience itself.[7]

VOCABULARY

Other factors must not be overlooked. Recent studies indicate that the social concepts gain in precision as the child advances in other studies; and that more especially the increase in his vocabulary has an important influence on the concreteness of these concepts. But it must not be thought that a larger vocabulary necessarily means a corresponding increase in definite concepts. For example, where one derisive nickname served the child of five, the child of ten may use a dozen such words without attaching to any of them a very precise meaning. The older children already have been subjected—to a degree which probably exceeds that which is usually assumed—to almost every form of stereotype-building influence. To them the sound and the color of the word and not only its meaning has a large variety of associations, not all of which are clearly present in the consciousness. What is worse, words and phrases are deliberately dissociated

[6] See, for example, the incident told on p. 22.
[7] Robert Morris Ogden, *Psychology and Education* (1926, p. 201).

from their proper meaning and connected up with new and misleading meanings by the arts of the propagandist.[8]

We have already seen how an insidious propaganda, whether intentional or not, operates through almost every one of the child's opportunities of social education. What here concerns us is the realization that language fixes in the mind the specific associations which the child is desired to learn. Apart from the particular meanings desired by his *particular* group (including all adults with whom he comes in contact, but more especially his parents and teachers), the child has no meaning for any abstract term. If the word "Negro" is always used with the implication of low social status or moral inferiority, it is psychologically all but impossible for that word to acquire also a more precise ethnic meaning for that child. Even later in life, one exposed to a frequent repetition of that social implication will have great difficulty in using and reading the word Negro in its purely ethnographic meaning. In the same way, frequent repetitions of historical associations between two terms may so firmly knot them together in the child's mind that one will always tend to suggest the other. For example, for many the often-heard phrase, "The Jews killed Christ," continually gets into the way of an objective observation of the Jews as an ethnic group. The mere idea that the mother of Jesus was a Jewess, though an obvious truth, becomes one of that large category of facts which many individuals, though they may be forced to admit it, never manage to incorporate in their private thinking.

It has been said that apart from all deliberate teaching of association between race or nationality with concepts of moral or any other kind of inferiority, the verbal associations which form the inadvertent attendant learning of all of us suffice to cripple our mental independence for life.

RACIAL ATTITUDES AND CHARACTER

A number of the contributors to the material of the present study have expressed themselves in regard to the effects which

[8] Of course, the *purposes* of propaganda may be altruistic in the extreme, and there are even textbooks by teachers of social ethics on the art of such re-combinations for the purpose of "Influencing Human Behavior"! But the great bulk of propagandist influences upon the average individual are undoubtedly the outcome of personal and group selfishness. See A. B. Wolfe, *Conservatism, Radicalism and Scientific Method* (1923, p. 225).

the various race attitudes absorbed or learned by children have upon their general mentality and morality. In the questionnaire, they were asked to give their views as to "the effects of adverse attitudes to those of different race or nationality, (a) upon children of the exclusive group and (b) upon those of the group excluded." This question was understood, as it had been intended, to refer more particularly to effects in the creation, reinforcement, or modification of attitudes, not to effects on the immediate situation.

The New Jersey parents' group came to the conclusion that the children of the exclusive group suffer most by these attitudes: Their own outlook narrows their vision and, in the long run, hinders the progress of the race toward an understanding of itself. The children of the exclusive group, says a child psychologist, become egotistic and self-centered, domineering, and lacking in sympathetic tolerance. The middle-western high-school teacher, repeatedly quoted for rather incisive remarks, does not believe that children think much about the effects of racial exclusiveness until pretty well matured. (Other correspondents agree with this.) The principal effect on the exclusive group, he says, is that they overestimate their own progress. They try to keep out of their consciousness, for example, the effort and, perhaps, the ability of the Jewish group to excel them, or the effort and ability of Negro children to equal them.

Selfishness and snobbishness as well as intolerance are mentioned as the effects in a Michigan report. One correspondent says that the Jews have a "superiority complex," but fails to describe it other than characterizing it as an "inverted inferiority complex." The southern settlement workers say, more specifically, that the children of the exclusive groups become snobbish, feel superior, form their own groups, and thus form an impassable barrier to real refinement and culture.

Somewhat more varied and documented are the opinions expressed concerning the effects on children of the excluded groups. There is much mention of the "inferiority complex" which is fixed into their consciousness and, according to the southern settlement people, becomes "the cause of so much delinquency among foreign-born children." They add: "Those children who have a strong will hate the exclusive group with a blind hate and anxiously wait for a chance to get even." For example:

Pauline was taken into the Busy Bee Club, a club of ten-year-old Syrian girls, because she had played a great deal with these children on the playground. In some way she was soon made to feel that she was not wanted and dropped out of the club. After that time, whenever the club was to have a party or a picnic, she did everything in her power to make it a failure. On several occasions she tried to break up a club meeting. Now she cannot be induced to enter any club. This unfortunate experience has probably ruined her club life for all time.

This report further suggests that adverse judgments about foreign-born groups should be reconsidered from the point of view of the effect on their character of the adverse attitudes to which they so often are exposed:

Some say, "Limit immigration, foreigners do not make good American citizens." If we face facts squarely where does the fault lie?

A case of "inferiority complex" in children is reported by a high-school girl in a Christian Endeavor discussion group:

There was a colored girl in my class at school who was all right, but she never would have anything to do with the white girls. We'd borrow from her, but she never would borrow from us. She and her sister lived on my street. They always ran to school—they were wonderful runners. I'd be late about every so often, and I'd have to run and try to catch up with them, but they never would let me. They didn't seem to want to associate with me. But finally one of them got on the basket-ball team, and then they got to going out more, and we got used to them, and they didn't mind us so much. I think they thought if we spoke to them we were pitying them. I know I don't like it if people that I know don't like me are nice to me!

The examples which have already been given in other connections (see especially Chap. II, p. 22 et seq.) in illustration of the stimulus to self-improvement which contempt or ridicule sometimes provide, we may here add yet another. A colored girl describes the effect produced upon her by the exclusiveness of the white girls in her class:

A teacher in one of the mixed grade schools of V. had a way of seating the children according to the rank made on their test papers. A girl who made the highest mark would have the first seat in the first aisle on the girls' side. The next highest would take the second seat, etc. One day my mark entitled me to the first seat in the second aisle.

A girl of the other race (I was the only colored girl in that room) had been given the last seat in the first aisle, and she asked the teacher if she could change with me as she couldn't see from a rear seat. The teacher said she could if I were willing. I changed with her.

At recess, the other girls surrounded her, wanting to know why she let me get in the first aisle. They also tried to persuade her to take her seat back. "Don't you know," they said, "if you let her have that seat, the next time she'll make a still higher mark, and the first thing you know she'll have the first seat in the first aisle? Why don't you let someone else change with you? Even next time if you make the same grade, she'll sit ahead of you if you let her sit ahead of you now." The girl censured replied that she had no right to ask anyone behind me to exchange with her as that would place them ahead of me, which wouldn't be fair.

I kept the last seat in the first aisle. Overhearing their conversation inspired me to try to make their words true. Before the term closed I reached the third seat in the first row.

Other reports referring more briefly to similar effects of adverse racial attitudes upon the group under contempt, expressly warn against the assumption that children can have an "instinctive" sense of the inferiority of their own group. One group writes:

The children treated as inferior unconsciously demand full self-expression. Restrictions limit self-expression. Everything else (i.e., in the way of interpreting the permanent depression that results from such treatment) is rationalizing. To hear a child say, "We are all entitled to the same things," is an example of rationalization. A child somehow feels that he is entitled to the use of the whole world. If he has a sense of inferiority, he has got it from without.[9]

The remarkable way in which educators differ in what they consider the best way of avoiding the depressing effect of contemptuous conduct upon children of despised racial groups is illustrated by the following contribution from the Cleveland discussion group:

A colored boy was the leader of an athletic group in one of our high schools. Just before a certain contest with another school he was approached and asked to give up his place on the team in order that the

[9] Floyd H. Allport in *Social Psychology* (1924, p. 369), describes the operation of the inferiority complex in the intellectual sphere in a way that is particularly characteristic of members of racial or national minorities which because of a long history of poverty or degradation, are popularly regarded as (and of course often are) culturally backward.

team might be given fair treatment. He did so. The question as to the ultimate results in character and attitude on the part of the boy and others we all thought was very serious.

In contrast to this, one of our colored members spoke of a teacher who had been so afraid that her colored pupil's feelings might be hurt that she had appointed a white girl to walk with her regularly.

Another colored member had had quite a different experience when her son bought a "bid" for a dance. Although he had been asked to do so by a number of his companions and was on very friendly terms with the class, the school principal called him aside and asked him if he did not realize he would be badly treated there. When the boy reported this at home, his mother insisted that he go to the dance nevertheless. The principal then said he had called the students together, and the consensus of opinion was that the colored boy should not attend. Accordingly, he stayed away. However, on graduation day his partner, as he walked up for his diploma, was a white girl. He is now in college, but full of racial bitterness.

One of our white members had a similar story of a white boy in high school who asked a colored girl to dance with him. Later the principal called him into the office and protested against his doing so. The boy insisted on his right to dance with anyone at the dance.

(In none of these cases was any motive of race prejudice imputed to the school principals and teachers, each of whom apparently acted according to his lights.)

Another group reports dishonesty as one of the characteristics which adverse attitudes toward them on account of their race may produce in children. In illustration, this incident is told:

A colored girl, ten years old, did not stand when her teacher, trying to ascertain the races and nationalities represented in the class, asked how many children in the room were colored. She thought that if the teacher and the children in her class found out that she was colored she would not be given an opportunity to take part in the little plays given by their dramatic club. This child is blond, and no one would have known she was colored unless he was told.

More serious still is another report which asserts (it may be said contrary to much evidence already given in these pages by others) that a hostile attitude toward them causes children "to lose ambition and hampers the achievement of success. A smoldering hostility burns within them and causes race riots, brawls and, in the final analysis, the overthrow of law and order."

Exactly the opposite is asserted by a middle-western high-school teacher: "The Negro is yet too willing to accept the attitude of the white." However, even he admits that this condition is passing with the increasing influence of national organizations that teach race pride.

The rebellious spirit, though opinions vary as to its acuteness, is mentioned in the majority of findings as the outstanding effect of race discrimination and hostility upon the minds of the children made to suffer from them.

The group of southern settlement workers, in contrast with many of the other interested people who have studied this matter through personal observation, warn us against taking too seriously the permanent influences of derogatory associations of their racial or national group by other groups upon one of the minority groups. They say, among other things:

Children are perfectly aware (or more than the too seriously minded investigator might give them credit for) of the comic exaggerations that with the mention of a nationality suggest a characteristic, or with a specific kind of action the nationality with which it is supposed to be habitual.

Perhaps this is true, in so far as the more superficial associations are concerned that result from movies and comic strips and others of the less intimate contacts. But the impression of a majority of the observers, backed by scientific opinion—in so far as it has expressed itself on this matter—is that the permanent influences of the larger factors in the shaping of racial attitudes, such as segregation and discrimination in treatment, are usually grossly underestimated. Their general verdict on this topic might be summarized by saying that associations between race or nationality and inferiority, formed in childhood, are exceedingly difficult to throw off later in life and interfere with the formation of new and sounder judgments as regards race characteristics.

In short, then, the evidence on racial attitudes in children (and the consensus of impressions given on some aspects in lieu of objective evidence) that has been brought together in previous chapters constitutes a volume of descriptive data concerning the nature of race consciousness in children and the processes by which many different types of learning, primary and attendant, contribute toward the formation of patterns of association which are retained in memory with different degrees of vividness and permanence. We have seen that it probably depends on their relative intensity whether later experiences and their learnings blot out earlier ones. We have seen, further, that the racial attitudes formed in childhood are different in quality from those formed later in life; and that, therefore, a society desirous to exterminate prejudice from the relations of its component groups, will have to deal with its sources in early life. There seems, thus, to be a case for an imaginative, thorough, scientific study of ways in which race attitude in childhood may be modified.

PART IV

HOW MAY RACE ATTITUDES BE MODIFIED?

CHAPTER XIX

A NEEDED SYNTHESIS OF AIMS

In the section just concluded we have surveyed the influences which school, home, club, etc., exert upon the race attitudes of children and have found operative in these influences certain common factors which inhere in the diversity and confusion of human purposes and educational objectives. We are now able to recognize more accurately the sources of child behavior which, according to much of the testimony in the earlier chapters, is puzzling parents, teachers, and other workers among children. Incidentally, our analysis of these common factors also has helped to simplify the educational task; for we are now no longer confronted with many disjointed experiences but with a coherent social experience for which we require a social program. Obviously, then, our next task is to state that problem and that program. The present chapter, therefore, is crucial; and while it may here and there state too dogmatically the author's own conclusions from the preceding study, these conclusions are intended rather as a tentative first draft for a much-needed agreement among those concerned for the integration and harmony of our American people.

After thus endeavoring to come to grips with underlying principles of educational program-making, it will be necessary for us to return at once to the actual situations that exemplify the problem lest our thinking be too abstract or insufficiently related to the specific situations in which the problem must be tackled. It is inevitable that in doing so we shall seem, here and there, to go over ground already covered in the previous section. But while we are obliged to deal with the same subject matter, such as the teaching of civics or the question of segregation, our approach and our purpose now are different ones: For, while previously we were occupied in analyzing the difficulties, we are now trying, in line with our fuller and more comprehensive understanding, to find the answers. Where before we focussed our attention upon failures of the educational system—including home and outside influences—we shall here focus it upon success—both in the avoidance of the evils and in their removal. Instead of inventing new methods and processes for the embodiment of an agreed set of principles, we shall look for existing examples of practices and theories seemingly in line with them. The partial duplication of subject matter, therefore, will—in the procedure adopted for the present discussion—be found to represent a review from a different angle and a logical step in a progressive dialectic treatment.

We have seen that the race attitudes of children present problems that are distinctly educational, in the sense of being amenable to processes of change that can be manipulated in the interest of larger and more accurate information, of the acceptance or rejection of theoretical doctrines, and of any desired habits of thought and behavior. But we have also seen that the racial attitudes of children reflect those of the environment in which they grow up and, in fact, are almost inseparable from them. What children feel and think about those of other national and racial groups represents for the most part what they have learned about them. If they are confused in this feeling and thinking, it is because diverse and even divergent influences have been brought to bear upon them. The innate character of the child plays its part in choosing between these influences, so that, for example, an exceptionally intelligent and sensitive child is likely to react in one way to the pressure of public opinion and a more stolid and stupid one in another, even where both are exposed to the identical environment. But generally speaking, even in those reactions that seem most closely bound up with the physiological equipment, the part played by individual character in the formation of racial attitudes is small, apparently, compared with that played by the weight of surrounding adult opinion and its conscious and unconscious influence.

It is easy to understand that under these circumstances the problem of changing racial attitudes must appear to many as a hopeless dilemma: The children, unless separated from their natural environment, are bound to absorb its attitudes—the adult community is too set in its ways to be expected to change much. Nevertheless, racial attitudes do change; in fact, today they are changing at so rapid a rate that the average American child is exposed to contradictory influences within the same narrow environment of home and school and neighborhood.[1] From the ob-

---

[1] See Franz Boas, *Anthropology and Modern Life* (1928, p. 183).

servation of these changes it should not be impossible to deduce guiding principles for a deliberate educational method of modification of attitudes. But while technically there is no impassable obstacle, we still have to consider the question: *Who* wants to change racial attitudes, and why? What part are we as parents or teachers or social workers or religious leaders to play in this process? Do we know for certain in what direction we, ourselves, would want to influence that change?

It is here that we meet with much loose thinking. Our libraries are full of textbooks on world friendship or interracial cooperation which simply assume that a large number of Americans, more especially those associated with churches, desire an application of "Christian" principles to race relations, and that they know what these principles are. In practice, as many of the examples given in the foregoing pages have shown us, Christians and non-Christians are equally perplexed as to what the application of their final convictions as regards human relationships would mean in concrete situations. Moreover, most of us are quite incapable of defining these "principles" in terms in which they could become applicable at all.

Frankly, the Christian in modern society has never faced the dilemma that arises from the contrast between the standards of value inherent in his religious faith and those inherent in his cultural traditions. Obviously a native white American community seeks to defend certain cultural heritages; but these are not necessarily Christian. They are not necessarily democratic either. For example, on Christian and democratic grounds it may be desirable that the child of such a group should associate with the children of other groups, if only to be prepared by a personal understanding for a future contact with them in adult life. But on the ground of cultural integrity it is undesirable that the child should have his language corrupted or his good manners impaired.

The educational question, in regard to children in communities or groups with marked attitudes toward race, then, is this: How far can educators go in preserving the child's natural curiosity, in keeping his mind flexible and open to new experiences, in making him desire fresh experiences, without alienating the adult group to which he belongs and thus, perhaps, having him withdrawn altogether from the liberating educational influences—or, what amounts to the same thing, having these influences countered by antagonism in the home? [2]   On the other hand, where parents—often because of unusual cosmopolitan experiences— are less circumscribed in their racial sympathies than their neighbors and desire to bring up their children appreciative to the values of variety and tolerant of differences in cultural standards, how far do they really wish to go in alienating their children from the prevailing social opinion of the community?   Have they not themselves, in the influences to which they expose their children in and around the home, more than one set of principles at work that cannot be harmonized?   Do they not, after all, leave the child subjected, as regards the formation of his attitudes, to the chance of contending forces in home and school and neighborhood?

But there are numerous institutions and organizations—including the public schools and many of the churches, the Boy Scouts, Campfire Girls, social settlements, playground organizations and many more—that presumably have for one of their major objects the creation of tolerant and cooperative intergroup attitudes.   At least they, it may be thought, are not confused in their own valuations but stand before problems of method alone.

Alas, a little inquiry shows that these institutions and organizations are not exempt from the general difficulty.   They are not, among themselves, or even each within itself, agreed as to standards and values.   There often is a certain "liberal" tone about their professed principles, but in every common problem of practical application there are on exhibit materializations of every known racial attitude from that of severest exclusiveness to that of the most absolute freedom.   To speak quite openly, there seems not to be today the possibility of agreement on a single line of action in relation to a given practical problem between the constituent local bodies of the Sunday School Union or the National Federation of Settlements, or the National Council of the Y.M.C.A. or the Boy Scouts of America, or any other national body that may occur to the reader.   It is impossible that there should be such agreement, for in each case the local Sunday school, settlement, Y.M.C.A., boy scout corps, etc., is bound to a certain degree to reflect local opinion; or it could not operate at all.   This is illustrated in the report of the southern settlement group:

[2] See, for example, *The Immigrant Child and the Church School* (Department of Religious Education of the Episcopal Church; pamphlet, 1922), p. 16.

In groups in our settlement, children of different nationality are not forced together, but because we are trying to make them all good citizens we encourage mingling as much as possible for a happy harmony. When there is parental objection, we do not attempt associations, however, because we have found that we do more harm than good, and the life standards and customs of the parents cannot be changed in a day.

And another reason why there can be no agreement is that our national life is not uniform in regard to conditions affecting race attitudes. As we have noted in many of the examples given, these nearly always are forms of economic, political, social attitudes. The factor of race or nationality often serves merely as a blind in the definition of classes, parties, sects. The status of a racial group is fixed by the occupations or wealth or religion or language or manners or tastes of its majority; and many of the individual problems in human relationships arise from the tendency to try and make the pattern of race composition in a community coterminous with the pattern of class or other social composition. Hence the question may be raised whether it is possible to separate education on race attitudes from the total of educational influences upon the child and to provide for it with a specific program. It is, of course, obvious that the ethics of race relationships are quite closely bound up with general ethics and that the mental qualities desired in the facing of race problems are mental qualities desired also in the facing of other life problems. In other words, we are really far more concerned with a good system of education in general than we are with a good program of education on a specific subject or within any other limits.

This is particularly true of educational influences on young children. Many experienced teachers doubt whether anything is to be gained from interfering with, or adding to, a really good method of education for the young child. Without any particular reference to social relationships which are far removed from the child's personal experience, the best educational practice already aims at the very qualities of mind which we recognize as valuable for satisfactory attitudes on race and nationality later in life. Others feel that essential likenesses can be stressed in early childhood in such a way as to prevent an excessive reaction to difference when awareness to it grows in later years.

But for older children, beginning perhaps about the eleventh or twelfth year of age, when as a rule the child begins to absorb information from many sources with an objective interest in things not necessarily of personal concern to him, when he reads printed matter not intended for him, listens to the talk of grown-up folk and forms abstract conclusions from his observations, it may be possible and worth while to direct attention to the subject of racial and national differences and to help in the formation of a receptive attitude of mind in regard to them. There is not as yet enough pedagogical experience on this matter to present a suggestion of this sort other than tentatively. The age at which a deliberate influencing of race attitudes may usefully begin can only be ascertained through more experiment and must depend, of course, not only on the nature of the school program in general but also on the character of the community.

Agreed Objectives

Clearly, the educational problem is not one of absolute choice between race "tolerance" and race "loyalty"; it is rather the problem of producing that kind of loyalty to the established and cherished standards of the group that will not close the mind to new experiences and their possible lessons—a loyalty that, while inevitably setting standards of valuation, will not stand in the way of the formation of new standards of value to take their place beside the old.[3]

A religious educator, in an inquiry similar to the present one, has formulated this objective as follows:

As nearly as I can formulate any philosophy of social education I should say that it involves two distinct and complementary processes: first, transmission to the individual of a social inheritance of ideals and convictions which will give him the benefit of the experience of his forebears; second, furnishing the individual with an equipment for criticism and evaluation of these elements in his social inheritance. The important point to be noted, then, is that the first of these processes involves a very considerable amount of emotional conditioning. That is to say, the social inheritance of ethical values is transmitted, not as a set of ideas or notions, but as a group of sentiments (using the word "sentiment" in the sense of a set of emotions organized about some concept, custom, or relationship). To express the matter in still another way, one's ethical inheritance consists of loyalties and repulsions which

---

[3] William Heard Kilpatrick, *Foundations of Method* (1925, p. 317).

necessarily involve a conscious or unconscious emotional conditioning.

It cannot be urged too strongly, however, that this emotional conditioning must not be of so violent a character as to make it impossible for the growing individual to scrutinize the objects of his loyalties with a critical mind and without disaster to his intellectual and emotional life. The evil results of a very positive emotional conditioning with reference to ethical values or religious beliefs has been made very clear by the psycho-analysts. What we want, I take it, is a definite bias in the direction of those values which have been well established in social experience, but a bias that is free from the "taboo" element.

The second part of the educational process, namely, the furnishing of the individual with the equipment for criticising and evaluating his socially inherited ideals requires chiefly that a habit of questioning and reasoning concerning moral propositions shall be encouraged from the moment it shows itself   It will be greatly strengthened probably if the emotional conditioning already referred to has resulted in an enthusiasm for learning and a bias toward scientific method.

The discussion method which we are now employing increasingly in our moral education is valid, then, if it proceeds upon the foundation of definite value attitudes that have been established in early training. Without this conditioning no amount of discussion or intellectualizing about life would be of any use.

It would seem, therefore, that we must begin by selecting those situations in the ordinary lives of our boys and girls which lend themselves to the development of those attitudes which we agree upon as immediately desirable. With the younger children these situations should be made use of in developing loyalties and inhibitions; with older boys and girls, in teaching moral discrimination in the light of values already established and in securing a re-examination of such values in the light of developing experience.[4]

Are there any attitudes which even the more broadminded of Americans can agree upon as "immediately desirable?" Without trying to discuss this question exhaustively, we can single out some major items of educational endeavor upon which probably every reader of this book would agree and which contain possibilities for a wide range of practical application:

1. *Sensitizing the regard for justice in the dealings between individuals and groups regardless of race.* In practice, of course, this at once gets into conflict with the inherent injustice of prevailing attitudes; but in theory every community will admit that jus-

[4] F. Ernest Johnson in a statement to the Commission on Christian Education of the Federal Council of Churches, 1925 (unpublished).

tice is a desirable thing and should be taught to children and young people.

2. *Counteracting influences that make for misinformation and misunderstanding.* Of course, there will be differences of opinion as to what constitutes correct information and right understanding; but in theory there will be common agreement that children should not be deliberately misinformed or prevented from arriving at true understanding.

3. *Creating appreciation for qualities and achievements in other groups which are in harmony with the cultural values shared by all groups.*

It is probable that emphasis on these three items will bring about a new situation, after a time, in which it will be possible to reach agreements on further educational advancement among more controversial grounds—as for example, personal association between members of different groups, the sharing of educational, recreational and vocational opportunities, and the like. It would be a mistake, however, for the reasons given, to include educational activities on those lines in an initial program intended to embody the agreement that may be expected in any American community. Individuals, of course, can enlarge upon the initial program with experimental excursions into a more difficult field, but institutions and organizations must guard against possible failure of their extensive educational work by too rapid an advance on principles which their clientele and their supporters may not share.

In practice, the three points mentioned would seem to permit of a variety of experiments and methods of approach.

First, *as regards justice,* every effort to establish a strong sense of fair dealing as between individuals will have a tendency to affect the thinking on dealings between different racial groups. If the problem were raised in the first instance in the form of group conflicts, the result might be less certain. But the teaching of a merely abstract regard for justice will not be helpful either, because it will be unapplied to actual situations. The effort, therefore, should be to utilize every possible opportunity, not artificially created, for leading children and young people to recognize what it is in their own thinking that changes a situation in which their sense of justice demands one form of action toward an individual rather than another when the fact that that individual is of dark skin or of foreign birth seems to change the situation.

Of course, to secure opportunities for such teaching, some contact between individuals of different groups is desirable; but it is not indispensable, and a vicarious solution of problems in conduct is possible in connection with the teaching of history, with Bible study, and through the reading of story books.

Second, *as regards counteractions to misinformation and misunderstanding*, this obviously is an element in any and every educational effort. But it can be sharpened as regards the knowledge of different racial groups by a deliberate seeking for opportunities to demonstrate the untruth of misleading propaganda and to expose the sources of misinformation, together with a cultivation of the appreciation for correct information in any field of interest.

Concretely, this means a confronting of the child who has been subjected to misinformation with corrective information, and this in the most appealing and dramatic possible form. For example, the introduction of an obviously educated and refined Mexican into a school or institution, to deliver an address or merely to be seen chatting with the principal, will have the effect of offsetting the notion, gained from moving pictures and general talk, that "all Mexicans are ruffians." Lessons bringing out the contributions of Italy to science, art, and statecraft will have the effect of undermining the impression that all Italians are illiterate, superstitious, and ignorant. Emphasis on the fact that Jesus was a Jew and comparison of His martyrdom at the hands of other Jews with other historical examples of persecution of saints and heroes by their own countrymen will destroy the idea of the Jews as a people quite apart and different from others in that they killed the Savior of Mankind. Other similar examples will suggest themselves.

Third, *as regards appreciation for qualities and achievements in other groups that are universally esteemed*, several methods have already been tried out and have been mentioned in previous chapters: the holding of exhibits of the arts of other groups, plays and pageants, dances, songs, and games that demonstrate their contributions to the esthetic and spiritual heritage of the human race; visits to museums and exhibitions where traces of their great past may be pointed out; the arrangement of special occasions for performances by visiting orchestras, choral societies, dramatic, athletic, and other groups representative of other races and nationalities; lectures by returned travellers telling appreciatively (and with suitable pictorial illustrations) of their contacts with foreign peoples and races; pictures and posters and other wall decorations as permanent reminders of the universality of contributions to enjoyment and inspiration; and above all books about other groups and by members of other groups.[5]

The three general suggestions here made will not seem to go very far to many of our readers who believe that personal association between children of different racial and national groups is necessary in education for racial tolerance, and that there must be agreement on so important a factor before any worthwhile modification of the prevalent race attitudes can be achieved. But it is precisely when it comes to personal association that agreement cannot be taken for granted. In fact, in situations involving personal contact lies the crux of the present disagreements. So, while here and there a leader may include in his program interchanges of visits to their homes by members of different racial groups, or the mixing of races and nationalities on teams, in games, in hikes and other forms of recreation, this cannot be made part as yet of any official program to which great national agencies or a majority of local institutions can pledge themselves.

For, the one thing most zealously to be avoided is the danger of hypocrisy. Few organizations are entirely free from it at the present time. Thus we have organizations that do not nominally recognize differences of race, yet in practice set up separate institutions for their colored clientele and refuse them the use of the facilities of the white institution. Thus we have national rules of tolerance disregarded by local officers who refuse colored or Oriental boys admission to white clubs or troops; churches which, while not admitting race discrimination, "tactfully" eliminate foreign-born casuals from Sunday school before they can come to regard themselves as regular members; institutional officers rationalizing their prejudices or preferences against certain particular groups by making out that some applicant for membership is undesirable on personal grounds when really it is only his color or his accent or the typical social status of his group that, they fear, may create friction.

If, to begin with, all national agencies working among children and young people were to concentrate upon a more modest

---

[5] These suggestions, by way of illustration, will be taken up in more detail in the following chapters.

program that leaves much to be desired from the point of view of some but incorporates the common sense of all of their officers and supporters, and if they were to carry through such a program with absolute honesty and completeness, they would make more rapid progress toward satisfactory relationships between different groups in the community than by a frequent forcing of issues or by high-sounding pronouncements that are continually at variance with practice.

It is for these reasons that we cannot rest satisfied with merely stating the conditions that make for a maximum of social integration and the means to achieve them. It is well to know what those conditions are, but it is necessary to know that statements of immediate steps to which people will consent are more important than statements of theoretical ultimate goals to which, for the present, only a few idealists assent.[6]

It may be well at this point to recapitulate the major educational objectives in the modification of racial attitudes upon which presumably there may be enough consensus to permit the working out of local and national programs in which home and school, church and recreational organization, will have their part. They were:

1. A general flexibility of mental responsiveness that would at least maintain an equilibrium, a state of curiosity, as between pleasant and unpleasant reaction to new experiences and impressions.

2. Sensitiveness for the demands of justice in the dealings between individuals and groups.

3. Substitution of correct information for misinformation and of understanding for misunderstanding.

4. Appreciation for qualities and achievements in harmony with the cultural values shared by all groups.

Merely to mention these objectives is not to indicate how they may be reached. In a sense, they incorporate the major aims of modern education; and to discuss them adequately would be to review the recent literature of educational method. While this is impossible within the frame of the present volume, certain principles, not generally understood, which bear more directly upon our problems, may be worth pointing out.

To begin with, the child is not a small adult. His psychological

[6] However, for a suggestive "ideal" program of educational conditioning for group integration, the reader may be referred to Charles C. Peters, *Foundations of Educational Sociology* (1924, p. 240).

pre-disposition is totally different. Too often those who are charged with the development of socio-ethical programs of education seem to overlook this simple but important fact.[7]

What, then, are we to do? First, and foremost, we must protect the integrity of the child.[8] The natural open-mindedness of youth must be allowed to establish itself as a mental habit.[9] And this more especially in all that pertains to human relationships.[10]

There is another psychological factor which, though elementary, is often overlooked in educational projects designed to create liberal or appreciative interracial attitudes, and that is the relative force of favorable and unfavorable impressions. This is particularly true of racial situations. Though he may a hundred times have passed a group of white boys without any incident whatever, the one time that a white boy calls him a derisive name and the others grinned, will be a remembered occasion for the small colored boy. It will for years affect his attitudes toward white people; it may forever mold his self-respect. But if soon after the unhappy occasion he should happen to be the center of an admiring group of white boys, anxious to try out his new boxing gloves, the later pleasant experience will go far to correct the earlier unpleasant one. This phenomenon holds good of all age groups, but it is particularly important in childhood because there is not as yet a full canvass of past experiences and impressions in the background of every new experience to correct any twist which it may give to one's attitudes.[11]

[7] John Dewey is emphatic on this matter. See *Human Nature and Conduct* (1922, p. 98). See also the passage quoted on p. 249.
[8] William H. Burnham, *The Normal Mind* (1925, p. 680).
[9] Arland D. Weeks, *The Control of the Social Mind* (1923, p. 34).
[10] George A. Coe, *A Social Theory of Religious Education* (1917, p. 106).
[11] See E. S. Bogardus, "Analyzing Changes in Public Opinion," *The Journal of Applied Sociology,* May-June, 1925, p. 381.

CHAPTER XX

WHAT THE HOME CAN DO

We shall assume in the discussion of this chapter that, perturbed by the evidences of intolerance, perhaps even of interracial friction, in the community, parents desire to do all that is in their power to keep their children free from adverse attitudes toward other groups than their own, to counteract the possible absorption of prejudice from sources outside the home and, in short, to cultivate those fundamental predispositions toward a liberal ethics of group relations that have been discussed in the previous chapter. We have already seen that such an objective far exceeds the occasions and resources of direct influencing in regard to race attitudes. It demands a totality of home influences that will make for open-mindedness, curiosity, sensitiveness to the demands of justice, appreciation of accurate information and desire of understanding. Since exigencies of space do not permit us to discuss the methods of home education in social ethics generally, we shall further assume that in these more general respects the home influences leave little to be desired, but that the question is asked whether some special means do not exist to reinforce, specifically in regard to race relations, the ethical teaching of the home.

It is important to keep clearly in mind the secondary nature of the things we are going to discuss. Too often a thoroughly bad environment, from the point of view of the formation of liberal race attitudes, is taken as a matter of course, as an inevitable condition; and a great deal of futile effort is put into elaborate schemes or tricks for undoing in part—usually as regards some specific behavior problem—what the general tone and teaching of the home does to the child. We have seen, in numerous examples, how confusing these contradictory influences often are to the childish understanding. If therefore some readers start their use of this book—as we are sure they will—by turning to these last few chapters for "constructive" suggestions for ways of modifying adverse race attitudes in children, we emphatically deny them admission until they have passed through at least some of the previous portals. There are no easy methods to do the trick. Those who believe that this or that activity in home or school, this or that book or form of contact, has in some magical way helped the child to rise above the mists of prejudice that surround him, merely deceive themselves. The only truly "constructive" way of going at this task is to go at it from the bottom up. If there is conflict between the standards of the home and those of the community, or of other groups with which the child associates, do not disguise it: life is conflict, and the child must learn to face life.

With the best intentions in the world, but lacking psychological training, parents often induce in their children the very state of mind they deplore in others. Aghast at the prejudices that surround them and at the force of prejudiced public opinion upon the shaping of their children's attitudes, they make a strenuous effort to make them appreciate "the other side." But, whatever the merits of the case, the method employed in impressing upon the child's mind what they consider the right view has the effect of creating habits of subservience to dogmatically stated principles, not of creating an inquisitive, alert, open mind. Instead of being liberalized, the child is merely conditioned for a favorable response to certain types of causes or principles which happen to be causes or principles contrary to those advocated by others. The whole business is uneducational and exposes the child to thoughtless absorption, later in life, of the very prejudices which parents fear. Habituated to choosing between dogmas, his intellectual life will consist in a series of conversions from one prejudice to another.

An experienced teacher writes:

If boys and girls are ever to attain to a larger and more comprehensive social view, it must come through their own experience. Parents, teachers and leaders must find what part they can play in this without infringing on children's liberties or lacking respect for their personalities. There are some influences that hamper, and some that aid; some that enslave and some that set free. If we expect children to be interested in the things that interest us, we hamper them, for they are not yet ready for these. If we hurry children toward the things we think are good for them, we hamper them. We can help most, perhaps, by providing an unobtrusive but suggestive atmosphere full of opportunity for the activities that children of their age enjoy. . . .

When we see children playing with other children, learning to share with one another, finding it fun to plan together, learning to appreciate the unique qualities in one another, getting acquainted with children of different backgrounds, we must recognize these things as steps by which they are growing as social beings. If they learn through quarreling with one another what *not* to do, that too is good. When we find children interested in what is going on around them, duplicating in their play the motorman, the fireman, the grocer, they are growing socially. Gradually, step by step, children will grow out of the interests they now have into others of larger social import, if our influence has been truly helpful.[1]

Another witness, speaking from much practical experience, says:

We are slowly realizing that the child can only truly learn through actual contact with reality, with the concrete sense experience which operates inevitably as cause and effect. We know that words mean nothing to him as symbols or images of the mind unless they are accompanied by the actions or deeds which correspond. The child, as is the case with primitive man, must learn from the concrete sensible fact, for sensation is the primary psychological function and not thinking or feeling or intuition. When parents and teachers give the child arbitrary commands, telling him this is right and that is wrong, and at the same time acting towards the child and in his presence in a way quite contrary to the teaching given him, the resultant effect upon the child is confusion, with the strongest influence that which he has experienced in the concrete, and not what he has been told.

I think it is not too much to say that the greatest error in the early education of little children is the almost universal one of the parent, usually the mother, nurse or teacher, placing herself between the child and his own experience. . . .

No child normally possesses any prejudice or discrimination as to the peoples of any other nation or race. This is something entirely acquired from his environment. The problem of his relation and attitude towards stranger peoples is fundamentally exactly the same as it is towards his ordinary personal relations. The uncertainty and suspicion, the fear and distrust manifested between alien peoples, are entirely the result of conditioned primitive emotions. The primitive mind fears the unknown, the strange and the unfamiliar. But human relations developed on merely an instinctive and primitive functioning of the mind have no secure basis because not rooted in individual achievement. As long as the primitive emotions and feelings which are normal

[1] Sara Lyman Patrick in *The World Tomorrow* for October, 1925, p. 306.

to the child remain undeveloped and uneducated, his inadequate relations with his fellows, both at home and abroad, will continue to be the crux of the problem of mankind.

When the little child is patiently taught by experience itself instead of preachings that consideration and regard for his fellows is equally important with that for himself, and that when he fails in this he himself suffers the loss equally and inevitably; when compromise and arbitration between the opposing wills and desires is the method of adjustment, instead of physical force and dogmatic authority, . . . it is certain that a new ethic and a new morality based on a profound alteration in the narcissistic feelings of the child, will be evolved.

As far as the child is concerned, our way is fairly clear; seven years and one generation would be sufficient to alter the entire attitude of humanity. But this implies parents and teachers not only capable of seeing a vision but of living it.[2]

Sometimes parents are overzealous in their efforts to counteract influences on their children's attitudes which they regard as nefarious. They make too much of an occasional reflection of an outside attitude that may express itself in the child's conversation without really having entered very deeply into his thinking. For example, exaggerated fear seems to be expressed in the following statement of a well known worker for interracial cooperation whose home unquestionably provides all the anti-toxin which his children may require against poisoning influences from without:

My little boy came home telling how superior white people were to Chinese—his teacher had told him that. And we had tried to guard our children against just that. The teacher probably did not mean to do this—she probably denies herself to give part of her salary to foreign missions. Yet, it will take a long time to get that idea out of the child's head. We have brought him up not to think that he is superior to anybody—and one idle word has upset all those years of home training!

How simply an incipient prejudice may often be corrected in the home is illustrated by the following incident:

Bessie, a girl of fourteen, heard her father tell of an experience in a restaurant which, contrary to the law, had refused to serve a colored man. She remarked she certainly would not like to eat in the same place with Negroes. Asked to give her reason, she said she often found colored people ill-mannered on the street cars. The father suspected

[2] Beatrice M. Hinkle in *Progressive Education* for May, 1925, p. 67.

that this was a rationalization and that really the child merely reflected attitudes current among her school friends. To provide the child with opportunity to correct impressions gained from too limited a contact with people of the dark races, he took the first opportunity to invite some refined colored people to the home.

The same contributor also at times employs very simple devices to correct prejudiced racial attitudes in the children of his friends and neighbors, as in the following case:

John, twelve years old, came around to sell tickets for an entertainment at the public school, to raise money for a school orchestra. Asked for the price of tickets, he said, "Seventy-five cents each," and without waiting for comment, added: "That will keep the Wops out." To his utter astonishment, the hand of his prospective customer, which already held two crisp dollar bills, went back to the pocket, and he was told that the p. c. much regretted not to be able to go or have members of his family attend. "You see," he said, "I am an immigrant myself, and I should not be welcome. I hope next time you give an affair it will be something for everybody." (As an interesting side-light on the state of our suburban civilization, the contributor adds that the exclusive entertainment to which only the elect of the neighborhood were to be invited was a minstrel show!)

How parents may themselves be educated by adopting a more liberal attitude toward the associations of their children is illustrated in the following, contributed from California:

In the neighborhood of Fresno, California, there are a great many Armenians who have been very successful on fruit ranches. Naturally, there is a great deal of economic jealousy in the community. Armenians are not allowed to own property in certain residential districts, et cetera.

In a certain part of Fresno an Armenian and an American family had been living side by side for several years. The American parents would not allow the children to associate with the Armenian children because of the race relation in the community. In each family was a boy attending high school. These boys were very friendly in school but were not allowed to associate at home.

The American boy was taken ill, and his Armenian friend was determined to see him. So he had his mother prepare some rare Armenian delicacies, and started forth. He met a cold reception at his friend's front door. However, at the urgent request of the American boy, he was admitted. The illness went on for some time, and little by little the American parents saw the joy brought into their son's life by the visits of his Armenian friend. The Armenian mother did many thoughtful things for her boy's friend, and finally the American woman felt called upon to express her gratitude. After making the acquaintance of her Armenian neighbor, she regretted the years she had missed knowing this family with whom she found she had much in common.

More widespread than excessive zeal in counteracting influences looked upon as undesirable is the superficiality of parents' interest in the attitudes of their children toward persons of other groups. They are more concerned that their children should be able to get on well—especially with those who will be likely to be helpful to them—than that they should have a real foundation of habitual tolerance for difference. It is difficult to tell the two kinds of concern apart. The one merely reflects the state of tolerance current in the set in which the parents move, the other reflects a more genuine desire for the intellectual independence of the child. Perhaps a comparison of two illustrations will make this clear.

The child of a merchant with many international connections one day at dinner mimicked a Frenchman and was applauded for the performance by some of the guests, who thought it amusing. Later in the drawing room there was quite a discussion of the incident. The mother was visibly embarrassed and tried to find an adequate apology for it. "I don't know," she said, "where Molly picked this up. Certainly, I never saw her do anything like this before. Why, only a week ago we had the X's (Italians) here in the evening, and Charles is constantly bringing home people from all sorts of countries. What would they think . . ." The child was duly reprimanded, presumably; but what she was made to feel, to judge from her mother's talk, was that it was bad form and dangerous for happy social relations to make fun of other people; she was probably not made to feel that her idea of the manners of Frenchmen was mistaken or too limited and objectionable because false. Nor was she made to feel, in all likelihood, that differences in manners and other things are starting points for new learnings.

A sociology student at a middle-western university contributes this reminiscence: I can remember my mother telling us, and telling neighbors, when the question of "Negro odor" came up: "Yes, white folks smell, too, when they work in hot fields and have no chance to take a bath. My brothers all had to have a clean suit every day in hot weather. They'd bathe when they came in from the field and put on clean white suits to wear during the evening, and then wear that suit to work next day. Yes, the washing and the ironing was terrible. Negroes don't have a white linen suit for every day. Of course, their clothes smell. A Negro worked for father one summer, and I ironed his shirts along with the others. There was no odor—even when the iron was on the under-arm part. And *my* mother said the same, and she was from Virginia. There is no more odor when they have a chance to be clean than that from white folks." All this, adds the student, impressed me as a child because it was first-hand proof, and I passed the argument on to other children who could not refute it with facts and were told so in no uncertain terms.

ABOUNDING OPPORTUNITIES

It is clear, then, that the home has opportunities for conditioning the race attitudes of children that are both more varied and more intimate than those of school and neighborhood. Practically everything that has been considered in the preceding chapters has aspects of parental influence; for by their selection of outside associations, studies, recreations and institutional affiliations, parents have it in their power to determine somewhat the social atmosphere in which their children are to grow up. But in the present chapter we are concerned with the opportunities contained in the direct contact between parents and children. First of all, there are obvious occasions for communicating feelings and thoughts on the matter. Several such examples have been mentioned incidentally. Here are two or three more:

It was Easter morning on the second-class deck of the *S.S. Olympic* en route to America. A New England mother was quietly reading the story of the Crucifixion to her three children. In the midst of the story one interrupted and asked, "So it was a bunch of Jews who killed Jesus?" The mother started to nod assent when her eye fell on the occupants of several adjacent steamer chairs and, like a flash, she said, "Yes, it happened to be Jews who killed Jesus, but He Himself was a Jew. If He had been living in America today, it would have been Protestant Christians like ourselves who would have killed Him."

A woman who is especially alive to the need of such corrective teaching through much experience as a religious teacher, contributes this incident:

My three children attend a school which is very fine, of high standing, with excellent equipment, teaching staff, etc.—a public school which is almost an institution. It has about 1,000 children. The Jews are moving into our neighborhood, and many small shops in it attract a class of Jews which is not of the high type of the resident Jews, who live in apartments or over the stores. One day my children announced, "Oh, mother, —— School is getting to be awful! There are so many Jews going there. Pretty soon it will be all Jews."

I asked them what was a "Jew"—they couldn't say exactly. An attempt by the six-year-old was, "They are like those awful Cadalics (Catholics)." I knew they had not heard criticism at home but from some one at school. Then I explained to them about the Jewish race and their connection with our Christian religion—their long history, etc. I explained that some were bad and some were good, as in any race, but that kindness and courtesy brought out a like spirit from them.

The oldest one, my boy of eleven years, was sharply rebuked when he began to "run on" them. I reminded him that when I went to the school to tell World-Friendship stories, a Jewish lad was the one who first came up to him in the yard to congratulate him on his mother's stories, and that later when I went again to tell a missionary hero story that boy was most appreciative.

After that I heard no more about Jews in such critical terms. But a month or so afterward I told a missionary story over the radio. It was advertised as a Christian Church Vesper Service, 5:00 P.M. Sunday, and that I would have a part. The Jewish lad listened for my story. The next day he praised the story to my son at recess. He is the nephew of a prominent rabbi here. My boy will no doubt be more and more friendly. If my boy were to continue his criticism of the Jewish race, the Jewish lad would soon build a wall between them, whereas now we have built up a link in the chain of race friendships and race good-will.

An inquiry into the effect of home teaching in a sociology class produced these two examples, à propos of direct teaching through talks:

A Chinese student has lived with us eight years. She was still away at the university this June when a girl of six years (mentally) came to spend the summer and be tutored. One day the neighbor children must have told her something which she didn't get quite straight, for at dinner she broke out in round-eyed amazement and horror, "Are you Chinese?" to my sister. "No." "Are you Chinese?" to me. "No." She was puzzled and silent. Next day came, "Is this a Chinese house?" with the attitude that that must be the solution and she was entrapped in something awful. When again she received a "No," she seemed to give it up and forget it after a time.

The neighbor children were asked not to puzzle her by talking about the Chinese girl and they evidently did not. Meantime we began to remark on various things that would be so much nicer for us "as soon as —— is home." She became very anxious for that day and was happy clear through when she did come. Now she considers her her special friend and would monopolize her if we let her. When the time comes that she learns —— is Chinese she will have some first-hand experience to counteract the stereotype she had gained, largely, I think, from many movies she had attended and heard her mother discuss.

As a child my mother would never let us say, in her presence, the rime that went with one game and contained the words:

> "When the nigger begins to run,
> Shoot him with a leather gun!"

She told us there was no such word as "nigger"—that it was "negro" but that they preferred to be called "colored people"; that they were no more likely to run than other folks, etc. As a child I resented her interference with a game the other mothers did not object to, but later I got the reasonableness of the argument against an undeserved slur.

In several of the examples given, the parent endeavors to arouse sympathy for members of another group by having the child imagine himself in their situation. Occasionally, especially where group conflict or the sense of group hostility is acute in the community, a useful educational end may be served by telling against one's own group a story of the type that is usually told about the other group, reminding the child that it is well at times to see ourselves as others see us.[3]

The typical American community is full of neglected opportunities of contact for teaching appreciation of other groups that can be improvised in the course of a shopping tour. An instructively guided walk along one of the shopping streets may provide occasions for pointing to the dependence of each group on the joint effort of all the groups. If parents happen to have tastes in that direction, they can point out the contributions of different peoples to American architecture and indoor decoration, to the clothes we wear or the foods we use. Miss Mary Chaplin Shute of Teachers College, Boston, suggests that the child's natural sense of dependence—which William H. Burnham considers a criterion for normal mental health [4]—be broadened in such a

---

[3] Such an example is given by Professor Bogardus in his collection of cases illustrating race friendliness. *Journal of Applied Sociology* for January-February, 1927, p. 284.

[4] *The Normal Mind* (1925, p. 667).

way as to overcome any tendency there may be to take excessive pride in his own group.[5]

A "tableau of world interdependence" is sketched in *World's Youth* (international organ of the Y.M.C.A.) for May, 1925. For the suggested pageantry small cut-out pictures might be substituted and, with appropriate explanations, pinned or pasted to each article—such as bread: western farmer; table cloth (cotton): American Negro; tray: Japanese; china: Chinese; sugar: West Indian; coffee: Brazilian; cocoa: African; tea: Singhalese; etc.

One contributor writes:

I have made it a habit to collect printed pictures of every kind and, from my children's earliest years, have found constant educational use for them. At first, esthetic considerations prevailed entirely, and we thought of nothing but the production of pretty picture books once or twice a year. Later, the interests of the family directed a system of arrangement so that, during the whole school years of the children, hardly a subject came up for discussion that we were not able to illustrate. In addition to the general geographical and ethnographic order, with an envelope for each country, we also have a separate envelope for the arts of each of the more important peoples or groups, and inclusive folders on anthropology, architecture, industry, shipping, etc., that permit of quick historical and cultural comparisons. The periodical sorting out and filing of new material has been a constant source of interest and education to the children and to myself. Our sources were limited to magazines, catalogues and other printed matter that comes to the house.

Even a walk through the fields—for one acquainted with the origins of our American flora—may produce material for an appreciative discussion of the contributions of different peoples to the wealth of America and the comforts and enjoyments of children.

The following extract, conversely, illustrates the effect in happy goodwill which such appreciation may produce in members of the minority groups:

I saw a throng of people crowding around the show-windows of the Oriental shop of a great hotel. We edged our way through and finally reached the interior of the shop. The first view made me think that some fairy had waved me into a Chinese dream of delight—right in

[5] *Childhood Education,* for February, 1926, p. 274.

America. The smiling clerk stepped forward and said, "May I serve you, Lady? Aren't you a Chinese? Probably these things will interest you." "Thank you," I replied, "I have recently come from China and would like to look around in your famous shop." "We have just received some new orders from your country," she added, "and I would like to ask you the meaning of a certain piece of embroidery."

Guided by the pleasant little saleslady, I went to a big case containing crystals, amber, jade, rubies, amethyst, matrix and ivory ornaments of all imaginable styles and shapes. They sparkled radiantly, struck by the light shining through the quaint colorful Peking lanterns. Walking over the delicately hued Tientsin rugs, we came to a room where the walls were decorated with gorgeous embroideries and paintings and beautiful Nanking tapestries. Here and there were highly polished and well-carved pieces of teak or ebony furniture, adorned with bridal skirts and coats as table covers. An emperor's throne of black lacquer, with insets of golden dragons, made one wonder whether the occupant had recently stepped down and could be seen sad-eyed and wistful in some secluded nook. Scattered on little tables and stands were jade trees, ivory statues, cloisonné vases, bronze incense burners and fragile Canton porcelain wares of all shapes and uses. Cunning little dolls with their almond-shaped faces and dreamy slender eyes, garbed in red embroidered coats, queer trousers and dangling head-dresses, smiled a welcome to me from my homeland. The whole atmosphere was Oriental. Numberless treasures of China gathered in this single room! Beauty of China displayed everywhere!

I was asked to explain a piece of embroidery to a group of anxious listeners circled around me. It was a huge, most exquisite embroidered birthday piece, representing the "Eight Fairies Crossing the Sea." As I related the story and explained the beauty, I could feel the thrills of appreciation and admiration. . . .

How proud I felt to hear all this appreciation of the art products of China! [6]

THE QUESTION OF DIRECT CONTACTS

For reasons already amply discussed, we enter upon a matter of more doubtful expediency when we come to the opportunities for creating direct contacts with members of other groups. For purposes of this chapter, however, we shall try to help those parents who consider such contacts desirable and necessary to create a lasting attitude of friendship for these groups in their children. Many of them are seeking suggestions as to possible

[6] Lily Ho, of the University of Southern California, in the *Chinese Christian Student,* January-February, 1927, p. 11.

ways of arranging such contacts with the normal resources of the home.

We must distinguish, in this respect, several possible purposes. It may be that what is desired is a complete unconsciousness of racial difference so far as behavior is concerned. Or it may be that friendly contact is desired but not a sense of equality. Indeed, between complete segregation and complete disregard of the racial element in the child's personal contacts, there lies an infinitude of shades of social distance. You can be friendly to foreign-born tradesmen, yet not think of associating with their children. You may countenance play with colored children, yet not for a moment wish to implant either in them or in your own children the idea that they are on an equal footing. You may desire your children to possess affection and respect for all groups in the community, to look upon them all as equally valuable to American civilization, and yet for good, practical reasons not want your child to be in the company of those whose language or manners do not come up to the level of yours. Moreover, different psychological attitudes come into play in contact with adults and in contact with children, and in contact with children of different ages.

In all practical efforts to permit a limited "tolerance" on the part of children for those of other races and nations, account must, of course, be taken of the fact that the childish mind does not automatically pigeon-hole different types of experience but readily transfers a pleasurable racial contact from one social plane to another and from one racial group to another.[7] And it is hardly honest to persuade doubtful parents that some small step in the direction of interracial contact, such as they might sanction, has no bearing upon the formation of race attitudes in the large.

For those who desire a maximum of all these contacts, or of any of these contacts, the next problem is how to make them of such a character as to have lasting educational effect. Perhaps the first requisite in the pursuit of that object is that the contacts must be pleasant. One or two examples will illustrate the intentional creation of pleasant contacts for the purpose of conditioning children to an eager acceptance of members of other groups into

[7] Cornelia Stratton Parker, in an article, "Take Your Children to Europe"—*Harpers*, August, 1928, p. 376—shows how readily the attitude of international appreciation, acquired abroad, is transferred to interracial relations at home.

their circle of friendly personal relations. (In each case, the action that is intended to produce an appreciative interest is given in italics.)

Up to a year ago, my work as a teacher has been singularly free from opportunities of seeing race antagonisms in children. But once in Kentucky—although in this district there are no Negroes at all—I began to hear for the first time of "niggers" and to feel an attitude of scorn and hatred on the part of some of the children whenever they referred to them.

At Christmas time a member of our faculty took one of the mountain children, Madgie, aged eight, home with her to Detroit for two weeks. As a preparation before starting, Madgie *was told* that she would see colored people on the train and at Miss C.'s home and *she must be sure not to* call them "niggers," for this might *hurt their feelings*. On the journey and during the visit Madgie grew to love the colored people because of the attentiveness of the porter and the waiters on the train, and because of the good cheer and genuine *kindness of the colored cook* and laundress at Mrs. C.'s. She asked Martha, the laundress, many questions about her home, her (blind) husband and what made her so happy. Before leaving, she begged Mrs. C. for a colored doll-baby "to remember Martha by; Martha is so kind and brave." She was given the colored doll, and on her return to the Center the other children laughed at it and called it "nigger." Madgie was furious! She defended it fiercely and said they should never call it that. And after she told them about Martha and her blind husband and how cheerful and kind she was, they seemed interested and the objectionable word was dropped—at least in Madgie's hearing.

A New York high-school teacher writes:

Home influences seem of the greatest importance. My nephews have been brought up in a rural district, where there are many colored people and a strong Ku Klux power. *Association* with colored children *has always been practised,* however, and I have noted *no instances of discriminations* against Negroes *in matters of courtesy*. I have heard one of my nephews report the use of the term "nigger" with disapproval as a "bad word." The home influence seems to have extended to a young German maid, who attended evening school in company with a colored fellow-servant, although this association was unusual in the town.

Frequently, the best and most important way of creating interracial appreciation and friendship is simply to permit the children to make and keep their own social contacts. This is by no means always a simple thing since the parents cannot, in the nature of things, be as equalitarian as are the children, who as yet may be unconscious of strong reasons for maintaining certain social distances.[8]

The influence of the parental example, both in behavior and also in hospitality to members of other groups, need only be mentioned to be grasped.

The son of a famous internationalist on one occasion expressed surprise when someone congratulated him on his cooperative spirit in interracial matters. "How could I be anything else but that?" he asked. "During the whole of my childhood we never knew whether father would bring home a man with a silk hat on his head or a man with a turban."

A Pennsylvania mother thus describes the influences of international hospitality on her sons:

There have been occasional, if not frequent, Negro guests in our home and at our table. Hindu, Japanese, Mexican, Jewish guests were often in our home, too, and I never detected the slightest natural aversion to any of them on the part of our children. Our oldest boy, now sixteen, is a sophomore at —— [Negro] College; he is the only white boy regularly enrolled, several others are "specials." He takes his lunch in the refectory with the Negro students but is not in residence in the dormitories because he lives at home. He occasionally brings a classmate home for a meal. He has been on a debating team and identifies himself in every way with the institution. He is quite conscious of possible social handicaps, going from here to —— University, and says, "I know every one will be horrified at my coming from a Negro college, but I shan't mind that."

I might explain that he has been at —— because of the unusual quality of the instruction there. It is infinitely to be preferred to our local high-school.

Our second boy is one of the specials there. He has said that he prefers not to eat at the refectory, but I am not sure it is race feeling since he has never shown the slightest aversion at our home. I think it is the crowd and the food.

[8] This problem is interestingly discussed by Sidonie M. Gruenberg, director of the Child Study Association, in *Sons and Daughters* (1926, p. *297 et seq.*).

For other examples illustrating a tolerant attitude on the part of parents toward the ripening of their children's chance acquaintanceships into friendships—apparently without hurtful effects on manners and morals—see *Journal of Applied Sociology*, January-February, 1927, pp. 276, 281.

It seems to me that race prejudice is entirely a matter of suggestion and imitation in children, that its roots are hidden far back in economic rivalries and conditions, and that it can be wiped out if children can be brought up without seeing or hearing of it.

The ways in which parents impress their children with the superiority of their own group and the lapse inherent in every transgression of its tradition of exclusiveness are, as we have seen in many of the examples given, as varied as the gradations between extreme forms of punishment and of reward. But the effectiveness of punishment and reward in efforts to create an opposite conditioning that is in favor of liberal attitudes, is not so clear. We cannot at this point enter into a full discussion of the values of these two kinds of incentive in general, except to draw attention to the increasing disposition of educators to rule them out altogether as unreliable factors in character education.[9] The reason for this is that it takes exceptional imagination and skill, not to be expected in the average parent or teacher, to anticipate the exact association that will take place in the child's mind between the nature and the cause of the stimulus that comes to him in the form of an unpleasant or a pleasant experience. Moreover, even if the direct learning is unmistakable, it may be accompanied by any number of associated, attendant learnings which are not only unintended but positively mischievous.[10]

A seemingly successful combination of threatened punishment with other educational influences is illustrated in the following account:

Two little Italian boys lived in a cottage in the rear of the big house, and the sons of both homes played together happily week in and week out. But one day when the mother in the big house said to her ten-year-old son, "You are having Tony and Alfred to your party on Saturday?" the son promptly informed her that he thought not. Why? Well, John's mother had not invited them, and so on. Mother made no comment, but half an hour later, when the four were having a glorious game of ball in the backyard, her sons were called in. "You must stay in your own yard and the boys in theirs," she announced calmly. "But why?" roared the indignant pair. "We ain't doin' nothin'; we

---

[9] See, especially, William H. Kilpatrick, *Foundations of Method* (1925), various references. Also *Outlines for Child Study,* manual of the Federation for Child Study (1924, Sec. 7 and bibliography).
[10] A good example of this is given by Mrs. Sidonie M. Gruenberg in *The Survey,* September 1, 1926, p. 588.

always play together after school!" "Yes, I know, but you must have discovered something about them which is not nice, or you would have had them with your other friends Saturday. I supposed they were nice boys, but if you feel that they are not nice enough to meet your other friends, they are certainly not the kind of boys for you to play with every day in the week. So after this you will just stay apart," she finished firmly.

Two very crestfallen, solemn sons went silently out of the house and into the garage for a period of thoughtfulness, and at dinner-time rather sheepishly admitted that they had added two to the list of guests, and that Tony and his brother would be on hand for the party. And on hand they were; positively scoured, clad in their best, and on the alert to catch every suggestion as to behavior on this wonderful occasion of a real American party. And never again was there any suggestion of the little new Americans being omitted from the good times in the big house.

Then something else happened. The mother in the big house asked John's mother to come and help her in Saturday's fun. She watched the dark-skinned guests closely; she did some thinking; and two little Italian boys were at John's party a month later. In a year a little leaven had permeated the whole neighborhood, and Tony and Alfred wondered that they had ever felt that America was a lonesome place.[11]

The illustration just given incidentally indicates the nature of an even larger task, that of education for parents. Sometimes it is incidental to and, indeed, inseparable from the task primarily discussed in this chapter. Sometimes nothing at all can be accomplished until parents have groped their own way out of a confusion of ideals for themselves and their children. And sometimes children have to take a hand in educating their parents! For example:

Into a lovely rural neighborhood, with quiet streets and backyards, in which the children of the whole neighborhood played together, there moved a refined, nice-appearing mulatto family. The two children of this family were about of the age of a little girl whom we will call Miriam—one of the older children of the block who previously had not had many children of exactly her own age to play with but who was extremely popular as general guardian of a troop of slightly younger ones. She at once played with the colored children.

An informal delegation of mothers of the block waited upon Miriam's mother to say that if this intimacy continued, they could not allow

[11] *Christian Americanization at Work,* a tract of the American Baptist Publication Society, Philadelphia.

their children to play with Miriam. Miriam's mother wisely laid the matter before the little girl herself. Miriam was wildly indignant, turning the fury of her wrath against her mother for even listening to the other mothers, let alone mentioning the matter to her. Her mother made her sit still and listen for some time. She told her to consider carefully whether she was willing to sacrifice her pleasure with this, that or the other child whom she had known all their lives, and whether she was strong enough to risk everything for a mere principle, remembering that she did not yet know the mulatto children well on their own account. Miriam sat on the edge of her chair with clenched fists and pink cheeks, saying only, "This is not the way you taught me; I think it's dreadful for you to talk this way to me. Now, may I go, mother; may I go now, mother?"

When she was released, she made a bee-line straight across the street and up to the new neighbors' house, giving as she went a signal call which rallied around her all the familiar little neighborhood clan. All that summer afternoon the group of children played with the new kittens and playhouse of the two mulatto children—and that was absolutely the end of the experience. No mother ever commented on it afterwards, and the children played in whatever yard was convenient from that day all the rest of the summer.

Parental Self-education

The present volume does, of course, serve the purpose of helping parents, among others, to come to a clearer understanding of educational needs in relation to race attitudes—but only in regard to the influences to be exerted upon or kept away from their children. This chapter would be incomplete if it did not emphasize that back of any new ideas in that connection which parents may obtain, it is even more important that they should be intelligent and reasonably consistent in their own racial attitudes and in their own behavior toward members of other groups. For, most of the education in these respects which they give their children is unconscious and unpremeditated anyhow.

No one can create tolerance in others who himself is engulfed in prejudice; and a blind man should not attempt to lead the blind. On the other hand, it is often through their interest in children that adults are, for the first time in their lives, made aware of the nature and influences of their attitudes and troubled about their relation to their fellow man. Many a person who has lived within the confines of his set, oblivious to the world outside, is introduced through his children into a larger range of perplexing social problems—not because the child has to face them necessarily, but because he cannot exclude the child from outside contacts that may either help or hurt. Incidentally, the impetus for the present study has come largely from a realization of parents and others responsible for bringing up children that they must educate themselves on this matter before they can be sure what educational policies to adopt.

This, often, means more than a preoccupation with rights and wrongs, with far-reaching ethical questions and problems of eugenics and sociology. Often it means an elementary self-education in the national and racial composition of one's own neighborhood and its influences on one's own life and that of family and community. Too many parents are well-disposed to all mankind on general grounds but totally ignorant of the foreign-born or the colored people at their own back door. Or if they know of their existence, they may know very little about them; and the first step in self-education may, therefore, well be to get to know them and also to get to know about them what can be learned from books or in other ways. This need is illustrated in the following incident:

A Parent-Teacher Association in a Pennsylvania city voted to give a scholarship. When it became known that the person eligible was a Russian youth, several members of the association gave voice to their feelings of resentment. One woman present at the meeting had professionally been brought into close touch with the foreign-born and did not share the prevailing view. She made a strong plea for fairness in the award of the scholarship regardless of the nationality of the recipient. A heated discussion followed, in the course of which this woman succeeded in arousing interest in wider aspects of the subject, with the result that for some weeks the topic of immigration was seriously discussed by the members.

At a meeting two weeks later, the woman member of the association who had been loudest in her protest against the proposed award, got up and said: "I apologize for the unkind remarks I made at an earlier meeting about our foreign-born neighbors. Since that meeting I have read three books on immigration and discussed the subject with my family. I am willing to acknowledge that I now have a vastly different opinion of the foreigner and am ready to help in his adjustment instead of retarding it. When I found out how much we owe to the foreign man in the development of our country and the progress he has made against obstacles which seemed almost unsurmountable, I think America should respect him and give him the same opportunities which Americans enjoy."

THE LARGER OBJECTIVE

We have thus far discussed attitudes toward persons of another race or nationality as though they involved problems in child behavior, distinct from other questions of antipathy and sympathy. This is not, of course, the case. These forms of association that have been considered are merely of one convenient subject category, not essentially different, as regards psychological reactions, from other categories. Sympathy, curiosity, consideration are qualities that do not require the relatively rare opportunities of interracial contact for their development; indeed, they cannot manifest themselves in interracial situations unless they are always brought out by experiences of a similar nature. The question is, can sympathy be trained or is it a natural attribute that some people have and others have not? Doubtless, physical constitution has something to do with it—smallness of stature, weakness, nervous sensitiveness are more predisposing to a gentle disposition than their opposites. Nevertheless, it does not follow that a big, burly, strong and healthy boy is necessarily more cruel than a boy of his age who possesses the opposite characteristics. As important as physical predisposition are early training and the gradual growth of habits of behavior; thus the weakling may be a cruel tyrant and the athlete a gentle nurse.[12]

Ellwood distinguishes three main types of sympathy: organic sympathy—presumably what Russell means by "physical" sympathy—; compassion, or feeling *for* others; and the rational sympathy which is neither organic nor impulsive but reflective. This highest form is, of course, derived from the other two which are more primary. He continues:

Rational sympathy is the most valuable form of sympathy in all the higher phases of social development, because it is subject to rational control. It can, moreover, be cultivated through the social imagination. It is indispensable in building up the higher social and altruistic sentiments which have characterized the most advanced civilizations.

[12] On the possibilities of training for sympathy see Bertrand Russell, *Education and the Good Life* (1926, p. 70). Also W. G. Carr, *Education for World Citizenship* (Stanford University Press, 1928, p. 58 *et seq.*), and sources there quoted.

Experience has shown that through the cultivation of rational sympathy we most surely direct the activities of individuals in an altruistic rather than an egoistic direction. It is the chief means of motivation of rational altruism.[13]

Positive instruction can prevent many wrong conceptions. If we wish a child to respect the Negro race we need not wait until he has built up an idea of the race from prejudiced newspaper reports. We can share with him the remarkable achievements of the race since the Civil War. We can show him injustices done to the race. We can make personal contacts so that he may learn that people of a different color think and feel much as he does. In all worthwhile play activities it is this positive side which the teacher is seeking to develop.

Sometimes it seems impossible actually to see and know a Japanese or a Chinese or a Negro or a miner. Sometimes life seems to fail to supply some of the vital contacts. A child, however, may gain the experience imaginatively through a story, through pictures, or through actually being the person as he takes the part in a play. Dramatization thus offers opportunity for increasing his sympathetic interpretation of the world.[14]

In short, whatever phase of the subject we take up in its relation to the educational influences of the home, one striking conclusion which we are entitled to draw from the evidence in previous chapters as well as the present one is that parents require far greater knowledge than they now possess of the child mind in general before they can successfully cope with any particular form of reaction that seems to them undesirable. This need is increasingly being recognized, as may be seen by the large number of books on the child mind that are being issued year by year, the popularity of study courses, the space given to the subject in women's magazines.

But unfortunately educational experts are themselves as yet in no certain possession of a technique of child training, especially for the earlier years of life in which so many unfortunate habits are acquired. The literature of applied and educational

[13] Charles A. Ellwood, *The Psychology of Human Society* (1925, p. 373). The whole chapter XII of this textbook, on Feeling and Group Life, bears upon our subject. Incidentally, the author denies the existence of a law formulated by Giddings "that sympathy between two groups is proportionate to their resemblance, or rather to their consciousness of resemblance, whether actual or potential" (p. 377).

[14] Edna L. Acheson, *Why Play? Some Play Experiences with Juniors in a Church School.* Board of Christian Education of the Presbyterian Church, 1926. Pamphlet, p. 35.

psychology is full of experiments; but there is as yet little consensus as to desirable and undesirable methods. Take the subject of fear, for example, which, as we have seen, is one of the earliest manifestations of an unfavorable reaction and one most difficult to eradicate. One recent experimenter reports as follows:

In our study of methods of removing fear responses, we found unqualified success with only two. By the method of direct conditioning we associated the fear-object with a craving-object, and replaced the fear by a positive response. By the method of social imitation we allowed the subject to share, under controlled conditions, the social activity of a group of children especially chosen with a view to prestige effect. Verbal appeal, elimination through disuse, "repression," and "distraction" were methods which proved sometimes effective but were not to be relied upon unless used in combination with other methods. It should be remarked that apart from laboratory analysis we have rarely used any of the above procedures in pure form. . . .[15]

This little sample of the experimental approach under laboratory conditions must suffice to illustrate how far we are as yet from a reliable technique. It must suffice also here to illustrate the kind of fundamental psychological consideration that enters into the practical problem of child training for those qualities of response toward persons of other racial groups which fall within the early years of home care. A discussion of these more general questions, important as they are for the purposes of this chapter, would lead us far outside the scope of the present study.

Our brief survey of the educational opportunities in the home has shown how similar many of the problems faced by parents are to those which have occupied the attention of schoolmen in recent years. We are gradually discovering, with the aid of psychological studies, how attitudes and mental habits are formed in childhood; and because of their more organized character and functioning, the progressive schools of the country have so far been in a better position to take full advantage of the significant contributions of science. We shall, therefore, in the following chapters, review some of the practical ways in which teachers are trying to tackle these common problems

[15] Mary Cover Jones, "The Elimination of Childish Fears." *Journal of Experimental Psychology,* Vol. VII, 1924, p. 390.

CHAPTER XXI

WHAT SCHOOL CAN DO

The Question of Segregation

In reviewing the many different ways in which the American public school contributes toward the fixation of race attitudes, we have recognized that it faces a particularly difficult task. (Chap. XI, p. 146 *et seq.*) It not only acts as the principal organ of the nation for transmitting to the young established traditions of democracy (and this at a time, let it be noted, when outstanding historians are disagreed among themselves as to the exact meaning of key passages in the Declaration of Independence and in other documentary evidence of the views held by the Fathers of the Country); it has to make these traditions known to children of immigrants with a background of both different political conditions and different political principles; and, in addition, it has to reflect in a measure the attitudes of majority groups that dominate the public school system without necessarily being able to take any other than a local or sectional point of view of desirable race relations.[1]

Under the circumstances, it is obviously impossible to lay down generally valid precepts except on the assumption that, no matter what type of association between children of different races, classes, denominations, nationalities, may seem desirable or unavoidable in a given region, certain broad educational principles are applicable to all who wish their children to be brought up as free as possible from prejudice.

In this undertaking, we shall do well, at the outset, to remind ourselves of the history of the American school in the adjustment between different groups—more especially between newcomers and older settlers. In one respect, the part which it played has proved decisive. Whatever influence we may ascribe to other

[1] The extent to which public education is controlled by limited class interests has recently been shown by George S. Counts in a study entitled *The Social Composition of Boards of Education* (University of Chicago Press, 1927); it is perhaps significant that in this monograph no mention at all is made of limited nationality and race representation.

favorable circumstances, it was undoubtedly the school, as Dr. Albert Shaw has so ably shown [2] that united the flood of ignorant immigrants and their children with their older established neighbors into an essentially solidary American citizenship.

We may note, in passing, the sacrifices often made by immigrants to assist their children in this process of adjustment:

Miss L. said her father and mother came to America thirty-eight years ago and were among the first Italian families to settle here. She has heard them tell of innumerable hardships endured during their first years of residence in Buffalo. They were greatly handicapped, of course, by their inability to speak and understand English. They were abused by the early settlers and exploited by their own group which had previously come to America. It is natural to believe that these conditions developed a clannishness among them which is noticeable to some extent even now, and perhaps their many handicaps have served as an incentive towards the education of their children. They have sacrificed the bare necessities of life in order to save something towards their children's tuition in the schools and many times the colleges. They realized that America is a land of opportunity and that one must be equal to the task of reaching for it and being as fully qualified as the next man.[3]

In a book primarily concerned with problems that remain to be solved, it is well to remember how much our American faith in democracy and mutual tolerance has already accomplished in producing a state of social harmony in a population composed of so many elements—and this not only through the efforts of the older residents who control the machinery of public education but also through the efforts and sacrifices of the immigrants themselves. Nor must we underestimate the modifying effect upon attitudes that is produced by the mere fact of racial mixture. Occasionally the prejudices brought into the system by the teachers from their earlier associations are gradually eliminated by the education they themselves receive at the hands of their pupils.[4]

[2] *Political Problems of American Development* (Columbia University Press, 1907, p. 61).
[3] From the unpublished notes of a nationality survey made in Buffalo by Professor Niles Carpenter.
[4] For a striking illustration see Dorothy Giles, *Adventures in Brotherhood* (Council of Women for Home Missions and Missionary Education Movement, 1924, p. 101).

Temporary Segregation

We must beware, however, not to let ourselves be swayed—either by such incidents or by the historical considerations adduced—into concluding without further reflection that, as between the children of native Americans and those of immigrants, there must be no segregation; that it is necessarily to the best interests of both and of the nation as a whole that they sit together in the same classes. Miss Grace Abbott has pointed out that in actual differences of previous training there may be good and sufficient reasons for segregation of immigrant children.[5] The larger social view-point underlying such separation has been stated by Professor Robbins who shows that the difference between a school system designed to embody the ideal of democracy and one designed to reflect the current social attitudes permits of various half-stages as well as an absolute choice.[6] That children recognize the reasonableness of segregation which has for its purpose the more rapid advancement of those who are possessed of the English language and to give the maximum aid to children retarded because of their lack of it, may be illustrated by the following incident:

A Jewish girl of fourteen was asked by a woman who had just moved into the neighborhood to which of two public schools that were about equally distant from her home she had better send her child. The girl recommended —— School because there the "Wops" were more or less segregated. This information was rather astonishing, for no one in the home of this Jewish girl, or among her associates, was likely to have given her a prejudice against immigrants. However, on further questioning it appeared that she had thought the matter out and was not speaking either from prejudice or with an intentional contempt for immigrants. —— School, being the larger of the two, she said, had so many pupils that each grade was subdivided into several classes, so that the children from American homes usually were put into those classes that got on faster while the "foreigners" who had language difficulties were in the other classes that did not advance so fast.

Sometimes segregation of foreign-born children may be justified on more subtle grounds of character-training. It has been pointed out that the segregated school or class for foreign-born children may be more sympathetic toward the viewpoints of the

[5] *The Immigrant and the Community* (1917, p. 223).
[6] Charles L. Robbins, *The School as a Social Institution* (1918, p. 90).

parents and thus prevent the tragic break between the foreign-born and their American-born children.[7] This argument has been applied also to colored children in northern cities when the colored community has only recently established itself and is, culturally, still of the South. Too often, in that case also, association with white native children, looked upon by the parents as desirable, has unfortunate results, because the white children who accept colored schoolmates into their intimacy are not always those who exercise the most beneficial influence upon them.[8]

In Chicago, and probably elsewhere, special classes have been established for children recently arrived from the South even in schools predominatingly colored. Their special problems are almost identically the same as those of white immigrant children from countries backward in their schools. In addition, these children often are timid in their contact with white children; being kept to themselves within the larger school community gives them the chance of gradually becoming accustomed to a new racial situation. The differences between children of the old-established colored families in the North and those of recent "immigrants" from the South are well brought out in the following extract from an unpublished report of the National Urban League concerning the situation in Milwaukee:

In certain schools, located in different sections of the city, may be found a few children of old residents who live apart from the colored community. These present no problem. In fact, their difference in race is hardly regarded. The principals and teachers appeared scrupulously careful to avoid calling attention to their race or making them conscious of it. One principal asserts that the colored children of northern parents show the same liveliness as white children. They are alert and active. The children from the South are timid and very reticent. The change of environment, he thinks, accounts for this.

Another principal thinks the colored children have a characteristic which, though admirable for some purposes, is not conducive to serious study, or "digging." They have, he thinks, a "happy-go-lucky air," and seem not to worry about anything. A decline in scholarship is noticed after the sixth grade is reached. This he would not account for. The children from Georgia have been placed in the backward classes, just as a foreigner would be. The problem met here is in the

[7] Mary Clark Barnes, *Neighboring New Americans* (1920, p. 44).
[8] Note also the experience of differences in physiological and mental maturing by members of different racial groups (see Chap. VII) and their effect on the race attitudes of adolescents.

overgrown children from the inferior schools of the South who would
be disgusted and further retarded if placed in the regular primary
classes. As a rule they learn rapidly. There is little truancy. Some
of the colored children have led their classes. In fact, at the Garfield
Street School, in an aristocratic German settlement, a colored girl was
leading the sixth grade.

The principal of one school in which there was a comparatively large
number of Negroes was "not sure that he knew what a Negro is."

When all has been said, however, in favor of a temporary segregation that permits each group to advance most expeditiously
along its own line of growth, we must not forget the educational
values that come from contacts through which children are made
aware of the rich variety of gifts and cultural traditions in the
world. Many students of the subject are so alarmed by the
danger of an American class stratification with the aid of the
public schools that, in spite of all admitted difficulties, they favor
the complete elimination of segregation in our public schools,
even of foreign children with language difficulties.[9] In short,
there is a huge difference between segregation on the grounds of
personal attainments and segregation by race without examination as to personal fitness and character. By far the largest racial
separations of school children in this country apply automatically,
without even permitting special opportunities for exceptional
children. (See Chap. X.) And the disadvantaged group is not
always mentally or otherwise inferior.[10] No personal inferiority
of any kind, obviously, caused the following incident:

A colored boy in Cleveland was the leader of an athletic group in
one of the high schools. Just before a certain contest with another
school he was asked to give up his place on the team in order that his
team might be given fair treatment. He did so.

At least one notable foreign critic believes that we do not go
far enough in this country in segregation according to differences
of talent. Graham Wallas quotes with disapproval an article by
Professor Dallas Lore Sharp in which that educator says:

The true end of American education is the knowledge and practice
of democracy—whatever other personal ends our education may serve.

[9] See, for example, Dorothy Giles, *Adventures in Brotherhood* (Council of
Women for Home Missions and Missionary Education Movement, 1924,
p. 107). Also Charles L. Robbins, *The School as a Social Institution* (1918,
p. 114).
[10] Sidney L. Gulick. "Japanese in California." *Annals of the American
Academy of Political and Social Science.* Vol. XCIII, January, 1921, p. 58.

. . . We must all go together to school, with a common language, a common course of study, a common purpose, faith, and enthusiasm for democracy.[11]

Commenting on this, Graham Wallas says:

I sympathize intensely with those American thinkers who fear the development of hereditary social stratification in America. And yet I am sure that if the political organization of America is to show itself compatible with the insistent demands of modern civilization it must be based on a theory of democracy more complex than that of identity, and nearer to the formula of 1848, "From each according to his powers; to each according to his needs." [12]

At this point the question may be worth discussing further whether it is desirable for the public school system to be more democratic than the community that supports it. Our theory of public education has assumed, for the most part, that there is a fundamental American ideal of democracy that must be taught the oncoming generation through the very organization of the school itself. It is true, this theory has never been fully applied; the Negro has not so much been deliberately excluded from it in the greater part of the country as he has never been considered in the South as a possible participant in the American democracy. The idea still sounds strange in the ears of many of our citizens. In other parts of the country, the theory has been stretched somewhat in application so as to permit the exclusion from the schools of particularly "undesirable" classes or races. Sometimes lavish provision has been made for the separate education of children of a given group so as to accomplish a segregation without injustice (as regards Chinese in San Francisco, for example). And sometimes the nonenforcement of attendance laws upon foreignborn parents has virtually meant exclusion through laissez-faire.[13]

While we cannot in this chapter enter into a full discussion of the question just raised, it is important that we do not answer it without an eye to all the aspects of the matter. For example, the question is often asked whether bringing children of different

[11] *Atlantic Monthly* for November, 1919.
[12] *Our Social Heritage* (Yale University Press, 1921, p. 98).
[13] See, for example, *Child Labor in the Sugar Beet Fields of Michigan;* National Child Labor Committee, 1923; and other literature of that agency (*e.g., Children Working on Farms in Certain Sections of the Western Slope of Colorado,* 1925; *Children Working in the Sugar Beet Fields of Certain Districts of the South Platte Valley, Colorado,* 1925). Also, *And Who Is My Neighbor?,* 1924, pp. 99, 100, 110 and 111.

social groups together in childhood, only to be alienated by social pressure later in life, is not going to stimulate desires in the disadvantaged group that can never be fulfilled and with it dissatisfaction with the place in life which they might fill happily and effectively. On the other hand, it has been contended that contacts in youth, even when they are likely to be crudely disrupted later, lay the foundations for a mutual understanding of the members of two groups which will help to harmonize their relations.

Teachers of Minority Groups

Many of the examples quoted in previous chapters have pointed to the existence of another problem of segregation concerning which opinions are divided, the employment of teachers of a minority group—especially if that minority, generally, ranks lower as to social status or recognition. For instance, we have briefly referred to the case of a body of colored teachers who were refused the privilege of a course of study provided by contract for the public-school teachers of their state at a university in a neighboring state. (Page 144.) We have recognized the difficulty which a teacher of swarthy features may have to win the favorable attention of his class of predominantly fair pupils. (Page 235.) We also have taken notice of the influence which a prejudiced teacher may exert on her class when there are in it pupils of a race she "can't stand." (Page 142.)

If we are more concerned about educational results than about a dogma or abstract principle of race relations, we shall not attempt, of course, to find a single answer to the question, Should race or nationality be allowed to influence the appointment and assignment of teachers? We shall rather endeavor to find out how different methods work in practice—what effects they produce on the race attitudes of pupils. But here we are confronted by the difficulty that the folkways of the larger part of the United States do not permit the gaining of experience through experiment. The appointment of colored teachers in the South, for example, to teach in white schools is nearly unthinkable in the present generation. There may be Indian teachers of white children in Arizona, Japanese ones in California, Mexican ones in Texas—but if so they would be rare exceptions. And this is not because somehow the teaching profession is outside the capacity of these groups, for there are excellent teachers in each of them, but because public opinion denies men and women of specific races and nationalities in specific regions the prestige associated with that profession.

Even where this sentiment is not so prevalent as to amount practically to an unwritten law, the instances in which persons from one of the less privileged groups teach in mixed public schools are rare. In northern cities where there is a large colored population, this is usually of recent growth; therefore, three factors react against the appointment of many colored teachers: Only a few of the families will have been in a position to give their children the requisite education and training for a professional career; the careers open for work in the colored community will be more lucrative than teaching in the public schools; the white community, because of the large number of colored people of low social status, will be apt to be prejudiced against the race. In a community with a small colored population, the situation will be more promising.[14]

New York seems to have gone further than most American cities in disregarding the color of its public-school teachers. In fact, no record of it is officially kept. It is estimated that there are about five hundred colored teachers in the schools of the city, and that about two-thirds of them are assigned to schools not predominantly colored. There has been no public discussion of the presence of these teachers in the city's school system in recent years; it must be assumed, therefore, that their relationship to their fellow teachers, to their superiors and, above all, to their pupils, is on the whole a harmonious one.

With this diversity of testimony it is not possible to come to any other conclusion on this matter than that which we have reached on the subject of segregation of pupils: Only a close study of local circumstances and social attitudes will reveal whether separation, complete or partial, or disregard of the color line is the more desirable policy. There are good reasons why in many—perhaps in most—situations progress in the education of children for justice, appreciation and open-mindedness can best be made within the frame of an existing system dominated by class consciousness. At the same time, the present trend to introduce divisions where there have been none before—simple

[14] For evidence on typical situations in northern cities, see *The Negro in Detroit*. Report Prepared for the Mayor's Interracial Committee. Detroit Bureau of Government Research, 1926, Section VIII, p. 17, and *The Negro in Chicago* (University of Chicago Press, 1922, pp. 247, 252).

as it is to explain it—will unquestionably make the task more difficult. With their rapid increase in prosperity, not only the Negroes but also other groups that now occupy the lowest rung on the American ladder to economic success will more and more demand the best possible education for their children; and that education nearly always will mean at least a measure of contact with children of other groups.

Indeed, in some cities, such as New York, there is now so large a group of wealthy, cultured and professionally distinguished Negroes and foreign-born people of almost every nationality that a keen demand has arisen for admission to the best private and semi-private schools (that is, schools partly supported from public funds). Many of these schools have racial quotas, some have an inclusive quota for children of foreign-born parents, some have a quota for Jews, and some for Negroes. But more of them exclude all children that do not come from "good" white, Gentile homes—even if occasionally they admit an exceptional Jewish child in contravention of their own rule. Here the increasing demand for admission and the increasing trend toward exclusiveness (sometimes induced by the presence of southern pupils but more often by the greater race consciousness of the dominant group due to the growth of the foreign-born and Negro population and to "Nordic" propaganda) are bringing about a regrettable conflict which some of the ablest and most broad-minded of educators are trying to cope with. Before they can permit purely educational interests to determine their decisions in this matter, many of them feel that they have yet to win to the side of educational liberalism parents and trustees; and that involves adult-educational tasks for which they are not always equipped. One of the purposes of the present presentation is to aid school principals, teachers, parents and administrative officers in such situations to come to grips with their own difficulties and the varieties of motive and interest that enter into the diverse attitudes that must be reckoned with.

MATERIALS AND METHODS

At the risk of tedium we have to start this section again with the reminder that no school and no teacher can by some process of magic undo the totality of community influences that shape the attitudes which children acquire toward social groups other than their own. And it requires more than special lessons or the use of specific books or extra-curricular activities or "talks" to counteract successfully what the general trend of the school organization does for social conditioning. To have splendid addresses at assembly on interracial friendship in a school that sedulously "protects" its pupils from contacts with the "lower classes" may serve the excellent purpose of flattering the self-opinion of teachers and pupils, but will not usually be of much effect on their behavior in situations in which interracial contact is unavoidable. Slogans concerning the golden rule, hymns of fellowship and lessons on Americanism, when offered in moderation, may help to set an idealistic tone—as well as provide a general glow of self-satisfaction; they may on occasion even provide a stimulus to interest in other peoples; but they are only rarely associated at all in the child's mind with the concrete tests that will confront his social attitudes now or later in life.

Efforts to create "race tolerance" may even over-reach themselves and by trying to produce a sense of equality really produce resentment of the favoritism shown the members of the normally less privileged group.[15]

The extraordinary difficulties which face a school system which systematically endeavors to stem a rising tide of race antagonism in the adult community were fully illustrated by the situation in the Chicago schools during and immediately after the riots of 1919. The report of that city's Race Relations Commission, already cited in several connections, contains evidence of an almost pathetic inability of teachers and principals to overcome attitudes which pupils bring from their homes and which often are reinforced by visits from parents, complaints to the school board, even street fights.[16]

More frequently, of course, the attitudes displayed in school management are simply reflections of those current in the groups from which the teachers are recruited. (See p. 142 *et seq.*) The problem of "methods" therefore begins in the normal schools. Teachers who are recruited from, let us say, a suburban, middle-class, Protestant, native-white social milieu do not by some miracle, after passing through normal school, suddenly find themselves "above the battle." They do not, as they enter the school room, shed all at once the characteristic prejudices of their class

15 Mrs. Sidonie M. Gruenberg in *The Survey* for September 1, 1926, p. 588.
16 *The Negro in Chicago* (University of Chicago Press, 1922, p. 255).

and group associations and become living embodiments, as it were, of a higher form of Americanism or of democracy or of applied religion. No matter how much consecration there may be in their calling, they remain subject to the thinking of their adult environment; and while the school may have an atmosphere and spirit all its own, it cannot separate itself from the common feelings and sentiments of the community it serves. All that we can expect of the school and the teachers is that they never lose sight of their primary function; that they place the *educational* objective before any other. If that really could be realized, if the schools really did train minds in habits of absorbing information relevant to life, we should not need to worry about the range of information which it takes up at different ages. This chapter might remain unwritten, because in comparison with the educational force of a teaching that keeps the mind spurred to intellectual effort, keeps it open to new impressions and feeds it with a constantly widening range of accurate and significant information, the specific place of race attitudes in the curriculum of the school would be of no great importance. Attitudes of curiosity and intelligent appreciation for likenesses and differences would grow of themselves. The school would create predispositions toward facing the facts of life which conservatives and radicals in the controversies around race relations would both recognize as desirable: open-mindedness, sensitiveness to the demands of justice, desire for knowledge and understanding, appreciation for cultural values that are universally cherished.

An interesting reflection on the way in which school teaching follows the changing folkways is contained in the summary of George B. Neumann's study of high-school students' attitudes, already quoted on page 31. He says:

The results of this study suggest the question whether or not a similar study made a generation ago would have revealed attitudes differing in important respects from those revealed by this study. There are no easily available data on which to base accurate answers to these questions. We seek to keep our schools progressive in regard to information given, skills developed and methods used. But an examination of the data resulting from this study raises the serious question as to whether or not the international attitudes now being developed belong to a generation past or rapidly passing rather than to the generation to which the students belong.[17]

[17] *The Negro in Chicago* (University of Chicago Press, 1922, p. 92).

He partly answers his own question by saying:

The tendency of each generation is to impose its own values on the succeeding generation, but if the new generation's needs differ from the old, can the old values adequately meet the new needs of the new generation? . . . Is the present generation right in inculcating attitudes based upon the old values of the present generation? Is there not rather a demand that the new generation be helped to discover ways and means of determining its own values to meet its own needs? [18]

Our more progressive educators begin to see that an erroneous ideal has in the past too often shaped educational objectives and methods. The assumption has been that the child is erratic, anarchical, and must be tamed to fit the demands of a stable environment. We now see that increasingly civilized life demands minds able to cope with a decidedly unstable environment. The task is not to create mental habits in conformity with a given set of needs, but to create personalities which, though stable in themselves, remain elastic and rapidly adapt themselves to changed conditions. The school cannot and should not function as representative of an abstract "ideal" state or society that is entirely fair, all-inclusive, and unspotted in the virgin purity of its democratic fervor. In other words, it cannot and should not try to free the children of a community from the prejudices, loves and loyalties that hold it together, nor can or should the school, in a civilization such as ours, exclusively represent the homes and their continuous war against the integrating tendencies of the community. Its function is, rather, to take the child as he comes from his early home associations and, while normally leaving him still subjected to its separative influences, gradually to socialize him, at least to the limits of the actual democracy practiced in that community. Without being able to substitute an entirely rational for a prejudiced relation to the facts of social life, it can make it easier for the child to face those conflicts of standards and ideals which he is bound to encounter as his experience outgrows the limiting bounds of home and neighborhood.

In this gradual enlargement of interests, knowledge, sympathies lies the most promising use of the school as an instrument of better race relations. If it fails in these respects, nothing it attempts of specific teachings on race relations is likely to be of consequence.

[18] *Ibid.*, p. 93.

The time-honored technique for accomplishing anything in the schools has been that of verbal suggestion. Many of us, however, are beginning to believe that, for the achievement of anything really profound and effective in our students, "saying it with words" is a fairly unfruitful technique. Nevertheless, in the well-meant effort to develop an international point of view, that traditional method will, one fears, be all too largely used. Teachers will set about to "teach" internationalism. They will proceed in various ways to talk about it, or have their students read about it. To cap the agony, they will have "lessons" on it and "examinations." As a result, the students, if they are not bored to extinction—or to rebellion—may annex a few valuable political concepts; but, one suspects, little more. What is necessary, of course, is a great deal more. For what we really need in the members of the coming generation is a new attitude toward human relationships; one which will so thoroughly permeate their lives that it will transform daily habits of thought and behavior, and make them, as individuals, less easily the dupes of myopic provincialism and thick-headed antagonism.[19]

All this may be admitted, and yet there may be much diversity of opinion as to the exact methods by which a school should proceed to fulfill this task of socialization. After all, a critical reader might here interject, while the dogmatic teaching of specific attitudes or forms of behavior in the matter of race relations may not be desirable, it is even less desirable to teach abstract notions of justice, wisdom and goodness; in so far as they are desirable, the consideration of these virtues must in some way be anchored in concrete subject matters. And why should not race relations be as good a subject for classroom discussion as any other? The point is a valid one in so far as it is a protest against a futile teaching of abstractions; but the point stressed in previous pages is that if all teaching of history, of English, of geography, of the sciences, in fact of any traditional school subject, were really educational in content and method, desired lessons on race attitudes would naturally grow out of them. Presumably, however, this is not going to be universally the case for some time to come; and so many teachers do desire to know whether there are not special opportunities in the normal routine of the class room for reinforcing the appreciation for those values that would, more especially, help the child to form desirable habits of reaction to interracial contacts. They realize the existence of

[19] Harry A. Overstreet in *Progressive Education* for May, 1925, p. 68.

many of the evils that have been described in Chapters XII and XIII—namely, the ease with which, either intentionally or unintentionally, the teaching of school subjects, some of them seemingly far removed from the subject of race, may become the means of fostering antagonistic, prejudiced attitudes. And they want to know whether, in addition to guarding themselves against these dangers, teachers cannot find some special resources in these subject fields for fostering the open mind, the sense of justice, appreciation of universal cultural values, and so on.

Such opportunities unquestionably exist. One of the earmarks of the good teacher is, in fact, that he is resourceful in discovering and in utilizing, what otherwise may be no more than the dry content material of a half-hearted subject teaching, as the significant rafters and beams in a rising structure of comprehension of life, and of the individual pupil's place in it. It is precisely because they are unimaginative in this respect that so many teachers fail to recognize and counteract those limiting and misleading tendencies that have been referred to. There are no easy tricks of teaching history, for example, which ensure that the pupil will not come out with a heightened contempt for peoples other than his own, and none through which the teaching of civics may be made immune against the absorption of racial prejudice. There are no fool-proof lists of books for supplementary reading. In short, there are no substitutes for psychologically sound methods applied by resourceful teachers. All we can attempt to do here is to illustrate with a few examples—none of them necessarily meeting the exigencies of other circumstances than those in which they were applied—some of the things that have been thought of and tried. The present author hands on these recipes without guaranteeing that they will cure; in fact, the only purpose which such examples can ever serve is that of stimulating the imagination and of suggesting to the reader possible methods which he, in his specific situation, might try out.

Building Up Resistance

Dr. Goodwin B. Watson, in a letter to the author, expresses the fear that in the preoccupation with teaching material the development of educational techniques for strengthening resistance to prejudicial influences might be overlooked.

It seems to me important to deal with the situation through building up resistance rather than through eliminating prejudicial factors in the environment. I suspect that inoculation and vaccination are sound principles in social health as well as in physical. Probably it will be easier for any teacher to help a group of adolescents become critically aware of the insinuating elements in moving pictures, press reports, novels, patriotic speeches, and even school textbooks than it will be to produce changes in those instruments themselves. In other words, I am suggesting that a part of every home, school and club program should be a unit on how to think straight in the midst of biasing influences.

This suggestion is important. Obviously, the task before us is not simply one of elimination and substitution. But on the other hand, a discussion of methods by which resistance to propaganda may be strengthened will be most effective if it is definitely applied to those subject fields and teaching traditions with which propaganda is most frequently connected. For example, the process of inoculation creating resistance to the misuse of public holidays by a selfishly motivated racial group in the community will require a different technique from that of making the pupils immune against the poison of propagandist story books. The processes of building up resistance and of eliminating the causes of disease go hand in hand in our most successful health campaigns; and both must be considered in relation to concrete situations, rather than *in vacuo*.

1. LANGUAGE AND LITERATURE

Here, for example, since we have just mentioned story books, are one or two things said on this matter of home reading and possible ways in which it might be used to make for "desirable" attitudes: Tales should be suited to the period of the child's mental development, and they should paint desirable behavior as beautiful and inviting—not as something characteristic of exceptionally good children.[20] The natural way for children to learn about strange people is to progress from fairy tales of all lands to folk tales, fiction, travel books, and thus to books about real people.[21]

[20] Katherine Dunlap Cather, *Educating by Story-Telling* (1918, p. 132).
[21] Mrs. Sidonie M. Gruenberg in *The World Tomorrow* for October, 1925, p. 304.

A student writes:

I was born in the South, which meant that I had a negro nurse and was accustomed to negro servants. As a child I had no especial attitude toward negroes, as a class. My feelings are perhaps characterized by lack of attitude. I just accepted them. As I grew older and became conscious of a wish for personal daintiness, and developed a strong sense of Puritan morals, negroes disgusted me. To aggravate this feeling men used to hint at horrible immoralities among negroes that I could not even understand.

It took nearly four years of college and extensive reading to change this attitude. I began to have an interest in the problems of the race. Then the presence of a polite young negress in a college class further broke down the old reserve. But the most vital influence was the reading of the life of Toussaint L'Ouverture. I became conscious of the fact that even a negro could be noble. Now I laugh at the whims and prejudices of my Southern friends but I would not meet a negro socially yet. The early training is too ingrained. However I would not mind meeting one in a business or intellectual way.

This contribution, which we give for what it may be worth, suggests that one should be careful not to exaggerate the influence of reading on one's attitude. No doubt, in retrospect it is easy to overestimate the impression received from books precisely because it is difficult to recall more illusive but perhaps more frequently repeated and in their totality stronger influences of the kind reviewed in our Chapters VIII and IX.

Fiction and Biography

It is interesting in this connection to consider the influence which books of fiction have actually had on the development of American race attitudes. Hardly two generations ago, the Indian was a feared reality in thousands of American homes. He had no qualities to endear him to the people; at least if he had such qualities they were not generally known. But to a generation not so exposed to danger from too close and unfortunate a contact, the Indian stands for the same heroic qualities that are admired, when translated into the past, in the history of both the Latin and the Germanic peoples of Europe. A single writer, Fenimore Cooper, has brought about this transformation in the attitudes toward the Indian by creating fictional Indians in the image of the accustomed hero of myth and legend. As might be expected, he captured the imagination of the distant children of Europe before becoming the children's idol in America. [In part this happened because in translations his stories were shortened and rendered more popular.] The love of the Indian which the immigrant brought with him, through this indirect contact, has helped to create a new American attitude toward the Indian, now reflected in an enormous literature of fiction for children and in the rites, crafts, names, and recreational interests of several nation-wide organizations of and for children.

On the contrary, the one internationally famous American book about the Negro pictured a faithful slave. No author, American or foreign, has created a heroic Negro figure in the fictional literature that children read. Though perhaps no more close to life than were Cooper's Indians, the Negroes of fiction have failed to transform the attitudes of the nation. Indeed, if anything, they are holding back such appreciation as may be considered due the Negro for his actual contributions of the picturesqueness and inward beauty of American life.[22]

There is just beginning to come into existence a new type of book in which the achievements of Negroes are featured; but they are not books of fiction which children read with absorption. Even so, biography, interestingly written, will play its part. Concerning the need for such literature for children of high-school age, and their uses, a Pennsylvania teacher writes:

There is a lot that can be done incidentally in schools to show the great contributions of Negroes through questions in "general information" tests on Roland Hayes, Burleigh, Dunbar, Booker T. Washington, Tanner, etc. But it must be done without "race prejudice" in favor of the Negro (it can work both ways) and with a real desire to be fair and to know the truth.

The important truth for children to get (this bears on tolerance in all fields, international and industrial as well as race) is that groups are highly variable within themselves: that Germans, Jews (I find M. E. Ravage's article in the *Century* about a year ago helpful to my thinking), Japanese, Negroes have as much variety of attitudes and dispositions as have "Nordics."

Another thing:
Books about children of other lands, while they tend to increase

___
[22] Interesting in this connection is the treatment of the Negro by Cooper himself and the contemptuous attitude toward him displayed in his stories.

the width of sympathies, never have the force on public opinion which stories of adult adventure are likely to have. The reason is that, after all, the child thinks and dreams of himself in terms of a complete, independent self-expression. The foreign child, even when pictured as adventurous, rarely is an entirely free agent and, therefore, much like children known at home. The Swiss Twins are decidedly less interesting than William Tell; and details of child-life in Japan cannot be as exciting as stories of headhunters in Africa.[23]

Nevertheless, books about children of other lands have their place—especially in the library of the younger ones; and it is an advantage to have available in cheap editions and in many languages the children's classics of all peoples. A movement to this end was started some years ago by Frau Helene Scheu-Riesz, of Vienna, who published cheap editions of the world's best books for children, first in German and later also in other languages. In this way, Hans Brinkers, Alice in Wonderland, Heidi, the Water Babies, the Seven Dwarfs, even Don Quixote, are becoming internationally known characters; the mention of the Black Forest evokes the same sense of wonder and mystery in France as it does in Germany, while little Italian children, coming to America, are already familiar in imagination with the clink of skates.

For older children the selection of corrective reading becomes important in view of the misleading character of much they have already read. In addition to biographies, even polemic writings that meet a high standard of style and dignity should be made available. There is no reason why a child of high-school age should only read colorless English or should meet with a more emotionally vivid style in relation to subjects of purely academic, historical interest. There are writings by W. E. Burghardt Dubois, in regard to the Negro, by Ludwig Lewisohn in regard to the Jew, by C. M. Panuncio concerning the Italian in America, by Edward Steiner concerning the immigrant in general, and by

[23] Children are realists. Pictorial representations of children of different races dancing together or blowing soap bubbles do not interest them as much as pictures of real people doing similar things in different ways according to the customs of their country. The old crafts of soil and sea offer the best bases for such pictorial comparisons. The Educational Bureau of the Cleanliness Institute (45 East 17th Street, New York) has put out a series of five drawings showing how different peoples wash their clothes; things of that sort arouse interest.

many other authors of both American and foreign birth, which increasingly find favor with teachers of English for the vividness and intensity of their style.

Professor John Erskine suggests that, since only a minority of children can hope to receive a higher education, and since the task of surveying all our common cultural heritages through the study of literature is too large, high-school teaching might well confine itself to our American literature from the Revolution to the present day.[24]

The Teaching of English

In these comments on reading we are merely skirting the real problem, of course, and that is how to make the study of language itself—usually limited to English—a means of creating a more liberal, appreciative, judicious attitude of mind in contrast with a closed, prejudiced and self-satisfied one. In the hands of a good teacher, a lesson in grammar can become an ethical inspiration instead of being the drudgery it usually is. It can demonstrate the beauty of organic growth in the construction of speech and the reflection of logical law in the arrangement of sentences. Indeed, it is for this reason that an education comprising Latin and Greek has for centuries been looked upon as a "liberal" education.

The power and beauty of Greek literature and the prestige of Latin as the language of culture through the Middle Ages have naturally given these tongues the first place in scholarly esteem. Moreover, the orderly arrangement of declensions and conjugations, and the readiness with which words may be classified by their endings into distinct "parts of speech," give an inflectional grammar an aspect of system and logic. . . .

Grammar can open the pupil's eyes to the fact that his progress in knowledge takes place largely by improving upon the half-truths of common sense: statements which are true in many but not all their applications. Much wordy debate would be brushed aside if more thinkers had learned in their language-study to recognize the small verbal defects that easily pass unnoticed in generalization.[25]

How even the teaching of spelling may at times contribute toward greater understanding is illustrated in a letter from a Pennsylvania teacher. He writes:

[24] *American Character and Other Essays* (Chautauqua Press, 1927, p. 166).
[25] Alfred Dwight Sheffield, *Grammar and Thinking* (1912, pp. 69, 188).

In my classes at the —— School, I have several times let the spelling of the word Negro without a capital letter be an excuse for a general race discussion.

Perhaps that is not, strictly speaking, according to the rules; but a queer spelling or a difficult word may, on occasion, briefly be explained with such historical or ethnographic facts as directly bear on it. Indeed, a study of etymology is an experience in internationalism.[26]

Foreign Languages

The teaching of modern languages, while it may lack some of the advantages which the classical languages and literatures have of enlisting appreciation for the finest qualities of mind, provides special occasions for other disciplines desirable from the point of view of social ethics. The more intimate insight into the mind of a people which their literature, read in the original, affords, will open the pupil's eye to the superficial nature of his knowledge of other peoples. He will be less sure of his generalization concerning, say, the Japanese, when he discovers how great is the difference between his impression of the character of the French before and after having studied their language and literature for three years. Moreover, the teaching of modern languages permits of specific references to differences in mentality and achievements, and prepares the pupil for an appreciative expectation of variety of viewpoint in his contacts with strangers. The question is sometimes raised whether, in view of the great need for such understanding, the teaching of modern languages might not be more varied, at least in the high schools of our great cities. Within a decade or so, the study of Spanish has enormously increased North American interest in the forms and varieties of Spanish culture, both in the Old and in the New World. Would not a more widespread study of Italian have equally beneficial effects?

The mere idea of studying foreign languages for other purposes than those of commerce and travel will strike many readers as curious.

---

[26] Supply teachers who have to fill in odd hours will be interested to know that classes of all age-groups have at times spent periods of fascinated absorption in such books as G. L. Kittredge's *Words and Their Ways in English* (and the older Trench's *History of Words*) or Ernest Weekly's *The Romance of Names*—tracing not only the descent of their own idiom but also its relation to the living languages of the world and to place names from Tibet to Patagonia.

A group of churchwomen, in one of the smaller but quite cosmopolitan cities of the East, endeavored through a series of group discussions to arrive at a program of joint activities with the general aim of helping the foreign-born. Many of the practical proposals made met with this seemingly insuperable difficulty that none of the women could speak any of the languages of the larger immigrant groups in the community. Finally, the suggestion was made that it might not be a bad thing if as many of the women as possible were to form a class to learn Italian—the language of the largest of the foreign-born settlements. This sensible proposal struck those present as so utopian that they laughed it out of court.

Some of the religious and social organizations, however, realize the need for more professional workers, at any rate, who are capable to communicate in one of the less widely known languages.[27]

What is holding back a more rapid increase of foreign-language study in American schools is an exaggerated notion of the difficulty of acquiring a working use of foreign speech. This, again, is due to a faulty tradition of teaching in which unessentials were stressed, and academic conventions retarded the progress of the pupil. If the same common sense were applied to foreign-language study in our public schools as to other subjects of useful knowledge—hygiene, let us say—the impetus to elect this subject would be considerable, with probably large gains to international and interracial understanding.

As a device to make more real and interesting the study of English composition and at the same time to stimulate a desire to learn foreign languages and to know about foreign peoples, is the exchange of letters between children of different nations. Suggested and attempted at various times, the idea was carried into practice more systematically and with wide participation when revived after the war. A brief account of the movement may be of interest:

The idea originated with Dr. Neil Van Aken, secretary of the Netherlands Chamber of Commerce in New York and a teacher in the high school at Glen Ridge, N. J. In Holland, English is a regular part of the curriculum in the schools that correspond to our junior high schools. Dr. Van Aken wrote to a number of Dutch schools, and met with ready

[27] T. J. Lacey, *Immigration and the Church*, in Neighbors—Studies in Immigration from the Standpoint of the Episcopal Church, New York Domestic and Foreign Missionary Society, 1920, p. 32.

cooperation. As one of the exercises in English, each pupil was told to write a letter to a child in America. The name, even the sex of the recipient, was unknown to the writer. These letters, each enclosed in a separate envelope, were distributed to the pupils in New Jersey and, in their English class, each of them wrote an individual reply. The next exchange of letters was personal in content, addressed to an individual child. Many of them contained snapshots.

After a year of continued correspondence, the matter was taken up with the Minister of Education in Holland who approved a proposal to make it part of the class work of all pupils in grades that study English.

Since then, the plan has been taken up unofficially also with educators in the British Isles, France, Germany, Italy, Belgium, Spain, Norway, Sweden and Czecho-Slovakia. Correspondence with the British, Scandinavian countries and with Belgium and Czecho-Slovakia is in English. With the children in France, Germany, Italy and Spain, American pupils correspond in the languages of these countries. The results throughout are said to be gratifying.[28]

2. HISTORY

A more modern technique of teaching history belongs to the same category of desiderata. Many educators have stressed the part which a less academic and more psychologically oriented teaching of this subject might contribute toward a widening of social sympathies. But the temptation to use the history-lesson as an instrument of propaganda for the social and political *status quo* is, as we have seen in an earlier chapter (XII), usually too strong for the penetration of more truly educational viewpoints.[29]

The whole subject of the reform of historical studies with a view to the objectives of a liberalized social ethics has been discussed suggestively by Professor David Snedden of Teachers College, New York, who doubts the legitimacy of any use of history teaching for purposes of social control.[30]

Apart from specific references to races and race relations in the teaching of history, the general reforms now under way in the teaching of that subject have an important indirect bearing upon our problem. It is being recognized increasingly that in the past the emphasis has often been laid too largely upon military exploits and insufficiently upon cultural progress. In the pursuits

---

[28] For a fuller account see *New York Times* for August 2, 1926, p. 10.
[29] See Frederick Elmore Lumley, *Means of Social Control* (1925, p. 193).
[30] *Teachers College Record*, January, 1924, pp. 3, 7, 9.

of peace the opportunities for fostering love of country are as great as in the pursuits of war; but while a history of culture will no doubt always be taught in such a way as to aggrandize the achievements of race and nation, this emphasis does not have for its inevitable counterpart the creation of enmity for other peoples. While the achievements of *our* science, *our* statesmanship, *our* technology, *our* literature and arts will rank highest, they have not been won in deadly combat but rather nearly always in cooperation, direct or indirect, with those of others.

As one specific means of counteracting the traditional and yet largely operative teaching of history as a record of hostilities, it is recommended by some educators that the largest possible use be made of biographical material. In the story of an outstanding individual the child will be more likely to recognize common human traits, desires and triumphs than in the story of a tribe or nation. Thus reading lists of biographical material have been prepared by peace societies and by children's librarians. That even anti-American prejudice may on occasion be overcome by a judicious use of biography was recently shown by the present incumbent of the famous City Temple in London:

History is best taught by way of biography. Great men are always akin, in their virtues and even down to their faults. The other day I had to lecture to a great audience in Liverpool upon Abraham Lincoln. It was at the moment when British minds were very much inflamed because of Mr. Mellon's unjustifiable statements. I remarked to my audience that, if I were to attempt to speak eulogistically of America, it was likely I should have difficulty in arousing their cordial interest; but I expected to succeed in telling the story of a man who was truly a great human being. It is safe to say that not a tinge of anti-American prejudice disturbed the minds of that crowd for that evening. Every significant man is an epitome of his country; but his humanity makes contemptible the parti-colors of the atlas. Give the children more biography and let intrinsic worth rather than the accident of birth set the great ones in their true niches in the Pantheon.[31]

There is a danger, however, that the effort to do justice to different national or racial groups may lead to a distortion of history. Nothing is to be gained, for example, from such a medley of significant and relatively insignificant historical personages as the present city administration of Chicago, in its effort to deal

[31] F. W. Norwood in *The Spectator*, June 18, 1927, p. 1071.

out justice to the different component groups of the population, proposes to present to its half a million school children. A committee appointed by Mayor Thompson has distributed a new "syllabus for guidance of teaching of history" which contains the following instructions to teachers of history:

Stress should be laid upon the fact that every race strain found in our citizenship has contributed much to the agricultural, artistic, commercial, industrial, material, moral, political, and scientific advancement of America. Our pupils should be led to realize how much of our progress in education we owe to Americans who were either born in Austria, Belgium, Bulgaria, Czecho-Slovakia, England, Esthonia, France, Germany, Greece, Holland, Hungary, Italy, Ireland, Latvia, Lithuania, Poland, Portugal, Rumania, Russia, Scandinavia, Spain, Switzerland, Wales and Jugo-Slavia.

To render these services of the manifold constituents of our population concrete and tangible to our pupils, it would be well to dwell upon the work of Commodore Jack Barry, Andrew Carnegie, Enrico Caruso, John Ericsson, David Farragut, Baron de Kalb, Antonin Dvorák, Patrick Henry, Charles Hughes, Thomas Jamieson, Thaddeus Kosciusko, Marquis de Lafayette, Pierre L'Enfant, Count Pulaski, John Boyle O'Reilly, Jacob Riis, Carl Schurz, Phil Sheridan, Hyman Solomon, Nathan Straus, Baron von Steuben, George Washington and Booker T. Washington.

The pupils should, however, be led to see that the great contributions of these various race stocks have been made not by illustrious individuals alone but by the great masses of these races.[32]

Practically worked out plans for making the most of the opportunities afforded by history teaching for the understanding of American race problems are, so far, experimental and, for the most part, unpublished. Indeed, in preparation of the present chapter we have come across only one syllabus that has a general aim in line with the objectives formulated above.[33]

[32] Revealing self-studies of college students as to the effects produced upon their race attitudes by history lessons received during their school years are given by Professor E. S. Bogardus in the *Journal of Applied Sociology,* May-June, 1925, p. 376, and January-February, 1927, p. 275.
[33] This syllabus comes from an experienced practical teacher and may offer suggestions for adaptation within the frame of the prescribed study courses elsewhere. It illustrates how considerations of race may naturally be introduced into a course of study that is primarily for the purpose of deepening understanding for the historical development of America. The author, Professor Edgar C. Bye, is head of the Department of Social Studies of the Coatesville, Pennsylvania, Public Schools. See *Opportunity* for April, 1926, p. 116.

CHAPTER XXII

WHAT SCHOOL CAN DO (*Continued*)

3. GEOGRAPHY

Closely allied with the study of history is that of geography. What an imaginative teaching of that subject can contribute toward interracial understanding and toward the formation of desirable mental habits, as regards attitudes toward persons and groups of strange appearance, language or manners, has been well summarized and illuminatingly discussed by one of the leading American geographers in an article on "Geography and the Higher Citizenship." [1] As a textbook for teaching geography to young children that goes further than most in embodying the point of view of "international amity," Miss Mary Chaplin Shute, of Boston Teachers College, recommends a course of study for Kindergarten and First Three Grades issued for use in the Baltimore schools. She says:

Under the subjects of Geography and History it states as requisite knowledge, "the idea of a world made up of countries and peoples differing in many ways but alike in more, and bound together by mutual esteem and need," and as a resultant attitude, an interest in the children of a few remote countries not merely for the novelty they present but as real children and potential playfellows living in countries of which they have reason to be proud. [2]

William G. Carr, in a suggestive chapter on the part played by the teaching of geography on world-mindedness,[2a] stresses two desiderata: the introduction of more of the commercial phases of the subject—which, as we have already seen, can be made of intimate direct appeal to children—and the de-mechanization of a type of teaching which assumes that children will, without aid, draw the significant conclusions from the facts presented.

[1] Professor J. Russell Smith in *Progressive Education* for April-June, 1925, p. 77.
[2] *Childhood Education* for February, 1926, p. 274.
[2a] *Op. cit.,* Chap. VIII.

4. Civics

Geography is linked up with history and with other social studies so intimately that it is almost impossible to discuss separately ways in which these studies might be used for the purpose of promoting interracial appreciation.[3] A study of migrations has been suggested as a particularly fitting means of creating understanding for the likenesses and differences in the evolution and character of different peoples and races.[4] The desirability of personal contact with problems in social relations as part of the teaching of civics (discussed by S. B. Butler, *loc. cit.*) is made the pivot of good civics teaching by Professor Albert Shiels, of Teachers College.[5] The object of civics teaching as a realization of group interests in the light of inter-group welfare has been well stated by Professor Daniel H. Kulp, II, also of Teachers College.[6] Some of the suggestions made by these and other educators may seem difficult. Therefore, before going on to our next topic, we will quote a teacher who has experience with children from three to twelve years old and who, apparently, has no difficulty in utilizing any of the social studies, or even a story-telling hour, for such sidelights on interracial questions as there may be occasion to touch upon. She observed the attitude of the younger children to a colored cook and that of the older ones to Jewish class members. With the younger group, she says, ridicule appeared as a spontaneous expression of the sense of unlikeness—"much the same as the normal comments of children on any physical deformity." This is how it was dealt with:

We have met it like any other form of rudeness by calling attention to the fact that it would make Margaret feel badly to be laughed at. If this was not sufficient, which it usually was, we would simply insist that the rest of us in school liked her too much to allow her to be hurt in that way, and the child could not come to school unless he would be polite. We have tried to supplement this with more constructive teaching, by telling stories about African, Chinese, Red Indian and East

[3] How the whole of the teaching for citizenship may be made a force conditioning for openmindedness, sympathy and appreciation of common values, is discussed very interestingly by Sylvester B. Butler, in *Progressive Education* for October, 1925, p. 211 *et seq.*
[4] David Snedden, Sociological Determination of Objectives in Education (1921, p. 235).
[5] *Teachers College Record*, June, 1925, p. 828.
[6] *Ibid.*, January, 1925, p. 415.

Indian children, with some discussion of the different environments in the way of climates, etc., as well as the different physical characteristics and languages. What the children of other races would think and feel about white children inevitably comes into the discussion, of course.

As we begin the study of American history stories—at about eight years of age—of course the Indian problem enters, and the children's sympathies seem instinctively with the Indians because of their romantic appeal. How much of this would carry over into a practical situation, however, we have had no opportunity of finding out.

The Jewish problem which I ran into this year for the first time seems to me more genuinely typical of what we meet in adult society and more an outgrowth of that adult attitude. There are three Jewish children and one half-Jewish one in a group of twelve twelve-year-old boys and girls. Early in the year the boys started teasing one of the Jewish boys who, it happens, is one of the most popular children in the group, by calling after him in the yard and elsewhere, "Geney the Sheeny." (His name is Eugene.) Because of his popularity, I thought at first it would pass over without comment from me, and I did not like to attack it directly for fear of hurting Eugene.

It did seem to me, however, that it would be a help if the whole question could be brought out in serious discussion, and the opportunity soon arose in connection with the study of German. One of the Jewish boys was so good at it that I asked him if he knew Yiddish, and he said he did. This led to a discussion of how the Yiddish language came to be so like German and consequently to the whole story of persecution of the Jews in the Middle Ages. Finally, in the course of the discussion, upon my remark that it always seemed to me that the medieval nobles had a good deal of jealousy and fear mixed up in their feeling toward the Jews, Eugene suddenly gave a personal turn to the discussion by exclaiming laughingly, "Aha, Frankie, you're jealous of me, that's why you call me a Sheeny!" This brought protests from others at once. "But, Eugene, you're a Russian, you're not a Jew," which he answered by insisting on his pure Jewish descent. This led to further discussion of Jewish history and the age of their civilization as compared with European. All entered into it seriously and with interest, and there has been no further manifestation of any race attitude at all.

The significant fact about the whole episode in this case seemed to me to lie in the fact that "Frankie," the ringleader of the teasing, was the half-Jewish boy. Consequently, an unconsciously defensive attitude probably had a good deal to do with it, especially as he was without the support of real racial pride which Eugene had from his home background.

5. Ethics

We have now come to the question as to the place which social ethics, without direct application to one of the traditional forms of social study, may play in conditioning the child for habits of unprejudiced, appreciative, fair-minded feeling toward members of other national and racial groups.   Should there be direct ethical teaching at all, or should the formation of moral attitudes be left to arise as a by-product from such studies as we have just surveyed?   Educators are not altogether agreed on this point.   Edward L. Thorndike, of Teachers College, some years ago wrote trenchantly in favor of ethics as a class-room subject.[7] Robbins, Butler, Shiels and others stress the need for direct contacts, personal associations as the only effective means of acquiring habits of social behavior and thinking.[8]

Robbins also advises on the type of school discipline that is likely to make personal association an educationally valuable experience and not a mere herding together of individuals with different home backgrounds.[9]   Another educator, Colin A. Scott, of the Boston Normal School, some years ago pointed out that the attendant learnings in the personal associations of school life are apt to be overlooked and require more careful watchfulness on the part of the teacher.[10]   To demand the utilization of personal associations for the purpose of developing social attitudes is not, however, knowing how.   Here again we must, in the main, rely upon the resourcefulness of teachers and upon new methods of stimulating it in teacher training.

As a sample of the sort of thing which a resourceful teacher with a sound fundamental knowledge of method may attempt in this direction, Miss Mary Chaplin Shute, of Teachers College, Boston, says:

Of course we cannot talk to kindergarten children of race relations, of international thinking, or of the abolition of war, but we have long since learned that doing "small things with small people" does not in the least mean doing unimportant things.   To any kindergartner with clear vision each small beginning is full of significance because it is

---

[7] *Principles of Teaching* (1917, p. 188).
[8] Charles L. Robbins, *The School as a Social Institution* (1918, p. 55).
[9] *Ibid.*, pp. 28, 39.
[10] *Social Education* (1908, p. 9).

seen to lead towards or away from the world ideals which she holds for herself and her children. . . .

However we word it, the essential point is that we do with our little children those things which, simple though they may be, will lay the foundation for an integrated self, an integrated society, an integrated world.

Let us see then what some of these things are, both the obviously important and the apparently trivial. First of all, and probably most important of all, comes the daily life in the kindergarten, with its contact with many other little personalities, for many children the first call to adjustment to the needs and rights of others of their own age. Every kindergarten, by virtue of bringing together many children of the same age, automatically furnishes endless opportunities for helping each child to learn that he is but one of many, that the others must have a turn at the slide even though he would like to monopolize it, that he must keep quiet if the others are listening to a story, that he cannot be unreasonably rough without endangering the comfort and safety of others. He learns, too, to be gentle and chivalrous towards those who are younger or weaker than he, often developing a remarkable degree of thoughtfulness for some crippled or mentally backward playmate, his sense of responsibility entirely overtopping any inborn feeling of superiority.

Justice, fair play, tolerance, responsibility—all these are the normal outgrowth of any intermingling of little children under wise guidance. But how greatly these may be heightened and broadened in the kindergartens where we find children of many races living as brethren of one family under the leadership of the kindergartner who believes in the potency of early attitudes, and who really cares to break down race and class prejudice! . . .

Here lies the kindergartner's opportunity, and by wise commendation of that which the "different" child has to offer, by her tacit assumption that in kindergarten we know of no differences except as they insure a pleasing variety, by her unfailing courtesy to the be-shawled and gesticulating mothers in the doorway, by her expectation that all are to be made happy and at ease in this new home, it is generally a fairly brief process to bring respect and friendliness into the little group in place of warfare and prejudice.

When golden-haired Isabel learns that little black Lily's voice is far sweeter and truer than hers, she learns to admire where she looked askance and forgets that she objected to a seat beside Lily in the story hour. John may have derisively called Izzy "a Yid," but when it proves that Izzy knows the one sure way to make John's bridge strong enough to hold his toy train, what cares John for race differences? Concetta and Veronica, who slipped into the corner church with their mothers to look at the beautiful altar flowers on their way to kinder-garten, find their little hearts expanding to a new type of tolerance when they overhear their loved "teacher" inquiring with interest and sympathy regarding the Passover celebration to which Celia and Sara have just been "staying out." And when it is discovered that shy little Olga and sturdy Ludovic can talk in two languages where most of us can use only one, a new sense of respect dawns in childish hearts for those who are "different" from themselves. All this is, of course, a matter of experience rather than of instruction, for we do not talk of racial and religious differences in kindergarten. . . .[11]

Obviously, both the volume and the quality of such "attendant" learnings as those described will differ according to the degree in which associations at school are or can be varied. The school may be poorer or it may be richer in interracial contacts than the child's home surroundings. It may provide the same amount of variety of types, but different types. For example, sometimes school is the only place where white and colored children meet; sometimes it is the only place in the community where they do not meet! Sometimes school provides the chance to meet indi-viduals of another people not generally represented in the com-munity, or the chance to meet persons of a group very different in social and cultural status from those more often seen in the community. The school made up of a racially homogeneous group seems to be entirely lacking in opportunities for helpful contacts. But even here the resourceful teacher can plan ex-periences that will produce the desired associations. Miss Shute says on this point:

Not all public schools and almost no private schools can offer so fine a laboratory for democracy as that just described, but it will not be safe for them to ignore the problem because its challenge is less obvious. On the contrary, it is perhaps even more essential that the kinder-gartner whose group is practically all American-born, perhaps even of the "privileged class," should face the coming life problem squarely, knowing that the attitudes she establishes in her children have more than a fair chance of holding over to later years. Having no "alien races" in her midst, she must plan all the more carefully her campaign against the intolerance and prejudice too often already inculcated in her children, young as they are; and with the need in mind, opportu-nities will soon open before her.

For example, as dolls are brought in or made in kindergarten, she will find some of her children relegating all those whose complexions fail to conform to Nordic standards to the positions of cooks or chauffeurs, in unconscious imitation of the unthinking and uninformed adults who, since they have not yet learned the amazing achievements both in art and business of our American Negroes, are still thinking of them in terms of "Aunt Jemima" and minstrel shows! . . .

The kindergartners who really understand that toys have a profound influence over little children's hearts and minds, have gladly welcomed a very pretty type of colored doll recently put on sale in some of our better stores, and have placed them in their kindergartens, dressed as prettily as the white dolls, noting with satisfaction the children's prompt acceptance of them as babies to be loved and tended with the same care which has been shown the more familiar white dolls. Why might not our kindergartens make a point of having dolls dressed to represent Chinese, Japanese, Negroes, Indians, and others, not simply to be looked at as "curiosities" but that through the familiar activities of dressing, feeding, cuddling, and tending them the children may come sooner to a realization that all babies need much the same type of care, regardless of what their color or style of dressing may be.

Such experiences of underlying identities can also be given through the use of pictures. All the talks on the family and the working groups should be illustrated with careful emphasis on the "ties that bind." To show only pictures of American mothers and children gives a very one-sided view of the great universal fact of motherhood, an idea which ought to be interpreted to our children through a carefully made collection of pictures, including a Negro mother and her baby, an Indian mother and her papoose, a Japanese mother and her tiny slant-eyed son, and as many other varieties of motherhood and babyhood as one can find. Pictures of the industrial world are particularly valuable when through depicting the work of various groups they bring home to the child a sense of his dependence upon these people outwardly so different from himself. . . .

The two groups of pictures referred to really belong together, for when the child sees the mother caring for her baby and the father working at his task that mother and child may live, he learns to know the family unit in its most characteristic forms of activity. Add to these some well-chosen pictures of the children of the world at school and at play, and pictures of homes which, from igloo to mansion, wigwam to palace, shelter family life, and you have gone far to make children feel that "differences" are full of interest but not divisive.[12]

So much for opportunities in schools that offer no opportunities for direct contacts. Of course, these illustrations refer to the

[12] *Childhood Education* for February, 1926, p. 273. For further discussion of the use of pictures see Chap. XVI, p. 208 *et seq.*

lowest age groups only.   As we have already seen in previous
chapters, the available resources are much richer in regard to the
higher grades.

More difficult are those situations where the interracial contacts
at school are exceptional, with no counterpart in likely outside
associations.   Often, as the explicit and implicit rulings of many
private schools indicate, there is strong aversion on the part of
parents and of the pupils themselves, if previously unprepared,
to such widening of their human relations.[13]

A Problem of Manners

A high-school teacher tells in some detail how one school administration, after studying the causes of a nascent group antagonism among the pupils, went to work to eradicate its causes:

An educational experiment in a large cosmopolitan city high school,
while not directly concerned with the question of race relations, has
had significant results which seem to some observers both to prove that
traits ordinarily considered as racial characteristics are really cultural,
and to suggest the extent to which the modifying of unpleasant cultural
group traits by educational means may result in the removal of very
real causes of supposedly "racial" friction.

This school draws its students from a wide variety of racial and cultural groups, but predominantly from families with immigrant parents
still out of touch with the language and ways of this country, and with
rather low economic and cultural background.   At the time when this
experiment began, the students in the main portions of the school (not
counting an annex in a "better" neighborhood) were four-fifths immigrants or children of immigrants.   Racially, three-quarters at least
were Jewish (eastern European, chiefly Russian); next came a fairly
large group of Irish (here for two or three generations, and standing
out as the conspicuously "American" group in the school); the remainder included Italian, Negro, Greek, etc.   Perhaps two or three per
cent were of English stock.

The school had been in existence for four or five years.   One of its
greatest problems had always been along the line of conduct and manners.   The first students admitted had been those rejected by neighboring high schools, or others dissatisfied with other schools.   This

[13] Examples of ways in which even in early childhood group contacts may
be introduced that foster appreciation, and of how, later, these contacts may be
developed in such a way as to substitute emulation that has an educational
value for group rivalries that foster prejudice, are given by Mrs. Sidonie M.
Gruenberg in *Sons and Daughters* (1916, p. 144).

meant an unusually high proportion of unruly and impertinent girls, and a tone of bad manners at the outset. Very few girls had home training in pleasant speech, gentle manners, or courtesy of spirit sufficient to hold against bad example, and voices in school were loud and harsh, language and manners vulgar. Self-assertiveness and conceit, with a tendency to grab every least honor or advantage without regard for one's neighbors, were unfortunately common and admired methods of behavior; a flashy, cheap type of effectiveness in dress and cosmetics, with no particular regard for cleanliness, were student standards of appearance. Discipline in classes was very poor, because there was a feeling that restraint by a teacher was to be endured only if one lacked the wit or courage to rebel or to be impudent; a sense of cooperative effort was almost lacking. The efforts of the teachers to establish better standards met with painfully little success, because student public opinion was so definitely against them. Often it was clear from the comments of the girls when corrected that they took their standards of appearance and behavior largely from sisters and friends a little older than themselves and considered their teachers wrong or old-fashioned when they disagreed with them.

Now, this sort of manners, appearance and attitude, when it occurs in a foreign or racial group, gets attributed to innate characters in that group by the average outsider who observes it. This school was no exception. For example, the teachers of the older American stocks, when they discussed their difficulties, would usually assume that the term "foreign," or "Jewish" (because of the large proportion of these girls) was a sort of explanation of why the students looked and acted as they did. Reactions varied from pity to anger, but in any case the impression of inborn group characteristics was made. Exceptions were looked upon as rather happy accidents. The idea was: "This behavior is terrible, but we shall probably have to put up with it as long as we have so many foreign—or so many Jewish—girls."

Then one day in a conference between the principal and some of the teachers, it was determined that the chief effort of all should be given to the problem of helping the girls see the importance of forming high standards of manners, appearance and conduct, and ideals of service, and striving to realize them. Since the aim was to help the girls see that school might prepare them for life not only in scholarship and business methods but in developing a strong, gracious personality which would be admired and respected by others, this experiment developed into what was known as the "personality campaign." The idea was explained to the girls, and they were asked to elect student leaders who would meet with the teachers to make plans for improving personal standards in the school. All sorts of methods were used. The faculty committee would suggest topics for discussion; the student committee would modify or develop these, discuss them under leadership of the teachers as problems of the school in which all, students and teachers, were concerned, and then the student leaders would return to the classes to lead discussions there, in which the girls were given a chance to see the problem from many points of view and to feel some responsibility for improving conditions. Among the topics so discussed were: cleanliness of person, cleanliness and orderliness of surroundings, dress, voice, courtesy, honesty, punctuality, reliability, initiative, cooperation, and service. These discussions were all practical, dealing with actual school conditions. The teachers took part in the discussions, but tried to make the girls feel that these were really their problems, and that not only the comfort and happiness of the school group but their own later lives would be affected by the ideals and habits they were discussing.

The tone of the school began to respond to this stimulus, and the girls were interested. Many of them began to realize for the first time how seriously people are judged by their appearance and behavior in the world outside school, and how important it is to form right habits. More than that, for the first time they saw that their teachers were actually trying to help them when they insisted on certain standards, and that they need not feel that restraint was always a cause for rebellion. Finally, it dawned on the public opinion of the school that it really was of concern to the girls themselves how they looked and how they behaved, and that cleanliness, orderliness, pleasant voice, courtesy, honesty, and cooperation were things which made for everyone's happiness and usefulness; and that by working together, the girls might help themselves and help each other to have a more pleasant time in school, and to form useful habits for life.

It took about a year for the girls to see this and feel that this "personality campaign" was something that they really wanted to have succeed. By this time they had also found out from their discussions that it is necessary to be very watchful and work hard to improve the habits of a group (or, from the individual point of view, to improve one's own habits), and also that a person cannot always tell her own strong and weak points without assistance. Then a rating system was established, and the girls were told that at the end of the term they would be rated by their teachers on those items of personality which had been discussed, so that they might learn how other people actually did judge them, and be able to improve their weak points. This very personal criticism was accepted, for the most part, in the spirit in which it was offered; the girls were pleased to have their efforts rewarded by praise of their strong points, and while they did not always agree with judgment of their weak points, they learned to take it seriously and without resentment, and as a stimulus to effort.

After two or three years the general spiritual atmosphere of the place had changed almost beyond recognition. Cooperation and the spirit of service had taken the place of the old self-assertive, grasping, devil-may-care individualism. And marked advance had been made on each point. The girls dressed more appropriately, were cleaner and kept their rooms neater, observed more of the conventional courtesies and showed the essential spirit of courtesy in considering others; even the loud voices had been somewhat moderated.

This experiment is now six or seven years old. Students of the same type, often from the same homes, come to the school, but one who had seen the place some years ago and returned now would never guess that the girls were of the same group. They are not perfect; but it is safe to say that no one would conclude from knowing this school now that "all foreigners are noisy and dirty" or that "Jewish girls always take everything they can get and care nothing for other people's interests"—both of which, certainly, formed an implicit part of the conclusions drawn by many people who saw this school in its earlier state.

Here, then, is a case where apparently rooted group characteristics have been proved to be not innately racial but cultural, and where they have yielded to education, and been modified, to the great and welcome removal of friction. How much of the common criticism of foreigners and of Jews depends on just these points or similarly eradicable ones? How much can be done, through social and educational modifications of undesirable cultural group traits, to remove causes of friction between racial groups?

This account incidentally suggests the importance of considering the by-products in group attitudes of any process of Americanization that may be deliberately adopted in the schooling of immigrant children or the children of foreign-born parents. Often, in efforts with that purpose, attention is too exclusively directed toward the remodelling, so far as possible, of the foreign child, as an individual, so as to fit him into the American life as the teacher sees it—often an antiquated picture at that, when he visualizes a sort of glorified "Anglo-Saxon" civilization that does not correspond in the least to the actual contemporary facts as regards the community. In the meantime, frictions between children of different parentage, or between children and adults, that must be dealt with by quite different social methods of approach, are overlooked. Since the process of Americanization can, at best, only be started at school and must be continued in

adult life, it follows that the relations established at school between those who will form the future citizenship are a more important element in their adjustment than equality of pronuncia-
tion or a like appreciation for the deeds of some American
historical figure.[14] It has been a frequent observation that attendance at the common public school makes for assimilation
without direct pressure to produce a preconceived "patriotic" attitude or to supplant all past appreciations and loyalties by new
ones.[15]

6. OUTSIDE THE CURRICULUM

Whether ethics be introduced as a separate school subject or
not, there are, as we have already seen, many occasions in the
public schools quite independent of the regular courses of study
that can be utilized for effective and specific teaching on race
relations. Hints have already been given in Chapter XX concerning the opportunities for comparative studies of cultural contributions that lie on every hand in the average American community. The school can systematize school walks and visits.
Local museums and exhibitions, moving pictures, and studies of
architecture provide resources but too little used.[16] Even the
classes in manual training can effectively be brought into the
circle of factors in widened appreciations:

A small boy, not more than nine years of age, who had the advantage of education at a modern experimental school where manual training was a strong feature, occasionally walked with his father along the
main shopping street of a large city. On one occasion he indicated
more or less correctly the origins of various rugs displayed in a window.
On another he criticized the lack of originality of textile designers who,
as he correctly pointed out, were at the time featuring patterns taken
from Egypt and from the Pueblos. He had no difficulty in naming
some of the more important categories of ceramics, and one day he
astonished his father by drawing attention to the mixed architecture of
several of the churches. This child had himself learned the rudiments
of rug weaving, of decoration, of pottery and, through a sensible general education, had even at that early age been made observant and
interested in the cultural characteristics of peoples and ages.

[14] See Franklin H. Giddings in *Teachers College Record* for February, 1925,
p. 452.
[15] Charles L. Robbins, *The School as a Social Institution* (1918, p. 121).
[16] The Newark (N. J.) Museum has developed special methods for encouraging visits by parents and children.

One correspondent suggests organized visits to a succession of workshops illustrating the major arts and skills of immigrant groups:

Not only the cobbler and the tinsmith, but also the oriental baker of rice cakes, the Greek cook, the colored janitor, the Italian market man, the Armenian embroiderer, the Russian worker "in pants," the Swedish foreman on a housebuilding job, not to speak of the machine tender and the laborer in mill and factory, might be visited in their haunts, so that their crafts and routines may be observed and the demands be recognized that are made by their jobs on their intelligence and faithfulness, and sometimes on their taste as well as the skill of their hands.[17]

Many museums, municipal and private, make a special feature of educational activities in cooperation with the school authorities which lend themselves to demonstrations of the interdependence between peoples and races. Unfortunately, these activities are as yet too often an afterthought and provided for somewhere in the basement while the museum in general is arranged from the collector's rather than the educator's point of view.

The first complete departure from the tradition of the museum as a cultural mausoleum is the Museum of Newark, N. J., which, under the imaginative direction of Dr. John Cotton Dana, has been made essentially a part of the city's educational institutions. Here a junior museum permits children not only to see but, to some extent, also to handle objects, and not only to listen to miscellaneous information but playwise to participate in foreign cultures.[18]

In this connection, we may recall that it was Hull House, Chicago, which, many years ago, pioneered with the demonstration of foreign crafts by foreign-born women in order to arouse the interest and respect of young folks for their cultural heritage.

There is much in the experience of pedagogically minded museum directors and of agencies for community organization which are practically applicable to school programs—especially to

[17] Where opportunities for such comparative visual studies are not available, appropriate literature may be drawn upon. For example, for several years *The Survey*, in its graphic numbers, brought frequent pictorial features, with descriptive text, of our foreign-born neighbors in their contributions to the industries and trades and arts of the country. There are passages in Lewis Mumford's *Sticks and Stones* (1924), and other books not primarily produced for school use, that tell of the influences of different waves of migration upon the development of the American city.

[18] Write for *The Junior Museum*. Illustrated pamphlet, 1928, price 10 cents.

organized visits, to celebrations, the arrangement of occasional exhibitions and other extra-curricular activities.

Mrs. Gruenberg, in a recent address to teachers, said:

It has been a favorite device to get children to enumerate the sources of the materials and services represented in their breakfast or in their wardrobes. We may go a step farther and get them to answer the questions as to the racial or national sources of our cultural or spiritual enjoyments. Who gave us the music, the pictures, the poetry, the drama, the architecture, the science, the dance? Whence the arts of printing and metallurgy and medicine, in general and in detail? From the highest to the commonplace, what we have of value is a composite to which not only all ages but also all peoples have contributed and daily still contribute. We have no right to disdain any of those through whom we actually get our living and our enjoyment of life day by day.

Such education is, of course, not a matter of lesson assignments and recitations, nor is it a matter of special subject of instruction. It means the continuous utilization of every opportunity presented in every subject of instruction; it means the humanizing of geography and history, of science and mathematics; it means the arrangement of pageants and art exhibits and entertainments in which all the children represent their respective groups as well as their individualities, and eventually the dramatization of situations in which the child may project himself whole-heartedly into an alien personality and acquire through his own creative action a genuine sympathy. Thus, through stories, through plays, through work, through discussion, through dramatics, the child learns something of what has been accomplished by human beings of various races and sects and nationalities. Through all this he should get some insight also into the common aspirations of mankind, the common efforts, the common difficulties and sufferings, and so arrive at an appreciation of what is essential in our humanity, to distinguish the essential from the incidental, the superficial, the separating factors.

Exchanges of Gifts

Where two racial groups within the country or state represent distinct cultures, the same methods of mutual correspondence and exchange are applicable that have been found helpful in widening international outlooks. The Junior Red Cross has been particularly successful in experiments of this sort which have for their primary aim to break through the isolation which segregation and geographical distance have created for Indian children.

In 1923 a special Junior Red Cross worker was assigned in the states of New Mexico and Arizona to organize Junior work in the Indian schools of that territory. Subsequently all of the Indian schools of the United States were encouraged to enroll.

Many white schools have taken over an Indian school as a "partner" with whom they exchange correspondence, hand work, samples of school work and various exhibits. Sometimes a white school will send material for handwork, books, magazines and class-room decorations, and the Indian school will respond by returning samples of their handwork or things gathered on the desert which illustrate their life and customs. Sometimes the initiative comes from an Indian school.

The United States Indian day school at Oraibi, Arizona, took upon itself the task of decorating a rest room in the new high-school in Hawarden, Iowa. They sent two cachina design cushion covers embroidered in wool yarn, one large table cover with embroidered bird design, two pairs of curtains to match the scheme of decoration, a plate the design of which was used to paint a frieze on the drop ceiling in keeping with the design on the curtains. The same designs were used also on flower boxes and flower pots. Two pieces of Indian pottery were sent, one Oraibi basket and two Oraibi wicker plaques. In exchange for this the Hawarden Juniors sent a victrola to Oraibi.

A school in Fitchburg, Massachusetts, made a fine five-tube radio set for the San Juan Indian School at Shiprock. In exchange for this the Indian school sent a Navajo blanket which had been woven by one of the Navajo girls attending this school.

The Western Navajo Indian School at Tuba City, Arizona, sent a beautifully woven Navajo blanket, pottery, plaques and dolls in exchange for seven hundred books given them by the Southwest School at Hartford, Connecticut.

Each year one of the monthly numbers of the *Junior Red Cross News* is an Indian number and contains not only interesting information but many suggestions for interracial cooperation. With each number the teachers of the affiliated schools receive a special supplement, *The Teacher's Guide,* which provides further opportunities for stimulating interest and cooperative activities.

Most delightful are the evidences of successful efforts to interest the Indian children in countries and peoples in other parts of the world and thus to link them up with that great international brotherhood represented by the Red Cross. Thus we read of a cheque contributed to the National Children's Fund by pupils in St. Patrick Indian Mission School who had earned the ten dollars by picking cotton for neighbors. This fund is used to send gifts to children in foreign countries. A portfolio of pictures, sent by fourth-grade Indian children in an Albuquerque school to the Philippines, was accompanied by an essay describing Pueblo and Navajo houses. Similar portfolios of pictures have been exchanged between fifth- and sixth-grade children of the Chilocco

Indian School in Oklahoma and an industrial school at Paracin, Jugo-slavia. An editorial note indicates that there are several hundred such exchanges with schools in Japan and in Czechoslovakia.

The "service activities" questionnaire filled in annually by the Indian as well as other schools in itself is a reminder to the school principals of varieties of possible cooperative activities. A collection of these re-ports contains references to dolls dressed in Indian costumes made for foreign schools, and the study of foreign dresses and costumes by means of calendar pictures and news illustrations received.

Individual Advice

Lastly, there are the unending opportunities for individual in-terview and counsel. Sometimes, where teachers and pupils have a relationship of mutual respect, a little private talk will do more than hours of classroom lecturing. And there are occasions when only in this way a catastrophe to the good feeling between the different racial elements that make up the class or the school can be prevented. Here, for example, is an illustration of a typical situation that was skilfully handled by a teacher in a private school in a northern city:

A high-school boy was going to give a party to his entire class but did not dare to invite the one colored member of the class because he was afraid that he would not accept and that there would be some strained situation. He and his mother consulted me because they were sincerely distressed at the idea of an omission. I told them by all means to invite the boy, and I would see to it that he did accept. I went to the colored boy and said: "Now you colored people, in your effort not to seem obtrusive, frequently make it very difficult for white people to treat you with the exact equality that they would like to do, because you defeat their efforts by withdrawing. You are going to be invited to this party. If you go, there may be some painful experi-ences for you, but I believe it is your duty to go and have just as good a time as you can rather than give the whole class a chance to say, 'Of course, he was in school with us, but when it came to a party he had to be left out.'" The boy and his parents cooperated perfectly, and the party turned out a great success, the only question being that of a girl who made herself somewhat unhappy by working up indigna-tion over the situation. Everyone else took the matter in exactly the right spirit.

Lectures and Demonstrations

The use of occasional special lectures may be illustrated as follows:

The most dramatic interracial story that I heard on my trip was that of the work of George W. Carver of Tuskegee. Professor Carver is in charge of the chemistry department and has engaged in important research, securing hundreds of products from the peanut and the sweet potato. Recently, he has been making paints of extraordinary brilliance from red clay. He is an elderly man, unassuming, a quiet, industrious scholar and a lover of men. The Interracial Commission secured an invitation for him to lecture on chemistry before a white college. He gave his talk, not a word of it remotely touching the race problem. But when the lecture was over the boys crowded around him, leaning over his shoulders, interested deeply in his subject and loving his personality. They have seen a great scientist and he is black. A man who was born a slave. They find him with those lovable qualities that the old-fashioned writers delighted to portray. They get to know him. And while he helps them as one of Joel Chandler Harris's or Thomas Nelson Page's old uncles helped his boys in the past, they see that he is not the servant sitting in the kitchen, but the chemist in his laboratory, Fellow of the Royal Society of Great Britain, recipient of the Spingarn Medal in the United States. Without saying a word on the subject of race, Professor Carver is the best propagandist for the doctrine of good fellowship that the Interracial Commission knows.[19]

The use of the morning assembly periods for education in race tolerance and world-mindedness has many advocates. The relative freedom of the occasion, the tradition of solemnity, the ability to bring in outside speakers, make this occasion particularly appropriate for educational efforts which have for their aim the setting of an ethical tone in the discussion of these topics.

At a boys' school, in which many nationalities were represented, a speaker took for his theme symbiosis—the mutual accommodation, adaptation and aid between different species. Drawing his illustrations from the surrounding woodlands and careful not to over-stress the comparison, he pointed out how humanity as well as the forest gains in power and beauty from the cooperation of its organic units.

On the basis of experiments extending over a number of years, the superintendent and the sociology teacher of the Woodbury, N. J., High School have published a suggestive program for a series of morning

[19] Mary White Ovington in *The Crisis*, April, 1927, p. 43.

assemblies, assuming that two or three days a week are given to the subject during a school year. In each part of the program one of the school departments is given responsibility for one period. For instance, the eight periods in October, all devoted to appreciation for the Italian people, and their history and culture, are taken in charge by the Latin, art, English, science, history, physical training and music departments. In the same way, other months are devoted to demonstrations of other racial contributions, not excluding the British—which so often are forgotten in such arrangements. (A similar program, but for adults, in another New Jersey city several years ago, brought the recognition that the devotion of an evening each to the cultural heritages of England and of Holland considerably strengthened the interest of the older residents of Nordic ancestry in the programs primarily intended to inform them of the cultural backgrounds of the new immigrant groups.) The American Indian, Jewish, German, and Negro contributions likewise are spread over a number of assembly periods each.[20]

How ostracism may be overcome by demonstration of special achievement is further illustrated in the following incident:

Several years ago we organized a voluntary orchestra which met after school. The director accepted all applications, among them a number from colored boys. The white boys balked; it should be white membership or they would leave. As it was near the end of the year the orchestra was dissolved. The next year I suggested to the teacher that he fill the orchestra places by a general try-out, so understood, but really with the policy of excluding the colored. This was done and a white orchestra organized. Shortly, the father of H. F., a colored boy who had been excluded, protested in my office, saying that his boy had been excluded because of race prejudice and that he was going to carry his protest to the Board of Education, for he knew his boy played better than any boy in school. I admitted that it was a choice in school of white orchestra or no orchestra, but that if his boy was the fine musician he said he was I would gladly see what could be done. Soon after that H. appeared on a school program and played with remarkable skill and technique. He was applauded enthusiastically and recalled three times. Straightway the orchestra members asked him to play with them. He became unusually popular throughout the school.[21]

Reference has already been made in an earlier chapter to the possibility of combining ocular demonstrations of openmindedness

[20] Copies of this program may be obtained from the Women's International League for Peace and Freedom, 79 Halsey Street, Newark, N. J.
[21] Evidence of a high-school principal given in *The Negro in Chicago* (University of Chicago Press, 1922, p. 255).

on the part of the teacher with such private interviews or other modes of influence.

Unable to check in ordinary ways a certain amount of antagonism to Italians because of their increasing number in the neighborhood and the enrollment of children of that nationality who were not particularly shining examples of either cleanliness or good manners, a public-school principal went out of her way to arrange for interviews with refined Italian teachers, social workers and doctors at her office during school hours so as to be seen in friendly conversation with them by children and—what was more important—by fellow teachers. Several times she invited one or the other of these educated Italians to speak in the assembly as she was in the habit of inviting other prominent citizens, and afterwards introduced them personally to some of the teachers. In this way she managed to dispel the growing feeling that Italians were not quite the kind of people with whom self-respecting people could associate.

More often, school principals and teachers, when they discover a growing antagonism to some particular group or underhand discriminations against pupils because of their foreign parentage, attempt to correct this feeling by going out of their way in being friendly, in the presence of children, to parents of that group. This is sometimes almost a necessity to preserve a loss of self-respect in a child of the minority who suffers at the hands of his fellow-pupils or to prevent a cleavage between foreign-born parents and their children. A high-school teacher says on this point:

We have had several instances of students in our school who were ashamed of their foreign parentage. In these cases we have sought to preserve their pride in their own families and their sense of dignity about their homes. Cases of this kind are more common with us than friction between individuals of different races.

Teacher Training

When all is said and done, the various hints that have been strewn out in this and in the preceding chapter as to methods of making the school a more effective instrument of the attitudes desirable in a progressive, democratic community, are no more than additional helps in a process that must, in the main, be inherent in the whole management of the school, in its programs of study, its pedagogical principles, and its selection of teachers. As we have seen, these specific methods of creating sympathetic in-

terest are distinctly minor ingredients, and the personality of
the teacher is far more important than any device that might be
invented for preventing conflict.[22]   We thus arrive, at the end of
this chapter, at contemplation of another very large need, and
that is the need for continuous self-criticism and self-education
of the teachers so that their own insufficiencies may not stand in
the way of their best potential influence.   And not only introspective self-study is needed, but also a decidedly objective and practical study of the racial and national elements in the community
from which the school population is recruited and which forms its
daily and hourly living background.[23]

How often may not the inability of a teacher to secure the
attention and reasonable progress on the part of colored pupils
be laid to an innate incompetency when what is really at fault is
the teacher's lack of regard for the different temperament and
home background of the colored pupils from those of the white
pupils.   Here also, more knowledge of neighborhood conditions
might help.

These considerations, again, suggest a possible need for changes
in the training of teachers, a subject too large for us to go into in
the present volume, since it embraces much more than preparation
for a given, specific task—namely the capacity of the teacher to
rise above the purely intellectual aims of his profession to the conception of his task as that also of a spiritual leader and an artist.
If teachers are to fulfill the tasks implied in many of the suggestions that have been made—fulfill them as a rule and not in the
rare instances of exceptionally gifted individuals—their whole
training will practically have to be reconstructed, so as to awaken
or preserve in them sensitiveness to those imponderable shadings
in taste and feeling that constitute the fabric of social conflict.
Resourcefulness and the technique of taking advantage of situations and given material would count for more than mastery of a
subject technique.

The one aim alone, of preserving in teachers a critical and curious attitude toward life, would involve a revolution in the substance and manner of their training.   Our educational system
today is making for the opposite qualities of mind.   While it is
not lacking in imaginative and highly intelligent practitioners of

[22] See also W. G. Carr, *The Negro in Chicago* (University of Chicago
Press, 1922, p. 109).
[23] Robert A. Woods and Albert J. Kennedy, *The Settlement Horizon* (Russell Sage Foundation, 1922, p. 283).

the art of teaching, its rewards more commonly go to the person who sticks closely to the rules and as rapidly as possible sloughs off what he may possess of originality, in the interest of a smooth, efficient routine. Instead of encouraging imaginativeness, it encourages a platitudinous and mechanical gesturing—a hollow mimicry of the real thing. Again, not all teachers answer this description; but it is because of their humanity that the norm of the "perfect" school system—from the point of view of the efficiency engineer—is not more fully realized. Eventually, if we really want democracy, intelligence, and good feeling as the common possession of Americans, we shall have to abandon much of our deadening school machinery and substitute for its technical perfection a more living relation between teachers and pupils.

Occasionally, as we have seen in several of the examples given, an unusual teacher or group of teachers even today, in spite of the system under which they operate, manage to get into their school a really warm sense of human fellowship, a combination of those qualities of mind which, at the outset of this section, we found fundamental to the integration of races and classes. This chapter may, therefore, fittingly be concluded with a further, brief example of this condition. A high-school teacher writes:

In the —— School, the principal and teachers are quite consistent in drawing no color line. They have been known to lean even the other way where there might be a question. It seems more than a coincidence that in this school there is the freest association of white and colored, gentile and Jewish girls. Moreover, while the students are rather inferior in home refinement to those of other high schools, I have never noted any discourtesy directed to those of another race. Even in the cases of fighting, I have not heard boys use opprobrious epithets toward one another. When a colored parent calls, he is treated with respect by the chance pupil he meets. There is a teacher who is a decided Mulatto, but I have not known of a single case of rebellion against his discipline or heard a disrespectful word applied to him. I have heard him spoken of as a "dark teacher," as if boys feared discourtesy in mentioning the difference of race. One of the clerks is a Mulatto, and, as far as I have observed, she is treated with the same respect as the others.

CHAPTER XXIII

WHAT CHURCHES AND VOLUNTARY AGENCIES CAN DO

Before discussing in detail the contributions of church, social settlement, playground and camp to the body of worthwhile practices in interpretive education, we must review briefly the problems surveyed in Chapter XIV. What we have seen there as symptoms of misleading influences, we must here consider as the product of educational and social philosophies and systems which in themselves are faulty and which in themselves must be modified before effective means can be devised to make them contributive to improvement in race relations. To some extent, reeducation of adults must precede the education of children. What has been said, at the end of the previous chapter, about the caliber and training of teachers is true also of ministers, social workers and all varieties of volunteer workers with children in churches, social settlements, and other institutions. With them the matter is even more serious: For too often they are trained—if trained at all— for other functions, and in their relations with children their good intentions must make up for what they lack in skill.

Unfortunately, many of these institutions do not even realize the nature of their problem. They recruit their workers as best they can from among those whose principles and moral character they can depend upon and then try to help them with such minor aids as they may be able to find available to improve the quality of their leadership. Many social organizations tend to limit their activities to the amount of trained, supervisory service they can afford to pay for. But churches still depend almost entirely on volunteers. As a result, we have, without exaggeration, thousands of institutes and lecture courses for volunteer religious teachers every year and a perfect avalanche of textbooks and ready-made lessons for their use. In so far as it is possible to make teaching material "fool-proof," the great denominational agencies have done all that can be done. But it seems to be true that the better kind of material only makes it the more tempting for those in charge of the educational work of churches and religious institutions to employ persons who otherwise they would not consider competent. It is always difficult to get good volunteers; the choice is enormously widened if all you require of them, as regards intelligence and skill, is ability to act as cog in a machine of systematic procedure, managed by some expert or other in a distant college or denominational headquarters who puts out the literature and tells exactly what to do from the beginning to the end of each session with the class.

We are not here concerned with this problem in its general aspects but only with its relation to the "teaching of race attitudes." And in that respect there is reason to believe that good texts by no means ensure good teaching. These expertly produced books, pamphlets, tracts, single lesson sheets or other pieces of literature too often discourage such originality and resourcefulness as the teacher may have. Everything, from the missionary lesson to the celebration of holidays, is cut and dried. The same pictures are distributed to children in Montana and in Florida; the same stories are told the Anglo-American children of Vermont and the Spanish-American children of New Mexico. A thousand churches produce the same pageant (since instructions have been distributed for making the paraphernalia for this pageant) whether particularly suitable for their constituency or not.

All right, you may say, that will make for a more uniform Christian Americanism, much to be desired. But when the pictures are accompanied by the same explanations in environments where the personal experiences of children are worlds apart, when the stories are told in terms familiar in one part of the country but constituting almost a foreign language in another, when no account is taken of differences in group psychology, in parental occupations and cultural backgrounds, the whole business is apt to become decidedly unreal. Quantity production ensures cheapness of material and does not stand in the way of effective use by teachers who adapt it to their own uses. But too often the uniformity of the lesson material in use is not one of felt oneness but of thoughtless conformity to a single pattern. The only thing that could make the use of uniform teaching material helpful in the development of like interests and mutual sympathies among children of different antecedents would be its use by skilful teachers, sensitive to varieties of childish understanding and able to take advantage of every available means to adapt the lesson to the specific circumstances of their particular locality and group. Such teachers welcome the time-saving device that suggests procedures without dictating them. But, unfortunately, a majority of Sunday-school teachers are insufficiently prepared to make fine distinctions and so are prone to follow slavishly whatever looks like a prescription. Moreover, where there is no confidence in their ability, they may be held closely to these texts and prescriptions by their superintendents. If so many fine and intelligent young people are nevertheless attracted to serve their churches in a volunteer capacity, it is because of an urge to be educationally creative, which even a somewhat dictatorial system cannot altogether squash.

What exactly is it that religious institutions are trying to accomplish as regards racial attitudes? We have already seen in a previous chapter (XIX) that their aims are not necessarily either clear or consistent. Yet, they must in some respects be distinct from those of the secular schools. However ineffectively and incompletely, the schools do represent to some extent the interests of society as organized in the state; their fundamental aim is to prepare future citizens. The churches are concerned with even larger interests; their fundamental aim is to prepare men and women for a religious attitude toward life and its responsibilities. Where the one will stress the claims of patriotism, the other will stress those of human brotherhood. They are apt to teach very emphatically and dogmatically an abstract equality of races and nationalities as well as equality of worth in individuals—even when contemporary society and the specific social environment in which they find themselves do not lend themselves to even an experimental application of that thesis. Here, for example, is a program formulated by a church discussion group in answer to the question as to what churches might do to modify or correct adverse racial attitudes:

1. Include definite training as to the fundamental likenesses of all races. (One member added: "With the recognition of the things which should keep them apart.")
2. Meet representatives of other races. (However, they add, there is no evidence in the experience of the church itself in its Sunday school that happy contacts between children of different races there lead to *generalizations* of mutual appreciation.)

3. Bring out the cultural values of other races. Call attention to the nationality of great people of other races (e.g., the Negro descent of Dumas).

4. Show how Americans have overcome some of the lower standards, which, seen in others, bring about a feeling of superiority; and point out that other peoples can do the same.

5. Teach the Christian basis in the brotherhood of children of a common Father. (This was considered the most important.)

6. It is vitally important that teachers should have unprejudiced attitudes and that the teaching material is suitable. (The personality of the teacher was felt to be the key to much of the difficulty.)

This program stresses the fundamental needs already discussed in this and in previous chapters: appreciation for cultural values, good teaching material, good teachers, etc. But it also contains prescriptions upon which there is agreement only so long as they are considered in general and in terms that have favorable connotations. There is no recognition here of such practical problems as the possible increase of miscegenation as a result of a greater recognition of potential equality, nor of the difficulty of combining the concepts of brotherhood and class division of society in a single social system.

Therefore, before we proceed further and endeavor to discuss possible methods of carrying into effect such principles as those suggested, we shall do well and reflect for a moment what would happen if the expected results of this kind of social teaching really did take place. It is all very well to think of them in terms of increased fairness and kindliness toward persons of other groups. But no effective instrument has yet been invented for arresting these dynamic qualities at a given desired terminal point. What would happen to established social institutions if the attitudes that are the objective of these educational activities really became general? Much of the discussion of education in social ethics draws a polite veil over those consequences that are likely to prove controversial. For the sake of realism, we must again remind the reader in this place of the fundamental difficulties discussed in Chapter XIX, and more especially of the dilemma that faces social education in a society which, in some of its main tenets, so far from being completely socialized, is not as yet even tolerant toward a completely social point of view. In short, if the teaching on human relations that takes place in most of our churches were effective, we should have nothing less than a social revolution.[1]

After the first glow of satisfaction over the fine phraseology of the unending texts on "neighborliness," "world-friendship," "adventures in brotherhood," it is something of a shock to return to so sober a consideration of their larger implications. One becomes more wary of the optimistic tone of programs and policies that avoid the real problems—as illustrated in this communication:

If the schools and Sunday schools make use of their opportunities, they can develop in the child a spirit of brotherhood. Through knowledge of the characteristics and customs they can be taught toleration for the racial differences. They learn to respect and admire the great people of other nationalities when they learn from books, movies, pageants, etc., of their heroic deeds. They see that in spite of outward appearance and diversity of customs there is a striking similarity in all human beings.

Many pages might here be devoted to a listing of textbooks, stories and other literature which somewhere or other are recommended as sure to make for more tolerant racial attitudes. Unfortunately, few of those who write such books or recommend them are specialists in educational method; and even educators, if they are glowing with religious zeal for human brotherhood, are apt to be swayed by other than strictly professional considerations of educational technique when it comes to texts of this sort. In short, disagreeable as it is to have to make this criticism, the literature that is put out in such enormous quantities for the religious and moral education of our children is not produced with anything like the regard for pedagogic principles as goes into scientific textbooks used in public schools. The great bulk of it is just sentiment put on with a broad brush—and sometimes sentiment that does not quite ring true.[2]

[1] George Albert Coe, *A Social Theory of Religious Education* (1917, p. 48).
[2] A book-list, too inclusive to be regarded as critically thorough, yet suggestive of the different types of literature that are available, is *The League of Nations Non-Partisan Association's International Guide to Material Descriptive of Many Lands and Peoples* (June, 1926; Price 5 cents). It contains bibliographies for different age groups, references to plays and pageants, folk songs and folk dances, games, pictures, posters, maps, periodicals, material for leaders and a directory of organizations interested in the matter. The league also has reprinted an article on "International Friendship Thru Children's Books" by Clara W. Hunt, of the Brooklyn Public Library.

Without looking at the books themselves, it seems probable that books referred to by a religious educator in the following terms cannot be relied upon really to produce the attitudes that make for understanding, appreciation and sympathy; they may have attendant learnings in quite different directions.

. . . Stories of a missionary character but which will help admirably in letting children understand their neighbors of all nations. Quite friendly in attitude toward children of all nationalities. . . .

. . . Teaches world brotherhood in a very beautiful manner, showing peoples of all nations to be brothers and the contribution each has made for the success of the other. Very illuminating. . . .

. . . Very friendly in attitude to other nations and races. Treatment is such as to bring out friendship of personal character with other nations and races.

Indeed, extremely few of the books of a definitely missionary character that have been surveyed in connection with the present study can be said to make for a really reflective sympathy, as defined by Professor Elwood (see p. 291). Even some seemingly innocuous books, just because they endeavor to arouse zeal for missionary work, emphasize the gifts which the American has to offer the non-American, or the white to the colored peoples of the world, and thereby make for self-satisfaction and a sense of national or racial superiority. A book that teaches "world brotherhood" is apt to be decidedly general and to avoid the concrete problems in human group relations that are likely to exist close at home. A "very friendly attitude" when taught by a religious textbook is apt to be one of benevolent paternalism toward foreign peoples; and when "friendship of personal character" is stressed, one may be sure that the book does not go into questions of group relations which, even for children, constitute ethical problems more real and concrete than expressions of abstract friendship for imaginary individuals.

Even where the endeavor apparently is to approach the religious teaching of human relations in terms of what is commonly called "life situations," the treatment is almost universally abstract and deals with the opinions of children or adults rather than with real situations of contact in which opinions and attitudes concretely express themselves through behavior. Words never are a sufficient substitute for experiences. Before a church authorizes its religious teachers to implant in children notions of universal brotherhood, let it ascertain whether the church, as the cooperative agency of its members, is really willing to have its children practice the nearest approach to it—namely a sharing of all their opportunities with other children, regardless of class, race, nationality! If that should be the case, then a vigorous teaching through actual associations is possible, and suitable reading matter and discussions will have their place as additional means of education.

Instead of having pageants, made up of children of a single, select group of the community, to celebrate world friendship, it will then be possible, for example, to have a real pageant of races and nations by inviting participation of representatives of other groups.[3]

The author recently witnessed (in Rochester, N. Y.) an admirable pageant in which children of some twenty-five or thirty nationalities participated; here the subject of national difference was not even mentioned, but the libretto dealt entirely with the enchantment of spring—and its cause in the richness of a varied flora.

The point to be stressed in this connection is that a merely verbal teaching of interracial friendship without personal association in any form, rarely is of much value. Better by far to use other, practicable forms of personal contact for a gradual training in social forms of behavior and to rely on the imaginativeness of the individual to expand later in life the types of association to which such behavior may be applied.

One of the most progressive church schools in the country, in a situation where both congregation and pastor are unusually sensitive to the need for education in interracial cooperation, does not even attempt to apply direct teaching to the problems in race relations. The school contains children of a great variety of nationalities and races; but their attention is never directed to this fact. Consideration, helpfulness, cooperation are taught in that great variety of ways known to the skilled, progressive teacher.

SECULAR PROGRAMS

If in the foregoing pages we have more especially concerned ourselves with the problems of the church school, we have not

[3] Such a pageant is described by Dorothy Giles in *Adventures in Brotherhood,* Council of Women for Home Missions and Missionary Education Movement, 1924, p. 143.

forgotten the similar and related problems of other institutions that have for one of their objects the moral or social education of children. While they differ somewhat in their aims, the main objective is sufficiently similar to speak of these organizations together as agencies designed to help in the formation of social attitudes. Social settlements, Y.M.C.A.s, boy scout, and camp-fire girl organizations, community centers, and other institutions of that nature usually have this advantage over churches—that they employ skilled workers—if not always persons trained in the art of teaching, at least persons with a higher education who are recruited from the more cultured and intelligent sections of the community. Nevertheless, even in these agencies—as many of the examples given in the present volume amply illustrate— there is the greatest diversity of opinion and, sometimes, real perplexity, as regards the best methods to be used for strengthening or bringing about racial attitudes favorable to cooperation.

HELPFUL CONTACTS

Especially on the matter of the desirability of personal inter-racial contacts, there is complete uncertainty. As has repeatedly been stated, it is impossible to blue-print a set of specifications in this respect that would fit all conditions—that is to say, all parts of the country, all types of communities and all kinds of social institutions. Absurd as it is, a demand for such prescription, nevertheless, is often made; and it is probable that many ministers and social executives will put this present volume to one side, disappointed because it does not tell them "in fifteen words" what to do in this matter.

The best we can do, however, is to direct the attention of these responsible workers to the enormous variety of contacts that may naturally arise in the experience of their respective clientele or may artificially be brought about as a means to its education. One of the main obstacles to a practical handling of the problems is the assumption that when the question of personal contacts between members of different racial groups comes up, it is a question allowing only of two answers, yes or no. Perhaps the mere awareness to the immense variety of contacts that may be countenanced or brought about will help to secure larger awareness to other resources than a plain yes or no.

Where a racial group is completely segregated, by the sentiment of the dominant majority in the community, it is hard to avoid keeping children segregated also in their recreational activities out of school hours. But the term segregation admits of many shades of interpretation. For example, in one place the only possible basis for social work among children may be the exclusive use of the premises for one group or the other. In another place, it may be possible to have the premises used at different times by both, or to have separate departments under the same auspices.

One of the simplest devices of providing an unobjectionable initial contact even when the sentiment of the community requires complete social segregation is the occasional introduction of speakers from other racial groups or walks of life. It is not necessary that in each case they should talk about "my people," but the mere presence of a cultured person of a group that is looked down upon—usually because of the generally low social status of its majority in the community—may have the effect of correcting a misunderstanding; such, for example, as that "all foreigners are dumb," or "all Negroes are dirty," or "all Orientals are a sneaky, thieving lot of people." Any subject of interest to children will do well for their discourse. On the other hand, there may be something a little too artificial when, for example, after a heated discussion in Sunday school over the rights of colored people, the following week a Negro speaker is introduced who lectures about some totally unrelated topic without once referring to the friction or misunderstanding between the two groups.

It has become a more frequent practice of late to arrange for interchanges of visits between white and colored or native and foreign-language clubs or classes.[4]

[4] In *The Congregationalist* for September 8, 1927, John Leslie Lobingier describes a rounded program of activities, containing different types of contact, which might be modified to meet the exigencies of somewhat different community situations. In the First Church of Christ of New Britain, Conn., an interesting project was recently carried out by boys and girls of the seventh grade in the United Week-day Church Schools. It brought young people of two races into contact in a worth-while task. . . . The enterprise began with a study of biographical material, and it was agreed that if any of the classes worked up appropriate dramatizations these would be given as part of a program to which they might invite their parents and also the members and children of the local Negro church. One class decided to work out a movie scenario of the life of Dr. Samuel Chapman Armstrong, including his influence on Booker T. Washington through Hampton Institute. A second class decided to learn to sing one good Negro spiritual. A third class worked out a dramatization of the life of Booker T. Washington. Other classes made their contributions, too, one being a display of pictures, with suitable readings or statements. . . . The colored Y.M.C.A. secretary of Hartford talked to them about the aspirations of his race; a colored quartet was secured for the public program.

The question whether it is desirable or not to include members of groups socially under the ban in Sunday schools with children of the more privileged group, has already been referred to (p. 173) and cannot definitely be answered except with reference, once more, to the necessity for a previous agreement on fundamentals. The Catholic Church refuses to recognize racial privileges, and where its classes for children are composed of those of one race or nationality only, this is either because of the accident of situation or because of practical language problems. Among Protestant churches, the Episcopal Church, though it is often regarded as the aristocrat among them, seems to have gone furthest in developing a technique of contacts where these are not likely to come about in a natural way.[5]

Where an occasional but not frequent direct personal contact is practicable, even common membership in a national or international organization has its psychological values. Thus, the gradual separation of Negro Protestant bodies from the major parent Churches has seriously lessened the sense of mutual obligation which existed previously. On the other hand, the increasing inclusion of churches with foreign-language ministers (self-governing churches, not missions) in the great denominational bodies is making for a fuller sense of fellowship among native and foreign-born congregations, even though they rarely meet. The values for children of common membership in a national body, even when divided into racially segregated units, is illustrated in the following letter to the editor of *The Crisis:*

I was the guest of the executive officer, a southern white man, of the only regular organized colored boy scout troop in the United States at the only colored scout camp in the United States. We went out to the camp. . . . At the camp I was served supper with my white friend, and at the evening camp fire I listened to an address of the executive officer of the white troops and to a white scout who had come from a near-by white scout camp to sound and explain the numerous bugle calls in the routine of the day. . . .

The colored boys related this story to me: In the afternoon they had been out on a long hike and in returning passed the white scout camp. These white youngsters signalled, "Who are you?" The response came back, "Colored Scouts." The white scouts signalled again, "Come over and visit us." The colored scouts went over and spent a half hour

[5] Thomas Burgess, Charles Kendall Gilbert and Charles Throley Bridgeman, *Foreigners or Friends*, Department of Missions and Church Extension, 1921, p. 223 et seq. See also *All Colors* (The Inquiry, 1926, p. 77 et seq.).

yelling and singing and talking with their white fellow scouts. These southern white boys, observing that the Negro scouts were tired and dusty from their hike, said, "Come on and take a swim in our pool." The colored boys responded and had the swim of their lives. The white scouts served the colored scouts with candies and sent a supply to the colored boys who had remained at the camp.[6]

Contacts across national barriers are likely to play, in times to come, an even greater part in the effacement of racial antagonisms than they can play today. The possibilities of international travel for children are as yet quite undeveloped. Efforts at organized travel have rarely so far extended down to children of school age.[7] The recent international conference of Boy Scouts (1926), attended by boys as well as leaders, has given the participants a little foretaste of what such international gatherings might mean in the future when the economic situation permits of a more frequent staging of such occasions. Incidentally, the mere consciousness of membership in an international organization of boys or girls that meets periodically cannot be without influence on international and interracial attitudes. In the members, the vaguest possibility of being able at some later time to participate in such a meeting will create a greater disposition to meet as equals a potential Japanese or Mexican fellow-member.

It (the scout movement) has become almost a kind of religion, and a religion resting on the simplest and also the most transforming of conceptions, that of the brotherhood of men and of Scouts. If any one doubts it let him go to one of the annual assemblies of the Scouts of all nations and of their instructors, the scoutmasters. There he will find not only the differences of nationality but, wonderful to relate, the differences also of race and color, completely ignored and overthrown. He will find the white man and the brown man (perhaps also—we do not know—the black man), boy and man, meeting together, playing together, learning together as brother Scouts and brother men. It is really rather wonderful, and people don't perhaps quite realize that here, beneath their eyes, is taking place a transformation which, if only

---

[6] *The Crisis* for March, 1927, p. 22.

[7] Such a plan has been inaugurated with considerable success of late by a German public high-school which includes foreign travel for senior pupils during the school year in its course of study—and is able to accomplish it at a ludicrously small cost. (See *The Survey* for June 1, 1927.) The success of this experiment also has brought organized vacation travelling in foreign countries under teacher-leadership into vogue with German high-schools of the more conventional type that cannot permit travel to encroach upon the formal plans of study.

it goes far enough, will fulfill the very ideal of religion and make war between nations an anachronism and an absurdity.[8]

How the admission of an exceptional representative of a foreign group may modify the thinking of a school in regard to his race is illustrated in the following contribution of a student:

In our town, there is a family of Japanese people—that is, the mother is American and the father is Japanese. The oldest girl came to our Senior Christian Endeavor, and we all became acquainted with her. Very soon she began to get right into things. She was our vice-president. Then some of the young people thought she was getting too strong an influence on our society, and we rather forced her out. She was not defeated by this but started an organization of Junior Christian Endeavor. She has done splendid work at this. Her group always wins prizes for membership and loyalty in conferences and mass meetings. All her membership of Junior Christian Endeavor would do anything for her. It makes the older society feel ashamed to think we fairly pushed her out.

How an observant and quick-witted Sunday-school teacher may turn to account a single experience of interracial contact which threatens to create friction, is told in the following example:

A social worker in one of our schools observed that as the pupils gathered one day for their lesson the girls were avoiding and the boys were making fun of a little lad of African descent who had come in with them. She saw her opportunity. Instead of the lesson planned, she told a story in which a little colored boy was the hero. She spoke of the fact that peoples of different color lived in different parts of the world, all children of God; that a single white boy in those regions might be very unhappy if the boys and girls there teased him because his skin was white, just as God meant it to be.

The change in the conduct and attitude of the class was apparent at once. But there was later assurance that the teaching had been effective. One of the boys ran home after the lesson, burst into the room where his mother was sitting, and cried out, "White isn't the only color in the world; there is black, and brown, and yellow, and if you were there you wouldn't like them to make fun of you!" His mother came

[8] *The Manchester Guardian,* February 25, 1927. This tribute is the more interesting since in years gone by pacifists used to express themselves in this as in other organs of British liberalism as hostile to the scout movement because it seemed to make for a spirit of militarism. In fact, this is an interesting example of a case in which international expansion is gradually transforming a movement which at the outset was distinctly chauvinistic.

to the teacher to tell the incident and ask what had been the lesson for the day.[9]

How the establishment of traditions of this sort may help to counteract efforts to introduce racial segregation is illustrated in an unpublished report of the National Urban League on the Negro in Westchester County, New York:

Colored boys have been, and are, on high-school teams and in the school orchestras. In the theatres, playgrounds, schools and in the county offices the colored report that there is little prejudice. Unfair treatment of Negro citizens is usually made a community matter and is so handled. . . .

One village reported the presence of a' branch of the Ku Klux Klan; but, as one of the oldest (colored) citizens expressed it: "I can see no difference that it has made. The son of the organizer of the Klan used to come to my home to play."

A similar occasional crossing of the prescribed barrier by an unconscious "revolt of youth" is illustrated in the following:

The secretary of a religious organization working among young girls recently started a separate group of colored girls because the parents of some of the white members objected to the colored girls that were distributed over the different groups. The members of one of these clubs asked that their two colored members, while joining the new colored girls' club, remain also members of their former club. Obviously, the officer of this Christian institution was not in a position to interfere forcibly with this arrangement, and one of the colored girls, in addition to joining the new group for girls of her race, subsequently also was elected officer of the mixed club.

There are, further, the most varied opportunities for combining normal segregation with occasional associations of a sort that are likely to create friendly mutual attitudes. An experienced leader will both take advantage of such opportunities as they arise naturally and also create opportunities of this kind. For example:

A California teacher writes: Last Christmas, the smaller children of our Sunday school entertained the children of a nearby Mexican colony at a party. This was a give-and-take affair, and the Mexican children

[9] Florence Buck, *Religious Education for Democracy* (Pamphlet, American Unitarian Association, 1919, p. 25).

were invited and treated exactly as the white children of the neighboring Sunday school might have been. For the Mexican children the white ones made small gifts of paper and cardboard. The Mexican children made a "Pineota" and some "Cascaronis" for presentation to their hosts. Both nationalities were much pleased with their presents and took great delight in their novelty.

In May, the Mexican children invited the same group to their colony to a May party. Both nationalities brought May baskets as gifts to the others. They were even more friendly than at the first party. We hope in the autumn to have a party at which each nationality may exhibit its homes to the other.

The following example comes from one of the oldest settlement houses in a middle-western city:

Among the older boys and girls (that is over ten years of age) I notice more "race feelings." I often hear an Italian boy telling another not to play with the "coons," or not to play with a "dirty Jew." The feeling among the Italian parents seems to be that they do not wish their children to play with the colored children. However, we make no separations in groups. The colored children register in groups, thus forming their own clubs, and the white children do the same. It seems to be a matter that they take care of themselves, without, no doubt, realizing it. I think they prefer to be with their own group.

We had a very interesting example this summer of real respect and regard on the part of members of one racial group for a member of a different one. Our summer work is organized on the plan of a junior city, self-governing. City officers, council and police are elected by the children. A colored boy of fourteen was elected chief of police by the "citizens" as a recognition of three years of faithful service as a member of the police force. Other names were suggested, but the general feeling was that Theodore should have the place. I wanted to bring out the reasons for this and discussed the others who had been suggested for the place. An Italian boy immediately said, "He's honest, Miss A.—he won't double-cross a fellow!" Theodore proved to be a capable chief of police; he was present at every meeting of his group and supervised the work of his department in a quiet "unofficious" way. At the next election of officers I was much surprised to hear his name suggested for city manager, a great honor and a position never previously held by a colored boy. I did not take it very seriously until I heard the children discussing his nomination. Italian boys were telling their friends why they believed he should be elected, Italian and Slavic girls told me reasons why they thought he would make a good officer. Among the reasons that they gave were the following: 1. That he was honest; 2. That he helped little children; 3. That he treated all alike, showed no preference, had no special favorites; 4. That he refused to let his own brother serve on the police force because he did not think that he would make a good officer; 5. "That he knew what he was doing and did it but wasn't bossy." One Italian girl of twelve who, I knew, had never played with, or liked colored children said, "Why, Miss A., Theodore is better than any city manager we ever had." Needless to say, he was elected by a big majority. Two weeks later election time came around again. Three names were put up for city manager, two Italian boys and Theodore. Theodore was reelected by a unanimous vote. Often the boys and girls do not seem to be much interested in the election, but this time I noticed that they were all interested; there was a certain tenseness in the air that showed a keen interest in the outcome. When Theodore was again named city manager there was loud cheering. Theodore has always been quiet, interested, unselfish and fair. My idea of the whole thing was that the children recognized in the boy a fair-minded, honest friend and when allowed to choose for themselves wanted that kind of an official, regardless of his color or nationality.

Another settlement experience also is to the point; it is particularly interesting in that it illustrates the limits set to the "liberalism" of an institution, as it expresses itself in its activities, by the "illiberalism" of the outside community:

Some time ago the Jewish children in a certain settlement would chase the Italian children away, bombard them with anything they could lay their hands on, make dire threats against them. The head of the settlement, at last, protected the Italian children at club time with the aid of a policeman. After a few times, the Jewish children let the Italians come in peace. A little later the children mixed in clubs, on the playground and in parties. Both races come to the settlement now as a matter of course, and the group that once had so much trouble are now associated into a Wednesday night dance club where the Jewish young people dance with the Italians, and the Italians with the Jewish, just as they would dance with anyone else. A group of Polish young people have come into the dance and are accepted in the same way.

A club of colored girls met on the same night as clubs of Italian, Polish, Russian and Jewish met. It was the custom to use the last half hour of the evening as a social time in the living room. All the clubs attended but the colored girls. One night it was decided to have stunts, and the various white clubs sent an invitation to the colored club to join with them. They did, and the colored club took the prize for the best stunt. Cordial relationships seemed established. The next week the colored club came to the social time. Apparently there was no feeling. After a few weeks the presidents of the white clubs met the girls' club leader and asked that she keep the colored girls away, otherwise they would resign and get out. The club leader would not ask the colored girls to stay away, but the white girls made it so uncomfortable that after a time the colored girls did not come. The girls' club leader went to one of the white girls and asked for an explanation of their objection.

"The colored girls are all right," she said. "They're very decent for darkies, but suppose the club has a visitor, what would the visitor say? We don't mind, but how would it look to the outsider?"

What about letting children decide for themselves what interracial contacts to tolerate or to avoid? This is something different from a mere drifting, letting each problem come up by itself to be handled as a unique test of the executive's skill and tact. To have no policy in the matter is a good policy only when the institution consistently abstains from interfering with the choices of its youthful clientele. This has been carried out with striking success in many neighborhood houses where either a too liberal or too dictatorially exclusive policy would have been offensive to some of the membership. Instead of either segregating or not segregating the groups in the different classes and clubs, it is announced that the house has no principles in the matter, that the children may organize themselves as they wish and will be accepted in groups for whatever instruction or leadership they may desire and require without selection from above as regards their racial or national composition. In this way, there is often almost complete segregation through a natural gang formation in keeping with the sentiment of the neighborhood, and yet an occasional inclusion of a racial minority and a free transgression of racial barriers for specific purposes or on specific occasions. In other words, while the children in their group formation reflect exclusive, and sometimes prejudiced, community attitudes, yet they themselves often provide first opportunities—such as joint councils of all the groups—for an educational process through which these attitudes may gradually be changed. Skilled group leaders use these situations to bring out the richness of experience that comes from diversity of background and points of view.

Is it not possible, after this brief survey of different types of institutional interracial association to deduce some generally valid principle as regards the desirability of personal contacts through religious and social organizations? Before we can answer this question, we ought to face, perhaps, the more difficult question, "Of what use are principles anyhow in a matter of this sort?" Unfortunately there is only too much ground for scepticism as to the value of formulated principles. In a majority of our largest and most representative national organizations, including both religious and secular enterprises, we have local practices that are decidedly at variance with nationally enunciated principles. Moreover, we also have local institutional practices at variance with the accepted principles of the local institution.

POLICIES AND PROGRAMS

The principles applicable to interracial contact are dependent, then, on the major aims of organizations and institutions. There are two possible inclusive aims in the work. They may consciously be working for social peace—whether in general or as between specific groups or classes—and they may be working in the main for the emancipation of the more backward groups or classes in their community or neighborhood. The methods adopted by a community center, let us say, must necessarily vary with one aim and the other. If social peace is the chief purpose, everything that can be done to reduce friction between the members of racial or national groups must be attempted. If social advance is the aim, intergroup friction often is not only a price that must be paid but may actually have to be increased for the time being, as an unavoidable by-product of an educational process.

Confusion as to aim will produce conflict of principles. But aims in religious and social work cannot always be clear-cut. Often the aim develops or assumes definiteness as the work proceeds. A concrete example will make this clear:

In a small and mainly residential city of one of the middle-Atlantic states there has for some years been a community center, at first conducted with definitely religious aims by a Protestant denomination, but in recent years carried on by a representative board of citizens on which Catholics also serve, and financed by a community fund. The clientele is almost entirely Irish and Italian, but lately increasing numbers of Negroes have come into the community. All three of the racial groups (if you like to think of them as such) are, as it happens, of relatively low economic and social status—more colloquially, the clientele of the center is looked upon as distinctly "rough."

Boys and girls, who go to the same public schools, have not been separated by race in this institution; but many of them are in boy scout and camp fire girl groups that insist on such distinction.

While these children play together on the school playground, complaints of parents have come with increasing intensity of feeling (due, presumably, to the gradual increase in the number of colored children) about the interracial associations on the playground and in the gymnasium of the community center. Friction between the children themselves also has been more frequent of late; clashes of a kind that used to be regarded as between individuals now take on a racial group complexion.

What are the managers of the community center to do? Inquiry as to primary aims brought out that the community center was not established originally as an instrument of community integration, that is, of social peace, but decidedly as an instrument of education for the least privileged groups of the community—at that time chiefly Irish. While the center has been instrumental through its activities to further mutual inter-group appreciations and friendships, its primary aim still is that of cultural advancement for those most in need of it.

At the present time, the Negro group as a whole is somewhat behind the immigrant groups in standards of home life, behavior, culture generally. But, as it happens, those who make use of the opportunities offered by the community center belong to the more ambitious and advanced families—the same that are anxious for a high-school education —while only the rougher elements of the Irish and Italian groups are now attracted to it. From the educational point of view, therefore, two aims have to be combined—thinking, for the moment, of the separate requirements of the groups: The colored people need more self-assurance, every stimulus possible to aid their ambition. The white people need not only similar aid but, in addition, education in tolerance for those whom they regard as their inferiors.

If social peace in the community were the primary objective, the policy of this institution probably would have to be a gradual sharpening of segregation so as to reduce the occasions for inter-group friction. But the colored people of the city are extremely sensitive to even the slightest signs of discrimination. To be excluded or herded further apart by a progressive institution would be likely to result in increased bitterness on the one hand and in a decided check to ambition on the other—twin symptoms of the oppression psychosis. They do not desire to associate with those who look down upon them; but to be told that they cannot associate would, for some of them, be a severe blow to their self-respect.

At the same time, in this case the institution was somewhat to be blamed for letting the matter of interracial association drift instead of developing a conscious policy upon it. For white and colored boys simply to be loose in the gymnasium to make up their own teams as best they could was almost an abdication of leadership. After realizing the situation, therefore, one of the first changes recommended was that there should be less individualism and more group organization. In other words, if boys were obliged to come in as members of a group, it was thought, those who were most race-conscious would be likely to join a club made up of members of their own race only. If, however, boys who played together at school desired to play together at the center, they could form interracial clubs.

Moreover, if race feeling were to become a strong factor in group associations and formations, the institution would have it in its power to introduce activities of strong emotional interest to individuals of both races and so to cut across the racial barriers. A boy really keen on playing in an orchestra will hardly notice whether some other boy in the orchestra is white or colored. Nature-study rambles will be equally exciting whether some of the participants are dark in hue or not; and a common search for a rare botanical specimen will make for a mutual understanding and sympathy in which race plays no part. In other words, a vitalization of the whole institutional program, it was decided, would be likely to result in a lessening of race friction—and that means, of course, the abandonment of activities that are merely routine traditions and substitution for them of activities that meet real, present desires and needs.

There were also, a discussion showed, unrealized opportunities for increasing the types of conscious group division, so that the contrast should be more varied than merely between white and colored. In one or other of the activities a Jewish group, for example, might participate as such, and groups representative of distinct neighborhoods might be set up—in civic activities, for example—to offset groups representative of race or nationality.

In all present and possible future activities, more attention might be given than had been customary to the attendant learnings. From a near-by large city, lecturers, musicians, and talented people of all sorts, of practically every race and nationality, might be drafted for an occasional contribution. It was pointed out that a demonstration of the variety of groups in American life even when not represented in the community itself would have a valuable influence on attitudes. While the presence of an oriental lecturer or class leader may not directly aid in the creation of a more sympathetic interest in the Negro, it will help to disperse the erroneous notion that all wisdom and charm resides in the so-called Caucasian race or in persons of fair complexion.

Even if there were no educated Negroes in the community, the community center could aid awareness to their existence by introducing interesting colored men and women from outside on occasions where they might contribute toward interests already in existence. For example, it was suggested that a well-known Negro sociologist in the nearby city be invited to take part in a discussion of a civics club of older boys that is interested in neighborhood improvements. In the same way, there were prominent colored teachers in the nearby city who could interestingly discuss ethical and educational problems with groups of older girls. And at times a colored glee club might be invited to take part in a purely recreational program or community celebration.

These suggestions do not, of course, exhaust possible changes and amplifications of the program. They merely are given as illustrations of the type of consideration that must enter into it if there is a gradual shift in major aim—in the present case from a religious-institutional one to one more extensively educational. A community center, a social settlement or an institutional church cannot suddenly change the attitudes of a community; but in a case such as that here envisaged, it can for a time hold up the developing tendency to friction while the despised group of new-comers—in this case Negroes with the cultural background of the rural South—adjust themselves to the higher level of living standards. Such a program calls, of course, for constant watchfulness and resourcefulness. Not every effort will succeed. At times it may seem as though racial antagonism had actually been increased; but a passing phase of friction in a situation kept in flux is preferable to a hardening of group divisions which prevents the rise of the oppressed group without giving security against encroachments to the dominant groups.

We have dealt at some length with this case because it illustrates the connection between four types of motivation that must necessarily enter into the work of such an institution. These are: first, appropriate *ad hoc* measures for dealing adequately and expeditiously with situations that arise calling for immediate action; second, deliberately planned methods for dealing with changing situations that are known in their main character and tendency; third, principles of administration derived from the major aims of the institution; fourth, convictions or first principles derived from the religious or ethical philosophy within—and out of which—the institution is growing into the life of the community. A "live" institution will rarely run smoothly because

these four types of motive for action at some point or other will
fail to harmonize. If there are no other discrepancies, there will
at least be diversity of motive on the part of the actual human
beings who make up the managing board, the staff, and the members who, in most cases, are drawn in, not after an exhaustive
preliminary examination of their views and purposes, but for
many reasons of expediency as well as of aptitude.

Efficiency will consist in doing justice to the four demands that
arise from the four types of motive: There has to be a satisfactory
promptness and *practical competency* in dealing with immediate
questions that arise from situations requiring adjustment while
they are yet moving, or as one might say, while they are yet
"warm." There has to be a *program* corresponding to the situation in the large. There has to be a *constitution* embodying the
major aims. There has to be a general appreciation for, and
sharing in, the *convictions* as to human destiny and human nature
from which the support, the administration, and the use of the
institution derive their common dynamic.

What has just been said must often be applied in the heat of
controversial discussion. "Expediency" and "first principles"
sometimes are held up against each other as though an institution or organization could be run successfully either without one
or without the other. A succession of minor situations which can
be met without a special concern for lasting values is apt to
create, however, a major situation when ulterior purposes are
frequently neglected in measures of dealing with them. Thus we
are sometimes told that a Christian institution is "defeating its
own purposes" by permitting some practice to prevail in a minor
ruling which many people recognize as contrary to what they,
and others, conceive of as essential to a life of Christian brotherhood. The relative strength of the idealistic concern may vary
considerably in two branches, almost identical in other respects,
of the same national organization because in some one respect
their situation is totally unlike. Thus, the situation pictured in
the example given above would probably not exist either a hundred miles further south or two hundred miles further north; it
only occurs in a zone where those particular race attitudes prevail
that have been described. This will be clear by a comparison
of that example with others in this and previous chapters.

Moreover, within the same institution problems of social contact which are seemingly or theoretically alike will on closer exam-

ination prove very different indeed because of the difference of the racial or national groups involved. One of the contributors to the present study reports, for example, that in a southern city he noticed a group of small colored children whose faces were pressed against the iron railing of a playground from which they were excluded because of their race. This playground happened to belong to an institution which is unusually thoughtful in the invention of new means of integrating the different white nationality groups represented in its neighborhood. It may not even have occurred to the board members and the workers in that institution that the methods which they are applying to create better understanding across the boundaries of nationality might also be applied to programs for better interracial understanding. They are so immersed in the traditions of the region that they can no more see anything incongruous in this omission than the Fathers of Our Country saw in declaring all men equal but owning Negro slaves. And so, while their ideal of fellowship is undimmed, it finds expression only in programs and experiments on behalf of those groups which they visualize as coming within the orb of their potential field of action; toward others their feelings remain unfocused. So, while the outsider may see two similar problems in their community, they see one problem closely, calling for the kind of social engineering in which they are competent, the other remotely, as something vaguely calling for better understanding but not primarily a thing they can do anything about. They will let two different sets of motives arising out of their primary principles on nation-building decide their attitude toward the two problems: One they will meet realistically by inventing practical means of dealing with it; the other they will refer somewhat ineffectively to a theoretical sense of tolerance or kindly helpfulness in themselves and in others without attempting to build up instruments for its practical expression.

It seems fairly clear that similar discrepancies exist almost anywhere, though they do not always lie on the surface. The folkways which in one community limit the interested social vision so as to exclude from it Negroes may, in another, exclude Orientals or Mexicans or Jews or French-Canadians. Here, for example, are two paragraphs from a report contributed to the present study by a settlement group who, in writing them, do not seem to have been aware that—as other portions of the report show—they were limiting their discussion to work with different European nationality groups and were not considering other racial groups in their community at all:

Race attitudes in children are modified through games, music, and art. In our library we have books and pictures showing the art and beauty of other countries to overbalance the sordid side of every-day life. In reading and telling stories we give authentic phrases, words, settings, etc. By an annual folk festival we are guiding hundreds of our leading citizens as well as the members of our clubs and classes to an appreciation of the customs, costuming and dances of different nationalities.

These attitudes are modified also through club teaching of general (moral) ideals and of broad-minded citizenship, correct parental teaching, school teaching and religious teaching of tolerance. An important method is good leadership in games. In play, because of its universal appeal, men can get closer together than in any other way.

NATIONAL PROGRAMS

Since we have indicated the special problems which arise when a national organization promotes purposes which locally must be modified in accordance with local or regional mores and folkways, it may be worth while in this place to consider briefly the special values which, nevertheless, the formulation of aims and programs on the larger national scale may have for the solution of local problems. There is a danger that the existence of a national—or international—point of view is entirely lost if the problem is attacked only with sensitiveness to local limitations. For, the officers and members of institutions and agencies are constantly subject to influences which throw a sharp light upon *some* racial and nationality contacts while they leave others in the shadow of unrecognized responsibility. Meeting from time to time with others engaged in similar efforts but in a different type of community, they are sensitized to the as yet unrecognized aspects of their own community's race problem. They may not at once recognize also appropriate measures for dealing with them, but their thinking will have been stimulated; and when opportunity arises to enlarge the scope of their activities they will be somewhat prepared to take advantage of it.

But there is more. A comparison of methods which in one community are applied to an improvement of relations between natives and immigrants, in another to that of relations between whites and Orientals, and yet another to that between whites and Negroes will overcome the feeling that the problem as it manifests itself in any one of these communities is absolutely unique. It will be realized that, while some of the phases may be unique, there is a larger area of concern which the workers in all these communities share. Whether they meet at an occasional national conference or are kept in contact through correspondence, this consciousness of oneness with a national movement has the advantage of emphasizing the larger stakes in the undertaking, whether seen locally or nationally, of strengthening those motives that have more to do with permanent convictions than with expedient programs or passing situations.

Too often, where this higher sense of responsibility is allowed to become submerged in the claims of the daily task, the idealistic motives of a permanent character suffer atrophy, and the enterprise sinks to the level of a useful but uninspired routine. There is special need, in these days of increased concern for "efficiency," to strengthen those national and international links that touch the deeper springs of action. For example, it may happen that a group of business men with a cool and materialistic, if well-intentioned, concern for the "success" of the local institution will influence its program in such a way as to over-emphasize the demands of expediency upon it and almost to disregard those of the underlying purpose of the institution as an instrument for the realization of human brotherhood. In such a case the contacts with a national movement may provide the necessary reminder that merely to see the wheels go round more quickly or more smoothly does not in itself serve the larger end.

A third value of the over-arching national movement to those who have to find the solutions for specific problems within the frame of a locally practicable program is that it helps the local group to discover not merely likenesses and unlikenesses but patterns of experiences which can become the foundations for principles of action. In addition to being aided to see their task as a whole and to recognizing the essential relations between their local effort and a national, or perhaps worldwide, movement, the interchange of information and suggestion through a national office also increases the ability of the local workers to recognize types of situations about which it is possible to do something and to know how to select the instruments most appropriate to the specific local need.

THE RESOURCEFUL USE OF SITUATION

Let us take, for example, the problem of personal contact as a means to better understanding.[10]   Local and regional attitudes on this matter are about as diverse as any social attitudes in our country that represent group loyalties and feelings.   Not only are some types of contact permitted in one region that are forbidden by public sentiment in another, but these taboos include different racial and national groups in different regions, and often are varied by class feeling and social status.   Thus, a rich white man in a southern community is more likely to permit his child to play with a colored child than a poor white; but both equally resent an association between their children and colored children in formal education.   In a northern community, on the other hand, public-school contacts between white and colored children are more likely to be tolerated as in the public interest while contacts outside school hours are frowned upon.   In a western community, the Negro may represent no particular problem, but there may be great agitation over contacts between white and Oriental children.   In a northern community, Indian children may be discouraged from attending the common schools for similar reasons.

We have, then, in these various communities a common problem of providing, if we can, direct contacts between children of different racial groups, in forms that will be outside the traditional taboos and yet possess elements contributing to a better mutual understanding.   We have here a type of situation that is very frequent and, where it exists—that is to say, where there are margins of potential contact between complete taboo and complete lack of segregation—has given rise to a new type of educational engineering.   How to bring together children of different groups who would not naturally meet in school and could not, because of too great a distance in home backgrounds and personal requirements, be brought together in the same institutions, provides a practical problem to which a good deal of ingenuity has been applied.   Here are a few examples of type solutions:

An experiment in contact through visits has in recent years been made in New York by the Rev. Clarence V. Howell, as part

10 For a tentative classification of types of interracial contact in their demand upon individual and group conduct, the reader is referred to The Inquiry's study outline, *All Colors.*

of his program of Reconciliation Trips.[11] To that program he has added special trips for boys and girls between twelve and sixteen years of age to Negro Harlem. The trip includes visits to a high-class residential section owned and inhabited by Negroes and to a printing plant, games with colored children, a concert of Negro songs by a chorus of colored children, and a story hour at the Harlem branch of the Public Library.

The fullest kind of association which it is possible to provide is, of course, through living together in camp. But even here different shades of association are possible. As between different nationalities, there is often so little adverse feeling that parents gladly consent to a camp life without segregations of any sort. An occasional colored or oriental boy may be found in a camp where members of these minority groups, if more fully in evidence, could not count upon an altogether friendly reception. In some cases, it has been found possible to include in mixed camps colored units, with their own tents and under their own leadership, but participating in all the social and educational activities of the white units.[12]

Obviously if it should happen that the white boys were the more experienced this would introduce an element of importance. They would naturally be looked up to and respected as seniors. If any of them were to assume a light air of superiority it might be explained with his superiority in age and attainments and so easily be passed over without giving rise to interracial feeling. On the other hand, the feeling of racial superiority which any of the white fellows might bring with them would, under wise leadership, be likely to be changed into a different and socially less damaging sense of superiority, that of an older brother over a younger one.

These examples must suffice to illustrate the way in which an experimental attitude toward typical problem-containing situations gradually develops solution-types among which the individual local institution may choose what it needs for its own purposes, in integration with its existing program. Here are two lines of suggestive effort—visitation and camping—which, according to circumstances, may serve to provide pleasant and

[11] See description in *All Colors*, Appendix II, p. 142
[12] The beneficial effects of a camp in which Mexicans boys were permitted to meet with native Americans have been described by Fred Eastman in *Unfinished Business of the Presbyterian Church* (Westminster Press, 1921, p. 46).

educationally stimulating contacts between children of different racial groups whom public sentiment, and in most cases, of course, also the sentiment of the organization, does not permit to meet in the more frequent associations of school and playground. Gradually, as experiments of this kind accumulate, it is possible to distil from the separate experiences common recognitions of what "works" and what does not. For example, we already know that contacts which stress the differences of the two groups in social status or contacts of an active-passive contrast in which one group consists of givers and the other of recipients, are apt to impress upon the children false associations between race and class, whereas forms of contact that stress similarity of interests are more likely to strengthen a desire for mutual understanding and cooperation.

How to choose within the potential varieties of action one that corresponds to the lessons of previous experience and therefore falls into an incipient or growing pattern of principles, or how to apply such principles to a situation which in some aspects is unique, is a task requiring skill. No agreement on aims, principles, or fundamental convictions as to desirable race attitudes will show the individual worker or institution how to formulate a program or even how to meet a particular situation: It can merely help to form the standards of judgment against which to measure and weigh suggestions for action that spring from the situation itself. But without such standards there will be a drifting with every current no matter where it leads, an unsystematic "dealing with every situation as it arises" which often is not, strictly speaking, a "dealing" with it at all but a partial evasion which leaves no guidance for action when the same situation arises next time.

General Principles

We have thus come to the point where we can, tentatively at least, answer the question which has forced itself upon our attention in several chapters of this book and which was formulated (on page 355) briefly: "Of what use are principles anyhow in a matter of this sort?" Must each situation problem stand by itself as a unique demand upon the skill and resourcefulness of the educator, the parent, or the social engineer?

Principles, we have seen, are the deposits of experience, and are most reliable where experience has been richest and has been analysed most thoroughly and objectively, so that causal trends can definitely be recognized. Principles are valuable to the practical movement for interracial understanding when they are used as standards of value, not when they are codified as rules. An imaginative parent or worker, in dealing with any aspect of the problem, may devise successful methods that are entirely novel and outside previous experience. But more often conformity with a tradition, even though it is a developing, growing tradition, will save blunders. In the one case, experiment will tend to modify the established principles as standards of value, in the other it is more likely to confirm them. In both cases, the values added to national experience in dealing with this problem will vary with the extent to which the four demands which may legitimately be made upon a successful form of action (p. 359) have been harmonized into a single, definite policy.

In this summary statement, it may be permissible to recall one or two other desiderata in social action which have emerged from our examination of examples. The effort must, in so far as this is possible, do justice to the different interests involved which are not exhausted when the aims of the organization have been named. For the organization itself, to be of maximum value, must be a living thing, continually re-adapting itself to the changing needs of the community. No ideal that finds expression in its program can be considered final except that which relates itself to ultimate convictions as to human power and destiny. Everything else must be conceived of as in flux—even those moves that seem most sanctioned by the authority of age or association. If new interests in the community make themselves felt, the far-sighted policy will recognize, not endeavor to suppress, them—provided only it is convinced of their genuine character. In this way, even though, as we have seen, even the religious institution is necessarily restricted in its functioning by time and place, it can always be a force for progress—at least in that it is exceptionally sensitive to interests and needs which are apt to be overridden by the overwhelming weight of established power and privilege.

Another desideratum: No form of activity that purposes to influence the race attitudes of children in the direction of responsiveness to human values outside those already highly appraised in their own group will be of permanent good unless it embodies sound principles of education. No solution of a problem of friction between children of different nationalities, for example, solves anything if it does not, together with the settlement of the immediate dispute, utilize the experience of strife for a better understanding on the part of children as to "what it was all about." Even where only a very small step in the direction of fostering understanding and sympathy is possible, that step is worth taking, provided it makes it a little easier to face that kind of problem next time. Provided the process of practical handling of such problems is a progressive one, the rate at which unfavorable attitudes are changed into favorable ones is relatively unimportant. Before we can get excited over problems of educational speed, much effort still lies ahead in seeing to it that the solutions applied to racial problems really are sound. And that, as we have seen, implies in many cases a change of spirit, a substitution of faith in the success of methods that integrate diverse and even conflicting motives for faith in the self-directive power of some single "right" principle.

Practically everything of constructive effort to which we have been able to direct attention in this chapter, in so far as it is worth considering at all as a possible example for wider application, was originally in the nature of an experiment—sometimes a daringly novel one. A warm feeling of human kindness is of no value whatever in social engineering unless it is accompanied by courage. Our institutions will go further than they have gone if they learn to care more for the spirit than for the form; if they more fully appreciate the importance of effective, not to say scientific, techniques; if they more frequently permit their gifted minor workers, paid and voluntary, to try out some of their own ideas; if they encourage resourcefulness and originality in meeting practical problems; if they have faith in youth instead of laboring under the self-imposed burden of equipping it for life with a ready-made set of attitudes.

Fortunately, there are now in every type of religious and social institution rapidly growing numbers of leaders who share this standpoint and realize the values of a valiant, cooperative process of reform, who are anxious to do their part in slowly building up better traditions and techniques in practical effort rather than to stand out as martyrs for an abstract theory of liberalism which nobody, least of all they themselves, could concretely apply. The hope of American democracy largely lies in these groups and in their influence on public opinion.

CHAPTER XXIV

SUMMARY AND CONCLUSIONS

Race attitudes in children present a baffling problem in social psychology only because we are as yet without an adequate technique for making observation and record truly scientific. Our technique fails us even more when we try to trace these attitudes back to their causes. The factual material with which we deal is neither permanent nor altogether open to inspection. The first expressions of aversion may be so slight as to escape even the vigilant eyes of a mother. The occasions of more obvious expression may be so trivial as to invite no thought and therefore no record. Moreover, it is the unusual which attracts attention, and a whole community or a whole generation may be living in an abnormal fear or an abnormal sense of its relation to an outside group without being aware of it.

Our information concerning a "typical" expression of race feeling in children, therefore, is typical only in the sense that the course of a disease may be said to be typical. Those who record it do not claim that it is representative for a majority of children; but they do claim that insofar as expressions of race feeling occur, such and such an incident is apt to be among the symptoms. They go further and, cumulatively if not individually, show that there are typical symptoms for different ages and for different situations as regard interracial contacts and other community conditions. Thus fear is the typical form of race feeling in very young children. This is followed by the characteristic attitudes of the pre-adolescent stage with its tremendous vitality. As the child enters adolescence, a complication sets in, for each stage of puberty has its own emotional concomitants; and at the same time, through the widening scope of his experiences, the child grows in wisdom and self-control. New problems in social relations arise in the later stages of adolescence when the eye is directed more constantly toward the future, when group membership becomes conscious and new adult influences are exerted upon the youth, and especially the girl, to condition them for the part they are expected to play in life. We thus are able to trace a progressive development of attitudes, fairly clearly marked in its main stages yet never completely lived through in real life because the typical experience and response for each age group is traversed by a shifting pattern of changing situation. The child of poor immigrant parents may already be out of school and at work when his native American chum absorbs the social idealism of a teacher who disposes him toward a deliberate seeking of friendships that bridge both class and race. A school building program, a new industrial development—bringing to the community a number of additional workers from outside—a new pastor, a removal to a different neighborhood, a single athletic event, may completely change the situation that conditions the child's feeling toward the members of another group. Ascending and descending levels of well-being affect racial pride and deference, and a sense of racial rivalry.

The acquisition of new race attitudes is cumulative, not substitutive, and old responses break through the newer habits of behavior when a situation reminiscent of former channels of thought and feeling also brings back the former stimuli. Yet there are also violent conversions, not least in adolescence, both up and down (whichever way you may measure these directions), from the acquisition of an expanding new feeling of human brotherhood to the exultation of combat against a racial foe. There are fine youths around the lynching tree as well as around the boy-scout camp fire.

SOURCES OF PREJUDICE

What makes for this immense variety of responses and feelings in our national life? Why is it that some children fear a person of dark color and others do not? That Jews are baited in one town and Chinese in another, while many towns are seemingly without a racial scapegoat upon which small boys may practice their shafts of humor? Many people, especially those of limited or uniform experience in the matter, believe that either a general feeling of aversion for persons of considerable difference in appearance or one for persons of a given race group can be explained by an inborn trait. As soon as we survey the variety of such aversions—even when we limit ourselves to content only and overlook the variety of forms—we discover that no single instinct, nor even a whole key-board of instincts, can explain so mixed an assortment of reactions. Modern psychological research here comes to our rescue and confirms our suspicion that much which people have assumed to be born with them in mental habits has really been acquired—and sometimes quite painfully—in the early years of life. Nevertheless it remains an open question which scientific observation and testing has failed so far to answer, whether normally physical difference does create a distinctive sense, either of aversion or of special attraction (both hypotheses have been defended); if this should be proved true, it is possible that with it would be proved the further contention of many observers that sexual maturing as well as greater social group pressure expedites the development of that racial feeling, whatever it is, in adolescence. In other words, the part played by instinct in race feeling, if it plays a part at all, is probably smaller in child life than in the later stages of adolescence and young adulthood; and, whatever may be the outcome of further studies of innate reactions of that kind, we already know that among the total environmental influences upon the child's race feelings they almost disappear into insignificance.

For, though we were prepared for much evidence concerning the pressure of adult attitudes upon those of children, the actual evidence of the staggering weight of prejudices with which it burdens the rising generation is beyond all expectation. One might almost say that it makes no difference whether the child is born with natural aversions or not; he is certain to have his mind canalised, even before he starts going to school, into habitual acceptance of the prevailing attitudes of the group within which he lives. Personal experience, when hedged around with prohibitions and protective care, is no gateway to realism. The average child is made to notice outer differences and to accept them as signs of inner differences of value. His very contacts are regulated for him, if not by precept then by example. So it comes that the child—since his experience is not the same in classroom and Sunday school, on the street and on the playground, at home and in the social center—acquires a mixture of contradictory attitudes toward those of other races which he is quite unable to explain to himself or to others.

But a child is perhaps less concerned with his own experience than is sometimes assumed. His daydreams are at least as much in the future and in the past as in the present; and the glimpses of romance afforded by the story-book may be more real to him than what little he carries with him of experiential memory. The significance of his personal experience must be striking for him to become aware of it: for example, the gradual growing away from him of classmates or playmates who are different from him in their rate of physiological maturing. Of two comrades of yesterday one has remained behind, a mere child, content to play as "kids" do; the other takes football seriously and scans the evening papers for the latest reports of his favorite team, or he may suddenly have moved up into an almost "grown-up" interest in girls which for the first is incomprehensible in one formerly so "sensible" on that score. Hence our inquiry into the psychological effect of the differences in physiological growth and our recognition that, alas, we know as yet all too little about it. We do not know, especially, to what extent these differences are biological, on the one hand, and, on the other, caused by diversity in environment, folkways and economic status.

In this and other ways the contact between children of different races produces its own influences upon race attitude; but the nature of these contacts is largely determined by a much larger and more inclusive influence: the adult-made environment. We have tried in the present study to distinguish between several categories of adult pressure upon the race attitudes of children— more especially between the absorption of adult attitudes by the juvenile mind, which is more or less automatic, from the absorption of attitudes that are definitely, if not always quite intentionally, being taught. Of course, such categories are of value only because they permit a more or less orderly arrangement of the evidence; in real life one type of attitude-acquisition so delicately shades into another that a sharp distinction cannot be made. However, we found that the less conscious forms of acquisition of race attitudes deserve special attention because they are much more neglected and, therefore, often vitiate what intentional educational effort is trying to accomplish. Furthermore, while it would not be safe at this stage of our knowledge to attribute a relative weight to different kinds of influences, the evidence makes it probable that the attitudes unconsciously transmitted are much more effective than those deliberately taught.

In our time as in no other, conscious education, in school, church and home, is saturated with unreality. The child is expected to admire values that count little in the life that surrounds him. The moral training is verbalistic and removed from the realities of daily life—or else artificially approximated to it in ways which the child does not recognize as reflections of the social obligations which adults recognize as guides to their own behavior. Hence the normal child is aware of a difference between precept and practice, between the moral teaching that is conveyed by words addressed to children and conveyed by the inescapable evidences of adult behavior, and it is the latter alone that he takes seriously when the two are obviously in conflict. In this matter of race relations, it is the gesture of the parent rather than the word of mouth, the smile of derision for members of another race in the adult group rather than the recital of the "golden rule" or a profession of cordiality, the adult's racial pride that comes to the surface in moments of exultation rather than lessons on human brotherhood, and above all the obvious facts of segregation and social division on racial lines that condition the child's attitudes. A refusal to admit members of another race to personal contact makes protestations of absence of race feeling ridiculous.

We have looked into the variety of existing forms of race segregation that especially comes to the attention of children; and while our factual study of the matter is not exhaustive, we have no difficulty in discovering that such forms of segregation, even where they are an established part of the folkways and therefore rarely discussed, leave a deep impression upon those whose attitudes toward other races and classes are formed in their shadow. We have examined the contradictions that often exist between the social principles embodied in school systems and those taught in the class-room and have found that usually they result from lack of clarity in aim rather than conscious hypocrisy. Lack of accurate knowledge is at the bottom of much uncertainty. Children are separated on the ground of assumptions as regards their racial character; and the objective truth of these assumptions is rarely investigated. Sometimes, the assumptions result from attitudes prevailing in the community which thus are strengthened by a school system presumably established to substitute for prejudice a responsible attitude to fact. A vicious circle is set going from which the only hope of escape lies in the fact that the school, though serving the fortification of established folkways, also carries within its own processes the dynamic of change. In our own country one of the main problems of public education is the preservation of the traditional ideals in an environment of ethnic flux; but this is also its main hope, for it forces a frequent reconsideration of these ideals in the light of new situations and of new contributions of Old World experience.

What the Child is Taught

In this functioning of the school, the civics class is a central, though not always the most important, factor. Some of the civics teaching gives us the most advanced and most realistic presentation of the task of nation-making in which all the rising young generation will have to play its part. But no school subject stands alone; and too often the information given and the attitudes taught in the civics lesson are offset in fact and spirit by the teaching of the history or other class periods. Moreover, too often the opportunities of teaching civics with the use of local resources, such as the ethnic diversity of the school population itself, are not fully utilized. The social experiences of the child are not made, as they might be, the starting points for inquiry into the nature and extent of civic responsibility.

To the controversy over the public-school teaching of history our inquiry contributes one or two pertinent facts: It is not immaterial whether one people rather than another is made the object of appreciative study, whether the influences of one rather than another are pictured as favorable upon the progress of western civilization. The child absorbs from historical study attitudes toward living peoples and their representatives in his own country and in his own community. Practically all history teaching is propaganda; but there are significant differences between the methods as well as the contents of different textbooks. Excessive emphasis on one type of facts and a corresponding suppression of others—the most frequent practice—conditions the child to preconceptions and false valuations which it takes much to unlearn. The more slyly insinuated expression of contempt for some national and racial groups is apt to create antipathies which cannot always later in life be traced to their sources and so, with others, are carried along as seemingly innate.

This is even more true of the prejudiced teaching to be found in textbooks on such presumably scientific subjects as biology, anthropology, or geography. There is much testimony to the effect that just because this teaching comes to the child not in the form of vivid narrative but in that of objective statements of fact in the vocabulary of science, and with pictorial illustrations not from "art" but from photography, its influence on attitudes is even more powerful. The heroes of history may merge with those of legend and fiction; but the naked savage pictured, in contrast with a fully dressed white man, as representative of the Negro race will have produced a mental impression which returns as the word "Negro" is mentioned.

Language teaching has its special influences on race attitudes which only rarely come to the surface, when, for example, the school use of a play or a story book becomes a matter for heated protest on the part of a minority group. Whether in this question, as in the related problem of the treatment of different national and racial groups in the moving picture, there is too much sensitiveness, or whether some of the stereotypes produced by derogatory treatments of this kind really leave a deep and lasting impression is still a matter for debate. But there can be no question that when stories and pictures reinforce an erroneous conception of racial character which is already current or which is assiduously propagated by an interested set, they do materially add to the effective instrumentalities of racial mis-education. The typical Mexican or Oriental pictured by the American school child, for example, is almost entirely the creation of this type of learning.

Particularly nefarious, from the point of view of substituting fictitious for realistic characterizations of races and nations, is the development of a teaching of public speaking which awards its prizes to those who in oratory or debating most nearly express the current prejudices and hardly ever to the child who has arrived at original conclusions on the basis of personal study and experience. In this field the effects of deliberate propaganda activities on the part of interested societies and individuals are obviously detrimental.

OTHER CONTACTS

Contrary to a wide-spread belief, we did not find the Sunday School so very different in its influences on racial attitudes from the day school. After all, the teaching of these institutions also represents the ideals of distinct classes and culture groups; and at most it can be said for them that idealistic aims of a humanistic character often are more stressed. But the opposite also is sometimes true; the day-school, maintained by all the taxpayers, is devoted to an ideal of democracy which the church that serves a distinctive neighborhood or set cannot adopt without losing the intimacy of its appeal. Some racial prejudices, thus, may occasionally directly be traced to the teaching of the Sunday School.

Again it is lack of clarity of purpose rather than false aim that is the cause of this circumstance. Too often even methods adopted in the belief that they will teach "world-mindedness" will be found on closer examination to implant in children attitudes of snobbishness and condescension toward the members of other races. A scrutiny of the textbooks used in religious education, more especially, reveals an appalling amount of vague sentimentalism in place of clear thought and single aim. The reason, of course, is that the teaching of a church on race relations must of necessity be somewhat self-contradictory. For one thing, it is difficult for a group that feels strongly the values of its own religious beliefs to regard as moral or intellectual equals those who do not share them. For another, the strongest religious feeling nearly always develops within the protecting cult of a distinct and intimate group, whether it be a sect or a rigorously limited "chosen people." But considerations of this nature must not blind us to the fact that for many of our adolescents the religious class is the first, and sometimes the only, occasion to bring the conflicts between sectional and general human ideals to consciousness, and to stimulate and develop unselfish attitudes toward unlike peoples, classes, and races.

To school and church a third socially planned influence has in modern times been added, especially in our cities—that of organized recreation. The popular notion that the morale developed by games and athletics carries into the relationships of every-day life an appreciation for fairness is well founded, as many examples show. At the same time, racial distinctions and segregations carried into the province of organized play are particularly effective in fixing in young minds the pride of race and the assumption that other races or groups are inferior. Experience disproves the belief that "gangs" are formed of the biologically similar; more natural, in neighborhoods with mixed ethnic population, is the mixed play group. The segregations in play-activities are nearly always adult-made if not necessitated by physical neighborhood conditions.

Standing outside the compulsions of school contacts and the

elevated tone of the religious institution, the playground and the club offer special advantages for observing the racial attitudes and behavior of children. It is here that the influences of the child's environment are most clearly reflected. But here also new stimuli are brought to bear. Games may be either favorable or prejudicial to interracial goodwill and appreciation. Plays and pageants, songs and social games as well as the activities of the playing field and the camp may be managed in such a way as to fix the existing limiting folkways in regard to interracial association and false concepts as to the character of other groups. Even in the individual play and hobbies of the child at home, society permeates pleasure with its teachings: Dolls and games show signs of propagandist intentions; story books, whether intentionally or not, produce stereotypes; the picture book and the comic strip cater to the small child's tendency toward derision for what is strange in appearance. Our survey, fragmentary though it was, produced an amazing variety of hidden attendant learnings which usually confirm rather than contradict those major influences that make for aversion and depreciation of those of dark color or of other racial distinctiveness.

Children are made to feel rather than to understand the consequences of different kinds of interracial contact. It is in the management of such contacts rather than on the plane of deliberate teaching that home and school and church are apt to be in conflict —and it is not always the same one of these institutions that is most limiting or most expanding in its effect on attitudes. But it is difficult to trace accurately where the child has got certain feelings. The various influences brought to bear upon him so interweave into a pattern of learnings that the contradictions and even the conflicts between them do not necessarily come to awareness. Thus the average American child goes out into life with ready-made associations between the concepts of race and those of moral value which, whatever their significance may be for the perpetuation of folkways or for other social ends, on the whole are objectively false.

MENTAL ASSOCIATIONS

Among these associations we may distinguish three types: those of racial inferiority with distinctive physical characteristics; those of racial inferiority with particular national origins; and those of racial inferiority with foreign habits. (See page 233.) Of these associations the first named appears earliest; the second cannot arise as a rule without a certain amount of book learning or deliberate teaching (such as war-time propaganda). The third comes half-way between these, and in it the personal experience of the child plays a larger part than in either of the others.

Throughout the present inquiry, attention was given to the question of relative permanency for the various learnings of children on this matter of race. Yet it is not possible to speak too positively of the permanent effect of this influence and the evanescent character of that. The race attitudes of the average adolescent are the combined result of so many voluntary and involuntary teachings that—in so far as they seem permanently engraved at that time of life—it is no longer possible to distinguish the various causative factors, or to evaluate them. But we do know that, contrary assumptions notwithstanding, *all* the influences on childhood that make for one kind of attitude are permanent in their effect unless they are counteracted by similarly effective influences. It is not true that personal experience or reading or more intelligent teaching or other new influences in later years can make up for a prejudicial teaching in childhood. Even a religious conversion, bringing with it a new attitude toward some other race or toward all races, rarely quite smooths out the ruts cut into habitual responses to situations of racial contact by successive, incisive attendant learnings. Though children do not react in the same way as adults and, in fact, react differently at different ages, their learnings are cumulative, not successive. The fear of the young child does not become transformed into some other response but still lurks in the more adventurous testing and teasing of the older child and lies dormant, to reappear later in life when some stimulus is sufficiently strong to evoke it.

The permanence of any such associations in memory is disputed by certain psychologists; but the evidence seems to confirm the more general conclusion that early impressions are especially lasting. The early associations between inferiority and some racial characteristic are likely to outlast all memories of personal experience to the contrary, even though at the time of each such contrary experience the disproof is felt in all its completeness. Thus the early stereotypes underlie the normal adult's changing opinions and are more difficult to dislodge than the results of faulty observation or of misinformation or of false reasoning. Moreover, they color other concepts and falsify experience. The feeling-response to the word "Mongolian" or "Russian" with which the individual enters into a situation of personal contact with a member of either of these groups affects that situation, makes it pleasant or unpleasant, furnishes for it from the start a background of attitude that affects the actual happening. Thus there are also material consequences which tend to reaffirm the preconceived association.

The conclusion is reached that race attitudes in children, in so far as they are regarded as prejudicial to the social peace or to a realistic grappling with the problems of race relations, or whatever may be looked upon as a desirable social goal, must be modified, if modified they can be, *in childhood*—and wherever possible at the very time of their first appearance or observation. The case has been made out for a thorough survey of possible means by which the race attitudes of children may be modified.

How to Modify Attitudes

The fifth and last section of the book is devoted to that theme. But before this is discussed in any detail, it is necessary to examine more closely what purposes are likely to enter into a program for the educational treatment of race attitudes in children. Once more we confront conflicting ideals, interests, motivations; and the difficulty of the task is seen to lie in the lack of clarity with which the problem is approached rather than in any lack of tools for applying an educational procedure. No organizations, not even those which have for one of their major aims the bridging of class and race differences, not even those with a decidedly "liberal" bent or those filled with the spirit of human brotherhood, can reasonably be expected to offset in their activities the divisive, unliberal, and clannish forces in the community—simply because they themselves cannot exist and function as though independent of the community. The group divisions in our American life are not accidental; there is a world of difference between bridging them and eradicating them; and public opinion does not always distinguish between these two processes. Thus an agency that seems to go counter to values that are cherished—even if only on grounds of recognized group selfishness—is deprived of support and finds itself without a sphere of influence. On the other hand, an agency that merely reinforces what public pressure already produces in fixed attitudes and ideas, is practically superfluous, from the educational point of view, and certainly contributes nothing toward keeping the folkways flexible and the folk-mind open to the lessons of new experiences. The problem, for such institutions, whether we think of school, church, social settlement, or individual home, therefore, is an insoluble one so long as it is posited in terms of absolute ideals. Opposite loyalties cannot be fostered in the human heart simultaneously unless the human mind is completely shackled by obedience to some authority with conflicting aims.

But to posit the educational problem in absolutes is false anyhow, for there are no two sets of desire, interest, objective, and motivation that clash on every point. Rather is there in the typical community a large variety of attitudes, and very often it is merely due to a chance of circumstance that one type of legitimate desire or interest finds full expression in community programs and pressures while others lie dormant or even repressed. It is the business of a progressive program of education on race attitudes to analyze that surrounding medley of social feeling and thinking and to help the community envisage the social facts. These facts will include all the psychological as well as all the material data—desires as well as seeming interests; they will embrace forces for change as well as forces for continuation of the status quo.

If such a study of all the influences on racial attitudes is made in a given community, it is probable that the desires which the community has for shaping the attitudes of children are not necessarily identical with the established pattern of adult attitudes. It is a notable fact in our American life, for example, that large numbers of parents—and especially fathers—deliberately subject their children to idealistic influences which they themselves shun. Even when conscious of a distinct predilection for the established cultural traditions of the older established, dominant, native American group, many parents desire to have their children grow up in an attitude of appreciation for other groups that have but lately come into the community so that adjustment to the actual situation may not be too difficult for them in later life. Moreover, when full allowance is made for all diversities of viewpoint and desire, certain fundamental objectives which make for a tolerant racial attitude are almost universally admitted as desirable. Among these we found, more especially, the desire that children should be sensitized for fair play in the dealings between individuals and groups, regardless of race; that misinformation and misunderstanding should be counteracted; that qualities of character and achievements in harmony with cultural values shared by all groups should be appreciated, no matter in which group they may be observable.

Of course, the way in which educational objectives are worded has a good deal to do with their acceptance. For example, many of those who in the abstract believe in justice between different racial groups, concretely deny it through their actions (and sometimes through their vote). It will be the business of an effective educational policy, therefore, so to reinterpret the demands of justice that every application in a concrete situation appears as the direct result of the accepted principle and not merely a slap in the face of some established custom or habit of behavior peculiar to that situation. In the same way, it is in relation to specific situations that an effective educational policy will help the child to realize the discrepancy between fact and fiction, between conclusions from observation and stereotyped opinions. Instead of insisting upon an abstract equality of all branches of the human family, it will on appropriate occasions—fairly and without an over-anxious emphasis—point to the qualities or achievements of members of some group not usually appreciated for traits that deserve approving notice.

But that is not all. An effective educational program will differentiate between situations upon which the child can both judge and act in the light of his own knowledge and experience, those in which the individual is powerless to modify his own behavior except as member of a larger group, and those situations that are surrounded by deep feelings, products of age-old experiences or superstitions, where even the group as a whole cannot without serious endeavor and struggle modify its accustomed point of view and resultant behavior.

To attempt more is to invite hypocrisy. And perhaps nothing stands as much in the way of a genuine educational movement on race attitudes as that too characteristic sin of our time. It is hypocrisy to stand for high moral principles if at least an effort is not made to apply them practically in every-day behavior. More frequent is another kind of hypocrisy, namely the employment of vague and presumably "diplomatic" terms to hide an adverse or prejudiced decision or attitude. It is often a temptation

in situations that call for tact so to wrap up in verbiage a negative, repulsive behavior toward members of another group as to
make it almost appear a positive, generous one.   Even where
tact is required in the engineering of situations which threaten
controversy or clash, the only truly educational procedure is one
in which all the participants are made aware of the exact nature
of the steps taken or advocated and the reasons for them in the
anticipation of further future opportunities for more adequate
solutions.

Especially with adolescents, the desirable aim is not so much
to supplant unsatisfactory attitudes by satisfactory ones but
rather to prolong the responsiveness of childhood and the state
of equilibrium between pleasant and unpleasant reactions toward
experiences and impressions; to stimulate curiosity for more and
better information as a basis for decisions.   And therefore it
follows that the proper method to pursue in the modification of
race attitudes is not limited to that subject but is the method
advocated and exemplified by our greatest educational theorists
and practitioners today.   We found how closely the educational
demands that seem to arise from the subject matter of this study
correspond with the demands put forth by John Dewey and
others as those of *any* truly educational process.

Truly Educational Aims

With this emphasis, then, on the method rather than the content
of an educational procedure that aims to modify racial attitudes
in process of premature stabilisation, we return to inspect once
more the opportunities offered for such a process by the different
categories of environment that surround the child.   We cannot,
in this summary chapter, repeat the hints for parents, teachers,
and others that result from this scrutiny.   They are given in
the respective chapters as samples of the sort of resource which
an observant adult or group of adults will discover at hand for
their use rather than as ready-made programs which lend themselves to adoption or adaptation in every kind of community and
neighborhood.

Above all, we have to stress the fact that, no matter what types
of personal interracial contact are practicable or seem desirable
with a view to the total situation in any given set of circumstances,
the possibilities of a truly educational procedure always are pres-

ent, though the means must differ. In one home it may be possible to promote actively pleasant interracial contacts of the children so as to condition them for an adult life free from race consciousness. In another, no kind of actual contact may be practicable, and yet by the use of many devices it is possible to predispose the child for an appreciative frame of mind toward the achievements of other peoples and races, for a habitual fair dealing with persons of unprivileged groups, for a sense of the value of fact as against superstition.

Such watchfulness and resourcefulness in both parents and teachers requires self-education. It is a surprising fact that, however much a community values attributes of liberal open-mindedness in the younger generation, it often quite disregards them in the appointment of teachers and others placed in charge of educational and recreational activities for children. And then the thistle is expected to produce figs!

Among the changes that may usefully be introduced into the programs and methods of institutions that influence the race attitudes of children we emphasize the need for a reconsideration of the program as a whole. Too many institutional programs are no more than a patchwork of heterogeneous and mutually conflicting items; and a general "spirit" of loyalty to the institution's "ideals" is supposed to make up for muddled planning. With the aid of a typical example or two we have suggested some of the considerations that will normally enter into such a program. This does not mean, of course, that under all circumstances all these considerations are either imperative or legitimate, or that they are all of equal weight. Nor does it mean that the same considerations in two different cases produce the same conclusions as regards desirable action.

In short, once more we must insist upon imaginativeness, resourcefulness, and courage in experiments (that may fail) as qualities more valuable than a slavish adoption of measures suggested by some one or other. There is too much demand for "fool-proof" teaching material and methods; and too often when such have incautiously been prepared or suggested, the result is the appointment of more incompetents to carry them out, while the appointment of alert and qualified practitioners in the first place would have made unnecessary any reliance upon outside advice. For example, in the present chaotic state of attitudes toward the desirability of personal interracial contacts, one com-

munity differs so sharply from another in the surrounding attitudes which are part of the "situation" that any general advice
on the subject would be absurd. All we can ask for is that people
and institutions do not fool themselves and think they are doing
one thing when they are doing another, that they are sincere with
the public, and, above all, honest with the children entrusted to
their care.

As has been indicated, there is room for more experimentation,
and that courageous. The exchange of practical experiences will
contribute more than any amount of general counsel to the
liberalization of policies, programs and practices. We have endeavored in the concluding section of this book to present a sufficient sample of varied experiment to induce others to go and do
likewise—not in the sense of imitating efforts which we merely
describe without either approval or criticism—but in the sense
of making up their minds after careful study as to the educational
needs toward which their own situation may point and to meet
these tentatively as best they can. All we have been able to do in
this first fruit of a national movement is to lay the foundation for
a more systematic study of the problem and to point to promising
ways of linking it up, in practical educational projects, with
experimental efforts of one kind or another.

As we close the book, however, it is not so much of technical
tasks that we think, as of a procession of boys and girls we have
met in these pages: Martha Lum, denied an education by decision
of the Supreme Court of the United States, the little boy who was
deprived of his white playmate, the bewildered southern boy in
the northern school, the Jewish adolescent who grew too quickly
into maturity to retain the friendship of his pals, the Chinese child
"made much of" as a pet and subsequently neglected, the Mexican boy who fought himself into appreciative recognition, the
Jewish and Italian gangs who could not come together on anything except to "beat up the niggers," the five-year-old in the
Baltimore street-car, the innumerable children frightened with accounts of "black men" and pictures of bloodthirsty savages, children often crippled in mind and future experience by propagandist tools wielded for the benefit of selfish interest.[1] Generation

---

[1] The *comprachicos,* according to Victor Hugo's novel, *The Laughing Man,*
were a wandering gipsy tribe of the seventeenth century, already well forgotten in the eighteenth, who plied a ghastly and horrible business. The word,
an abbreviation of the Spanish *comprapequenos,* means a buyer of children.
These loathsome people never stole children, as certain gipsies are supposed to

after generation, we see them pass by—children who are given the stones of fictitious stereotypes when they ask for the bread of knowledge, children of all races and all nationalities made the potential cannon-fodder of future wars because they are not permitted to develop in themselves those qualities of mind that make for a sense of fair play, for mutual appreciation, for mental flexibility in response to changing situations. It is to these children, burdened with the material costs of past wars and with the inheritance of limiting social attitudes that society owes its greatest unacknowledged debt.

have done; they bought them, but for a terrible purpose. As our plastic-surgeons seek today to eliminate physical defects and so to render the human face more beautiful, so these *comprachicos* studied how they might take the fair forms of the children they had purchased and convert them into monstrosities and hunchbacks at whose antics the courtiers of Europe might be amused.

The day of the *comprachicos* is happily long since past. We would no longer tolerate the conversion of the young into hideous oddities. We insist on the right of all children to a normal and natural physical development. But there are still some who would force the spiritual and intellectual development of the child into the cruel channels of dogma and curriculum, instead of allowing adequate opportunity for its individual nature to express itself.—*The World's Youth,* April, 1926.

INDEX

INDEX

*Asterisks are used to indicate a topic dealt with so extensively that the page numbers which follow it do not exhaust its treatment. Cases affecting Negroes or attitudes toward Negroes appear too frequently to cite every instance.

Abbott, Grace, 158, 296
Abernethy, Ethel M., 81
Acheson, Edna L., 292
Addams, Jane, 11, 247
*Adjustment of attitudes to new environment, 44, 305, 358
*Adolescence, 19-42, 45, 92, 265-266, 370; see also Puberty
*Adult attitudes, absorption of, 7, 9, 14, 17, 20, 25, 28-30, 35, 37, 38, 42, 47, 56, 64-66, 75, 76, 77, 93-114, 115-124, 230-247, 262, 274-275, 370-373
*Age, relation to specific attitudes and their expression of, 6, 13, 20, 26-28, 33-42, 190; see also Physiological influences, Puberty
Allen, Richard D., 88
Allport, Floyd H., 255
American Hebrew, The, 163
American Indian, children, 87, 90, 133, 320, 331-333, 363
American Indians, attitudes toward, 7, 97, 212-213, 218, 226, 300, 309, 319, 324, 331-333, 335, 363
*Americanization, 35, 51, 85, 90-92, 104, 120-121, 146, 169, 172-173, 222-225, 254, 288, 290, 294-297, 326-329, 340, 361; see also Civics
Anglo-Saxon, see British, Nordic
Anthropological questions, 79-92, 132-137, 190-191, 262
Anthropology, teaching of, 159-161
*Appreciation for racial difference, 24, 35, 42, 95, 174, 180, 184-188, 202, 225, 229, 268, 269, 275, 281-284, 292, 304, 313, 322-324, 329-336, 341-343, 349-350, 357-358, 361
Arabs, attitudes toward, 218, 226
Armenian children, 17, 277
Armenians, attitudes toward, 238, 277, 330
Art, 72, 187, 204, 208-213, 222, 269, 281, 311, 324, 329, 331, 340, 343, 361; see also Illustration
Assembly programs, 303, 334-335
Association for the Study of Negro Life and History, 155
Association of color with uncleanliness, 8, 10, 67, 70, 232, 234-236, 278-279, 336, 347

Association of race with badness, 9, 74, 97-98, 110, 112, 113, 154, 160, 197, 227, 231, 242, 244-245, 309, 347; see also Fear
Association of race with religion, 40, 50, 95, 111-112, 141, 178-182, 218, 238, 252, 280, 303, 353
Association of racial inferiority with foreign habits, 15, 26, 151, 224, 231, 239, 242-247; foreign language, 9, 43, 68, 102, 168, 205-206, 235, 238, 243-244; national origin, 31, 112, 122, 154, 159, 224, 237-242, 376-377; physical characteristics, 4, 8, 15, 68, 69, 102, 115, 150, 159, 207, 214, 233-238, 377
Athletics, effect on race attitudes of, 22, 23, 24, 46, 69, 70, 73, 126, 191-197, 219, 254, 255, 269, 298, 351
*Attendant learnings, 93, 107-108, 111, 168, 174, 181, 198, 233, 252, 257, 287, 289, 321-324, 357, 376; see also Adult attitudes, absorption of; Association; Institutional Influences; see also Segregation

Balch, Emily Greene, 104
Baldwin, Bird T., 41, 80, 83
Barnes, Mary Clark, 297
Barnum and Bailey, 218
Becht, George, 225
Behaviorism, 60
Bible teaching, effect of, 108, 174, 177-183, 185, 252, 267, 279, 350
Biography, 66, 74, 151, 165, 169, 184, 308-311, 316-317, 347
Bitterness acquired through experience, 17, 22, 253-254, 256; see also Inferiority sense, School strikes
Boas, Franz, 80, 81, 85, 87, 96, 132, 262
Bogardus, Emory S., 21, 25, 67, 74, 103, 104, 242, 272, 281, 317
Brabin, Charles, 201
Brandes, Georg, 18
Briggs, Thomas H., 91
British, attitudes toward, 69, 154, 155-156, 164, 208, 210, 224, 225, 335
Brown, Gilbert, 89
Buck, Florence, 351